THE SINGING ATHLETE

BRAIN-BASED TRAINING FOR YOUR VOICE

THE SINGING ATHLETE:
BRAIN-BASED TRAINING FOR YOUR VOICE

Andrew Byrne

Andrew Byrne Studio Inc. 2020

COPYRIGHT

Copyright © 2020 by Andrew Byrne Studio Inc.

The Singing Athlete™ is a registered trademark of Andrew Byrne Studio Inc.

All rights reserved. This book or any portion thereof may not be reproduced or used in any manner whatsoever without the express written permission of the publisher except for the use of brief quotations in a book review or scholarly journal.

The following is intended for general information purposes only. Any application of the material included herein is at the reader's discretion and is their sole responsibility. To the fullest extent of the law, neither the publisher nor the author assume any liability for any injury and/or damage to persons or property as a result of methods described in this book. Do not use this book to diagnose, treat, or cure any illness or health condition.

The author takes full responsibility for representing and interpreting ideas related to Z-Health Performance Solutions, LLC. The author's interpretations and representations of Z-Health may vary in intent and accuracy from the writings and presentations by Dr. Eric Cobb and his employees.

At the time of initial publication, the URLs displayed in this book link or refer to existing websites. The author is not responsible for, and should not be deemed to endorse or recommend, any website other than those owned by Andrew Byrne Studio Inc. While every effort has been made to provide accurate internet addresses, the author assumes no responsibility for errors or for changes that occur after publication.

First Printing: 2020

Print Edition: ISBN 978-1-7346369-0-1

E-book Edition: ISBN 978-1-7346369-1-8

Editor: Jon VanZile

Cover Design: Stephanie Layton

Publisher: Andrew Byrne Studio Inc., 161 West 54th Street, Apartment 603, New York, NY 10019

www.andrewbyrne.com

I dedicate my life to improving human performance so that people can do what they love, always.

I dedicate this book to everyone who believes that they can be better, feel better, and sing better.

WHAT PEOPLE ARE SAYING ABOUT ANDREW AND *THE SINGING ATHLETE*

"I've turned to Andrew at many points in my career because he understands that there is no 'one size fits all' vocal toolkit. I have so valued the immediacy of Andrew's technique; he provides real, tactile exercises that I can do in mere minutes to prepare for my 'game.' In a single lesson, the additional tools and skills I walk away with are invaluable. Andrew creates one of the most efficient and yet extremely comfortable and trusting environments for a singer to explore and grow in. I cannot thank him enough."

>-Erika Henningsen
>*Mean Girls* (Cady Heron, original Broadway cast)

"There are some people who are born to be teachers. Andrew is one of those people. The lessons within this book are a revelation and are sure to leave an enormous and permanent mark on the entertainment industry. It has been a personal joy for me to watch Andrew go from affecting deep change in individuals to affecting masses. And while there is a tiny part of me that doesn't wish to share Andrew – my secret weapon – with the world; the world will certainly be better for having read and put into practice the contents of this book."

>-Cecelia Ticktin
>*Wicked* (Elphaba stand-by)

"Andrew is a vocal ninja and my savior! He understands the demands of the performer and also the connection between the body and voice. He's helped me focus my sound and support in places within my range where I've had a constant struggle. He looks at how your body or your mind can be affecting the voice or holding you back. His studio almost feels like vocal pilates for the performer. It's incredible!"

>-Marja Harmon
>*Hamilton* (Angelica Schuyler)

"I'm an actor with no background in singing. Whenever I have a job that requires me to sing, I run to Andrew Byrne. Whether it's contemporary pop songs or old standards from the 1930s, Andrew knows exactly how to get me there. He can work with a beginner like me as well as the most seasoned professional; his toolbox is infinite. Directors are always thrilled to have him, as he is extremely flexible and a creative problem solver. With hard work and Andrew's expert guidance, I've been able to develop skills that give me the confidence to stand up and sing, which is no small feat."

>-Kerry Bishé
>*Penny Dreadful: City of Angels* (Showtime), *Halt and Catch Fire* (AMC)

"When I work with Andrew, I know I am in the hands of a one-of-a-kind expert. His research and study have formed a specific and holistic approach to singing that is detailed and yet easily applied. He has found a recipe that connects the analytical with the physical, engaging the brain, the nervous system, and the whole body. I leave his studio with practical, innovative exercises that produce real results: even tone, greater vocal agility and ease, and a deepened connection to the material."

>-Stanley Bahorek
>*Company* Broadway revival

"Andrew Byrne is a voice magician. He is the most intelligent and inspiring voice teacher I have ever studied with. His approach through the physical body and nervous system has transformed the way I sing and was essential for the success of my last Broadway role. Any singer or teacher of any level would gain a great deal from reading this book!"

      -Marissa McGowan
      Kiss Me Kate (Lili/Kate u/s—2019 Broadway revival)

"I have been taking lessons with Andrew Byrne for almost a decade, and there is no one like him. He is the most specific, educated, and clear voice teacher I have ever worked with. An hour with him is like months of training with anyone else. My work on a song before and after seeing Andrew is like night and day. He has an incredible way of drawing out my most authentic vocal interpretation of a song. Not only has he taught me about myself as a singer, but he has also taught me so much about specific areas in my body to target with relaxation or strengthening. To me, he is an amalgamation of a physical therapist, life coach, and superb vocal teacher. I'll never stop working with him!"

      -Kayla Foster
      The Deuce (HBO), *Spring Awakening*

"Andrew Byrne is my national treasure. He is, in my opinion, THE vocal wizard. His love of all things anatomical coupled with his unending knowledge of the voice makes him the most valuable tool a performer can have. His approach is unlike any other voice teacher I've ever experienced. If his superior skill isn't enough, Andrew is one of the most supportive and thoughtful people on the planet, who goes out of his way to make sure that those he calls students are taken care of. It's because of working with Andrew that I made it to my Broadway debut."

      -Stephen Scott Wormley
      The Lion King (Simba u/s—Broadway)

"Andrew's expertise in human physiology and his attentiveness to the current industry landscape make him an invaluable member of my team. His approach of utilizing the full body as an instrument for singing has allowed my voice to feel free and healthy while maintaining strength and endurance. I leave every lesson feeling inspired and empowered."

      -Emily Borromeo
      School of Rock (Broadway)

"Working with Andrew was one of the most creatively gratifying experiences of my career. With Andrew's teaching method, my voice developed in ways I could not have imagined. His tools to pinpoint areas of physical and mental tension as they related to my vocal strength were nothing short of mind-blowing. Our work made me a healthier artist and reframed how I tackle vocal challenges."

      -Ahna O'Reilly
      The Robber Bridegroom (Rosamund), *The Help*

"Andrew Byrne has been my vocal coach for over a decade. Andrew's ability to pinpoint how to address a vocal challenge in a song, both physical and emotional, never ceases to amaze me. And his knowledge of the physiology of singing is unparalleled. He continues to add to his arsenal to help to bring the best sound quality out of his students. I am grateful and fortunate to be able to have sessions with Andrew to this day. You will greatly benefit from his expertise and care."

      -Pearl Sun
      Come From Away (Broadway)

"Andrew is by far the best vocal teacher I've ever had. In October I had invasive vocal surgery, knowing four months later I was contracted to play the title role in a huge production. In this short amount of time, Andrew revolutionized my voice. I trained like an athlete, using his techniques three or four times a day, and I am now singing the way I did 20 years ago. My voice is never tired, hoarse, or raspy, and I am belting the way I did when I began my career on Broadway. Thank you, Andrew; you saved me, and I use your techniques every day!"

      -Jodie Langel
      Les Misérables, *Cats*, founder of *Making It on Broadway*

"Andrew Byrne has taught me how to reach a higher level of a true, conscious, and intelligent understanding of vocal technique. His knowledge of the nervous system and its kinesthetic response to the voice is mind-blowing. Singing is such a personal yet athletic art form, and Andrew teaches with such integrity and knowledge. He is a true voice builder, and I wish I met him earlier in my career."

      -Jessica Bishop
      Phantom of the Opera (Meg Giry—Broadway)

"The body of work and masterful teaching of Andrew Byrne provides a direct path to elite vocal training for today's singer. Andrew does more than connect the dots between neuroscience and the voice/body relationship. He has married neuroscientific principles and vocal pedagogy to create a whole new paradigm for how we can both learn and teach vocal technique. He does all this using straightforward, accessible vocabulary and physical/vocal tasks that produce immediate results for the singer. This work is game-changing for singers and teachers of singing alike.

Time and again, I've been the beneficiary of these seemingly 'magical' results in my singing as a veteran musical theatre performer, as well as being able to incorporate Andrew's work in my teaching studio readily. Another plus here is that *The Singing Athlete* negates no other system, no other technique, and no other pedagogy. It can be used to meet a singer 'where they are.'

I wholeheartedly encourage singers and singing teachers interested in fact-based pedagogy to investigate and experience *The Singing Athlete*. Decades of experience lead me to enthusiastically endorse Andrew Byrne as one of the most important vocal pedagogues of our time."

      -Lisa Rochelle, NYC
      Voice Teacher/Singing Voice Specialist

ACKNOWLEDGMENTS

Everyone needs a coach, and I train with some of the best.

I'd like to thank my teachers and mentors in the singing world over the past thirty years, especially Dr. Christine Carlton, Darleen Kliewer-Britton, Penelope Bitzas, Victoria Clark, Mary McDonald Klimek, Kim Steinhauer, and Joan Lader.

Gary Ramsey and Emily Whyte have been my invaluable guides in the Alexander Technique. Lisa Anzelmo has helped me master yoga poses I never thought I could do. Jen Waldman and Molly Mahoney are teachers who make me a better businessperson and human. Amy Rogers has been my trusty artistic partner in countless creative endeavors. Thanks to Zachariah Salazar and Bryan Thomas for being my brilliant coaches in nutrition and metabolism. Knight-Thompson Speechwork has provided me excellent training in spoken voice and accents.

The instruction of Dr. Eric Cobb has been life-changing for me. Z-Health Performance (zhealtheducation.com) is his company, and I highly recommend you check out their coursework. A shout-out to Cecelia Ticktin for originally introducing me to Dr. Cobb and Z-Health.

My beautiful readers helped me shape this book: Theresia Daniel, Rosie Harris, Chris Nolan, and Jessica Raaum Foster. Jon VanZile (editingforauthors.com) went above and beyond as my marvelous editor. Thanks to Brandon Davidson for working through *all* these drills with me. The multi-talented Stephanie Layton did the beautiful cover design.

I am unbelievably indebted to the performing artists I work with every day in my NYC studio and around the world. I treasure my time with you.

And thanks and love to Mark and my family!

CONTENTS

1. Stories 1
2. Brain Basics 5
3. Practice 20
4. Breathing 33
5. Diaphragm 46
6. Exhalation 57
7. Inhalation 68
8. Larynx and Palate 81
9. Tongue 99
10. Jaw and Teeth 116
11. Nose and Skull 130
12. Scars 146
13. Ears 152
14. Eyes 174
15. First Brain 198
16. Second Brain 211
17. Feeling 218
18. Next Steps 225
About the Author 227
Drill Worksheet 228
References 234

BEFORE WE START

The exercises found in this book are ones that I have been doing with singers for many years. I strongly feel that they are safe and effective for vocal training. That being said, I'm not there with you in person, and I don't know your history. As with any exercise program, consult your physician or health-care professional if you have any concerns over the material covered here.

Some of these drills may be a lot of work for your nervous system, so modify or stop them if you get any strange symptoms. There are around 100 billion neurons in the brain; no one understands how it all works, so you may encounter surprises. Above all, pay attention to your experience and take care of yourself.

Anatomy is a statistical conglomeration. A whole bunch of bones/muscles/organs/larynges get measured, and averages are found. If you don't feel what I'm describing, or you notice something different in your body, be curious and trust your own hands.

I am not a professional neuroscientist, neuroanatomist, or neurologist. My degrees are in music, not medicine, so obviously nothing in this book should be construed as medical advice. The information contained within is my distillation of years of study, reading, and practice in the realm of brain-based training. It is founded on the excellent teaching of many, especially Dr. Eric Cobb, but the views expressed in it are solely my own. I hope to take a complex subject and make it practical and fun, all in the service of improving your voice.

Learning movement is a visual process. As part of your purchase of the book, you get free access to videos of all the drills at thesingingathlete.com. If you're interested in the pieces of gear I mention along the way, you'll find links for them on the website as well.

I drew all the illustrations you'll find in the book. Skin is always depicted in uncolored line drawings. I intentionally simplified some anatomical structures to represent all people.

To get a ton of value out of this training, all you need is a willingness to play and experiment. Don't just read the book. Do the drills.

-Andrew

P.S. As I'm publishing this book in 2020, it bears mentioning that the immune system takes cues from the nervous system.[1] I believe you can support your overall health with the targeted neural education you will learn here.

1. STORIES

If you sing, you are an athlete. By definition, voice requires movement. Your breath flows. Your vocal folds open and close. Your tongue and lips form words. Muscles that are well below your consciousness are coordinating a kinetic symphony that would make Mahler jealous.

How would it feel to call yourself an athlete? Would it make you proud? Uncomfortable? Excited? Ashamed? In my Singing Athlete™ course, I've had all these responses. The word "athlete" can be a loaded one. If you feel that way, I can relate. Although I was tall for my age, I didn't make the basketball team in junior high school. I ran track but struggled to complete a mile in a competitive time. I loved tennis but never played with enough consistency to be on the high-school team. I identified as a musician but not an athlete.

My perspective on the value of physical training shifted when I developed an injury that almost ended my music career.

MY STORY

Although I sang growing up, piano was my main instrument. My teachers wrote fingerings in my score and provided accountability to practice, but none of them gave much instruction on the mechanics of how I was playing. I sounded good at the keyboard, so they seemed happy to have a student who could crank out some Brahms and Beethoven. Starting in high school, I began to play for singers and fell in love with it. In college and grad school, I was a voice major, and I earned money accompanying for voice lessons. I was fascinated by vocal technique; I would ask the teachers if I could come early and take notes on the exercises they were giving the students. I spent hours every week playing and listening, absorbing the wisdom of countless excellent voice technicians.

Along the way, though, I began to have pain in my left elbow. It would show up on a heavy piano week and then go away, so I ignored it. I soon moved to New York and started playing in Broadway pit orchestras. It was a fantastic career boost but came with more stress than I had ever dealt with at a keyboard. The stakes felt so much higher playing for *Les Misérables* than banging out "Caro Mio Ben" in a voice studio, and the pain started showing up more often. At this time, I was also taking jobs conducting and music directing from the piano. In 2002, I booked a dream gig doing *Ragtime*. During the show's run, my elbow started throbbing; this time, it wouldn't stop. I started wearing an elbow brace (in hindsight, a bad idea), and then my shoulder started aching as well. I tried to survive by getting massages and physical therapy, but there wasn't much improvement. I developed nerve symptoms, with heat and tingling in my fingers. At the end of the show, my left hand would be bright red while my right was a normal color.

When I returned to NYC, I reduced my schedule to the bare minimum and dealt with some pretty severe depression. I feel like I'm put on this earth to work with singers; there is truly nothing else I've ever wanted to do with my life. The thought that I might never be able to play the piano again without pain was devastating.

After a bit of wallowing around, I decided to figure out how to fix myself. I started taking Alexander Technique lessons, which began to ease my discomfort. I also began taking private Pilates and Gyrotonic sessions, where I realized that I had much less strength in my left abdominal area than my right. I had the first inklings that a childhood inguinal hernia on my left might be contributing somehow to my left-side arm pain.

With the help of some excellent coaches, I developed a physical training regimen and started to think like an athlete. As I unpacked my history and trained with more precision, the pain lessened and finally went away. I've now been playing for seventeen years with no recurring issues.

My recovery gave me a passion for learning about the physical self however I could. I continued my Alexander lessons for twelve years and studied with personal trainers, bodyworkers, and physical therapists. What started as a goal of fixing myself turned into one of bringing athletics into the voice studio. I wondered what singers could learn from the same ideas I used to get myself out of pain.

Eventually, I was introduced to the work of Dr. Eric Cobb and his company, Z-Health Performance, which is a training program dedicated to functional applied neuroscience. Z-Health looks at anatomy, physiology, and kinesiology through a brain-based lens, teaching you practical ways to assess and affect the nervous system for performance enhancement. From my first Z-Health class, I was hooked. With other modalities, the applications for singers were there, but it took a bit of translation to get to a useful tool. With a neural view of movement, everything immediately seemed so relatable to performers. The same perspective that could be used to create an efficient golf swing could also produce a killer high belt.

As I learned more about the nervous system, I changed the way I practiced my singing. I started using sensory drills as a part of my warm-up. I incorporated joint mobility and isometrics into practicing high notes. I included brain-based breathing, tongue, and jaw exercises instead of only the ones I had learned from singing teachers. Learning specific, tangible drills that train the brain has been one of the finest educational explorations of my life, and it forms the basis of this book.

YOUR STORY

I never had a voice teacher who asked me about my medical history, and there were things in it that were affecting my voice. I ask my students to tell me anything from their own stories that they are comfortable sharing because this often gives us a faster path to vocal progress. I'm interested in any previous vocal fold issues (e.g., nodules, polyps, cysts, hemorrhages, etc.), but I also ask the following questions. Take a minute to think through them for yourself.

1. Do you have any history of:

- Clearing your throat/phlegm

- Heartburn

- Trouble swallowing

- Sinus issues
- Allergies
- Asthma/breathing problems
- Jaw/TMJ issues

2. Have you experienced any of the following?

- Major surgeries
- Broken bones/fractures
- Sprains/torn ligaments or tendons
- Major accidents
- Concussions/head injuries
- Major illnesses

3. Do you have any scars or tattoos?

4. Have you had orthodonture at any point?

5. Are you aware of any spinal curvature (e.g., scoliosis, hyper-kyphosis, etc.)?

6. Do you wear corrective lenses (contacts/glasses)? Do you have other visual issues (e.g., blurriness, dry eyes, surgeries, etc.)?

7. Do you have any history of ear infections, hearing problems, or balance problems like vertigo, getting dizzy, etc.?

8. Do you have any history of stomach/digestion/GI issues?

9. Are you aware of any other sensory deficits (problems with smell or taste, areas of numbness, etc.)?

The answers to these questions may give you some clues as to which sections of the book will be most useful for you.

The reason I called this book *The Singing Athlete* and not *The Byrne Method* or whatever is that you are the center of this process, not me. Keep your goals in mind as you work through the drills. You are looking for exercises that remove barriers and help you become the kind of singer you want to be.

This book is going to give you a lot to work on, but before we get into the material, I want to let you know a few things it will not be giving you:

- **A comprehensive guide to laryngeal anatomy:** This subject has been covered thoroughly and brilliantly elsewhere. Check out my Reading List at andrewbyrne.com if you'd like further recommendations on this topic.

- **A list of vocal exercises:** A prescription for specific musical and vowel patterns for vocal exercises is not the perspective I have taken here. If you are interested in learning the vocalises I teach, you can join my Online Studio or take my 30-Day Vocalise Challenge. My Online Studio also provides specific instruction on how to develop head voice, chest voice, belting, etc., which I will not be covering here.

- **Advice on repertoire or professional development:** I have a series of Rep Lists that will tell you which pieces I think are best for auditions. I've also written extensively for Backstage about professional development, and I've done a bunch of videos for them as well.

2. BRAIN BASICS

Think about the best singing experience of your life: it may have taken place in a performance, a voice lesson, or just driving around town. Can you remember the euphoria you felt when, suddenly, everything worked the way it should? This state of effortless flow is what you are seeking every time you open your mouth to sing.

And yet, no matter how vocally skilled you get, there are inevitably days when singing feels challenging. The issues you experience on a "bad voice day" may not be noticeable to those who hear you, but you'll be aware that you're not at the top of your game. If you know how well you can sing, why isn't it perfect every time? The reason is simple: humans are survival-based organisms. Staying alive is more important than performing well. The majority of your brain doesn't care if you can float a high C; it cares that you survive the attempt.

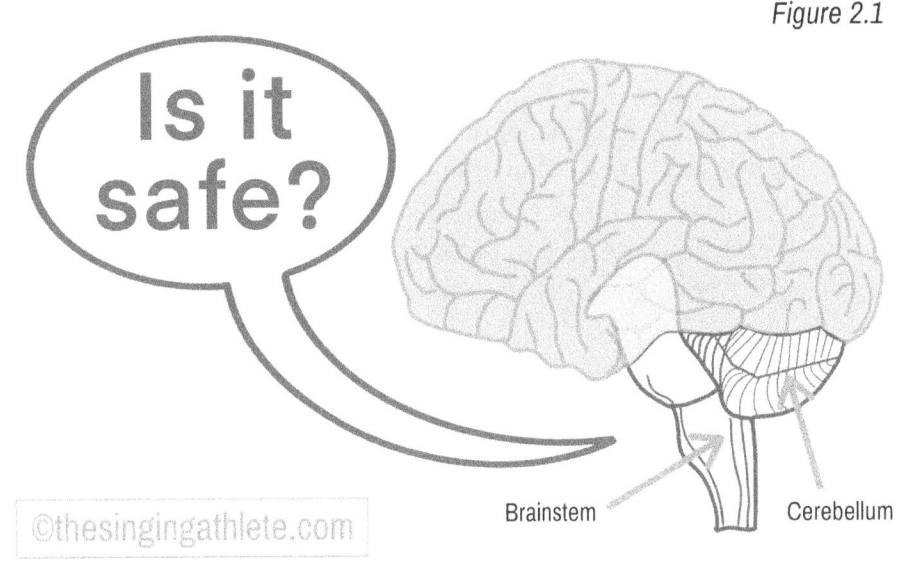

Figure 2.1

On a subconscious level, your brain is constantly assessing your environment for threatening signals. Is that person walking toward you friendly or crazy? Do you hear the sound of fireworks or gunshots? Are you smelling a cozy bonfire or a forest ablaze? These assessments occur in an ancient, reflexive part of your nervous system that we will call the ***first brain*** *(Fig. 2.1)*. This first brain, which includes the brainstem and the cerebellum, is always asking the question, "Is it safe?"

Let's say you've been struggling to belt a high note without strain. One day, all the stars align, and it happens. When it finally comes out of your mouth, you're not even sure how you got there, but you think, "Yes! I've figured this out!" The next day, you get up and vocalize, excited to go for the same phrase again. It cracks. You sing it again. It cracks again. You're crestfallen; you can't understand how your voice can be so inconsistent.

From a neural perspective, this inconsistency makes sense. The lion's share of your brain isn't interested in high-level performance. It's invested in keeping you alive right this second, not tomorrow or twenty years from now. Depending on the health of your nervous system, your first brain may have even interpreted the novelty of your big, beautiful note as a threat. The next day, when you approached the same phrase, it may have impaired the coordination of your vocal folds to dissuade you from ever trying that freaky thing again.

So, what can you do about this? How do elite performers get around the brain's survival mechanism to consistently sing their best? The first step is to understand threat and how the nervous system responds to it.

THE THREAT BUCKET

Have you ever felt like you were going to die when performing a song? On the one hand, it's ridiculous; clearly, no mortal danger is going to come from going flat on the last note of "Bring Him Home." On the other hand, the feelings of dread that can creep up as you approach a problematic vocal passage can feel real and terrifying. From your nervous system's perspective, there may not be much difference between falling down a flight of stairs and nearing the climax of "She Used to Be Mine." Both situations can produce a threat response.

Threat is anything your brain thinks might be dangerous. As you go through your day, your brain is looking for patterns and making predictions based on what it perceives. When new information enters your field of awareness, the brain compares this novel stimulus to previous experiences and to what is expected in this environment. If you see a deer in the woods, you may marvel at the beauty of nature. If you see one in your kitchen, some different thoughts will probably arise.

Based on the clarity of its predictions, the brain can react to potential threats as vehemently as real ones (e.g., performance anxiety). One of the goals of brain-based training is to improve your nervous system's predictive capacity. To form accurate plans, your brain needs trustworthy information and proper fuel, and all of your body systems need to participate. Erroneous data from any area can increase threat and degrade performance. Some things that can make prediction difficult are:

- Lack of sleep
- Dehydration
- Poor dietary choices
- Stress
- Injuries that haven't been rehabbed completely
- Underdeveloped motor control/weak muscles
- Issues with vision/hearing/smell/taste
- Lack of sensation/numbness in areas of the body

You probably read at least a couple of those items and thought, "Yeah, that's me." Maybe you've worn glasses since junior high, or you've sprained your ankle three times, and it still bothers you. When these issues begin to compound with other stressors, some nasty consequences can show up.

Let's imagine that your brain has a container in it called the ***threat bucket*** *(Fig. 2.2)*. The level of water in this metaphorical receptacle reflects the total amount of threat coming your way. Didn't sleep well last night? Threat increases, and the bucket starts to fill. Got up too late to eat breakfast and grabbed a donut as you ran out the door? More water in the bucket. Your train stalled underground for a half-hour and made you late to work? Now the level is rising fast.

As threats start to accumulate in the bucket, your first brain will begin to get very scared; it believes that if the water reaches the top, you could die. So, it will create a spigot, and liquid will drain out in the form of some kind of output. Some of the possible threat-bucket outputs are:

- Pain

- Sickness

- Breathing problems (asthma/allergies/reflux)

- Fatigue

- Anxiety/depression

- Loss of flexibility (physical or vocal)

- Poor balance/dizziness/motion sickness

- Migraines

- Hormonal problems

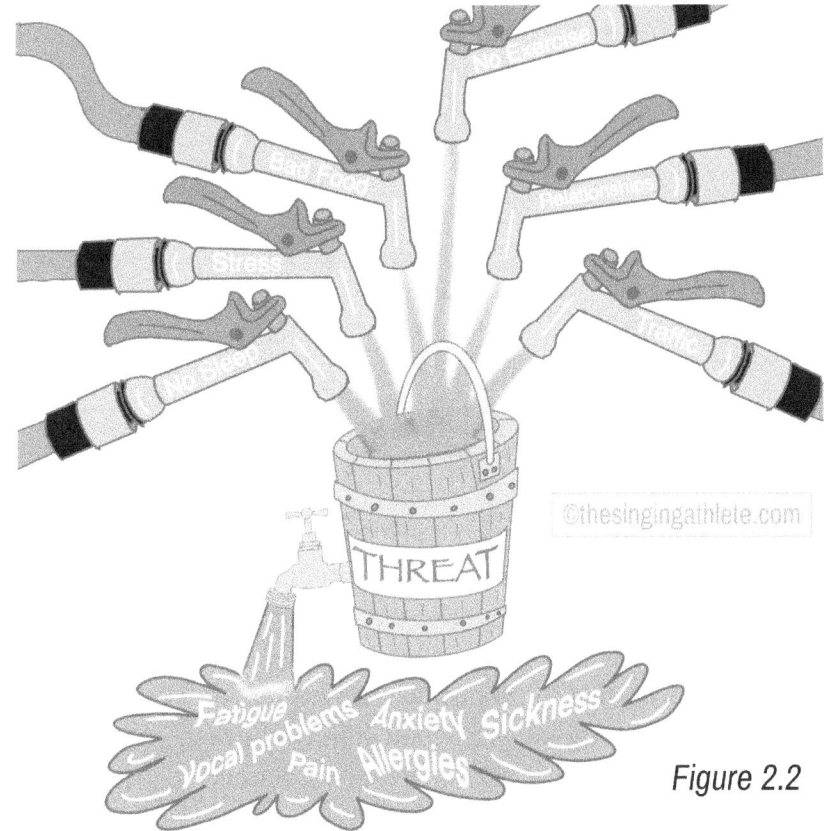

Figure 2.2

Nothing on this list is very much fun. But from a neural perspective, it makes sense why your first brain might give you these outputs. If you're in mortal danger, the best strategy to keep you alive may be to stop moving. Think of an antelope and a lion on the African plains; if the predator gives chase, the prey will attempt to flee. If the lion succeeds in capturing the antelope, the animal will go into a state of shutdown, basically playing dead. This ancient reflex is based on the hope that a sudden change in vital energy will be enough to create a brief distraction, allowing a final possibility of escape.

If you have ever had migraines, chronic fatigue, or frequent illnesses, you can understand how hard it is to move in the throes of these maladies. Even though there is no lion with its jaws around your neck, your threatened first brain reacts like that of the captured antelope. It thinks that the pain, illness, or fatigue it's giving you is necessary for your survival.

Performers are especially prone to threat-bucket outputs that are outside the realm of body pain. Almost all professionals have had to go onstage injured at some point, ignoring the brain's advice to stop moving. If the signals continue to be disregarded, the brain may think, "Wow, I gave you a ton of ankle pain, but you still tapped in *42nd Street* every night for weeks. Since pain didn't work, it's time to try something else to keep you still." It may hinder your immune system, give you depression, or mess with your hormones. Unresolved high threat eventually leads to a shutdown of some sort.

To avoid these unpleasant outputs and sing your best, you have to lower the level in your threat bucket. This is why many other body systems beyond your two little vocal folds can have a substantial impact on your voice. Threat levels can be reduced through improvements in the following systems:

- Movement maps (moving your joints through a full and controlled range of motion)

- Sensory capability (e.g., vision, hearing, taste, smell, touch)

- Balance

- Respiration habits

One of the goals of this book is to help you discover drills that lower threat in your singing and your life.

NEUROPLASTICITY

The term *neuroplasticity* refers to changes in brain structure or function that are either directly measured in individual neurons or inferred from measures taken across neuronal populations *(Fig. 2.3)*. In essence, it means that the brain can change. You wouldn't be reading this book if you didn't believe in this concept: education is neuroplasticity in action. Until fairly recently, it was thought that neuroplasticity was exclusively the claim of youth. We now know that to be untrue, and that your brain can and will change until the day you die.[2]

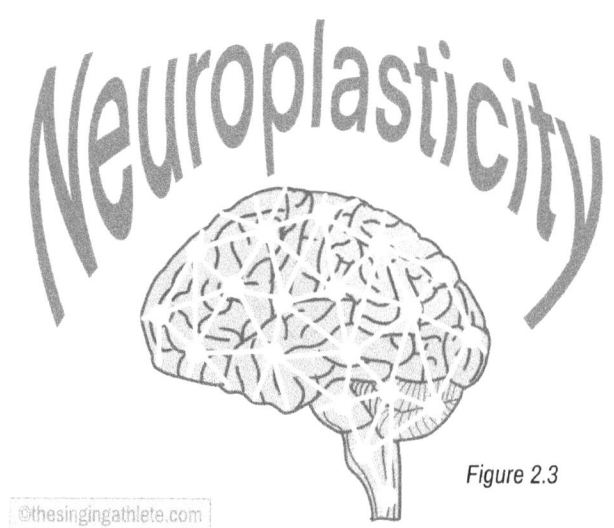

Figure 2.3

Neuroplasticity isn't good or bad; it just is. You can make positive plastic changes that improve performance and reduce pain, but you can just as easily have negative plasticity. Here's an example:

> Maybe you found a song that you learned and fell in love with; everything felt smooth, and the words seemed like they were written for you. When you took this winning new tune to an audition, you forgot to give a proper tempo, and the accompanist played too slowly. The dragging pace led to a lack of breath coordination and a cracked high note, which made the director involuntarily wince. Ugh. The next thing you know, your new favorite song goes in the garbage; the negative plasticity of the performance experience would make singing it again too painful.

You can reduce the harmful effects of negative plasticity by being more present in the positive moments. When something goes well in your singing, what happened before the breakthrough? What did it feel like in your body? The goal here is less a concrete verbalization of steps ("I lifted my palate and rounded my lips") and more a subjective and experiential reflection ("I felt my voice farther away from me"). Singers have more neural activation in the right cortex, where images and spatial relationships are stored, so describing vocal gains in less concrete terms can make them more "sticky."[3]

Another fantastic concept for performers is ***metaplasticity***, or the plasticity of plasticity. The more you practice putting yourself in new circumstances, the better your brain becomes at adapting to change in all areas of your life. Every time you learn a new song or tackle a role that you love, you improve your metaplasticity. Studying singing is a great lifelong brain-health strategy.

THE NERVOUS SYSTEM LOOP

There is nothing in the nervous system that isn't a loop *(Fig. 2.4)*. At an elemental level, the nervous system does three things:

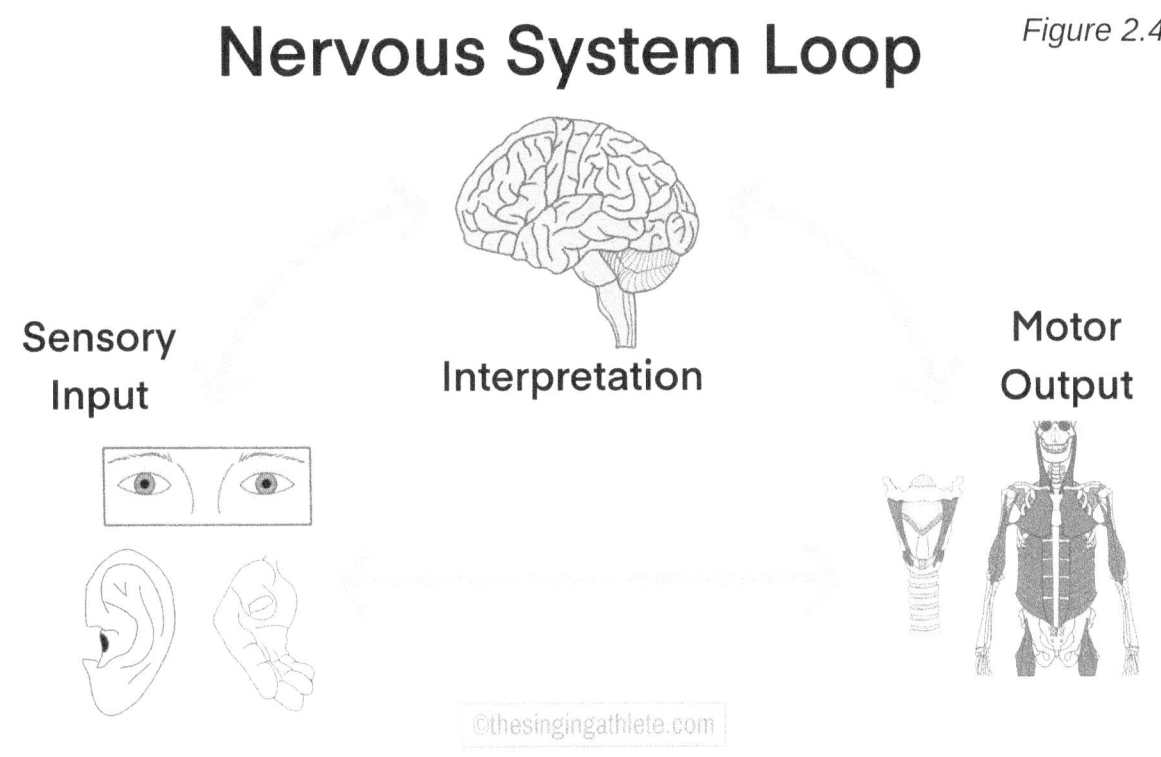

- Receives sensory input

- Interprets the input and decides what to do about it

- Creates motor output

A brain-based approach to training gives equal weight to sensory, interpretive, and motor elements. Traditional voice training tends to treat singing exclusively as a motor activity. Singers are instructed to "open the throat," "engage the diaphragm," and "move the tongue forward." This type of guidance will work for some students, but what if that's not you? Motor instructions like these can fail, and if your teacher starts to express frustration that you're not responding as expected, you may feel like you're untalented. The truth is there could be things in your sensory or interpretive systems that aren't working the way they should. After these systems are put back online, motor instructions like "lift your palate" may work great for you.

SENSORY INPUT

Let's begin with the sensory aspects of the nervous system. There are three main types of sensory input your brain receives, which form a triad *(Fig. 2.5)*:

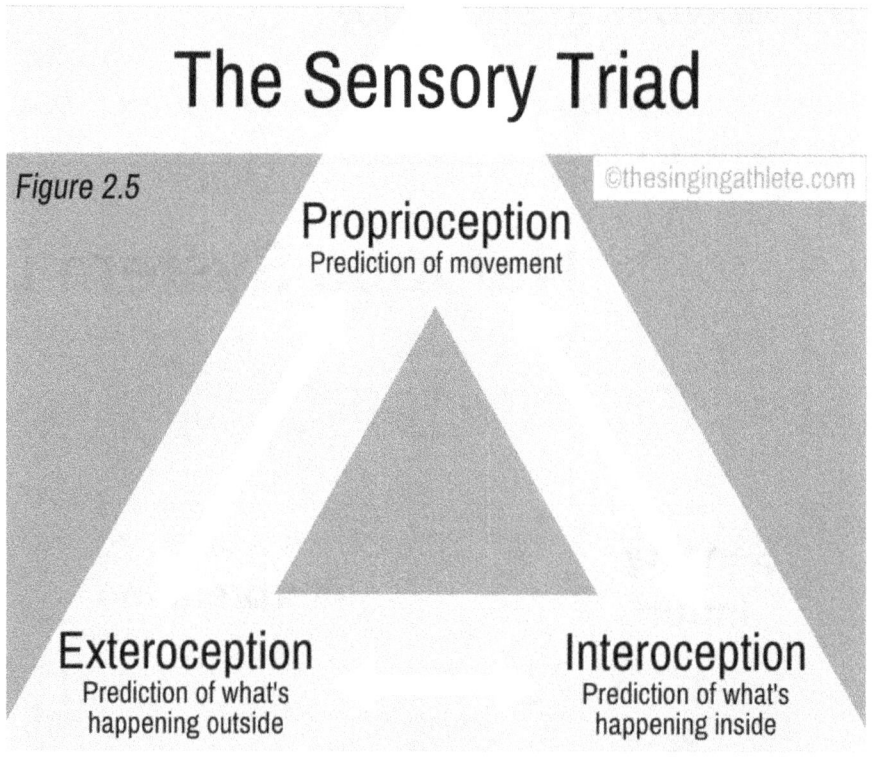

- ***Proprioception:*** Information about your 3D body position in space and time. You have proprioceptive nerve endings to sense movement (***mechanoreceptors***), pressure (***baroreceptors***), temperature (***thermoreceptors***), chemical substances (***chemoreceptors***), and threat (***nociceptors***). The two most important to remember are mechanoreceptors and nociceptors. Vocal control depends mainly on sensory feedback from laryngeal mechanoreceptors.[4] Nociceptors pick up any unpleasant stimulus, including (but not limited to) pain.

- ***Exteroception:*** Feedback from the external environment, including vision, hearing, taste, smell, and touch.

- ***Interoception:*** Awareness of internal sensations and feelings. Interoception includes gut function, breathing, balance, and your sense of purpose in life (see Chapter 17).

All of these sensory inputs are predictive in nature. Your brain is looking for patterns in the world and within yourself. It uses information from these sensory systems to streamline its predictions:

- ***Proprioception:*** Prediction of movement

- ***Exteroception:*** Prediction of what's happening outside

- ***Interoception:*** Prediction of what's happening inside

Data from the sensory triad is processed in a complex pattern that we can reduce to a simplified rule:

- ***All sensation eventually goes to the opposite side of the brain, except smell.***

Rub your left hand on top of your left thigh. The sensations on your palm and leg were processed in your *right* brain. Take your right hand and scratch your right foot. The sensations on your fingertips and foot were processed in your *left* brain. Plug your left nostril and smell something in your right nostril. That sensation was processed in your *right* brain (smell is the only sense that stays on the same side).

INTERPRETATION

Your brain is divided between the *first brain* and the *second brain* (Fig. 2.6). The first brain is also known as the old brain or reptilian brain; it is a relic from earlier evolutionary days. The first brain is the home of all the automatic processes that keep you alive, like reflexive breathing and pumping blood through the heart. It is non-rational and is the seat of primal emotion. This part of the brain includes the brainstem and the cerebellum (see Chapter 15). The primary concern of the first brain is your safety in the present moment.

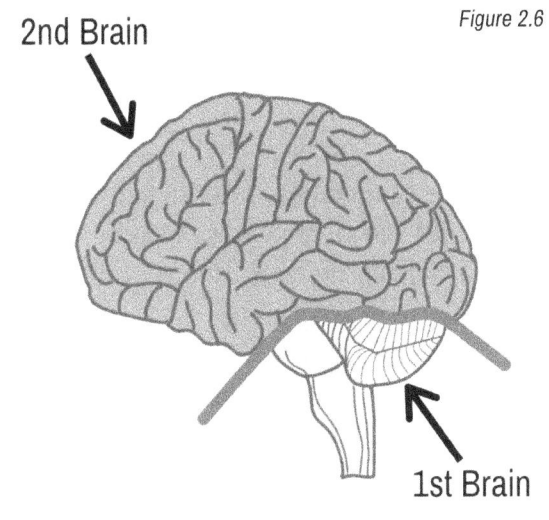

Figure 2.6

The second brain is also called the new brain or neocortex. Conscious thought, language, and creative impulses live here. If you unfolded it, it would be about the size of a dinner napkin and the depth of six business cards. All of the thrilling music and art ever created was dreamed up in this relatively tiny area of neural real estate. One of the second brain's primary jobs is to inhibit the first brain and its more primal emotional responses. If you only had a first brain, you would basically be a crocodile.

When the brain is interpreting sensory input, the data goes initially through the first brain, which then decides if the input is worthy of the second brain's attention. This decision happens in a part of the brain called the *thalamus*, which serves as a gatekeeper to the second brain. To get a sense of how this works, take a moment to notice the pressure your body is making against the chair/couch/bed as you read this. That force is being registered by baroreceptors in your skin. Your first brain sends the information to the thalamus, which decides there is no need to pay attention to this pressure, so you are not even consciously aware of it. Now imagine that a pin pops out of the surface against which you are resting. The sharpness of this object would trigger threat (nociception), and your thalamus would pass the first brain's message along to the second brain so you could get your butt up and avoid injury.

We receive a ton of information continuously (around 400 billion signals per second). We are unconsciously aware of about two thousand signals and are consciously taking in around forty. Most humans are capable of approximately seven conscious thoughts per second. It is the job of the thalamus and the second brain to decide where attention should be focused. If you spend your seven thoughts per second on the right things, that's when the vocal breakthroughs occur.

MOTOR OUTPUT

The reason you can move is either to enact your will on the world (performance-based outputs from the second brain) or to avoid danger (threat-based outputs from the first brain). The threat-based outputs take precedence over performance-based ones; this means that the first brain is really in charge of most of your neural output. Think of your first brain like an elephant and your second brain like a rider sitting astride. The rider might think they're steering the elephant, but our pachyderm friend probably has other ideas.[5]

Here's the rule when it comes to motor output *(Fig. 2.7)*:

- *The **right brain** controls voluntary movement on the **left** side of the body and sets reflexive muscle tone on the **right** side.*

- *The **left brain** controls voluntary movement on the **right** side of the body and sets reflexive muscle tone on the **left** side.*

Lift your left arm. That command came from your right brain. Wiggle your right toes. That command came from your left brain.

When a motor command leaves the brain, there is a division of neural activation:

- ***10 percent of brain output goes to voluntary movement.***

- ***90 percent of brain output goes to reflexive stabilization.***

Press your right arm up to the ceiling, like you're doing a shoulder press. As you perform this motion, most of your neural output is going to stabilizing the rest of your body; only a small fraction is directed at your right arm. Of the roughly 100 billion neurons in your brain, only around 1 million (.001 percent) are devoted to voluntary movement. The vast majority are given over to first-brain systems that keep you alive and reflexively steady.

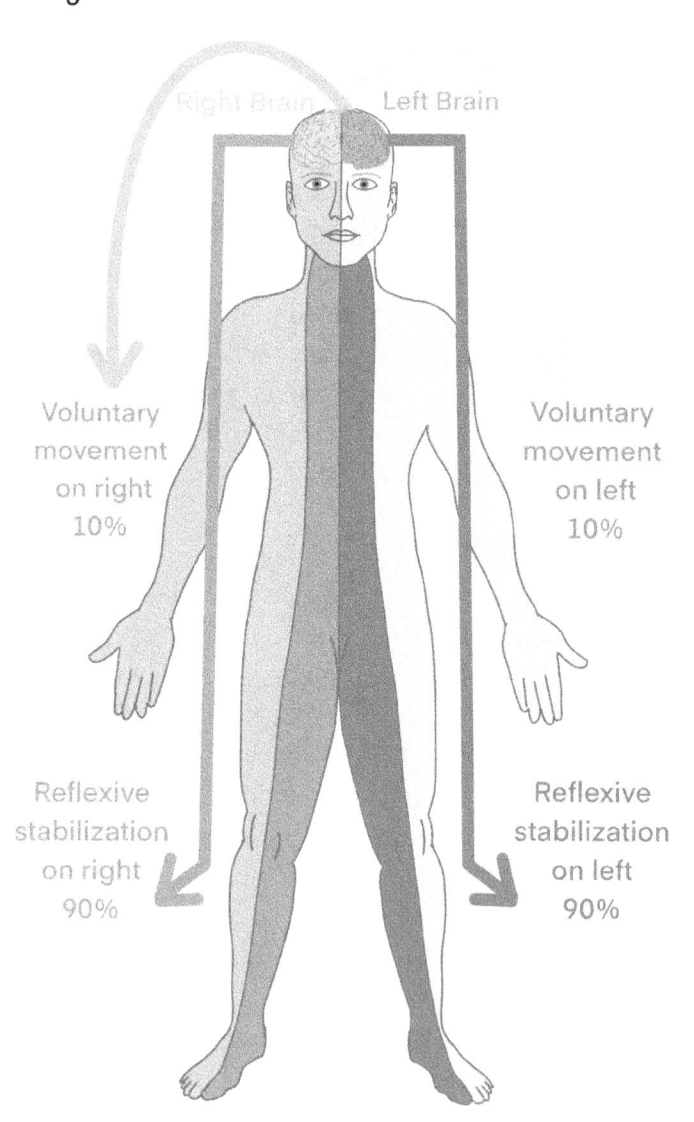

Figure 2.7

Think about the often-given voice instruction to "support the high note!" If 90 percent of the output from your brain is about *reflexive* support, not conscious muscle contraction, does this instruction make sense? Is it efficient to use 10 percent of your brain's output to "support the high note" using voluntary muscles? Or would it be better to connect with the other 90 percent of your muscles that provide subconscious stability, thus training the vocal support mechanism through reflexive activations?

Go online and watch some of your favorite performers; when choosing who to watch, select people who've been performing consistently at a high level for at least ten years. (If they've been vocally successful for that long, they're doing something right.) When you watch them sing, do they look like they're thinking, "Support the high note!" in the big phrases? Or does it seem to be happening automatically, without any apparent effort? Using voluntary muscle contraction makes singing feel stiff and hard. Improving your reflexive stability makes it feel free and easy.

BRAIN ANATOMY

Let's go over a bit of neuroanatomy *(Fig. 2.8)*. These are the first brain areas we'll be discussing:

Brainstem: Consisting of three divisions (midbrain, pons, and medulla), the brainstem is the seat of the reflexive systems that keep you going. It is also the originating point for most of your cranial nerves, which control many of the structures involved in singing.

Cerebellum: Also known as the "little brain," the cerebellum is positioned near the top of your spinal cord. It is an active integration hub for many sensory and motor inputs. The cerebellum is always asking, "What is the most appropriate motor response to keep me safe or achieve my targets?"[6]

In the second brain, we'll be focusing on these lobes:

Frontal Lobe: The frontal lobe is the home of conscious thought. Decision-making, problem-solving, and higher-order thinking all take place here. The frontal lobe also contains the motor cortex, which controls

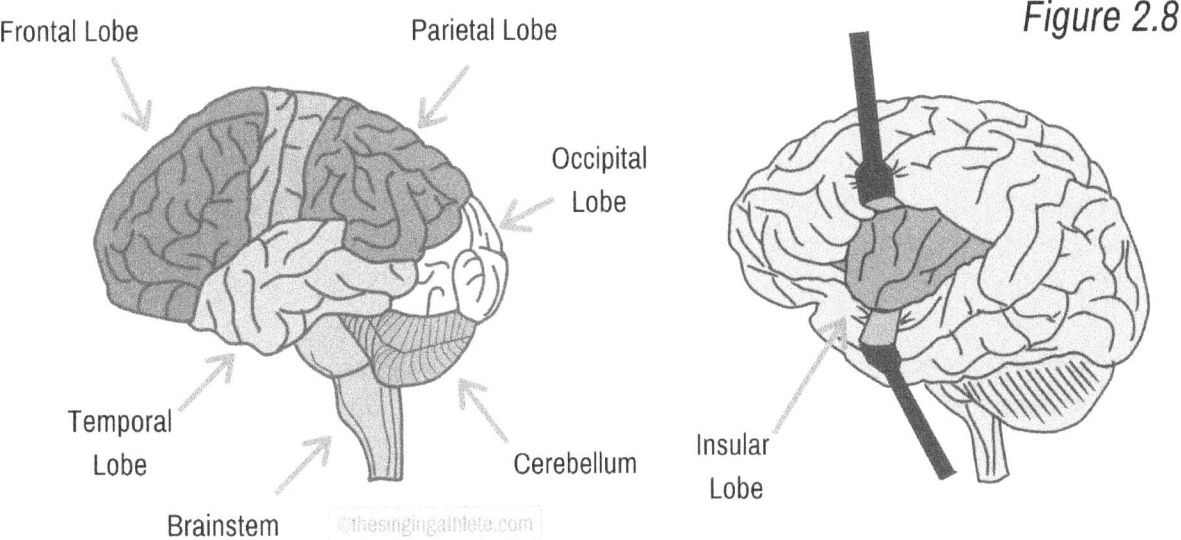

Figure 2.8

voluntary movement. Another essential function of the frontal lobe is to inhibit primal emotions from the first brain.

Parietal Lobe: The parietal lobe is where sensory information is processed. Touch, pain, and temperature are all assessed here. It's the "Where is it?" lobe, helping you create spatial representations of the world around you. Singers rely on this brain area more than instrumentalists.

Temporal Lobe: The temporal lobe is the music lobe; auditory processing happens here, as well as your sense of balance and rhythm. It plays a role in memory; if you always forget lyrics, you may have a left temporal lobe that needs some love. It also has significant functions in learning, language comprehension, and the sense of smell.

Occipital Lobe: The occipital lobe is the main home of visual processing. It contains the primary visual cortex and is involved with color and spatial perception.

Insular Lobe: The insular lobe is now considered by some neuroanatomists to be the fifth lobe of the brain, and it integrates with a tremendous number of body processes. It is the main seat of interoception and helps control your breathing, heart rate, and gut function. Any digestive issue (reflux/IBS/Crohn's) has an insular component. The insular lobe is also integral in social connection and giving you a feeling of purpose in your life.

HOW YOUR BRAIN STAYS ALIVE

The brain needs two things to keep going

- *Fuel* (oxygen/carbon dioxide balance and glucose extracted from food)

- *Activation* ("Use it or lose it" principle)

Fuel: Running your brain takes a lot of energy, and a steady fuel supply is the key. This is doubly true if you're in the market to change some of your habits. A brain that is in a transformation process requires about 25 percent more fuel than one that is plopped in front of a screen.

To have a happy brain, you must maintain the right balance of oxygen and carbon dioxide, which we will address in the breathing chapters. As singers, we are often told to "take a big breath," and we tend to think that taking in more air is always better. I'll show you how to test this assumption. The brain also needs a steady supply of glucose, which is a sugar that is extracted from the foods you eat.

Activation: The brain relies on neuronal activation to stay alive. A *neuron* (nerve cell) is the basic unit of the nervous system. The brain is estimated to contain around 100 billion neurons, making a potentially limitless amount of connections. If certain zones of neural real estate are habitually underused, your brain will assume you no longer need that area, and a loss of ability will result.

As an example, get on your hands and knees and press your palms into the floor, like you're about to do cat/cow in yoga. Rock forward slightly, putting a little weight on your palms and look at your thumbs. Are you able to completely extend (straighten) the thumbs while pressurizing your palms? Due to constant texting, many of us are losing our ability to activate our thumb extensors fully. If we keep our thumbs in constant flexion (thumb flexion is the bent position you use when you text), the brain assumes that extension is no longer a priority, and the neurons devoted to that movement get repurposed.

When you play a belt role for months in a show, your brain may think, "Hmm, you're never using your head voice anymore, so I guess those neurons can be put to better use somewhere else." To avoid a loss of vocal range and quality, you have to use all parts of your voice regularly. If you're a belter, sing a classical piece. If you're an opera singer, study a pop song. Vocal versatility isn't a party trick; it's a sign of neural health.

THE BRAIN'S FEEDING PATTERN

The brain is a greedy organ that demands a lot of resources to keep going. The oxygen, carbon dioxide, and glucose it uses as fuel enter in a "Bottom-to-top" and "Back-to-front" pattern *(Fig. 2.9)*.

The back half of the brain controls sensory processing (visual/auditory/balance/autonomics), while the front half controls motor output (planning/decision/voluntary movement). The back half is fed first. Even when you are asleep, automatic body processes like breathing and blood circulation must continue unabated.

The area that gets nourished last is the frontal lobe. From a survival perspective, this makes sense: long-range planning and thinking aren't nearly as important as reacting. (It doesn't matter if you can create an excellent twelve-month business plan if an avalanche is barreling toward you.) Thanks to this front-to-back feeding pattern, we can say that "***Sensory feeds motor***."

Therefore, we must include sensory testing and drills in voice training. Let's say your teacher asks you to lift your palate (motor instruction), and the sound gets worse. Maybe you've got an issue in your glossopharyngeal nerve that is preventing you from feeling your palate. Or maybe you had your tonsils out, and you never did sensory rehab in your throat after the surgery. Perhaps you had chronic ear infections as a child, and your balance and hearing are off. Rehabbing sensation in these areas may be all you need to "lift your palate."

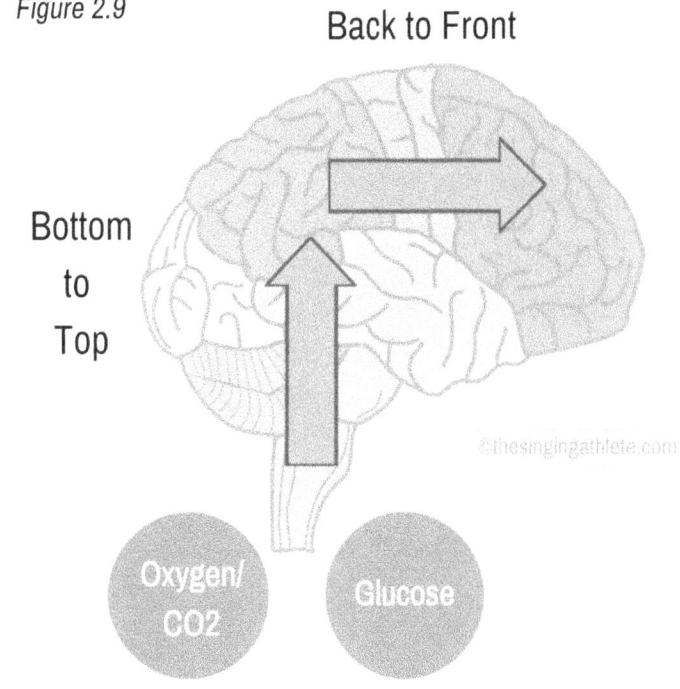

Figure 2.9

After an injury, the sensory component of rehab is often ignored. The typical focus is on regaining your range of motion, not on returning sensations to the surrounding skin. You can quickly check this in yourself: take the area of an old injury and test the sensation by putting something cold/warm/sharp/dull/ticklish on it. Does it feel the same as the skin areas around it?

If you can't feel something, you can't fix it. Your sensory awareness is crucial to good singing, and *everyone* has areas that need work. I've worked with thousands of singers at all levels, and no one has it all nailed. Remapping your body takes commitment, but it's what elite athletes do, and that's what I'm going to ask of you as you progress through the book.

MOVEMENT MAPS IN THE BRAIN

Think about the last time you got a paper cut on your finger. Do you remember how much it hurt? If you got the same size paper cut on your back, you might barely notice it. This disparity in sensation is because your brain has maps of your body parts, and they are not equal.[7]

You have a **somatosensory cortex** (in the parietal lobe), where sensation is processed, and a **motor cortex** (in the frontal lobe), where your brain initiates voluntary movement *(Fig. 2.10)*. Trained singers rely more

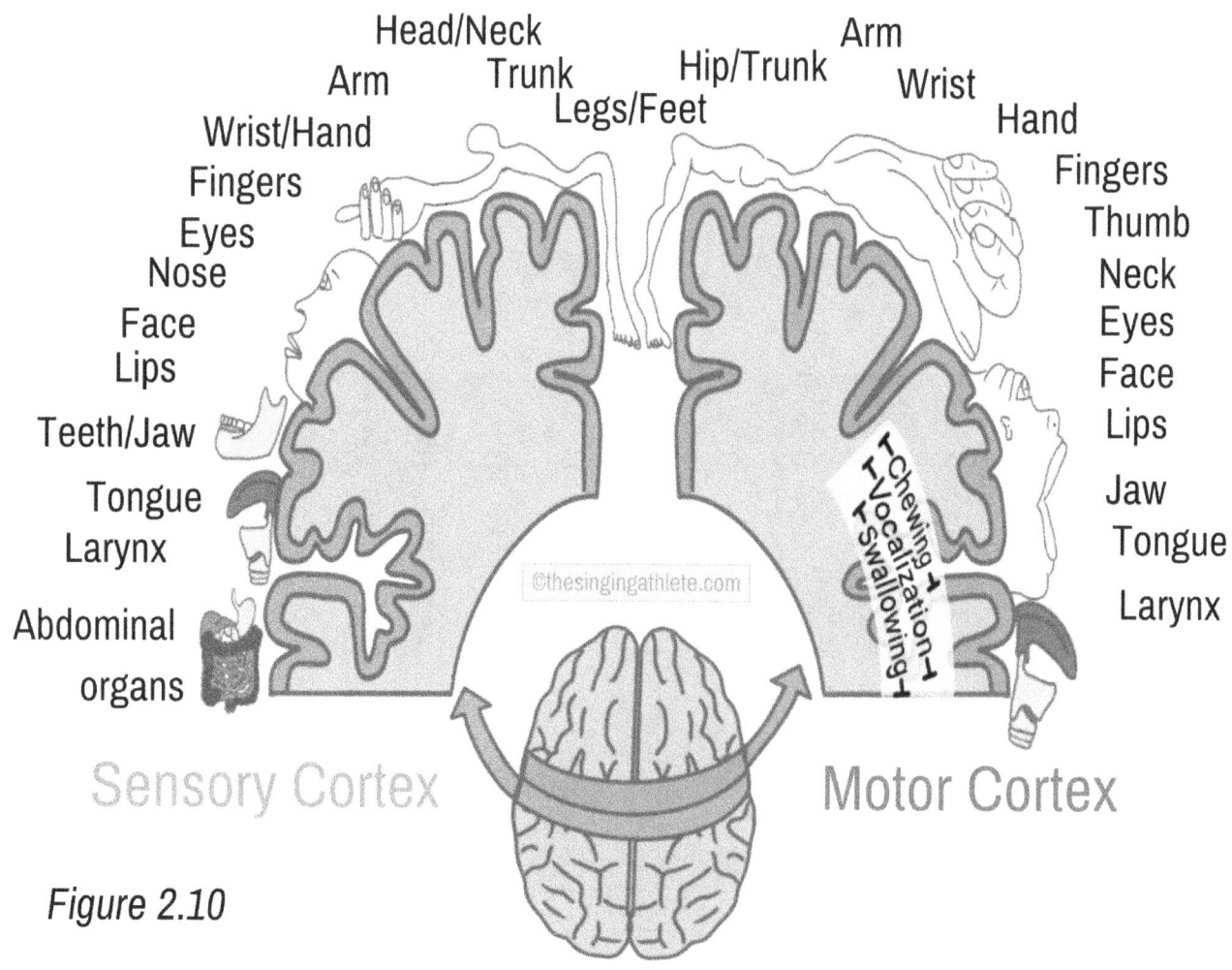

Figure 2.10

on these two brain areas than novices. As your voice study deepens, your ability to "feel" the note increases (somatosensory cortex).[8] Your motor cortex handles the subtle motions necessary for great vocal control. You've probably had to sing in less-than-ideal acoustics before; having a more developed set of sensory and movement maps prevents vocal pushing.

Each part of your body has a corresponding location in these brain areas. Let's look at the sensory cortex first, which is where sensation is processed for each body part. The larynx and tongue are right next to the abdominal area; this is why digestive issues can be so debilitating for singers. The larynx is also near the teeth, gums, and jaw, which tells us that rehabbing a dental surgery or a jaw issue can be important for a vocalist (see Chapter 10).

Now let's look at the motor cortex. The facial muscles live right near vocalization, which helps to make the coordination necessary for speech easier. Notice also that chewing and swallowing overlap with the voice; we will be checking your jaw and swallowing movements later. Going a bit farther up, do you see how the neck and the hands are the next neighboring structures? If you take a video of yourself singing, you may see extraneous hand motions, and this close relationship may explain why. Adjoining areas of the brain influence each other—or "neurons that fire together, wire together."

The development of fMRI (Functional Magnetic Resonance Imaging) technology has allowed considerable leaps in our understanding of the brain since its invention in the early 1990s. An fMRI machine creates a visual map of brain activation by perceiving changes in cerebral blood flow. When we look at musicians' brains on fMRI, we see mapping differences between singers and instrumentalists. For an instrumentalist, the motor cortex is quite active. Violinists show changes in the right motor cortex (remember, the right cortex controls the complicated fingering patterns that violinists do with their left hand).[9] The two-handed playing required for piano creates bilateral changes in motor-cortex activation.[10] However, the neural pattern in singing is strongly correlated with an increase in the activation of the somatosensory cortex.[11] For a singer, sensory feedback is essential.

Do you have injuries in your history that may have blurred your brain's maps in that corresponding body area? In one study demonstrating this concept, neuroscientist Michael Merzenich sewed two of a monkey's fingers together. After a while, the brain remapped the two fingers as a single finger, thus losing any ability to distinguish between them.[12] Other studies have shown that when two fingers are taped together, this blurring can start to happen in as little as thirty minutes.[13] Remember when I braced my elbow when I was playing in pain? That made my elbow maps worse, and I started having pain elsewhere as well. Have you ever spent any time in a cast or brace after an injury? Do you have areas that have been surgically altered? If so, it's worth thinking about how good your sensory and movement maps are in those areas of your body.

THE HOMUNCULUS

Figure 2.11 shows my representation of the *cortical homunculus.* This model is used in neuroscience to graphically depict how much of the nervous system is devoted to a particular body part. The distorted proportions refer not to that body region's actual surface area or volume, but rather to how many nerve fibers are found in that zone. You can think of it as a body map that lives inside your brain; the bigger body parts have more neural resources dedicated to them.

Figure 2.11

The sensory homunculus shows which structures get the most real estate to process sensation; let's look at it first. The tongue and lips are big because we use taste receptors to decide if the mushroom we're consuming is portobello or poison. The hands need to differentiate objects, so they get a lot of sensory brain space. The eyes and ears earn their size because we see and hear the hunting tiger before we feel it. The nose will help us smell a fire, so it's a priority as well.

Now let's take a look at the motor homunculus; the bigger the body part, the more important the brain thinks movement is in that area. The large hands make sense; that whole "opposable thumb" thing allows us to grasp and use tools. But why do you think the lips and tongue are so massive? There is one thing that made us apex predators: language. Being able to talk to each other allowed us to coordinate while taking down a woolly mammoth or two. The large eyes make sense from a threat-assessment perspective because we have to be able to look around our environment easily. Are you surprised by the size of the nose? Why would moving the nostrils be so important? Humans are supposed to be nasal breathers; mouth breathing is to be reserved for emergencies only.

Looking at the homunculus, think about how much brain activation occurs in singing. On a neural level, an hour spent vocalizing and moving the muscles of your face, throat, and tongue may be more stimulating than an hour spent running. It's also important to understand that areas with the smallest homuncular representations are the most likely to be in pain. Think of how often people complain about sore backs. If something detrimental happens in an under-represented area like the lumbar spine, the brain can quickly lose clarity there and send off alarms.

PERFORMERS AND CHRONIC PAIN

Pain comes in many flavors. In acute situations, like when you cut yourself, pain is a highly useful thing. When you feel a knife slice through the skin, your reflexive, immediate recoil prevents further tissue damage. But in chronic pain situations, a different process is at work. The nerves may have gone through a neuroplastic change where now they are hyper-excitable and firing constantly. The body may even convert movement receptors (mechanoreceptors) into threat receptors (nociceptors), triggering pain with each motion. This can cause you to fear that you are creating more damage every time you move (most likely you are not).

One of the first steps on the path of healing pain is to realize that pain is an action signal created in the brain, not necessarily a sign of tissue damage. Pain is your brain's *opinion*; your cortex has decided that you need it for some reason. Pain feels so real that we tend to believe that something dire is happening, but your brain can choose to create a nociceptive signal by merely being stressed out. You may notice that you're more aware of pain when you are under pressure or in environments that scare or irritate you (e.g., hospitals, court, the DMV). This can be summed up as: **Pain does not equal injury, and injury does not equal pain.**

If you are interested in resolving chronic pain issues, find a trainer on thesingingathlete.com, or meet with someone who understands these concepts. Pain is a private and personal experience. No one has the right to tell you how much something bothers you, and anything you bring to your healing team should be treated respectfully. My two favorite books on the topic are *Explain Pain* by Butler and Moseley and *Pain Neuroscience Education* by Louw et al.

Chronic pain sufferers tend to have a problem distinguishing left from right; determining left from right occurs in your parietal lobe, where sensation (including pain) is processed. Drills that improve your sense of left and right can also improve the clarity of your brain's sensory maps, thereby reducing threat and pain. The *Recognise* app is also a great tool for this. The app shows you a series of pictures of a body part (hands/feet/backs, etc.) shot in isolation, and you have to determine if the left or the right is being shown. It's fun, harder than it seems, and can be an excellent drill for pain reduction.

3. PRACTICE

To uncover the best possibilities for your voice, you have to practice. Even beginners understand that repetition is required for improvement, and yet there is often confusion about what this means practically. Do you just sing scales for awhile? Do you belt out your song over and over again? How much is too much or too little?

I can tell you that shorter, more frequent practice sessions provide better results. If you have two hours a week to devote to your singing, spend twenty minutes practicing, six times a week; this is more effective than a single two-hour session. And when you do practice, I want your training to be potent. Much like a drug, practice is designed to affect the nervous system. You want the effect to be palpable and clear. To achieve a potent practice routine, remember these elements:

- *You have to love it:* Nothing good will come from your practice time if you dread opening your music. Use the drills from this book and find something new to investigate every time you sing.

- *Rote practice is not potent practice:* If you're distracted or on autopilot when you're training, progress will be slow or nonexistent. You have to be present.

- *Failing sometimes is useful:* This is hard for the perfectionists among us, but if you're never falling short, you're not training at the right level. Potent practice can feel uncomfortable because you should be interacting with music that is right at the edge of your current capabilities. Some experts in motor learning think that a 50 percent success/failure rate means that you're practicing at the right difficulty level.

- *Practice needs to feel safe:* Do you love singing when you're alone in the car? Part of the reason may be because no one can hear you. Sing in a space where you are not self-conscious about making experimental sounds. If you're in an apartment with thin walls, get a white noise machine. You will achieve no gains as long as you're afraid of judgments from your boyfriend/girlfriend/roommate/neighbors, etc.

- *Feedback is essential:* I often record myself (either audio or video) when I practice. As I listen or watch back, I inevitably learn something new. I also work with various coaches to give me live feedback. If you are a teacher, you need a coach for yourself. No exceptions.

ASSESS AND REASSESS

There are a whole bunch of drills in this book. Your goal is not to do all of them in every practice session. You have to figure out which ones work best for you. Since I'm not there with you, we will be using a process called "Assess and Reassess" to test the efficacy of an exercise for your nervous system. In the assessment phase, you will sing a scale or a phrase of music to see how your voice is feeling. Choose something that presents a technical challenge but that won't exhaust you to repeat many times. Because motor learning improves when you create variety, I suggest rotating styles and songs during your assessments. Here are some examples of phrases that I use in my practice sessions:

- The final section of "Lonely Town" from *On the Town*

- The "ah" vocalise in the bridge of "It All Fades Away" from *The Bridges of Madison County*

- The opening lines of "Dear Me" by Eric Hutchinson

- "Stars" by Grace Potter

- The end of "Von Ewiger Liebe" by Brahms

- The last page of "Avant de Quitter Ces Lieux" from the opera *Faust*

I also intersperse traditional vocal exercises (e.g., nine-tone scales, arpeggios, sustained notes) into my rotation of vocal assessments. If you're a beginner and you don't know what to sing, you can assess with any favorite song. "Happy Birthday" is fine.

> Let's take a moment to talk about musical style as it relates to this book. I work predominantly with musical theatre performers, but these exercises can be applied to any style of singing. When it comes to using these drills, there is no difference between Adele's aria from *Die Fledermaus* and "Rolling in the Deep" (by Adele…see what I did there?) You can also apply them to stage speech or any other vocal demands.

Once you've assessed your voice, you will do one of the drills described in this book. Then you will sing the same musical phrase again as a reassessment.

There are three possible outcomes from the assess and reassess process:

- If your voice improved on reassessment, you know it was a drill that lowered threat for you; we will call that a ***high-payoff drill***. You will use your high-payoff drills before performance.

- If there was no perceptible change, it is a ***neutral drill*** for you. This doesn't mean it has no value, as I'll explain below.

- If there was a negative reassessment (loss of range/tightness in throat/increased sense of vocal effort), it is a ***rehab drill***.

A rehab drill is one that your nervous system is currently finding a bit scary. The drill increased threat in your brain, so it degraded performance. It is NOT okay to ignore rehab drills. Mammals are designed to move, so none of the motions you'll be doing throughout the book should test poorly. Having a threat response to a movement implies there are mapping errors in that area. Fixing these rehab drills may be the key to resolving issues that have been holding your voice back.

To improve a rehab drill, you have to regress it until it tests as neutral or high-payoff. Regressing a drill means making it easier until the threat you experienced dissipates. Some ways to regress drills are:

- Try it again for less time, do it more slowly, or move through a smaller range of motion (e.g., instead of moving your jaw all the way to the side, move it halfway).

- If you were doing the drill standing, try it seated. If you were seated, try it sitting on the floor with your back against a wall and your legs stretched out in front of you. You can also do most of these drills lying down on your back, which is the lowest-threat position.

- Be more conscious of slow, low breathing through your nose.

- Close your eyes.

Your neutral drills can be used to reset yourself after discovering a rehab drill. For example, if you have a threat response to doing pectoralis minor breathing (Chapter 7), but pectoralis major breathing was neutral for you, you can do the pec major breath to get yourself back to a balanced state.

Work on a rehab drill for a few weeks in one or more of the regressions above, possibly followed by some neutral drills. If no improvement shows up after a few weeks of diligent practice, you may need help from your high-payoff drills. From a neural perspective, the statement, "If you exercise something, it will get stronger" isn't necessarily accurate. If an area of the brain has been dormant for a long time, the signaling may not be robust enough to create change in the underused territory. The solution is: ***Do something good before you do something bad***

If you struggle with a certain vision exercise, but you always get a great result from a jaw glide, do your jaw drills (high-payoff) first and then work on your eyes (rehab).

When it comes to timing:

- Do your high-payoff drills right before you perform, exercise, or need a boost of energy.

- Separate your rehab drills from performance situations by an hour.

So, if you have an 8 p.m. curtain, you can practice your rehab drills in the afternoon and then do your high-payoff stuff right before you walk on stage.

For some of us, a vocal reassessment will be enough to notice changes. Sometimes, though, you may need a secondary confirmation. For this, I suggest using range-of-motion testing. You can refer to the videos on thesingingathlete.com to make sure you're doing these properly:

- Forward bend
- Torso rotation
- Shoulder flexion
- Shoulder abduction
- Shoulder internal/external rotation
- Neck rotation/lateral flexion

As you go through these movements, you are trying to identify limits. Can you get your palms flat on the floor in a straight-leg forward bend? Does one arm get stuck in front of your ear as you go into shoulder flexion? When you've identified something that feels sticky, use that as a secondary reassessment after the drills. If your high note flies out of your mouth and your neck rotates 30 degrees farther, you will definitely know it is a high-payoff drill for you.

If you are super-flexible and all of the range-of-motion tests feel easy and symmetrical, you can use balance or strength as a secondary assessment. Try standing on one leg with your foot in parallel and your eyes closed, or hold a static squat or plank as a strength test.

In most of the drills in the book, I start with the instruction "Assess your voice and body" and end with "Reassess." This is what that will look like *(Fig. 3.1)*:

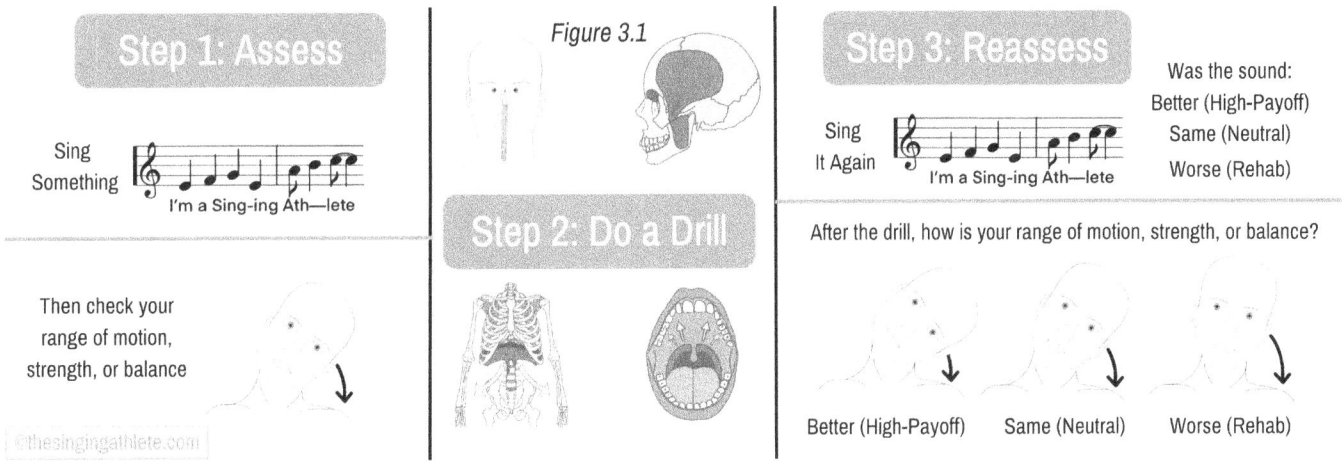

1. Assess your voice and body (Sing a scale or a phrase of music and then check your range of motion, strength, or flexibility).

2. Do the drill.

3. Reassess (Immediately sing the phrase again and recheck your range of motion, strength, or flexibility as a secondary confirmation).

I'm hoping the assess/reassess process will feel clear. If you are getting mixed or confusing results (one day a drill is high-payoff, the next day it's rehab), that usually comes back to fuel. Invest deeply in doing the drills in the breathing chapters and see if that makes results more consistent. Also, having a snack before or during training may be a good idea. To keep track of which drills are currently high-payoff, neutral, and rehab, there is a chart at the end of the book. You can also download it at thesingingathlete.com.

While this may seem like a simple idea, the assess/reassess protocol is quite powerful. The challenge in our lives today isn't access to information; it's knowing whom to trust. You have ten million opinions at your fingertips every time you look at your phone. The issue is sorting through all of this noise to get to something that makes sense for you. Luckily, your brain will tell you precisely what you need; you just have to know how to listen. A high-payoff reassessment means you are on the right track to lower threat and perform to your full potential.

EFFICIENCY AND ITS ENEMIES

When I saw Sutton Foster in *Anything Goes* on Broadway, I was floored by how easy she made the Act I finale look. After an intense five-minute tap routine that she performed with a big smile on her face, she had the vocal stamina to flawlessly belt a D at the end of the number. By this point, I had seen countless Broadway shows, but her performance took my breath away. It was efficiency personified.

In the Z-Health curriculum, efficiency is defined as "Doing just the right thing at the right time with just the right amount of energy." What can get in the way of efficient singing? The first thing is something called the ***startle reflex***, which is a hard-wired response to threat that is characterized by two main movements: flexion (closing the front of the body) and adduction (pulling the sides of the body in). You can think of it as "the hard, bony bits protecting the soft, squishy bits." Figure 3.2 shows the startle reflex in action:

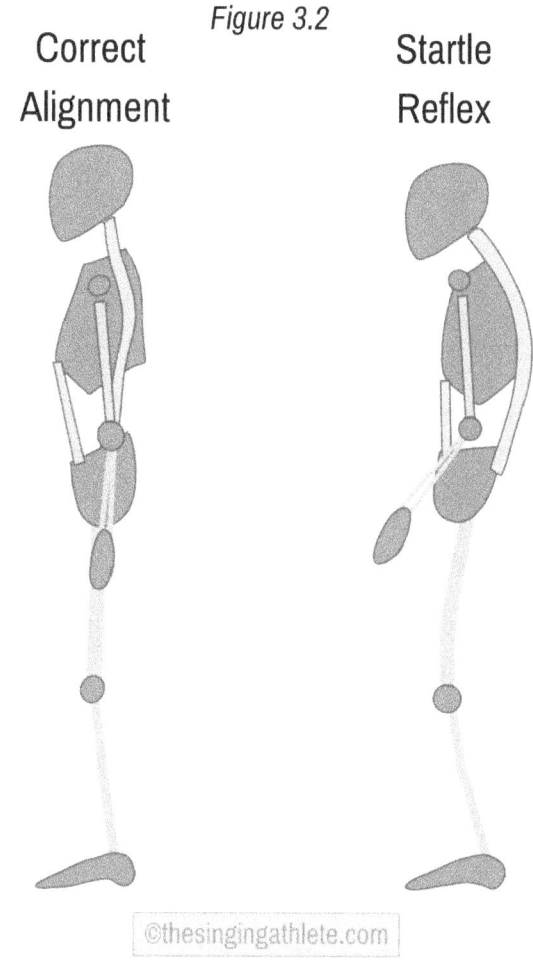

Figure 3.2

- The head is pulled down and forward to protect the throat.

- The shoulders are bilaterally elevated and rounded.

- The chest muscles are tight and squeezing the ribs.

- The abdominal muscles are locked.

- The butt and the inside of the legs are squeezed.

- It's not pictured, but the facial muscles will also be tense.

When you watch yourself sing on video, you may see some elements of the startle reflex. You might see a tight forehead right before that one high note. Or you might notice your head creeping forward when you get to that emotionally vulnerable passage. Maybe you see how your shoulders look more slumped than you think.

Once you are in a startle reflex, you are in a threatened state and will not acquire any new skills. Your brain doesn't think that whatever is happening is safe, so it will close off the neural pathways that create performance improvements. (This is also why a secure environment is so important in educational experiences.)

If you're working through the drills in this book on your own, you need to watch out for the elements of the startle reflex. The best way to do this without a coach is to shoot a video of yourself doing the drills. Watch it back with the postural elements listed above in mind. Is your face relaxed? Are your shoulders lifting when you breathe? Is your neck pushing forward?

The second enemy of efficiency is known as **sensory motor amnesia**, a term coined by Thomas Hanna.[14] If we are not regularly moving our joints through their full ranges of motion, the brain may forget how to control them. Life is driven by habit, and all of us have some movements that are being underused. Let's do an experiment:

Finger Circles

1. Put your non-dominant hand out in front of you.

2. Begin to make a slow, controlled circle with only your pointer finger, not moving any other finger. Go both ways for 3–5 reps, making sure you are not skipping any part of the circle.

3. Repeat with the middle finger, ring finger, and pinky.

How was that? Some of you may have found it surprisingly challenging. You might have noticed some of the following things:

- Shaking or tremors in the fingers

- Skipping part of the circle

- An inconsistent rate of movement (suddenly speeding up or slowing down)

- Forgetting to breathe

- Compensating with another body part (*"Why is my jaw tight while I'm moving my finger?"*)

In this book, we will be training the muscles of the trunk, neck, and jaw. Look for areas of sensory motor amnesia in your movement patterns. If you find a forgotten gesture, try these steps to fix it:

- Do the drill more slowly or using a smaller range of motion.

- Give yourself an external target (e.g., move your jaw toward an object in the room).

- Rub, scratch, or tap on the body part in question (remember that sensory feeds motor).

A Drill to Improve Efficiency: Long Spine

Pretty much every style of bodywork has a version of what can be called a long spine drill (*Fig. 3.3*). Alexander Technique describes the head moving "forward and up," while the *Tai Chi Classics* say, "The spine should be like a necklace of pearls hanging from heaven."[15] I support any way of experiencing this sensation, known technically as axial extension; it is a hallmark of all great athletes and performers.

There can be a difference in efficiency, however, between an internal and an external focus in a long-spine drill. An internal focus of attention is defined as training yourself to notice the movement or position of a specific body part. An external focus is directing your attention to the effects of your movement, or to specific objects in the environment around you. Let's do an experiment to see which type of focus feels better for you:

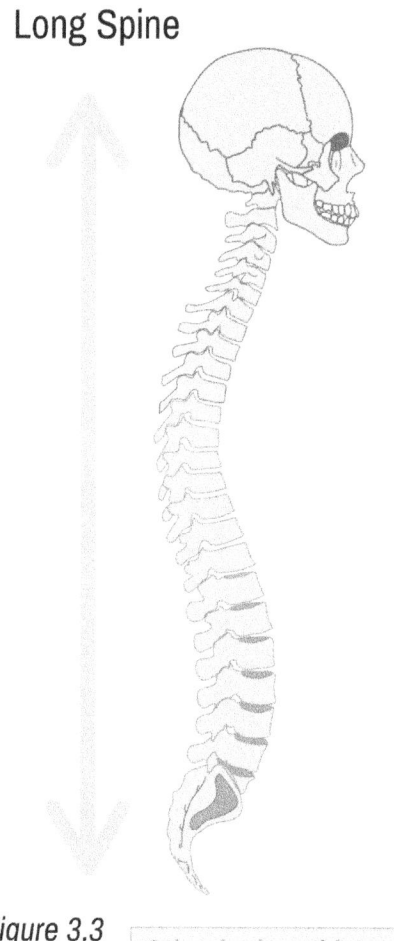

Figure 3.3

Long Spine Version 1 (Internal Focus): Sit up tall with your feet in parallel, flat on the floor. Imagine your tailbone moving gently down. Starting in your lower back, imagine each vertebra moving apart from the one above and below it. Scan mentally through the vertebrae in your mid-back, upper back, and neck, moving each apart as you go. Finally, imagine your skull floating off the top of your spine.

Long Spine Version 2 (External Focus): Take a light object (a small pillow or a wadded-up piece of clothing) and put it on top of your head. Elongate your spine by pushing the object toward the ceiling. At the same time, push the waistband of your pants toward the ground. Keeping pushing the object up and the waistband down.

Which one felt better? There is evidence that when you focus on building proprioception internally (e.g., trying to move each vertebra apart), there can be a negative impact on flexibility and an increase in muscle tension. Focusing instead on creating change in the external environment (e.g., pushing the pillow toward the ceiling) can promote fluidity. External focus also seems to make athletes and musicians more resilient when it comes to performance pressure.[16] This improvement in movement fluency that comes through external focus has also been demonstrated in oral-motor[17] and vocal performance.[18]

Here are some ideas on how to bring an external focus to your practice:

- *Add a visual component:* I'll give you a bunch of options in the chapter on eyes, but you can start with something simple, like singing to objects that are varying distances from you.

- *Add an auditory component:* Listen for something new in the accompaniment. Pay attention to the effect of your voice filling the space in which you are singing.

- *Use an external target:* Take a book and slide it along the top of a piano/table/desk as you sing a long musical phrase.

- *Focus on moving clothing instead of your body parts:* When I instruct a front-to-back pelvic tilt in my studio, I usually say, "Lift and drop your belt buckle," instead of, "Tuck and tilt your pelvis." The brain seems to make a distinction between clothing, which it considers external, and the name of a body part, which it deems internal.

- *Tell the story:* When you are singing lyrics, communication should always be paramount. Concentrate on the words and the effect they are intended to achieve. Basically, be an actor.

This idea of external targeting can also be applied to any areas of sensory motor amnesia. For example, if you struggled with the finger circles, try putting a rubber band around your finger and think of moving the band instead of your finger.

Does all this mean there is no value to an internal focus? Not at all. An internal focus can help you develop interoceptive awareness (your ability to feel the internal state of your body). Interoception is key for singers, especially when it comes to the emotional connection of music and voice.[19] And although an internal focus can promote more muscle tension, sometimes that is a good thing. We don't want to get the idea that tension is always bad and relaxation good. Muscles are designed to contract, and taking yourself into a strong activation can create a better movement map. (If internal focus tested well for you, pay special attention to Chapter 17.)

YOU SAID IT

One of my favorite quotes from Dr. Cobb is, "The body you have is the body you've earned by the way that you move." Since voice is movement, we can adapt this quote for singers: "The voice you have is the voice you've earned by the way that you move." *(Fig. 3.4)* I love this statement because it gives you ownership over your story. Whatever is happening with your voice, positive or negative, comes back to you and how you move through the world.

You might hear a singer say, "I have allergies, so I haven't been able to sing all spring." or, "I have reflux, so my cords are always swollen." If the singer accepts ownership of their movement patterns, these statements could change:

- Instead of, "I have allergies," how about, "I'm in a stubborn habit of mouth breathing, so I end up taking a ton of allergens directly into my lungs and my vocal folds are suffering."

- "I have reflux" could become, "I've been ignoring my diaphragmatic movement throughout the day and the muscle has gotten so weak that now I'm experiencing reflux symptoms."

You don't "have" reflux, allergies, or swollen vocal folds. These are all movement disorders; efficiency is not being maintained. The movements that are causing the problem may be below your consciousness, but that doesn't change the facts. If you're going to take responsibility for your movement, understanding the **SAID Principle** is essential.

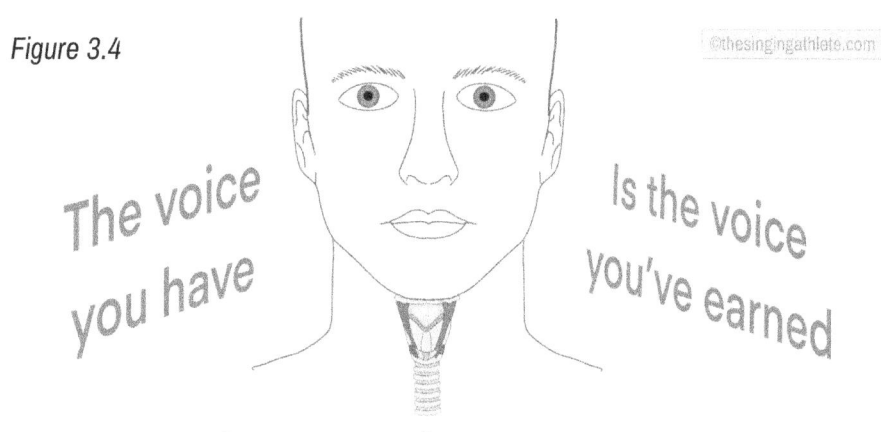

Figure 3.4

The SAID Principle stands for "specific adaptation to imposed demand." You can think of it as "form follows function." Whatever we do habitually (function) is supported by our physical selves (form). If we move for years in an inefficient way, the nervous system starts to lay down bone (called **Wolff's Law**) and soft tissue (called **Davis' Law**) to support these lines of chronic stress. An example would be a heel spur that develops due to faulty gait patterns. The brain sends signals to lay down extra bone in the heel to support the movement pattern, even though it's dysfunctional.

Another example of the SAID Principle is vocal nodules. If someone uses an inefficient pattern of vocal production, the brain may decide to lay down extra tissue in the vocal folds, creating a callus at the point of stress. When speaking and singing habits improve, the nodules usually disappear. The brain has decided there is no longer a need for additional tissue support at that location.

All training is SAID-specific. The ability to do something flawlessly in one context doesn't mean it will necessarily translate to all situations. For me, I've been doing tons of breathing work for years, and I'm pretty good at it when I'm standing, sitting, etc. However, I noticed a while ago that I tended to hyperventilate in my yoga headstand practice. So I started doing breathing drills before and during my headstand, and the hyperventilation pattern improved.

Let's say you're about to play Elphaba, and you can sing "Defying Gravity" like a goddess. Can you sing it that well on a narrow platform? How does it feel to hold a heavy broom in your right hand? Will the green stage lights affect you? (I'll talk more about color and the brain later.) Practicing in a narrower stance, holding a broom, or wearing green glasses would all be good ways to bring the SAID Principle into training for that role.

If you meditate, you've probably practiced regularly in low-threat arenas (at home, in a quiet and dark room). Make sure you also sharpen your mindfulness skills by using them in intense situations (in NYC, the subway is always a solid choice). The characters we play onstage are generally in very heightened circumstances (otherwise, why are they singing?). When you bring awareness into high-stress situations, the carryover to your performing is greater.

THE THREE STAGES OF MOTOR LEARNING

Sing a note on "ah" in a comfortable range. How did you do that? When you think about it, doesn't it seem magical? You had to reflexively coordinate inhalation and exhalation muscles, creating sufficient pressure to bring the vocal folds together. Several muscles of your larynx needed to variously engage or relax to create the pitch you intended. Your tongue muscles had to form the correct shape for an "ah." Your mouth had to open the proper distance. Your palate had to decide whether to close off your nose, your mouth, or hang out somewhere in between. Beyond these more obvious players, tons of stabilizing muscles needed to wake up to provide a solid base for the sound. The human body is friggin' amazing.

At some point in your development, this all required conscious thought, but now it feels automatic. You went through a process of **motor learning**, and it happened in three stages *(Fig. 3.5)*.[20]

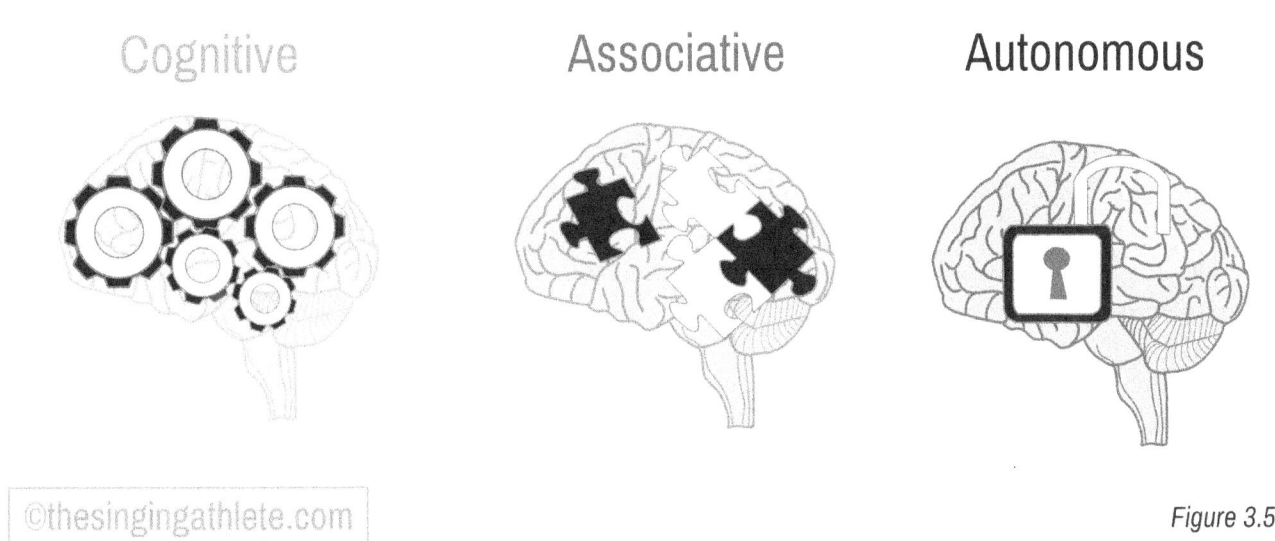

Figure 3.5

The **cognitive** stage is where you need to think consciously about what you're doing. You've probably come across some vocal skills that only happen when you focus on them intensely. Maybe you've mastered that one low note when you're thinking about it, but when you go to act the song, it leaves the building. This cognitive stage is where an internal focus of attention can be helpful. You need lots of opportunities for concentrated practice, with minimal distractions and a space where it's okay to fail.

The **associative** stage is where you relate the skills you're learning to previously mastered things. Let's say you're working on the end of "Hold On" from *The Secret Garden*, but the last B, on the word "a-**way**," keeps going flat. Shoot. But you also sing the title song from *Cabaret*, and that ending feels effortless on the same "ay" vowel ("life is a ca-ba-**ret**."). That song ends on a B-flat, a half-step down; your first brain may have decided that a B-flat is safe, but a B-natural is threatening. What if you sing the end of "Cabaret," but do it up a half-step, so now you're belting a B? It may feel less scary because the melody of "Cabaret" is an old friend (or should I say "old chum"). If the B comes out in "Cabaret," now go back to "Hold On" and try it again—it just might work now.

Finally, there is the **autonomous** stage, where no conscious thought is required. When singing autonomously, it feels like your voice is leaving your body without any effort at all. You already have lots of autonomous singing skills; think of that "ah" you sang at the beginning of this section. Practice is about guiding any song, role, or performance through these three steps: learn it slowly and carefully, make connections, and finally let it go (…the cold never bothered me, anyway).

I'M A F.A.N.

If you want to progress quickly through the stages of motor learning, there are three elements you are going to need in your practice:

- *Frequency*

- *Attention*

- *Novelty*

Frequency: Making vocal changes means you need to go over the correct form many, many, many, many times. A career as a singer is finding joy in repetition. It requires tons of reps because your brain wants to save calories; there is a constant subconscious concern about where the next meal will come from. Your brain will resist spending resources on making your high G shimmer because it views that glorious note as unnecessary for survival. It sounds silly, but your brain needs to be constantly reminded that you want to sing better. If you don't keep coming back to the drills, it will think you don't want to make the learning permanent.

Attention: Even though some singers tell me they do their best work while cleaning the house, that's not how elite athletes do it. Countless studies have shown that the best of the best are fully present when they are training. They are working hard to build a mental model of what the perfect race/game/event would look like and create an environment where anything else is an error. When you practice, I want your phone on silent, your girlfriend out of the room, and your brain ready to make some serious change.

Novelty: Humans rely on new experiences. If things never change in training environments, you stop caring, and a plateau or a backslide occurs. This is where a great teacher comes in; they can adjust exercises with just enough freshness to wake your brain back up.

As you practice your high-payoff drills over several months, some of you will find them to be working very consistently. Others of you will get great results, and then the drills will stop being effective. When this happens, it's probably still a good drill for you, but you may need to add novelty to it:

- Do it somewhere else or face a different direction.

- Do it at a different speed.

- Focus on a different part of the movement.

- Use a different breathing pattern.

- Add a different eye position.

- Add a rotation or tilt to your head, neck, or torso.

- Smile.

Using novel locations also convinces your nervous system of the value of training. If you work on your breathing drills in the park, in your lesson, in bed at night, and on hold with customer service, your brain will say, "Alright, fine! You keep doing this breathing thing everywhere you go, so I guess it must be imperative. I'll spend the calories on rewiring the circuits to make that pattern your default mode."

MINIMAL EFFECTIVE DOSE

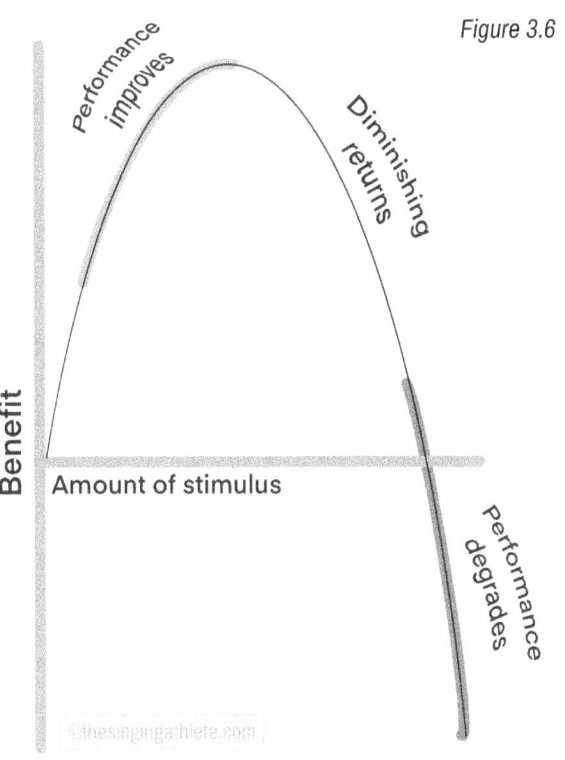

Figure 3.6

I'm obsessed with the unintentional comedy of drug commercials. I love the juxtaposition of a young couple frolicking on the beach while a voice-over lists all the possible horrific side-effects. (Look at them splashing in the waves while we hear about skin rashes and diarrhea!)

One of the main goals of drug trials is to determine the correct dose. That can be a tricky issue because different bodies metabolize drugs very differently. One person's overdose may barely be felt by someone else.[21] Training your voice is very much the same. It is most certainly not a "one size fits all" kind of endeavor, and allowing for individual differences is part of the game. When you practice, you are looking for the ***minimal effective dose*** of the exercise *(Fig. 3.6)*. If you do too little, your brain will be bored, while too much will cause frustration or depletion of resources.

Since I am not there watching you, you need to listen to your nervous system and look for signs of overdoing a drill. If you start to OD on an exercise, you may experience:

- Body tension (especially facial tension)
- Fatigue
- Pain/headache
- Change in skin color (turning pale or red)

- Sweating
- Swaying/loss of physical stability and balance
- Light-headedness
- Tunnel vision

If this happens, rest for a bit until you feel more steady, or grab a snack. And don't be alarmed if emotional responses come up as you do some of the exercises. We will be working in areas that can cause shifts in body perception and self-awareness. The nerve endings in your skin, connective tissues, and muscles talk to the emotional centers in your brain. Experiencing some effect is perfectly normal, and it may mean that you're on to something great.

LET'S DO THIS

Now that you understand a bit about the brain and how it works, we're going to move into the training portion of the book. The Singing Athlete is a big system; the reason I included this much material is that humans are so varied. I've seen every drill in this book be the key for at least one singer, and I want you to have the chance to explore many possibilities. If you're feeling overwhelmed, take it slow. Pick a chapter that interests you and invest in that area for a while. The rest of the book doesn't have to be done in order, so if there's something you know you need to work on, feel free to start there. Eventually, spend a little time with each chapter, and you may be surprised by what you find. Keep experimenting till you find your high-payoff drills.

Although it's fine to skip around, there is a logic to how the rest of the book is organized, so let me lay it out:

- We'll start with breathing because it's foundational to everything.

- Next, we'll move through some traditional structures that are studied in singing: the larynx, soft palate, tongue, and jaw. We'll also take a look at the nose and skull.

- After a look at scars, we're going to study the intersection between voice and the auditory, vestibular (balance), and visual systems.

- The last main section delves into how to train different brain areas as well as what to do about performance anxiety.

I'm not going to lie to you—there is a lot of anatomy in this book. Some of you are going to geek out on that, and some of you are going to find it challenging. All the material I've included is for practical reasons; it's because I think you can do something with the information. If your brain is hitting a wall, skip to the drills and then go back to reread the descriptive sections. The factual data may make more sense once you experience the exercises in your body.

Take a moment to think about what your vocal goals are; it can be anything from starring in a Broadway show to feeling more comfortable singing in the shower. To achieve these goals, I'm asking you to invest your time, curiosity, and passion. You have to earn the right to perform at a high level; I think it's worth it, and I hope you do, too.

4. BREATHING

As you read this passage, you are breathing (unless you are so rapt with excitement about learning neuroscience that you're holding your breath). It's something we do continually, and yet many of us don't do it well. The next time you're out, take a moment to watch the respiratory habits around you. Do you see calm, slow, nasal breathing in the lower belly or shallow mouth breaths that lift the shoulders with each inhalation?

Hyperventilation has become the norm in our culture, and a lot of it traces back to that little rectangular object in our pockets—our phones. There was a study done in which researchers monitored college students during texting. Everyone breathed faster and higher while buried in their phones, along with a more rapid heart rate and sweatier skin. Most of the people they tested were completely unaware that anything had changed. Eighty-three percent also reporting hand or neck pain while texting.[22] No wonder we're all stressed out.

This heightened state is created by the ***sympathetic nervous system (SNS)*** or "Fight, flight, or freeze." This is one branch of your ***autonomic nervous system (ANS)***, a control structure that is mostly unconscious and influences a sizable array of bodily functions. The nerves that control the SNS live primarily in your thoracic spine. The SNS is responsible for the following body processes:

- Increasing energy
- Raising heart rate and blood pressure
- Increasing blood flow to muscles
- Inhibiting digestion
- Dilating pupils
- Constricting all sphincters (eyes, throat, anus)
- Stimulating orgasm

As survival-based organisms, the SNS is essential. If you're swimming away from a shark, you clearly need more energy in the muscles, and your heart better start pumping blood as quickly as possible. Absorbing food and taking a nap would be a low priority at that moment.

The SNS is balanced by the ***parasympathetic nervous system (PNS)***, also known as the "rest and digest" system. Unlike the spinal location of the SNS, the PNS is guided by nerves in your brainstem and sacrum (tailbone). This may be one reason why craniosacral therapy can feel very calming. Digestion kicks in when the PNS is the dominant system, with more blood flow going to the gut and saliva filling your mouth.

Remember that relaxation (PNS) isn't inherently good and tension (SNS) bad; you need both. Getting away from danger is crucial, and the ability to increase blood flow to your muscles is what makes athletic movement (and singing) possible. The problem comes when you are continually living in an aroused state. When this happens, you can't sleep, your digestion suffers, and you get anxiety symptoms (e.g., sweating, shaking, dry mouth) when you sing.

Think of how often you receive a digital alert of some sort throughout your day. Your coworker texts you, an ad flashes on a screen as you walk down the street, or a loud voice blares at you while you wait at an airport. It's a monumental challenge to maintain low, slow breathing when our senses are under continuous assault. So, before we get to breathing exercises, there are a few actions I suggest you take.

> *Andrew's Digital Rules:*
>
> - Turn off all unnecessary notifications on your phone. Do you really need to be alerted to a President's Day sale from your favorite shoe company?
>
> - Put your phone on silent one hour before bed, when you are practicing your voice, and when you are working out.
>
> - If you are going to be looking at a screen at night, make it as dim as possible and put some kind of red-light filter on. I love f.lux for computers; Night Shift for iOs is okay, but it's much better to set a red color filter on your phone.
>
> - When you have a little break in your day, don't reach for your phone. Do some favorite drills from this book instead.

Okay, let's get to breathing.

WHY SHOULD YOU WORK ON YOUR BREATHING?

The most important reason to focus on breathing is that it is an extremely high-rep activity. You are going to take around 20,000 breaths a day; you can do 20,000 good reps or 20,000 bad reps. If you had to squat 20,000 times a day, wouldn't you want to be educated on the mechanics?

Working on breathing also has a relevant neurological component. Your vagus nerve is responsible for all the muscles that control phonation, but the nerve also has a significant role in moving the diaphragm. While the laryngeal muscles are mostly below conscious control, some of the diaphragm's muscle fibers can be activated voluntarily. Conscious breathing work can improve the connection to your vagus nerve, potentially boosting communication between your brain and your larynx.

Proper breathing also does these things:

- *Fewer headaches:* Good breathing lowers cranial pressure, making you less likely to get headaches. It also improves jaw function.

- *Reduced vocal swelling:* Breathing is one of the main drivers of lymph, which is the fluid that reduces swelling and improves your immune system. If you are experiencing swollen vocal folds that aren't responding to rest, it may have to do with how you're breathing.

- **Better energy:** Breathing issues are the number one reason we fatigue quickly. How often do you hear people say things like, "I'm always tired." You can translate that into, "I'm a lousy breather."

- **Increased control over food:** When you breathe well, your body may demand less food. Since the two types of fuel your brain needs are a good oxygen/carbon dioxide balance and glucose from food, it stands to reason that better breathing can reduce overeating.

- **Better decisions:** Good breathing makes you a better decision-maker under stressful conditions. Do you remember the brain's feeding pattern (top to bottom, back to front)? The frontal lobe (where conscious decisions happen) gets fed last. If you're not breathing well, you're getting less food to your frontal lobe, and it's going to affect your decisiveness. I spent many years of my life playing in professional auditions. What I noticed in callbacks was this: the job was won or lost on how well the actor could take adjustments from the creative team. If you don't breathe well, your underfed frontal lobe may steer you the wrong way in a critical moment.

BREATHING ANATOMY

When you breathe, air flows into the body and down the trachea, or windpipe *(Fig. 4.1)*. Take a moment to feel the rings of your trachea (you'll find them in the lower front part of your neck). These rings are flexible but very strong. If they were not so resilient, the vacuum created by the air pressure entering and leaving the lungs would cause them to collapse in on themselves. The trachea splits into two tubes called bronchi, which branch off at the level of your fifth rib (roughly in the center of your upper chest). The right bronchus is broader and shorter, delivering air to the three lobes of your right lung (superior, middle, inferior). The left lung only has two lobes (called the superior and inferior) and is slightly smaller since the heart takes up some of the room in the left side of the chest.

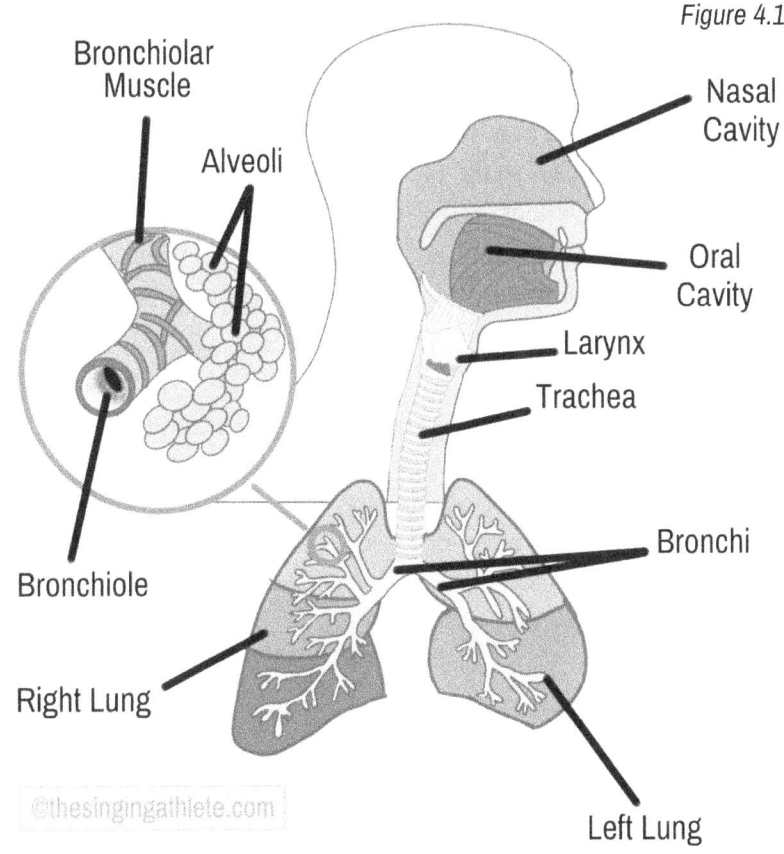

Figure 4.1

Further divisions of the bronchi take place as they enter the lungs, becoming bronchioles and eventually terminating in small air sacs called alveoli. The alveoli (of which there are around 300 million) intersect with capillaries that transfer oxygen to your blood. If you spread out the area of contact between your alveoli and your capillaries, it would cover an area as large as a tennis court.[23]

My view on breath training is that we're looking for respiratory competence in all levels of oxygenation. We need to be okay with a big inhalation and also be cool with having almost no air. Most singers are already familiar with the sensation of taking a big breath, but what tends to be more uncomfortable is working with lower lung volumes. We have arbitrarily agreed as a culture that running out of breath is a mark of vocal failure, which can make having less air feel threatening. But should we always take in enormous breaths for all singing styles? After all, the vibrating edges of the vocal folds are around the length of a penny; a structure that small shouldn't need tons of air to vibrate. And are there other unwanted systemic effects that chronic over-breathing may cause for singers? Could there be a relationship between common voice complaints (e.g., asthma, allergies, reflux) and the large oral inhalations taken by many vocalists?

WHAT IS HYPERVENTILATION?

Your brainstem is where the brain meets the spinal cord, and it controls the subconscious rate and volume of your breathing. Chemoreceptors found in your brainstem are tasked with balancing the blood levels of oxygen and carbon dioxide (CO_2). CO_2 is a gas produced in your tissues as the food you eat gets broken down and used by the body. Excess CO_2 is returned to the lungs via the bloodstream and released back into the atmosphere on exhalation. The key point here is that *excess* CO_2 is expelled during exhalation, not *all* CO_2. To maintain optimal energy for your body systems, some carbon dioxide must be retained in the tissues.

When you are in a pattern where breathing exceeds the body's demand for oxygen, it is called ***hyperventilation***. The traditionally observed hyperventilation breathing pattern is fast, shallow, and centered in the upper chest. However, singers who frequently take in large gulps of air through the mouth may also be overshooting their oxygen needs.

Hemoglobin is a protein in red blood cells that binds with oxygen and carries it around the body. When hemoglobin meets CO_2 in the bloodstream, it picks it up, simultaneously releasing oxygen into the tissues; it then takes the CO_2 back to the lungs. If there is not a sufficient level of CO_2 in the body, oxygen "sticks" to hemoglobin, and it doesn't get delivered. Since all tissues require oxygen, the body asks for more, and a cycle of over-breathing begins. When you hyperventilate, you're taking in tons of air, but none of it is getting where it needs to go.

> Hemoglobin can be a bit confusing, so here's an analogy; your body is an apartment building, and your larynx is the penthouse. The penthouse dwellers order some supplies (oxygen) to be delivered by a courier (hemoglobin). The courier shows up to deliver the supplies, but they won't drop them off unless they get a tip (CO_2). If a tip is offered, the courier collects it and drops off the supplies, making everyone happy. If no tip is given, the courier keeps the supplies—and now the inhabitants of the penthouse don't have the things they need to live.

Breathing heavily for a short period is not necessarily a problem. If you're running away from danger, you're going to take bigger breaths, and your system will rebalance once the threat has passed. But in our chronically overstimulated society, the brain may eventually go through a plastic change where the set point for CO_2 intolerance shifts.

As you exhale, your brainstem registers the increase of CO_2 entering the bloodstream. Let's say that you usually can tolerate 4 percent CO_2 in the blood, but during a stressful period you start hyperventilating for several weeks. The excess oxygen depletes CO_2 levels. Now, when you exhale and the blood CO_2 level reaches 2 percent, your brain is already telling your diaphragm to inhale again. You have become more intolerant to the feeling of increased CO_2, so you are now over-breathing all the time. When this becomes a long-term pattern, these body compensations will show up:

- Your abdominals and pelvic floor will get weaker, with your back muscles tightening up and possibly causing a swayback.

- Your stress response will increase because the sympathetic nervous system lives in your spine, and now most of your ribs and spinal segments aren't fully moving.

- The neck muscles will become overly tight, and a "hump" may appear in your lower neck.

- When this lower cervical segment stops moving, the output of the vagus nerve will be disturbed, and vocal quality will suffer.

Singers also need to know that CO_2 is a vasodilator, which means that it opens up blood vessels and body tissues. The "open throat" feeling that we all look for in singing can be related to your tolerance for carbon dioxide. The goal of this chapter's drills is to make you more okay with building CO_2 levels in the blood. If you can learn to be less threatened by lower lung volumes, I believe you will see an improvement in your health and your voice.

Let's assess your current breathing habits.

Breathing Assessment 1: Breathing Quiz

You'll find my breathing quiz at thesingingathlete.com. Take it if you are interested in assessing your tendency for hyperventilation.

Breathing Assessment 2: Tempo

An adult should take around 9–12 breath cycles per minute. Sit quietly for sixty seconds and count your breath cycles. Since you are cognitively aware of your breathing tempo as you do this drill, it's not a foolproof assessment. A more precise test is to watch a minute of yourself on video and count your breaths when you're not conscious of respiration.

In your usual breathing pattern, your exhalation should be around 1.5–2 times longer than the inhalation, and there should be a brief pause at the bottom of the exhalation. If your inhalation lasts for two seconds, your exhalation should be around three or four seconds, with a 1–2 second pause at the end of the exhalation.

Breathing Assessment 3: Low, Slow, and Through the Nose

Sit tall and place one hand on your belly, with the other resting on your chest. On an inhalation, you should feel your bottom hand moving out more than your top hand. The motion should be measured and distinct, and the air should be entering and exiting through your nose. The dimensions of your torso should increase on inhalation and decrease on exhalation. The mantra should be *"Low, slow, and through the nose."*

Watch for any the following problems on inhalation:

- The upper hand moves before the lower hand

- The upper hand lifts toward the chin rather than moving slightly forward

- The upper hand moves more than the lower hand

It is also possible that the lower hand will move in on inhalation, instead of out. This is known as ***paradoxical breathing***, where standard breathing mechanics get reversed. Our cultural worship of a flat stomach can cause confusion as to the correct respiration pattern. To be clear, the abdomen is supposed to expand in all directions on an inhalation, not contract.

Breathing Assessment 4: Pulse Oximeter

You can get the most objective view of your blood oxygenation levels by using a pulse oximeter *(Fig. 4.2)*. When you use one, you will see three numbers come up:

- ***SpO_2 (Peripheral Capillary Oxygen Saturation):*** SpO_2 is the percentage of oxygen-carrying red blood cells (hemoglobin) compared to the total amount of hemoglobin in the blood. Because oxygen is supposed to continuously release from the blood into the cells, an oxygen saturation of 99 or 100 is an indication of hyperventilation. The hemoglobin is holding on to too much of the oxygen. A good SpO_2 target is between 95 and 97.

- ***PI (Perfusion Index):*** PI is the ratio of the pulsing blood compared to the non-pulsing blood in the fingertip, indicating blood-flow strength. The lower the perfusion number, the less blood is flowing to your finger, signifying a stress response. When the threat bucket is full, the brain will pull blood away from the extremities and into the larger skeletal muscles, in case the need arises to run away from danger. Every model has its own proprietary formula for determining your perfusion. If you get the model I use, a PI number that is 6 percent or above is a good result (you can find a link at thesingingathlete.com)

- ***bpmPR (Pulse):*** A pulse that is high (above 90) at rest can be indicative of a threat state and issues in your brainstem. However, a low pulse at rest (below 70) can relate to metabolic and thyroid problems. I like to see a resting pulse somewhere in the 70–90 bpm range.

In Figure 4.2, I took my measurements and then did two minutes of bag breathing (which I'll explain later in this chapter). As you can see, my SpO_2 lowered from 98 (a little high) to 95 (better). Also, my PI

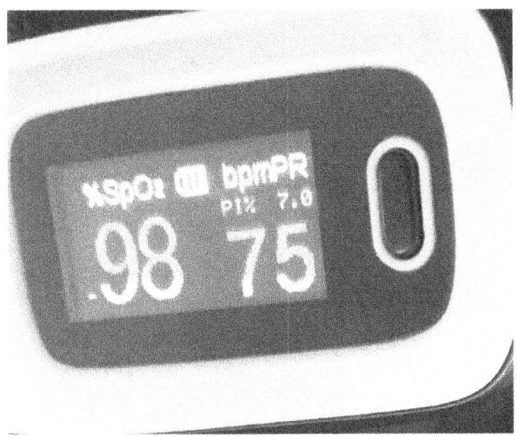 

Figure 4.2

increased several percentage points, indicating that my body was using oxygen better. My pulse didn't change much. I felt calmer and more focused after the bag breathing.

A few tips on pulse oximetry:

- Keep still and calm when testing.

- You should test both sides, as each side of your brainstem controls the blood pressure on that side. The comparison can be a useful piece of information.

- If you have certain kinds of nail polish/gel coatings on your nails (anything that blocks light), a pulse oximeter will give anomalous readings. Try flipping the oximeter over and see if you can get a reading this way.

- If you have particularly meaty fingers, the machine can restrict blood flow, affecting the results.

FUNCTIONAL INHALE AND EXHALE

As singers, we don't want to find either inhalation or exhalation scary. These two assessments will give you a window into a possible threat response to air entering or leaving. As you do these tests, notice your time, but more importantly, stay aware of your emotional reaction. It's a good clue as to how your breathing goes in performance. If you want to do these tests with their accompanying songs (who doesn't love a song?), go to thesingingathlete.com.

Functional Inhale

1. Sit tall in a chair with an upright, comfortable posture.

2. Exhale completely through your nose.

3. Start a timer and inhale slowly through your nose for as long as possible. Stop your timer when you can inhale no more.

4. If your inhalation was under ten seconds, that is a sign of threat around the act of inhalation. I'd like to see you be able to go for 20–25 seconds.

Functional Exhale

1. Sit tall in a chair with an upright, comfortable posture.

2. Inhale completely through your nose.

3. Start a timer and exhale slowly through your nose for as long as possible. Stop your timer when you can exhale no more.

4. If your exhalation was under ten seconds, that is a sign of threat around the act of exhalation. I'd like to see you be able to go for 20–25 seconds.

If either your functional inhale or exhale time was under ten seconds, you could use it as a reassessment as you work through the rest of this chapter, as well as Chapters 5–7. Do a drill and then recheck your functional inhale or exhale; if the time gets longer, you've found a high-payoff drill.

BREATH-HOLDS AND ASTHMATICS

We're about to do some breath-hold drills; I believe they're excellent training, but keep an eye out for these responses:

- Chest pain
- Dizziness
- Lightheadedness
- Dry mouth
- Numbness or tingling around the mouth or in the arms
- Palpitations
- Shortness of breath
- Weakness

If any of these show up, it means you are beyond your minimal effective dose. Regress the drills; do them seated or lying down, or decrease the length of time.

If you have asthma in your background, some of these may feel intense; asthmatics are understandably scared of not being able to breathe. Fixing an asthmatic pattern requires more training on exhalation, which can be uncomfortable. The idea of these drills is to make you voluntarily breathe less so you won't be so afraid of not having air. Listen to your body and stop when you've had enough.

AIR HUNGER

Air hunger is the sensation of not getting enough oxygen (and, in reality, being intolerant to rising blood-CO_2 levels). It is one of the scariest feelings for a human; we can go for days without food but only minutes without air. Hyperventilation patterns are essentially caused by a fear of air hunger. Your survival-driven brain believes that even a small rise in CO_2 levels is too threatening, so it keeps you continually over-breathing.

To be able to hold long, steady notes, a singer needs excellent air-hunger tolerance. If you sing a long phrase and think you're out of breath, you're not. It's impossible to empty all the air out of your lungs. The reason you are not making it through a phrase may be your subconscious panic from the rising CO_2 levels.

Air Hunger Test

1. Sit down and rest for two minutes before beginning the test.

2. Pinch your nose closed at the bottom of an average exhalation.

3. Start a timer and see how many seconds you can hold your breath comfortably.

4. Release your nose when you feel the first distinct desire to breathe. You will know it's time to release when your brain says, "Enough!" You also may feel a spasm in the diaphragm; this is your brain telling your diaphragm to resume respiration. You might even notice a constriction in your throat or a desire to swallow.

5. Pay attention to the first breath after the release. Did you need to gasp for air? If so, you held too long. The first breath back should come in through the nose; it should feel normal and under control.

The goal of this test is to make it comfortably to forty seconds. Anything over thirty seconds is considered pretty good, over twenty is borderline, and anything below twenty seconds indicates a threat response to increased CO_2 levels.

Now, let's do a breathing drill, and then we'll reassess the Air Hunger Test:

In for Two, Out for Eight

I recommend performing this drill using a metronome app—I usually set it between 80 and 90 beats per minute.

1. Sit in a comfortable upright position.

2. Inhale a small amount of air through your nose for two beats.

3. Exhale through pursed lips (think of a pucker) for eight beats. You should feel your lips providing resistance to the air, and your abdominals should be squeezing most of the air out of your body by the end of the eight beats.

4. Repeat for ten reps. Take a small breath in through the nose for two beats and exhale for eight through pursed lips.

5. Redo the Air Hunger Test. See if your numbers changed.

For many of us, after doing the "In for Two, Out for Eight" drill, you will find your Air Hunger Test numbers improved. You may have been able to hold your breath for longer, and you may notice that you felt less panicked in the breath-hold. Because your resisted exhalation was four times as long as your inhalation, and because your inhalation was modest, the receptors that control breathing were rewired. Rising CO^2 was no longer perceived as such a major threat.

I suggest this drill for students who have identified breathing-related issues like asthma, allergies, and reflux. It is also handy when performance anxiety is an issue; better CO^2 levels create calm in the brain. When I'm walking to a stressful event, I do ten rounds of "In for Two, Out for Eight" on the way. I breathe in for two steps and out for eight, ten rounds total. Afterward, I inevitably feel more relaxed and focused.

Variations

- If you're in a place where blowing air out through your lips feels weird, you can do this with nasal breathing only—in for two through your nose, out for eight through your nose.

- There is nothing magical about the numbers two and eight. I start there because, for most people, it's a mild challenge. If this feels too hard for you and you're getting some negative symptoms, try doing "in for two, out for six," "in for two, out for four," or "in for four, out for eight."

- Conversely, if "in for two, out for eight" feels too easy, try going beyond eight to breathing out for ten, twelve, etc. I like to do "in for two, out for twenty" as a challenge.

INCREASE YOUR VOCAL STAMINA

Have you had situations in your vocal history where stamina was an issue? Maybe you could do a challenging section of a song just fine in isolation. When it was put together with the rest of the piece, however, you may not have had anything left in the tank by the time you got there. This type of issue is similar to what long-distance athletes face. It's why many of them follow a "live high, train low" program, where they live at high altitudes to benefit from the positive physiological changes of elevated atmospheres. When the body experiences a reduction in oxygen, it adapts by producing more red blood cells. A hormone called erythropoietin (EPO) is secreted by the kidneys, causing the spleen to release more red blood cells into circulation. The result is a more substantial delivery of oxygen to the muscles, giving the athlete greater stamina.

One method of illegal blood doping is to take synthetic EPO. But there is another (perfectly legal) way to get many of the same effects called ***intermittent hypoxic training.*** In addition to many athletic applications, hypoxic training is being used to treat metabolic conditions such as diabetes, hypothyroidism, obesity, and autoimmune diseases.[24]

Like the Air Hunger Test, the basic idea of intermittent hypoxic training is to be more okay with having a higher level of CO^2 in the body. By loading yourself with athletic movement during a breath-hold, more EPO may release into your bloodstream, which can improve your vocal and physical stamina.

Hypoxic Drill 1—Reduced Breathing

1. Assess your voice and body.

2. Sit quietly and place your finger under your nose. Make sure your finger isn't blocking the flow of air.

3. Breathe lightly and quietly through the nose. Try to feel as little warm air as possible on your finger for each exhalation. Keep the lung volume very small on the inhale.

4. Continue for thirty seconds.

5. Reassess.

Hypoxic Drill 2—Walk and Hold

1. Assess your voice and body.

2. Take a walk; as you are walking, exhale and hold your breath at the bottom of the exhale. You can either pinch your nose closed or use your lips and palate to block off your mouth and nose.

3. See how many steps you can take while holding your breath before you feel a strong desire to inhale.

4. When you've gone as far as you can, inhale through the nose. Try to get your breath back to normal within one breath cycle; you don't get to gasp air through the mouth to recover. If you had to mouth-breathe, you went for too long.

5. Repeat for two more sets.

6. Reassess.

If you are a jogger/runner, try this same drill with running. You can also do it with brisk walking or skipping.

Hypoxic Drill 3—Squats

1. Assess your voice and body.

2. Blow most of your air out and hold your breath.

3. Perform as many bodyweight squats as you can while holding your breath before you feel a strong desire to inhale.

4. Try to get your breath back to normal within one breath cycle. Your first inhalation should be through the nose, and you don't get to gasp on recovery.

5. Repeat for two more sets.

6. Reassess.

Hypoxic Drill 4—Push-ups

1. Assess your voice and body.

2. Blow most of your air out and hold your breath.

3. Perform as many push-ups as you can while holding your breath before you feel a strong desire to inhale.

4. Try to get your breath back to normal within one breath cycle. Your first inhalation should be through the nose, and you don't get to gasp on recovery.

5. Repeat for two more sets.

6. Reassess.

The idea of hypoxic training can apply to any type of exercise. I use it when biking or swimming, I do hypoxic yoga poses, and I bring it regularly into gym sessions. When I take tap class, I notice how far into the combination I can get without needing to breathe. And on days that require a lot of vocal stamina, hypoxic drills are reliably high-payoff for me. See how you respond to this style of training.

Bag Breathing

Your heart rate is supposed to speed up on inhalation and slow down on exhalation (known as heart rate variability, or HRV). When you hyperventilate, you are focusing on inhalation and are putting more attention on the part of your breath cycle that speeds up your heart. When the focus shifts to the exhalation, the heart rate slows, and anxiety dissipates. Rebreathing exhaled air is one of the quickest ways to calm the autonomic nervous system, and all you need is a paper bag.

1. Assess your voice and body.

2. Open a paper bag and place it over your nose and mouth, so that the short ends of the rectangle are on the top and bottom.

3. Seal it around your mouth and nose using both hands.

4. Find a comfortable position. If I am seated, I prefer to do it with my elbow points resting on my knees, so I'm slightly hinged forward. Experiment and find what feels right to you.

5. Breathe in and out through the nose, recirculating the CO_2-rich air that is in the bag.

6. If you feel comfortable, try pausing at the bottom of the exhalation. Wait until you feel a slight air hunger and then inhale.

7. Continue for 2–3 minutes.

8. Reassess.

This drill also works with a plastic bag, which will build CO_2 much more intensely and quickly. Paper allows some air through, and plastic doesn't.

If you get a negative response from these hypoxic drills, it's worth reassessing again a few minutes later. There can be a large threat response to having less air, and yet many of us are over-breathing all day long. In this case, what seems like a rehab drill may actually be high-payoff after the brain has had a little while to adjust.

5. DIAPHRAGM

Whenever I talk with personal-trainer friends who know that I work with performers, they will say things like, "It must be so nice to be surrounded by singers. They all know how to breathe so well." That's true to a point. As singers, we are probably more aware of our breathing muscles simply through more frequent use. Most of us also have a sense that we should be breathing diaphragmatically. However, there is a big gap between knowing what we're supposed to be doing and actually doing it.

In lessons, I'm interested in watching a student's breathing when they are vocalizing, but I'm particularly focused on their habits when they are talking about their audition from last week. What shows up in everyday interactions is often more telling. As an artist, you need to train your respiratory competence in life, not just in your voice lesson. And when it comes to better reflexive breathing, the diaphragm is the most important muscle.

DIAPHRAGM BASICS

The diaphragm is the primary muscle that brings air into your body. Around 70–80% of your ability to get a full breath occurs through diaphragmatic movement. The lungs are passive organs that don't self-inflate; they cling to the diaphragm and ribcage, and as the muscle contracts, air flows in. The diaphragm has both somatic and autonomic innervation; this means that it will bring air in automatically, like when you're sleeping, but you can also train its muscle fibers consciously.

The diaphragm is a broad, thin, domed muscle whose shape has been compared to a jellyfish, a mushroom, or (my favorite) a shower cap. It contracts on an inhalation and relaxes/stretches on an unresisted exhalation *(Fig. 5.1)*. When you inhale, the dome of the diaphragm descends and widens in both a lateral and a front-to-back direction, creating a vacuum that sucks air into the lungs. This causes the abdominal organs to descend and the pelvic floor to drop and widen (assuming it is relaxed enough to do so).

During exhalation, the diaphragm moves up and in, with the organs and pelvic floor following. To get a feel for the movement of the muscle fibers, try the following:

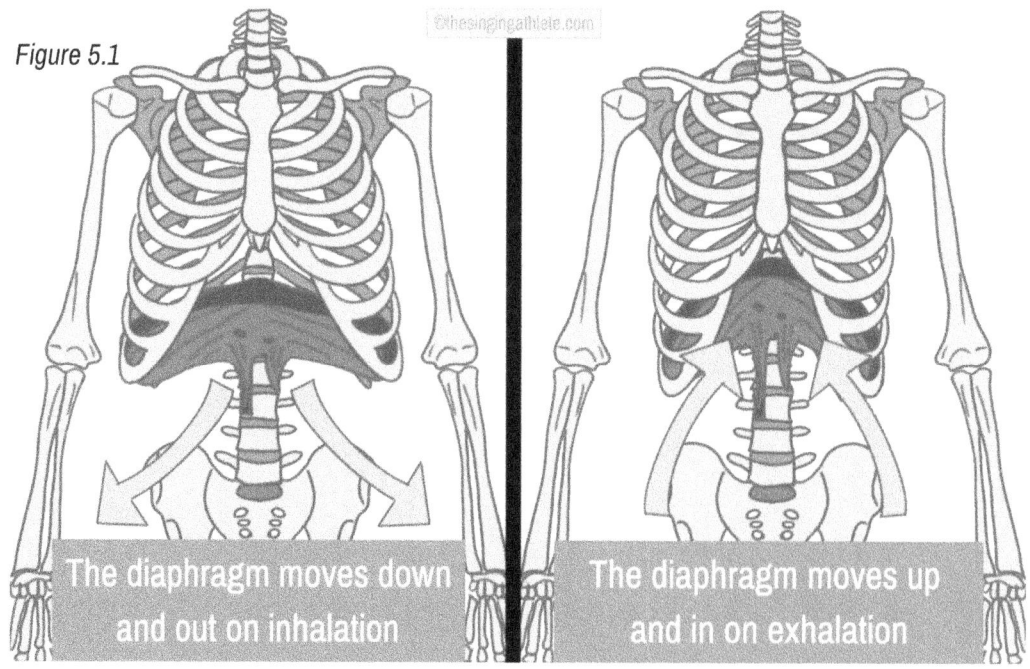

Figure 5.1

1. Clasp your fingers in front of you (like in prayer) and bring your elbows in toward the midline.

2. On an inhalation, begin to widen your elbows. You will feel your fingers start to spread apart and your hands lower. This is the motion of inhalation for the diaphragm.

3. As you exhale, draw your elbows together. This is the motion of exhalation. Notice that your fingers start to push together and your hands rise.

The diaphragm lives higher than many people think. If you touch your xiphoid process (the bone that comes off the bottom of your sternum, or breastbone), you have found an attachment of the diaphragm. On an exhalation, the dome rises quite high, up to the fourth or fifth rib in the front (roughly the center of your chest). It also has direct or indirect connections to ribs 7–12. If you take your fingers back to your xiphoid process and walk them out under the edge of your rib cage, you are finding more attachment points. Tucked under the left side of the diaphragm is the stomach and spleen (a small organ that plays a role in filtering your blood and in your immune and lymphatic systems). Under the right side is the greater portion of your liver.

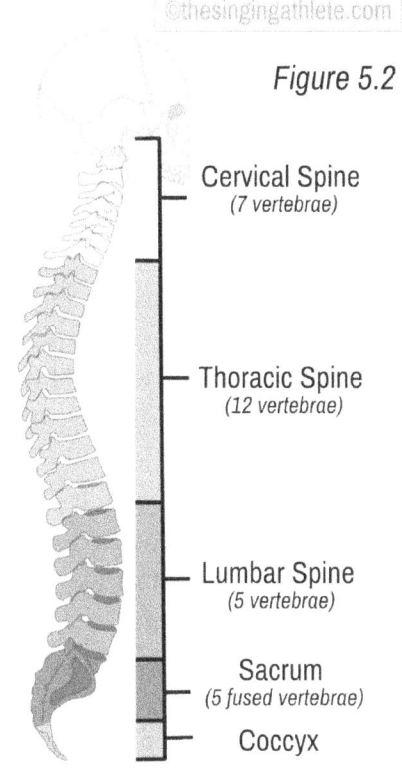

Figure 5.2

I'll be using some spinal terms as we go through the book, so let's take a brief pause to learn what's where (Fig. 5.2). Your spine is made up of thirty-three vertebrae, and these are the divisions from top to bottom:

- **Cervical:** Neck—7 vertebrae (C1–C7)

- **Thoracic:** Chest segments that carry a pair of ribs— 12 vertebrae (T1–T12)

- **Lumbar:** Lower back—5 vertebrae (L1–L5)

- **Sacrum:** Upper tailbone—5 fused vertebrae (S1–S5)

- **Coccyx**: Lower tailbone—4 fused vertebrae

In the back, the diaphragm's dome rises to your seventh thoracic vertebra on exhalation (T7 is roughly between the bottom tips of your shoulder blades.). It goes down to your second and third lumbar vertebrae, which are located around the level of your navel. L2–L3 are the attachment points for the pillars of your diaphragm; the right one is more robust and attaches to L3, whereas the left is a little smaller and attaches higher at L2. This difference could be due to organ placement or could be related to the fact that we have that extra lobe in the right lung. L1–L3 are the least flexible parts of the lumbar spine, which make the more-pliable L4 and L5 common areas for disk herniation. These two lowest lumbar vertebrae also don't have a lot of local muscular support, especially in the front. It is the air pressure created by the diaphragm that is supposed to keep this vulnerable area stable.

The diaphragm communicates through fascia with many other body areas. In an upward direction, it connects to the scalene (neck) muscles and the occiput (the area under your skull in the back). Toward the lower body, it interweaves with the psoas, the transversus abdominis, and the pelvic floor. Your diaphragm connects to everything in one way or another, and training it can have a profound global influence.[25]

Let's review a few anatomical terms that I will be using throughout the book:

- *Anterior*—toward the front
- *Posterior*—toward the back
- *Medial*—toward the midline
- *Lateral*—away from the midline
- *Superior*—above/farther from the ground
- *Inferior*—below/closer to the ground

ASSESS YOUR DIAPHRAGM'S MOVEMENT

In Figure 5.3, you can see that the diaphragm has fibers that run anteriorly, laterally, and posteriorly. To assess the strength of different areas of the muscle, you're going to find three landmarks with your fingers:

- *Front*: In a standing posture, find the front upper edge of your pelvic bone (anterior superior iliac spine, or ASIS) with both fingers. Move your fingers one inch (2.5 cm) toward the midline from both sides. Take a deep breath and notice if there is a bilateral expansion of this part of the abdominal wall. Are both sides moving the same distance out? Is one side moving first or lagging?

- *Sides*: Put your hands on your hips and slide them up until you feel your lowest full ribs (tenth ribs). Take a deep breath, and notice if your hands move out laterally. The average total amount of excursion should be around 1.5–2 inches (4–5 cm), and the hands should moving mostly out, not up. Are both sides moving the same distance out? Is one side moving first or lagging?

- *Back*: Now place the palms of your hands on your bottom ribs (eleventh and twelfth ribs) in the lower back; your fingers should be on your low back, in the area right above the back of your pelvis. Take a deep breath and notice if there is bilateral expansion here. Are both sides moving the same distance backward? Is one side moving first or lagging?

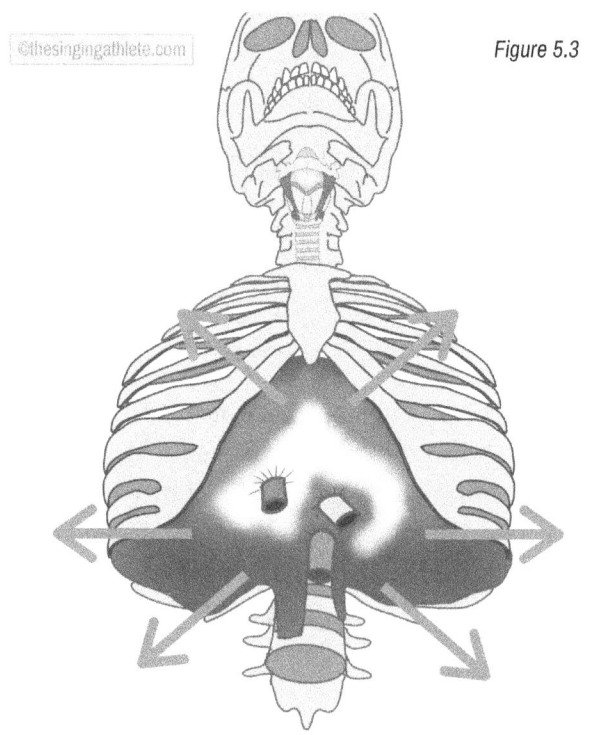

Figure 5.3

The stronger your diaphragm is, the more able it should be to displace the visceral contents in these areas. If you felt less movement on the left or right sides in any of these spots, write it down and reassess as we go through the drills. If it all felt even, challenge yourself by using some different body alignments and see if you can still maintain a full diaphragmatic excursion. I practice this in squats, lunges, plank, hanging from a pull-up bar, yoga poses, etc.

THREE DIAPHRAGM FUNCTIONS

There are two functional units of the diaphragm. The *costal region* attaches to the ribs and is focused on expanding the torso for inhalation. The *crural region* attaches to the vertebral column and is involved with digestion and preventing reflux. These two parts work in conjunction to perform three separate but related diaphragmatic functions *(Fig. 5.4)*:

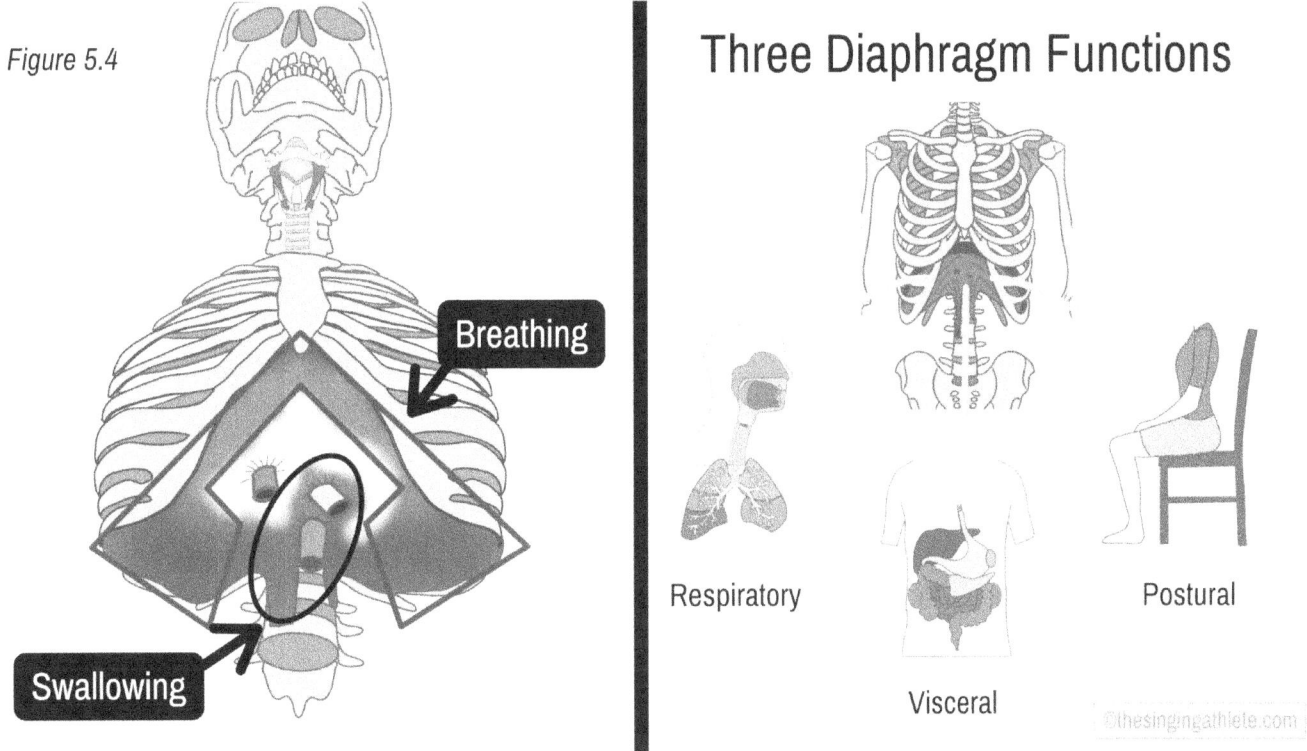

Figure 5.4

- *Respiratory:* Getting air into the body

- *Visceral:* Keeping the abdominal organs where they are supposed to be

- *Postural:* Working with the pelvic floor, abdominals, and back muscles to provide the top end of the cylinder that keeps the torso stable

Most singers are familiar with the diaphragm's respiratory function, so we'll start our training there.

Diaphragm Stretch 1

In these stretches, we'll be focusing on a full, complete exhalation. A strong exhalation causes a stretch of the diaphragm, bringing it firmly up and in. On the inhalation that follows, the air should reflexively enter fully and deeply, with a sensation like filling a vacuum.

1. Assess your voice and body.

2. Lie on your back, knees up, with the soles of your feet on the ground in parallel. In this drill, you have some options when it comes to your lower back. You can do a posterior pelvic tilt, bringing your lower back into contact with the floor (this is what I do because it gives me a greater diaphragm stretch). You can also leave a small space between your lower back and the floor (this keeps you in a neutral spine).

3. Place your hands on the sides of your waist and inhale.

4. Exhale fully and forcefully through an open mouth and throat. You should be using the shape of an "ah," but there should be little to no whispered sound. Your goal is to get the air out as quickly and completely as possible.

5. When you think you've exhaled all you can, keep exhaling. With your hands, squeeze in on your waist in a "lobster claw" action, encouraging the diaphragm to stretch up and in.

6. When you can exhale no more, let the air come back in as quickly as possible; it should feel like a sudden rush of air entering your lungs. If your inhalation happens slowly, you need to exhale harder before inhaling.

7. Repeat this cycle for four more breaths.

8. Get up and reassess.

Diaphragm Stretch 2

Version 2 is the same as version 1, except we'll add an opening of the chest by lifting your arms and resting them on the floor above your head. If you're not flexible enough to get your arms straight and on the ground above your head, you can bend your elbows, put your arms out by your side, or put a pillow under your arms.

Once you feel a comfortable stretch of your chest, repeat Steps 4–7 from Diaphragm Stretch 1 in this "arms-overhead" position. This time, you won't use the "lobster claw" action since your arms are resting over your head. Do your best to squeeze as much air out as possible before inhaling again.

Diaphragm Stretch 3

In version 3, we are going to go for a deep stretch of the lumbar attachments of the diaphragm. If you have any history of lower-back issues, do this drill carefully. Watch it on thesingingathlete.com to make sure you have the form right.

1. Assess your voice and body.

2. Lie on your back, knees up, with the soles of your feet on the ground in parallel. Maintain whatever lower-back position you used in version 1.

3. Place your arms over your head like in version 2.

4. On an inhalation, lift your butt off the ground and bring your hips high into a bridge.

5. Stay in the bridge and exhale fully through an open mouth and throat. Again, there should not be a whispered sound; the exhalation should be almost silent.

6. Once you've fully exhaled, begin rolling your vertebrae back down to the ground, but continue exhaling through an open throat as you go.

7. Once your butt hits the ground, inhale; allow the air to rush back in. Rest for a moment and exhale.

8. Repeat Steps 4–7 for four more breaths. Bridge up on an inhalation, stay in the bridge for the exhalation, roll down, and keep exhaling. When your butt hits the ground, inhale.

9. Reassess.

These diaphragm stretches are performed on the ground to allow you to feel the sensory aspects of moving this muscle. Once you've got the feeling of this stretch, you can do it seated, standing, or in any of the athletic poses listed earlier in the chapter. Also, since training is SAID-specific, if you are staged in a show to be in a specific physical position for a challenging vocal phrase, practice the diaphragm stretch in that alignment.

Diaphragm Push-up—Respiratory

In the diaphragm stretch sequence, we focused on creating a reflexive inhalation by starting with a complete and firm exhalation. Now, we will provide a direct challenge to the voluntary muscle fibers of the diaphragm on an inhalation. This drill is much easier to do with someone else because the angle of resistance they can create is greater than what you can do for yourself. Watch it at thesingingathlete.com and grab a friend, or give it a try by yourself. The goal is to use your hands and fingertips to provide physical resistance.

1. Assess your voice and body.

2. Sit tall and curl your fingers under the bottom edge of the front of your ribcage. Your pointer fingers should be about an inch (2 cm) to the sides of your xiphoid process, with the rest of your fingers curled under the ribs. Depending on your frame, it may be easier to find this position if you slump over a bit, letting your neck hang slightly forward.

3. As you inhale, you should feel the diaphragm displacing your fingers out of the space beneath your ribs. Is it moving an equal distance simultaneously on both sides?

4. Now that you've got the feel of it, keep your fingers where they are but use the rest of your hands to traction the ribcage down and in. Maintain this down-and-in resistance on the next inhalation. You should feel your diaphragm being challenged to move out by the pressure you're creating with your hands. If you need to adjust your hand position to create more resistance, go for it.

5. Repeat for five breaths and reassess.

THE DIAPHRAGM AND REFLUX

Since the diaphragm bisects the body, it has to have some hiatuses, or holes *(Fig. 5.5)*. The inferior vena cava moves through the diaphragm at the level of T8. If you get varicose leg veins or cold feet, you are experiencing venous stasis (slow blood flow in the veins) and may not be moving your diaphragm well at T8. The aorta passes through at the level of T12, becoming the abdominal aorta; a glossy appearance to the lower limbs or strong sock-line imprints on your calves can indicate poor diaphragmatic movement at T12.[26] (Try the Breathing Wave exercise that is coming up to fix these things.)

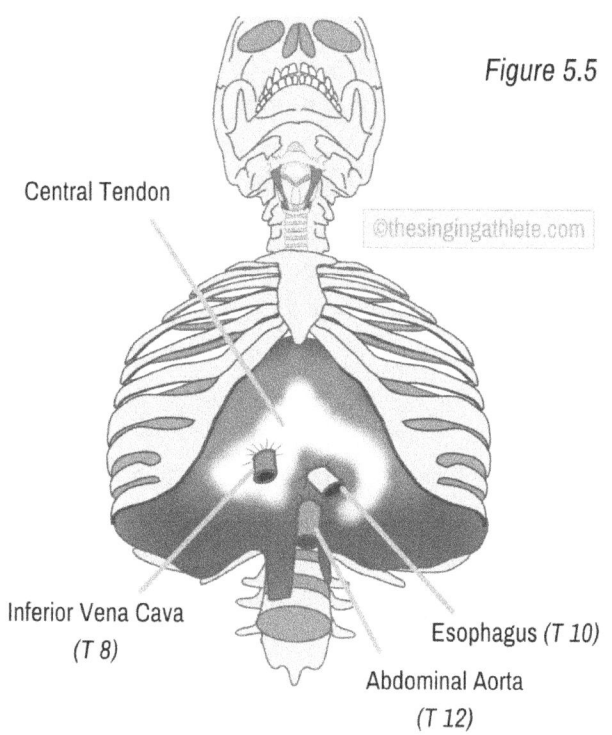

Figure 5.5

The esophagus passes through the diaphragm at T10, along with the vagus nerve. The hole for the esophagus, called the esophageal hiatus, is tasked with keeping the stomach contents in place throughout the breath cycle. A problem happens when this muscular hole in the diaphragm becomes weak. If this sphincter starts to lose tone, stomach acid can back up into the esophagus, and you may feel the telltale symptoms of reflux.

If you do experience reflux, a question to ask is, "Do I notice it more when eating with others?" When you're out to dinner, you are simultaneously holding a conversation (requiring coordination from the respiratory part of your diaphragm) and eating (requiring coordination from the visceral part). If all goes well, the competing muscle functions will balance beautifully, and you'll enjoy both time with friends and some delicious shrimp tacos. If not, the diaphragm may get confused and allow those tacos to head back up the wrong way.

Now is an appropriate moment to clarify the terms GERD (gastro-esophageal reflux disease) and LPR (laryngopharyngeal reflux). GERD is a failing of the lower esophageal sphincter (LES), the band of muscle where your stomach meets your esophagus. The main symptom of GERD is heartburn. LPR is an issue with the upper esophageal sphincter, which is where your esophagus and your pharynx meet. Those experiencing LPR often don't notice heartburn but do complain of hoarseness and a feeling of a "lump" in the throat. The laryngeal tissues don't have the same protective coating as the esophagus, so they are quite susceptible to stomach acid.

While GERD and LPR are technically different, they are related from a brain perspective. If you have better muscle tone in your diaphragm, both types of reflux improve, and the need for medication reduces. Proton pump inhibitors (PPIs) are the main class of drugs used to control reflux symptoms. They are among the most commonly prescribed medications in the U.S.; some brand names are Prilosec, Protonix, and Nexium.

Your stomach contains parietal cells that secrete hydrochloric acid (HCl). All vertebrates produce acid in their stomach; it is the key to healthy digestion. Proton pumps are present in your stomach, as well as in all cells of your body (except red blood cells). The stomach's proton pumps stimulate the parietal cells to produce acid for digesting fats, proteins, and carbohydrates.[27] The theory of proton pump inhibitors is that stopping the proton pumps from working will reduce the burning sensation associated with reflux.

There are a couple of problems with this approach. Firstly, the vast majority of people who seek treatment for reflux have *low* stomach acid levels, not high. It is not that they are producing too much acid, but that they are susceptible to the small amounts that they are producing. By further lowering acid production, digestion suffers further.

The second issue is that almost all of your body's cells have proton pumps, so inhibiting the ones in your stomach can disturb all of them. Proton pumps are a vital player in the production of ATP (the body's main form of cellular energy), so hindering them comes with a host of dangers. Long-term use of PPIs may cause an increased risk of bone fractures, kidney disease, intestinal infections, gastric cancer, dementia, and problems absorbing vitamins and minerals.[28, 29, 30] They are one of the most negatively reviewed classes of drugs in existence. If it were me, I would try a whole lot of other reflux solutions before taking PPIs.

When there is a history of reflux or bloating, there is a subconscious tendency not to move the diaphragm through a full excursion. After all, if your stomach isn't working correctly, you can be afraid to "poke the bear" and make things worse. This creates a cycle where the diaphragm muscle fibers weaken through disuse, making reflux even more likely. The crura (or pillars) of the diaphragm create a canal where the esophagus enters the abdomen, wrapping around it like a scarf. When the crural diaphragm contracts on inhalation, it can create an external sphincter for the LES through the phrenoesophageal ligament.[31] In other words, proper diaphragmatic movement keeps the stomach contents where they are supposed to be, without drugs. To test your visceral diaphragmatic strength, we're going to combine breathing and swallowing.

Diaphragm Push-up—Visceral

1. Assess your voice and body.

2. Find the same hand/finger position from version 1. Maybe slump over a bit and let your neck hang forward.

3. Inhale against the resistance of your fingers like in Version 1. At the peak of the inhalation, swallow.

4. Exhale. At the bottom of the exhalation, swallow.

5. Inhale and swallow.

6. Exhale and swallow.

7. Inhale and swallow.

8. Exhale and swallow.

9. Reassess.

This drill is a coordination test between different areas of the diaphragm, and many people find that adding the swallow is surprisingly tricky. If you didn't have enough saliva to keep swallowing, that dry mouth is a sign that threat is increasing. Start with two or four swallows instead of six, and work your way up. If your stomach gurgles when you do this drill, I take this to be a good sign. It's an indication that your vagus nerve (which controls your parasympathetic, or "rest-and-digest," function) is waking up.

Even if you don't have reflux, this can be a great drill. Volitional swallowing (swallowing on demand) activates the areas in the homunculus related to your throat and your diaphragm. Practicing your swallow may improve reflexive communication between the larynx and your breath. Additionally, swallowing on cue has been shown to activate the right insular lobe.[32] The right insula integrates sensory feedback from the larynx and is involved in the emotional content of singing. A well-developed right insula makes your performance more engaging.

Breathing Wave

The nerves in your spinal cord send information to your brain regarding the state of your digestion and visceral organs.[33] The breathing wave can help you identify which areas of your spine are the least mobile. It is done face down, making it a great way to train the posterior diaphragmatic fibers that contribute to spinal movement. This drill also engages some smaller spinal muscles that help with inhalation. You'll need something with a slight weight and that can spread out a bit (e.g., a pillow, a bag of rice, a folded-up blanket, etc.).

1. Assess your voice and body.

2. Lie face down on the floor. Rest your forehead on your hands (put your palm on the back of your other hand to make a "pillow").

3. Take a deep breath. You should feel a "wave" motion starting on the sides of your lower back and flowing up all the way to your neck on inhalation. Do you notice areas that aren't moving or that move as a block?

4. Place the pillow/bag of rice/etc. on your lower back.

5. Take five breaths, focusing on moving the weighted item up toward the ceiling on inhalation.

6. Move the object up to your mid- to lower back and take five more breaths, moving the weighted item up toward the ceiling on inhalation.

7. Move the object to the middle of your back between your shoulder blades and take five more breaths, moving the weighted item up toward the ceiling on inhalation.

8. Move the object to the upper back and take five more breaths, moving the weighted item up toward the ceiling on inhalation.

9. Before you get up, take the object off your back and see how smooth the breathing wave feels now. The motion should start in your lower back and flow up to your neck on inhalation.

10. Get up and reassess.

DIAPHRAGMATIC NERVES

The diaphragm is innervated by both the **phrenic** and the **vagus** nerves. I'll be addressing the vagus later, so let's look at the phrenic nerve now *(Fig. 5.6)*. It originates out of your third, fourth, and fifth cervical vertebrae (C3–C5). To find your C3–5, start your search at C7, your seventh and lowest cervical vertebra. Put your fingers on the back of your lower neck and look for the bump that sticks out the most. (If you can't find it, let your chin drop toward your chest; it should stick out more now.) Walk up two vertebrae toward your skull, and you've found C5. Bring your head up, look straight ahead, and turn your neck from side to side with your finger on C5. Does this vertebra move easily in both directions? Now try tilting your ear toward your shoulder in both directions. How is the quality of movement in this plane? Try the same motions with your fingers up one vertebra higher on C4 and then up one more on C3. The more

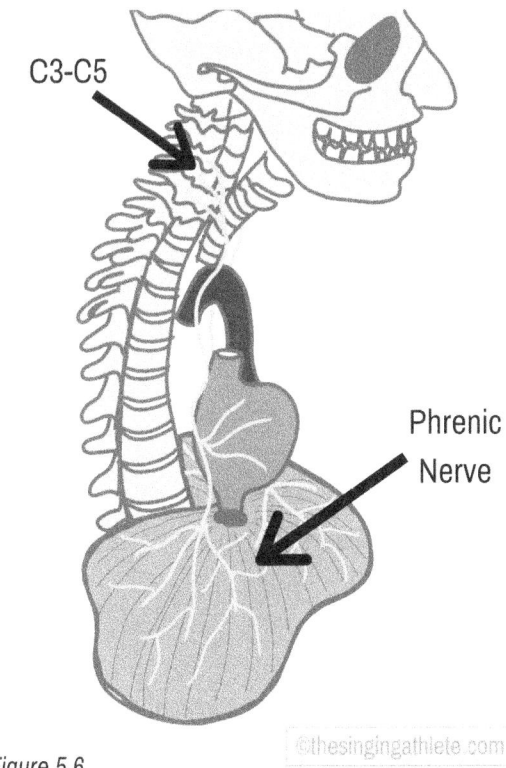

Figure 5.6

well-mapped you are here, the better your diaphragmatic breathing will be.

The phrenic nerve receives sensory input from the pericardium (the sac containing the heart), the liver, and the peritoneum (the membrane lining the abdominal cavity). The phrenic motor units also contribute to swallowing, vocalization, coughing, and sneezing. One of the primary jobs of this nerve is to help create appropriate intra-abdominal pressure for all movements of the body, including singing. If you're not familiar with the concept of **appoggio**, it's a support technique taught in bel canto training where the singer tries to resist letting the torso collapse on exhalation. The ability to create appoggio is partially dependent on the function of the phrenic nerve.

The phrenic nerve receives its commands from a portion of the brainstem called the medulla.[34] This is one reason why releasing suboccipital muscles (the area right under your skull at the back, near the brainstem) can often improve breathing. The phrenic and vagus nerves also provide sensory feedback to the parts of the brainstem dealing with the eyes (medial longitudinal fasciculus) and the mouth and jaw (spinal trigeminal nucleus). Furthermore, the phrenic nerve sends signals to the hypoglossal nerve, which controls tongue movement. Fixing diaphragm issues can also fix a whole lot of other stuff and vice versa.

In Greek, the root "phren" refers to both the diaphragm and the mind.[35] At one time, the mind was thought to live in the diaphragm and, although that's not anatomically correct, there is a certain truth there. Our breathing connects intrinsically to our thinking.

You can create a stretch of your right phrenic nerve by going through the following sequence.

Phrenic Nerve Glide

1. Assess your voice and body.

2. Place your left fingertips on C3–C5 (count up from C7 if you've lost your place).

3. Rotate your head to the left from C3–C5 (you should feel your fingers rotating).

4. While maintaining the rotation, also tilt your head to the left from C3–C5 (you should feel your fingers tilting).

5. Lift your chin a little bit.

6. Nod your head in that position while taking a few full inhalations. Do you feel your fingers (and the C3–C5 vertebrae) moving?

7. Reassess.

Reverse these steps for a left phrenic nerve stretch (right fingertips, right rotation, right tilt, lift your chin, nod and breathe).

6. EXHALATION

One of the instructions I was given early in my voice training was to imagine a string on the opposite wall that was lifting my sternum. The idea was to achieve a "noble posture," and because I wanted to be an A+ student, I spent hours and hours in a practice room ingraining this movement into my body. In the process, I ended up pushing my sternum so far forward that I flattened the curve of my thoracic spine until it was almost non-existent. Through Wolff's Law and Davis' Law, my brain laid down additional bone and soft tissue to support this aberrant pattern, which ended up contributing to the chronic pain I developed in my elbow.

An instruction to lift the sternum isn't inherently wrong, and it can be useful for someone who is kyphotic (slumped) and needs to open their chest. But I was already quite lordotic (swayback) with a hypertonic set of muscles in my lower back. The teachers who told me to open my chest were well-meaning, but they were not looking closely at the body in front of them. If I had known about the assess/reassess protocol back then, I could have quickly figured out that efforts to "open the chest" don't test well for me. The exhalation-focused drills in this chapter, however, are always great for my body and my voice. If you stand in swayback, can't do a full forward bend, or feel tight in your back muscles, see if you respond similarly well.

ABDOMINAL ANATOMY

Singing happens on the exhalation, and the abdominals are the main muscles of exhalatory control. The name for this muscle group comes from the Latin word "abdere," which means to conceal or stow away. The abs "hide" your visceral organs and provide protective layers for the vulnerable open space at the center of the body.

Although these muscles are often treated as a unit, you have eight abdominals, four on either side:

- *Rectus Abdominis* (2)

- *External Oblique* (2)

- *Internal Oblique* (2)

- *Transversus Abdominis* (2)

Sometimes one of these muscles is the key, so they need to be engaged and assessed individually. For my body, if I contract my right internal oblique, not much happens. If I do my left internal oblique (remember my left-side hernia?), my back opens up, and I sing and move better.

I'm calling the breathing drills in the next two chapters "awareness drills," because body mapping is both a motor and a sensory process. Before we strengthen the breathing muscle, we will do some "sensory priming," where you will rub, scratch, or tap the skin that lies above the muscle. (Remember that sensory feeds motor, so you will get a fuller experience of the core musculature if your skin is awake first.) You will use the picture I drew of each muscle as a guide for where to provide sensory stimulus.

Then we'll go into movement; we'll be using internally focused cues, asking you to draw bones together. (This internal focus is because we are working on strength-building.) While some of these will feel like workouts, also stay aware of the sensation of the contraction. Remember that singers respond more to the sensory elements of training than instrumentalists do.

Exhalation Awareness Drill 1—Rectus Abdominis

The *rectus abdominis* muscles (aka the "six-pack") run in a straight line up the front of your body from your pubic bone to your fifth rib, which is higher than most of us realize. There are two rectus abdomini, a right and a left, split down the middle by connective tissue called the *linea alba*. The muscles run close to the surface for most of their path (hence, the potential for visible bulges). However, at an area below the navel called the *arcuate line*, they dive below all the other abdominal layers, forming a direct path into the pubic bone. This deep connection means that the rectus can flex the trunk and help with pelvic stabilization.

Sensory Priming

Using Figure 6.1 as a guide, rub/scratch/tap your skin along the line of your rectus abdominis muscles.

Strength

1. Stand tall, with one hand on the right side of your pubic bone (the bone above your genitals) and the other on the right side of your sternum around your fifth rib (mid-chest).

2. Think of forming an open "ah" in your throat but don't make any sound. Exhale in this mouth position while pulling your fingers together, lifting the right side of the pubic bone up toward your head as the right fifth rib moves toward the floor.

3. Repeat 3–4 times, getting a feel for the contractile strength.

4. Repeat steps 1–3 on the left side. Does one side feel stronger/easier to contract?

If you found a weaker side:

1. Assess your voice and body.

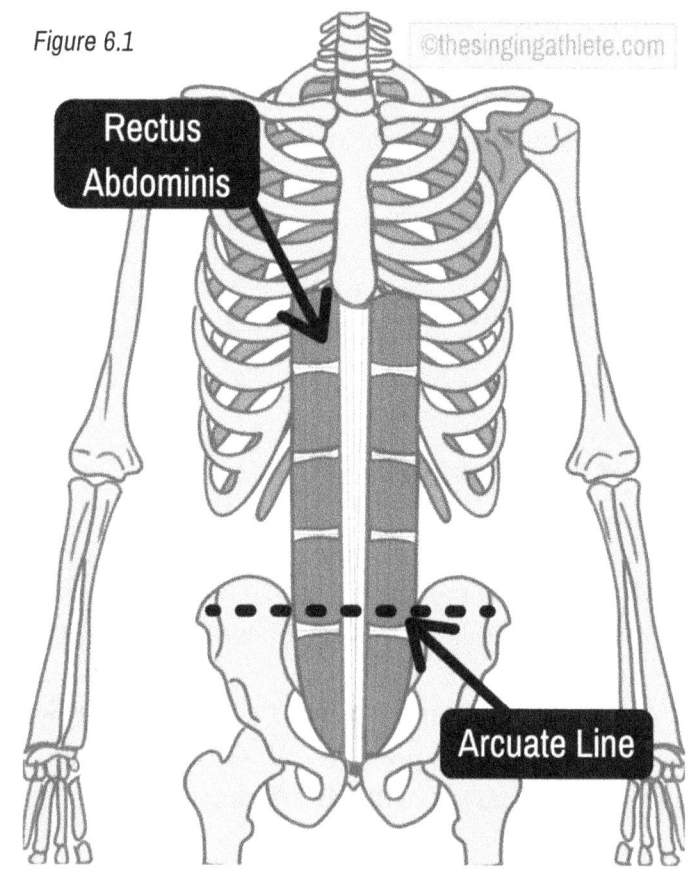

Figure 6.1

2. Put your fingers on the bony landmarks on the weaker side.

3. Perform five more full exhalations, focusing on pulling the fingers together on the weak side.

4. Reassess.

Exhalation Awareness Drill 2—External Oblique

The *external obliques* are the largest abdominal muscles, connecting your pelvis with your rib cage. Much like the rectus abdomini, the external obliques bring the pubic bone and the ribs together, only in a diagonal direction. The external obliques also attach much higher than you might think, all the way up to your fifth rib. These higher attachments make them crucial for controlling airflow in the mid-thoracic area (ribs 5–7). The right external oblique creates lateral flexion (side bend) to the right and rotation to the left, with the left external oblique doing the opposite (lateral flexion to the left, rotation to the right). The external oblique also interweaves with the serratus anterior at ribs 5–9 (see next chapter).

Sensory Priming

Rub, scratch, or tap your skin along the line of your external oblique muscles *(Fig. 6.2)*.

Strength

1. Assess your voice and body.

2. Stand tall, with your right hand on the side of your right middle ribs and your left fingertips across the center line on your right pubic bone.

3. Bend your knees and tuck your pelvis under slightly.

4. Without losing the tuck, lean your torso over to your right and then rotate your ribs back to your left. As you rotate, keep your pelvis facing forward; the rotation should only be coming from the ribs.

5. Flex forward as you pull your hands toward one another on a full exhalation. The action you are looking for is to pull the right ribcage and the right pubic bone toward one another.

6. Hold here for 3–5 more strong exhalations.

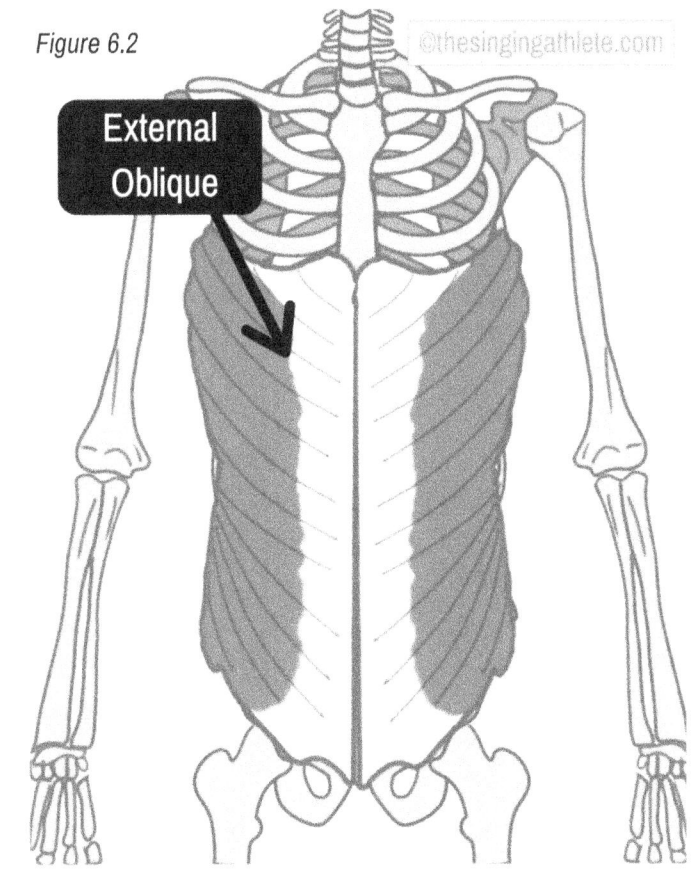

Figure 6.2

External Oblique

7. Reassess.

8. Repeat on the left side. Your left hand goes on your left middle ribs and your right fingertips goes across the center line on your left pubic bone.

9. Bend your knees, tuck your butt under, lean over to the left, and then rotate the ribs back to the right.

10. Flex forward and bring your hands together on 3–5 full exhalations.

11. Reassess.

Exhalation Awareness Drill 3—Internal Oblique

While the external obliques are closer to the surface and more of an anterior/lateral muscle, the ***internal obliques*** run deeper and further around the torso. They attach your lowest three ribs (ribs 10–12) to the pubic crest of your pelvis and your lower back (deep layer of thoracolumbar fascia).

For the upper two-thirds of its surface area, there is a split in the internal oblique. Its aponeurosis (broad, flat tendon) divides into a posterior layer that goes behind the rectus abdominis and an anterior layer that goes in front of it. This means that the internal oblique assists with both the creation of intra-abdominal pressure and the transfer of that force to the outside world.

The cremaster muscle, which raises a male's testicles in toward the body, is formed from a branch of the internal obliques. Irregular testicular height can be a sign of uneven function in the internal oblique muscles.

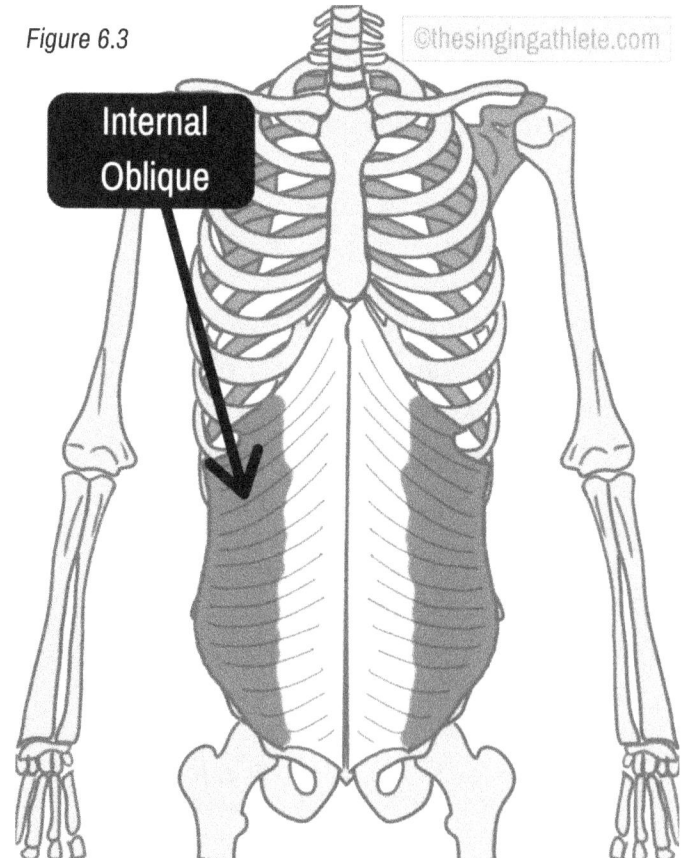

Figure 6.3

The internal oblique drill is pretty much the same as the external oblique drill, except that the contact points are different and you will be doing the opposite rotation.

Sensory Priming

Rub, scratch, or tap your skin along the line of your internal oblique muscles *(Fig. 6.3—they also go around to the lower back)*.

Strength

1. Assess your voice and body.

2. With your right hand, grab the top of your

pelvis. Your right pointer finger should be on the ASIS. The ASIS, or anterior superior iliac spine, is a bony projection off the upper front edge of your pelvis. Your right thumb should be around toward your back. Put your left hand across the midline to the lower front right ribs.

3. Bend your knees and tuck your pelvis under slightly.

4. Without losing the tuck, lean your torso to your right and rotate your ribcage to your right.

5. Flex forward and pull your hands toward one another on a full exhalation. The action you are looking for is to draw the right pelvic crest and the right lower ribs toward one another.

6. Hold this position for 3–5 more strong exhalations.

7. Reassess.

8. Repeat on the left side. Your left hand goes on the top of your left pelvis, with your left pointer finger on the left ASIS (top front of the pelvis) and left thumb toward your back. Your right hand goes across the midline on your lowest left ribs.

9. Bend your knees, tuck your butt under, lean over to the left, and rotate your ribcage to your left.

10. Flex forward and bring your hands together on 3–5 full exhalations.

11. Reassess.

Exhalation Awareness Drill 4—Transversus Abdominis

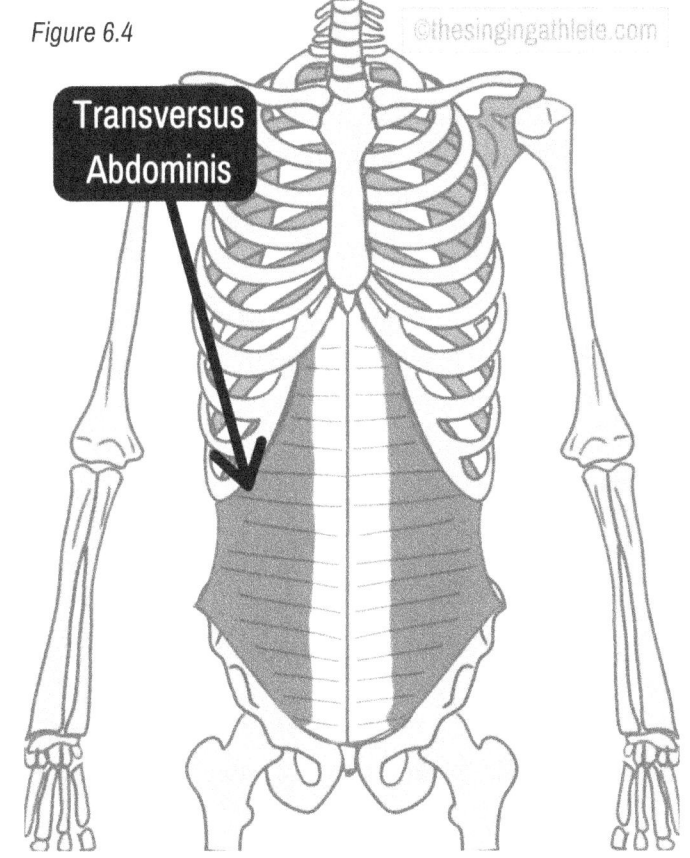

Figure 6.4

The *transversus abdominis* (TVA) is the deepest layer of abdominal musculature for most of its path, and it is the most thoroughly connected to the diaphragm. It attaches the deep layer of thoracolumbar (back) fascia to ribs 7–12 and the front of the pelvis. The main action of the TVA is to compress the abdominal contents on exhalation. With this in mind, you could also think of the diaphragm stretches we did in Chapter 5 as strength work for the TVA.

Sensory Priming

Rub, scratch, or tap your skin along the line of your transversus abdominis muscles *(Fig. 6.4—they also go around to the lower back).*

Strength

1. Assess your voice and body.

2. Stand tall, with your hands grasping the area under your ribcage on both sides (like the "lobster claw" position from *Diaphragm Stretch 1* in Chapter 5.)

3. On a full exhalation, draw your waist in as hard as you can in all directions.

4. Release and repeat four more times. Are both sides moving equally?

5. Now point your fingertips down and place your palms on the sides of your lower ribs (7–12).

6. On a full exhalation, draw your lower ribs directly down toward the floor.

7. Repeat four more times. Are both sides working equally?

8. Reassess.

Exhalation Awareness Drill 5—Internal Intercostals

The *internal intercostals* are small, flat muscles that lie deep to the external intercostals, forming a continuous chain with the internal obliques. Different parts of the muscle can either depress or elevate the ribs, but we will think of them here as mostly exhalation muscles. They do not work in quiet breathing, only in forceful exhalation.

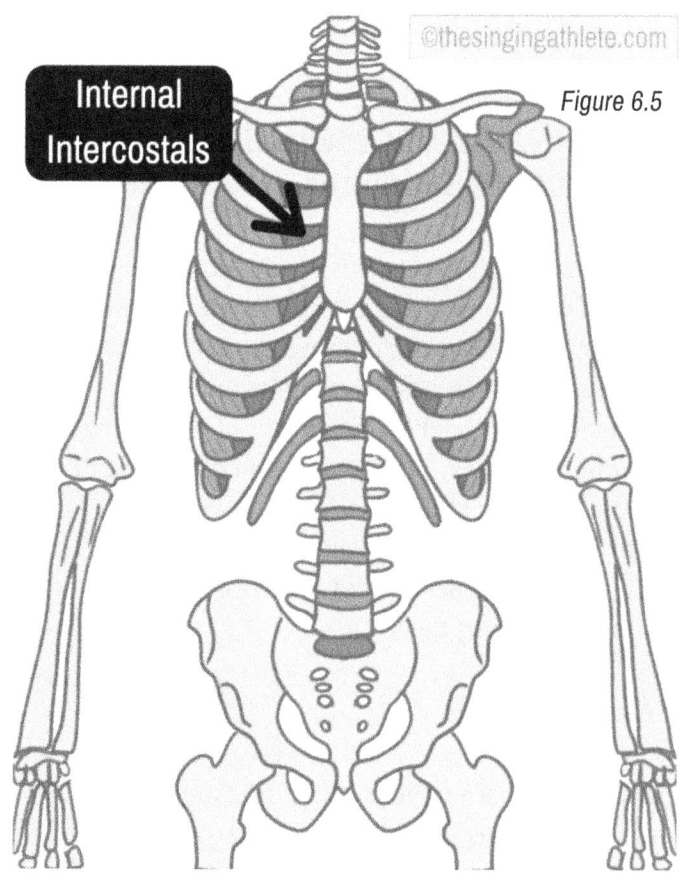

Figure 6.5

Sensory Priming

Rub, scratch, or tap your skin along the line of your internal intercostal muscles *(Fig. 6.5–they lie under your entire ribcage)*.

Strength

1. Assess your voice and body.

2. Place your left hand across the midline on your right ribs.

3. On a hard exhalation, imagine every rib moving toward the one below it.

4. Rotate your ribcage to the right and side-bend to the right. Exhale three more times as strongly as you can.

5. Reassess.

6. Repeat the setup on the left side. Right hand goes on the left ribcage; draw each rib down on a hard exhalation.

7. Rotate your ribcage to the left and side-bend to the left. Exhale three more times as strongly as you can.

8. Reassess.

Exhalation Awareness Drill 6—Transversus Thoracis

The *transversus thoracis* *(Fig. 6.6)* is a muscle that lies on the inside of the ribcage and sternum, in the same layer of muscle as the deep internal intercostals. It attaches to the inside surface of ribs 2–6 and pulls them down. The transversus thoracis is given short shrift in most anatomical literature (its Wikipedia page currently says it is "almost completely without function"), but I have found it to be immensely helpful for myself and many other singers.

Remember the instruction of imagining a string pulling your sternum to the opposite wall? By working the transversus thoracis, you may find a more balanced muscle tone in the upper chest if it is pushed too far forward. The first time I did this drill, I felt immediate relief. When you do this one correctly, you should also feel a stretch in the uppermost vertebrae of your back, which tends to be one of the hardest spots in the body to mobilize.

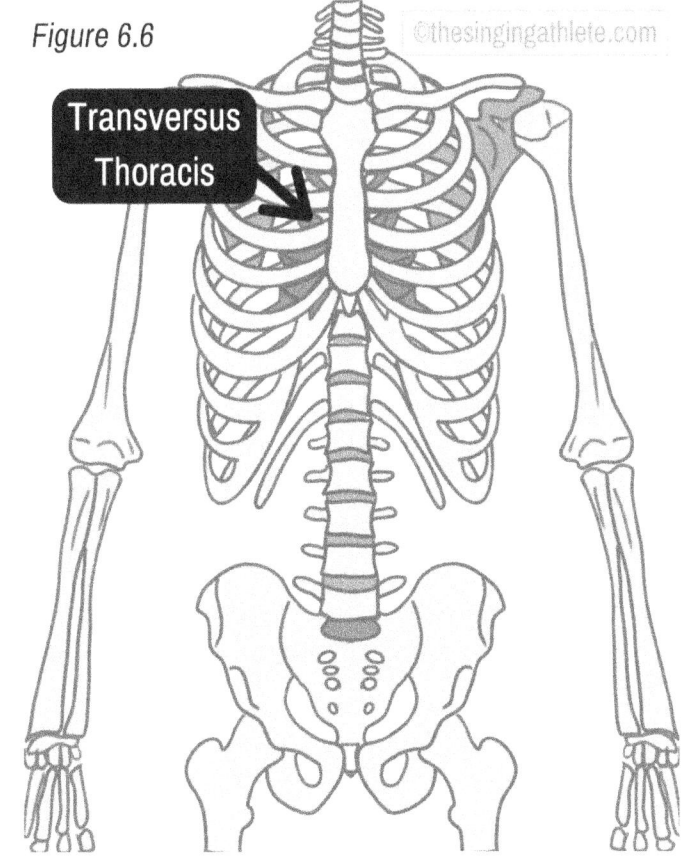

Figure 6.6

Sensory Priming

Rub, scratch, or tap your skin along the line of your transversus thoracis muscles *(Fig. 6.6)*.

Strength

1. Assess your voice and body.

2. Stand tall and place the fingers of your left hand on the top of the right side of your sternum at the level of your second rib and the fingers of your right hand on the bottom of the right side of your sternum.

3. On a forceful exhalation, pull your left (top)

fingers down toward your right (bottom) fingers. You are looking to feel a pulling down of your top ribs toward your bottom ribs. If you're doing it correctly, you will start to feel a stretch in the very upper portion of your back. Do three strong exhalations.

4. Reassess.

5. Switch sides, placing your fingers on the top and bottom of the left side of your sternum.

6. Repeat Step 3 on the left.

7. Reassess.

Exhalation Awareness Drill 7—Quadratus Lumborum/Serratus Posterior Inferior

Although the abdominals go all the way around your midsection, you have two muscles that are more exclusively in the back line of the body that help with exhalation *(Fig. 6.7)*. The lowest one is the *quadratus lumborum (QL)*, which technically forms the very back of your anterior abdominal cavity and connects your bottom (twelfth) rib to your lumbar spine and pelvis. The QL is assisted by the *serratus posterior inferior*, which pulls ribs 9–12 in and down toward the lower back.

Sensory Priming

Rub, scratch, or tap your skin along the line of your QL and serratus posterior superior muscles *(Fig. 6.7)*.

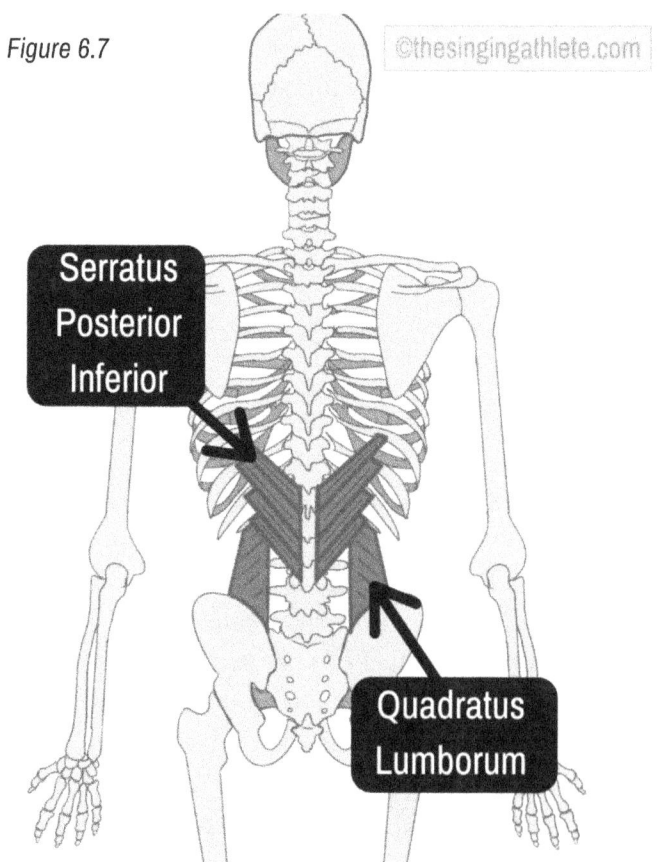

Figure 6.7

Strength

1. Assess your voice and body.

2. Stand tall, with both hands on either side of your lower back.

3. Place your right hand on the right posterior upper edge of your pelvis, next to your tailbone. Place your left hand across the center line on your right lower-to-mid back.

4. On a strong exhalation, draw your right lowest ribs down toward your posterior pelvis. Repeat 3–4 times.

5. Reassess.

6. Repeat on your left. Your left hand finds your left posterior pelvis and your right hand goes to your left lower back. Do a few strong exhalations, bringing your lowest ribs down toward the pelvis.

7. Reassess.

Exhalation Awareness Drill 8—Pelvic Floor

The *pelvic floor* *(Fig. 6.8)* is a diamond-shaped area bordered by your pubic bone, your tailbone (coccyx), and the two sit-bones (ischial tuberosities). It functions as a support for your organs and contains passageways for your urethra, your rectum, your sex organs, and for a baby during childbirth. In terms of breathing, the pelvic floor exists in a reciprocal relationship with your diaphragm. When the diaphragm contracts on inhalation, the pelvic floor should sense the downward motion and release. As exhalation begins, the pelvic floor should coordinate with the abdominal layers to gently draw in, with the diaphragm rising and relaxing.

Pelvic floor dysfunction (e.g., incontinence, pain, constipation, sexual dysfunction) is quite common. In a 2007 study, up to 50 percent of women reported pelvic floor dysfunction of at least one major type.[36] Although not as commonly self-reported in men, on average, 4–10 percent have admitted problems (the real number is probably much higher).

I find that the pelvic floor anatomy is very blurry for many people, so before we do these drills, I'd like you to locate some landmarks on yourself:

- Find your *pubic symphysis*, where your two pubic bones come together; you're feeling for a bony spot right above the genitals.

- Reach your hands under your butt and feel around for the two sit bones (*ischial tuberosities*). Using your fingers, palpate the curve of the bone; it is shaped much like the bottom of a rocking chair.

- Take your fingers farther back and toward the midline and reach under until you feel your *coccyx* (the point of your tailbone). Your fused coccygeal vertebrae are the remnants of a vestigial tail(!).

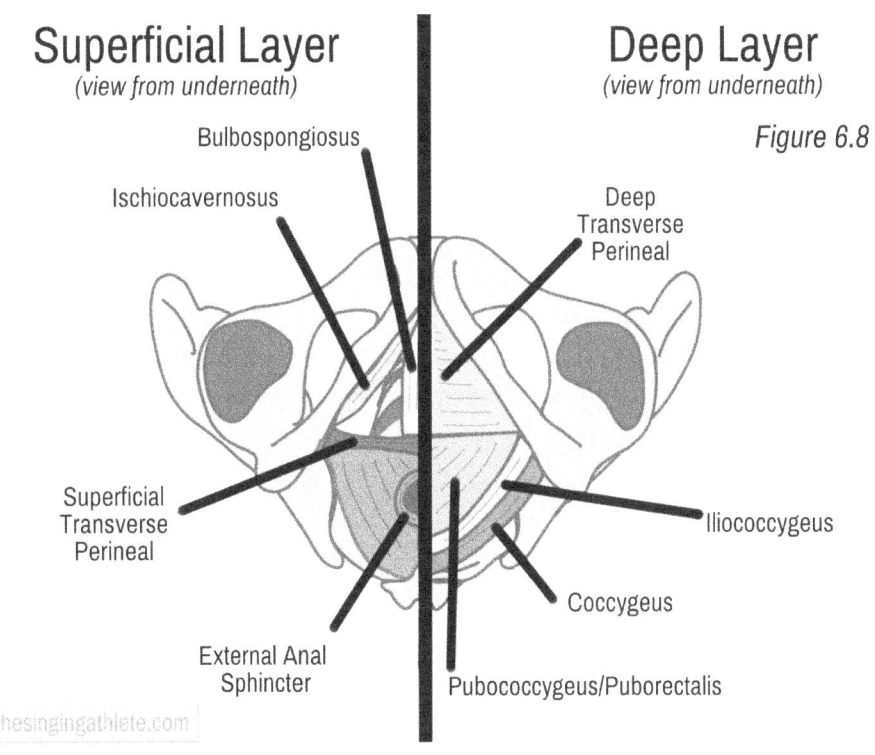

Figure 6.8

65

- These four markers (e.g., pubic symphysis, right and left tuberosities, coccyx) form the points of a diamond. Palpate the pelvic floor muscles that are internal to these landmarks, especially the front quadrants. Does one side or area feel tighter?

Did you discover tight areas in your pelvic floor palpation? Those tense muscles may be stuck in an inhalation or an exhalation position. If you often feel like you have to pee but not much comes out (urge incontinence), some of your pelvic floor muscles may be stuck in inhalation; focus on the contraction portion of the drills below, drawing the bony landmarks together. Conversely, if you "forget to pee" and go for many hours without remembering to urinate, you may be stuck in an exhalation position; focus on the relaxation portion of the drills below, allowing the bones to move apart.[37] We have poor proprioception of this area (the pelvic floor gets very little space in the homunculus), so the relaxation can take 2–3 times longer than a contraction.

The pelvic floor is one of the most neurologically and muscularly complex areas of the body. For this book, we will be simplifying things to two depths: a superficial layer right at the surface and a deep layer about 2 inches (5 cm) up from the surface. So you can discover the anatomical structures most easily, learn these drills lying down. As I describe pulling the bones together, some of you will do better by physically touching and guiding the landmarks with your fingers. Others will find it easier to avoid physical contact and use the imagination to draw the bones toward one another. Once you have mastered these drills in the supine position, try them seated, standing, walking, etc.

Version 1—Superficial Muscles

1. Lie on your back, knees up, with your feet on the ground and your spine in a neutral position. Check your lumbar curve by placing a hand under your lower back. There should be a slight curve away from the floor, and your hand should be able to slide in between your lower back and the ground.

2. Use the force of your exhalation to pull your pubic symphysis and your coccyx together. This contraction will be a front-to-back motion and should feel surface-level, centering the contraction right below the skin. Relax completely on an inhalation, allowing the bones to move apart. Repeat four more times.

3. On an exhalation, pull the bottom points of your tuberosities toward one another. Visualize the bones pulling together laterally on the exhalation. Relax completely on an inhalation. Repeat four more times.

4. On an exhalation, pull all four corners of the diamond together, guiding the front, back, and sides toward the center. Relax completely on an inhalation. Repeat four more times.

Version 2—Deep Muscles

1. Lie on your back, knees up, with your feet on the ground and your back in a neutral position.

2. Use the force of your exhalation to pull your pubic symphysis and your coccyx together in a front-to-back motion. Now, the contraction should feel deeper, imagining a layer about 2 inches (5 cm) up

toward the head from the superficial layers. Relax completely on an inhalation, allowing the bones to move apart. Repeat four more times.

3. On an exhalation, pull the midpoint of your tuberosities laterally toward one another. Imagine this about 2 inches (5 cm) up toward the head from where superficial contraction was. Relax completely on an inhalation. Repeat four more times.

4. On an exhalation, pull all four corners of the diamond together, guiding the front, back, and sides of the deep layer toward the center. Relax completely. Repeat four more times.

It's very common to find differentiation of the pelvic-floor muscles difficult. If you're struggling to find clear maps of the superficial and deep layers, here are three neurologically based additions you can try:

- **Teeth vibration:** Vibrating your teeth wakes up a part of the brain called the **supplementary motor area (SMA)**, which is involved in coordinating midline structures such as the pelvic floor. I use an oral motor tool called a Z-vibe for tooth vibration, but you can also use an electric toothbrush. Try one of the pelvic floor drills with and without biting a vibration source between your teeth. For me, the dental vibration makes the pelvic motions feel clearer. Tooth vibration is also an excellent strategy to improve gut motility and relieve constipation.

- **Warmth on your stomach:** Sometimes the reason it's hard to feel the pelvic floor is due to issues in your insular lobe. One of the most helpful ways to wake up the insular lobe is through warmth on the abdomen. Grab a hot water bottle, heating pad, or a friendly pet (here kitty, kitty) and place it on your stomach while you do the pelvic drills.

- **Listening to your heartbeat:** Another effective insular drill is becoming aware of your heartbeat. As you go through the exercises, count the beats of your heart. In my studio, I use a stethoscope for this purpose.

7. INHALATION

Like everything, breathing is SAID-specific. There is no perfect way to do it in every circumstance; breath is supposed to be responsive to thought and action. You need a very different type of respiratory competence when lying in bed compared with competing in a triathlon. And while the diaphragm is supposed to be the primary driver of inhalation, the surrounding muscles also deserve attention. When you're onstage, you may be in an emotional state where a higher, shallower breath makes the most sense in the given circumstances. If you have no training in accessing these upper lung fields, you're missing out on a juicy character-development opportunity. Proper breath training gives you a map for all possibilities.

As I said in the last chapter, I call these exercises awareness drills. The goal is to improve the mobility of your respiratory muscles while also giving you a sensory experience. As you do these drills, be aware of asymmetries. If you watched someone do a pull-up, and one arm was significantly lagging, you would know that person has some work to do on contractile strength on that side. It's the same with breathing; this is a muscular activity, and we're looking for evenness.

IS A LOWER BREATH ALWAYS GOOD?

In everyday life, "low, slow, and through the nose" should be the breathing pattern you adopt. The lungs are essentially shaped like a triangle, with the wider, two-pointed end at the bottom. This means you will get the most efficient oxygen exchange in the lower lung fields. A low breath also can create an aerodynamic drag that lowers the larynx; as the pelvic floor and diaphragm descend, the larynx goes along for the ride, lengthening the vocal tract.

The question is, do you always want to lower the larynx? In a classical singing aesthetic, I would say the answer is generally yes. Still, when you belt (i.e., call), it can be easier to achieve this quality on a higher laryngeal position. If you're a belter (and men and women can both belt), reassess a belted phrase after doing the drills in this chapter.

It's also worth saying that, although you should breathe primarily into the lower portion of the lungs, we do have lung tissue in the upper fields as well. I've seen some singers who breathe low to a fault, with no movement at all in the chest. Your sympathetic nervous system lies in your thoracic spine, so recapturing the small breathing movements of the upper ribs can reduce stress.

Inhalation Awareness Drill 1—Pectoralis Minor

The *pectoralis minor* muscle attaches ribs 3–5 to a front-facing protrusion from your scapula (shoulder blade) called the coracoid process. (Coracoid means "crow" in Greek, as its shape resembles a bird's beak.) The pec minor is generally thought of as a protractor of the scapula, meaning that it slides the shoulder blade forward around the ribcage. However, if the shoulder blade is fixed in place, the pec minor can lift and open the upper ribs on inhalation.

Sensory Priming

As in the previous chapter, we'll wake up the sensory system by stimulating the skin above the muscle we are training. Rub, scratch, or tap your skin along the line of your pectoralis minor muscles, using Figure 7.1 as a guide.

Strength

1. Assess your voice and body.

2. Stand with your right shoulder blade against a wall; it's easiest to do this by turning 45 degrees to the right. (The reason to put your scapula against the wall is to stabilize your shoulder.)

3. Place your left hand across the midline on your right upper chest.

4. Inhale and feel for an expansion of ribs 3–5 on the right. You should be focused on a feeling of inflation in the lung tissue between the wall and your hand when you inhale. You should also feel a slight elevation of the ribs but not of the shoulder. Take five breaths in this position.

5. Reassess.

6. Switch the setup, placing your left shoulder blade against the wall at a 45-degree angle and your right hand across the midline on your left upper chest.

7. Inhale and feel for an expansion of ribs 3–5 on the left, taking five breaths and filling your upper lung fields to move your hand and the wall apart. Is one side moving more than the other?

8. Reassess.

If you have a shoulder problem on one side, it is quite likely you will have noticed less mobility in the lung field on that side. This makes the pec minor inhalation an excellent shoulder rehab drill. Check your shoulder range of motion, redo the drill on the problem side and reassess.

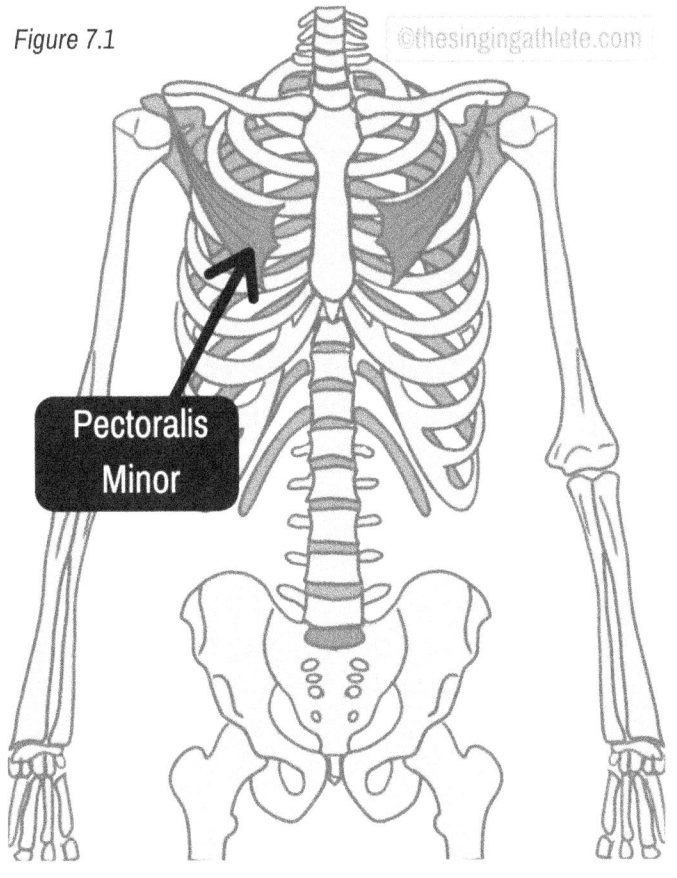

Figure 7.1

Inhalation Awareness Drill 2—Pectoralis Major

The *pectoralis major* is a much broader muscle than the pec minor, with attachment points at the clavicle, the midline of your sternum, your top seven ribs, and the humerus (upper arm). In terms of inhalation, the pec major acts mostly as a rib widener, especially in the mid-to-lower chest.

Sensory Priming

Rub, scratch, or tap your skin along the line of your pectoralis major muscles *(Fig. 7.2)*.

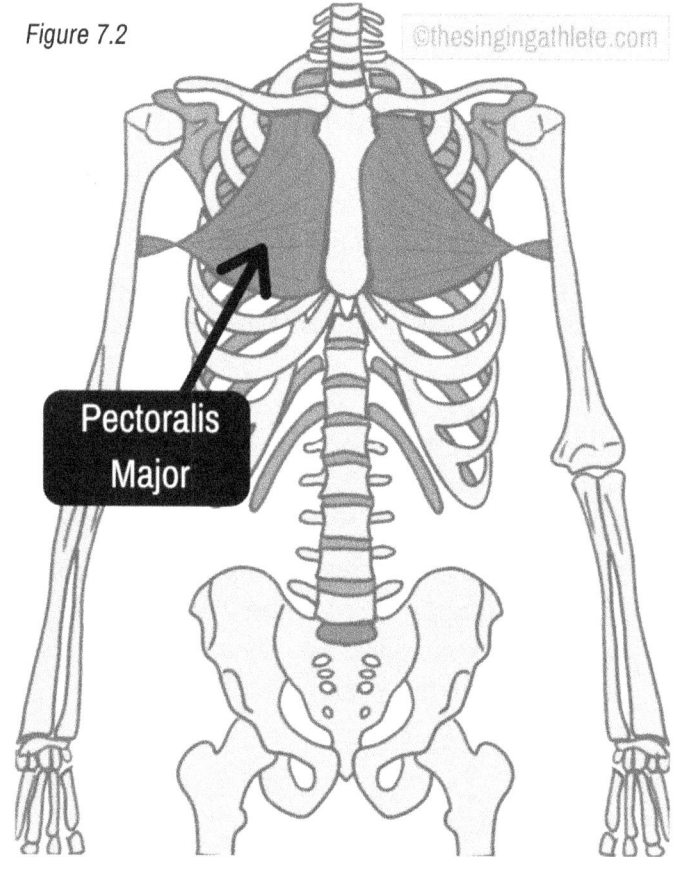

Figure 7.2

Strength

1. Assess your voice and body.

2. Stand against a wall, with both shoulder blades pressed into the wall. This time, you want to be facing directly out from the wall, not on an angle.

3. Roll your shoulder blades back and down, getting as much contact as possible with the wall.

4. Take your left hand, crossing the midline to wrap around your right middle ribs.

5. Inhale and feel for a lateral expansion of the ribs on the right. This sideways expansion should feel different than the more vertical movement of the pec minor breath. Take five breaths.

6. Reassess.

7. Switch your hands so your right hand is across the midline, wrapping around your left middle ribs.

8. Inhale and feel for a lateral expansion of the ribs on the left. Take five breaths. Is one side moving more than the other?

Inhalation Awareness Drill 3—Serratus Anterior

The *serratus anterior* attaches from the middle border of your shoulder blade to ribs 1–9, wrapping around the back and side of your ribcage like fingers. Along with the pec minor, it can protract your scapula, sliding it around your ribcage. However, when the scapula is stabilized, the serratus anterior lifts the ribs up, out, and backward on inhalation.

I find that this muscle is often hard for singers to isolate. As a prerequisite, we'll first practice protraction and retraction of the scapula:

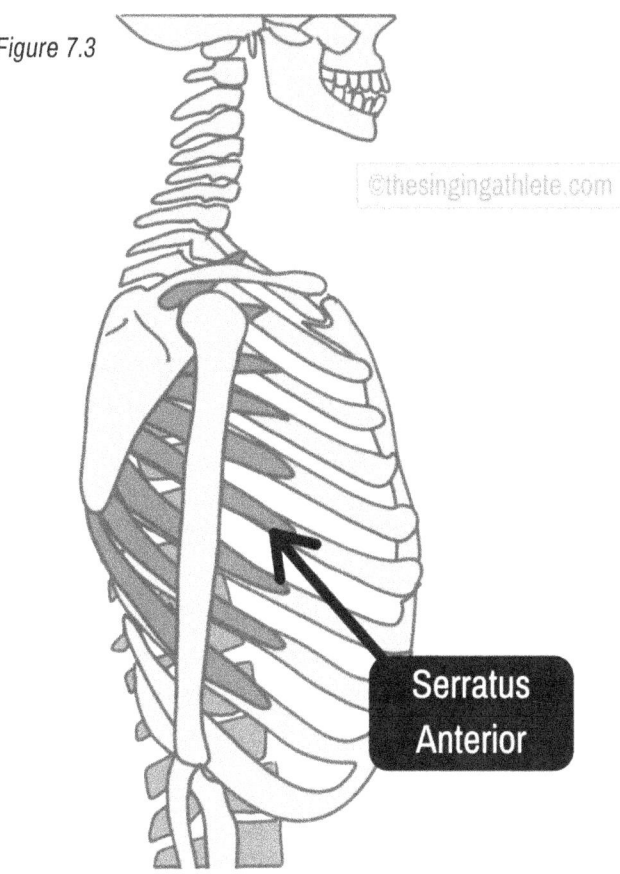

Figure 7.3

1. Place your right arm out in front of you, parallel to the ground and out to the side at about a 45-degree angle. Make a loose fist and turn it so that your thumb is facing the ceiling.

2. Slide your shoulder blade forward around your ribs; your fist will move away from you on that 45-degree angle. This is called protraction of the scapula.

3. Now, pull the shoulder blade in toward the midline of your back; your fist will move toward you on that 45-degree angle. This is called retraction of the scapula.

The protraction of the scapula is the main non-breathing function of the serratus anterior. If you max out this function before you find the breathing function of the muscle, it can be easier to appreciate what the breath possibilities are.

Sensory Priming

Rub, scratch, or tap your skin along the line of your serratus anterior muscles *(Fig. 7.3)*.

Strength

1. Assess your voice and body.

2. Place your right arm in front of you, parallel to the ground and at about a 45-degree angle. Make a loose fist with your thumb facing up to the ceiling.

3. Slide your shoulder blade around your ribs; your fist will move away from you on that 45-degree angle.

4. Once you are at your maximum protraction, wrap your left hand across your body and onto your right back ribs. Breathe in and inflate this area of the ribs out and back as much as possible.

5. Leaving your left hand where it is and keeping the ribs inflated, relax your right shoulder, letting your hand drop to your side. You will now have trapped your left hand in your right armpit.

6. With the right shoulder staying stable yet relaxed, see if you can lift the right ribs any farther out and back on an inhalation. Repeat for three more breaths.

7. Reassess.

8. Switch the setup to the left side and repeat Steps 2–6.

9. Reassess.

Inhalation Awareness Drill 4—External Intercostals

The *external intercostals* run along the same path as the external oblique. They may become active in a forceful inhalation, helping to expand ribs 2–12.

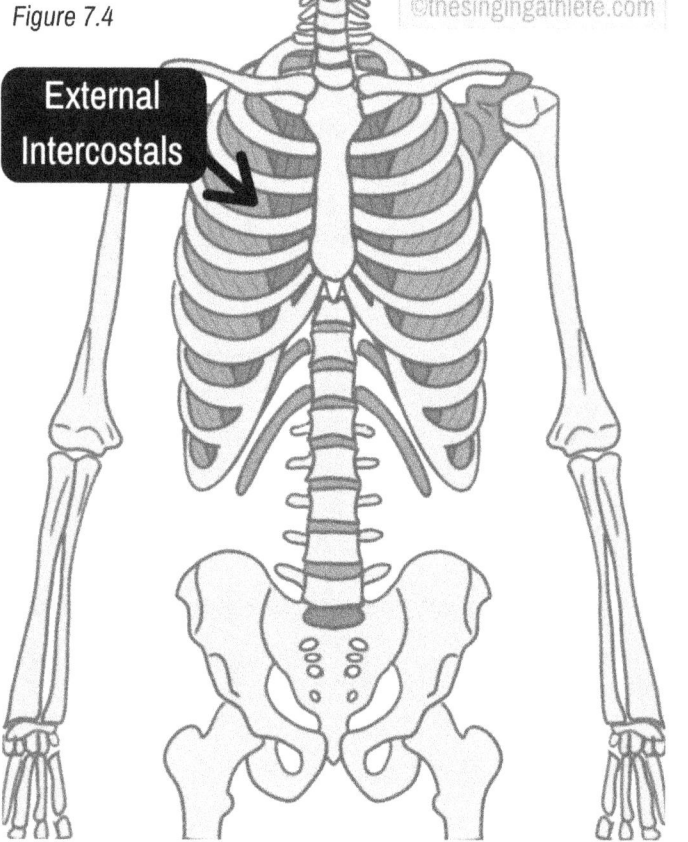

Figure 7.4

Sensory Priming

Rub, scratch, or tap your skin along the line of your external intercostal muscles *(Fig. 7.4)*.

Strength

1. Place your right pointer finger as high in your left armpit as possible. Look for the space between the two highest ribs you can find. Palpate this space; is it tender at all?

2. Inhale and see how the quality of the rib movement feels. You should feel the lower rib moving a little bit up and out toward the higher rib, slightly closing the space.

3. Walk your fingers down the ribs, taking an inhalation in each rib. Take note of any stuck or sore areas.

4. Repeat with your left pointer finger in your right armpit, walking down the right side of the ribcage. Take an inhale in each rib and assess the movement.

If you found a rib or two that was moving less or was sore:

1. Assess your voice and body.

2. Put your finger(s) back in the space between the ribs that need the most work.

3. Laterally bend about 20 degrees TOWARD the side you're working on, and then rotate about 20 degrees AWAY from the side on which you're working.

4. Take five more full breaths in this position, focusing on expanding the lung tissue and moving the ribs under your fingers.

5. Reassess.

Inhalation Awareness Drill 5—Serratus Posterior Superior

The *serratus posterior superior (Fig. 7.5)* is a small but significant muscle in your upper back that participates in moving your uppermost ribs. When I watch singers moving their thoracic spines, the area that is often the hardest to mobilize is the upper thoracic (ribs 1–4). Most of us have a poorly developed map of this area of the body, possibly resulting in stiffness or a stooped posture. Mapping this muscle can improve these issues dramatically.

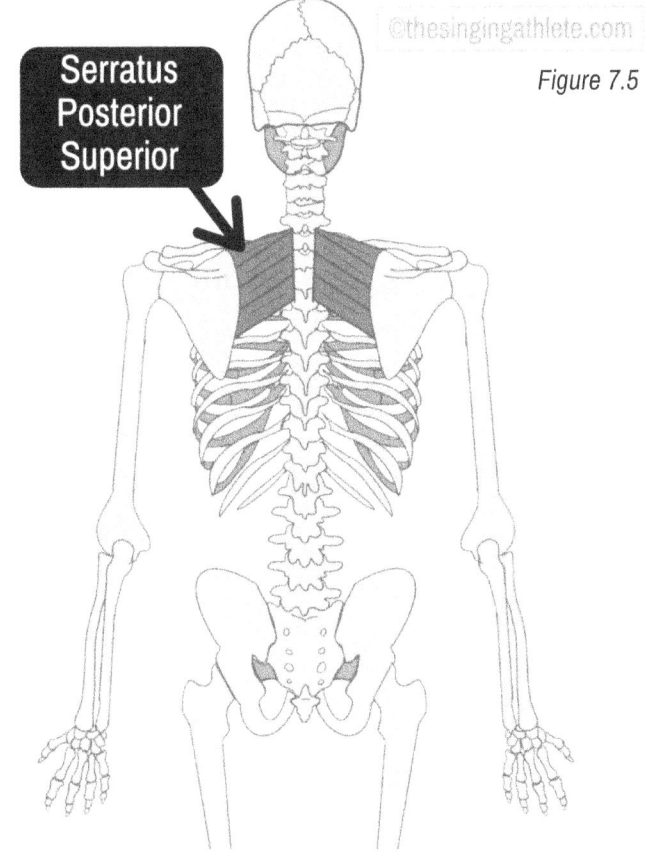

Figure 7.5

Sensory Priming

Rub, scratch, or tap your skin along the line of your serratus posterior superior muscles *(Fig. 7.5)*.

Strength

1. Sit tall with your hands reaching over your shoulders and placed on your upper back ribs. The goal is to feel at least the top four ribs, but if you are not flexible enough to do this, get your hands on as many as you can.

2. Take in several slow inhalations through the nose. You are looking for an expansion of the upper back ribs (not a lifting of the shoulders). Is one side moving more than the other?

If you found a side that was moving less:

1. Assess your voice and body.

2. Put your hand only on the weaker side.

3. Take five more breaths in through the nose, focusing on a subtle widening motion in the back ribs under your fingers.

4. Reassess.

If you're struggling to find the serratus posterior superior muscle, you're not alone; it's covered by the trapezius and can be difficult to separate from other nearby muscles. If you put your fingertips closer to the center of your spine, sometimes it's easier to feel the movement of the muscle there. You can also try this drill in child's pose. Kneel on the floor, sit on your heels, fold forward, and then place your hands on your upper back while you breathe.

THE STERNOCLEIDOMASTOID AND THE TRAPEZIUS

There are over 600 skeletal muscles in the body. The vast majority located below the head are innervated by spinal nerves, which come out of various locations along the spinal cord. The two exceptions are the *sternocleidomastoid (SCM)* and the *trapezius (Fig. 7.6)*, which originate in the brain. The reason for this direct neural connection may once again go back to survival. These two muscles create head rotation; being able to quickly turn and assess a threat is a big part of staying alive. (Think of looking both ways before you cross a street.)

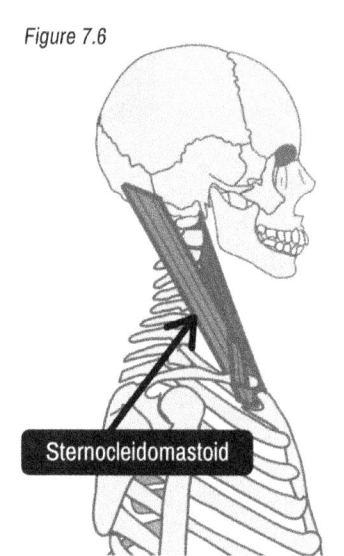
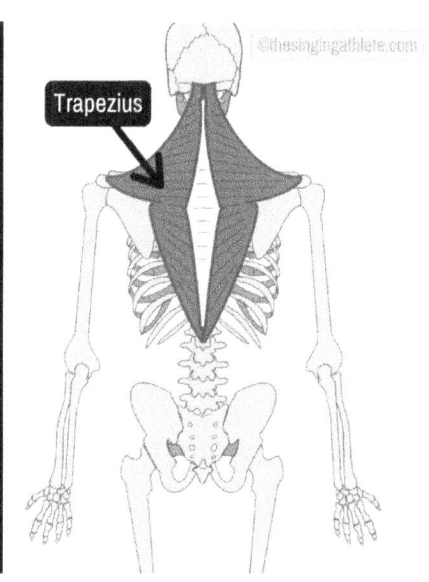

Figure 7.6

The SCM and the upper trapezius make up the outer ring of the neck. A tight SCM pulls the head forward, which squeezes the nerves coming down from the brain. It's like someone stepping on a hose when you're trying to water your garden; the flow of neural information gets interrupted.

The SCM can create a slight inhalation, lifting the clavicles/sternum when the mastoid process (the bony protrusion behind the ear) is the fixed point. The trapezius is not a direct inhalation muscle, but I have found that dysfunction here can prevent proper breathing habits. The SCM and trapezius are innervated by the accessory nerve, which is located right next to your vagus nerve in your brainstem. (Remember that the vagus is partly responsible for moving the diaphragm.) As these nerves leave the brain, a couple of the branches even share a common pathway. Nerves that fire together, wire together.

Stretch your SCM

This should feel like a pleasant stretch and should not hurt. Go slowly, and stop when your brain tells you to.

1. Assess your voice and body.

2. Place your left fingers across your body to rest on top of the center portion of your right clavicle (collarbone). Pull the right collarbone down toward the floor with your left fingers.

3. Slide your head backward, like you are trying to make a double chin. You can think of someone pulling an imaginary ponytail directly toward the wall behind you.

4. Tilt your left ear down toward your shoulder. Your right ear should be moving up to the sky.

5. Rotate your head toward the right. Spin your right ear toward the wall behind you, so your nose moves toward the ceiling.

6. Make some small nods/rotations from the very top of your spine. You are trying to pull the right collar of your shirt apart from an imaginary earring in your right ear.

7. Reassess.

8. Repeat on the other side. Right fingers on the left collarbone, head slides back, tilts to the right, and rotates left. Nod and rotate while pulling the left shirt collar and left earring apart.

9. Reassess.

STRENGTH FOR THE NECK

Let's talk about strength training for a muscle that is chronically tight. At first glance, this might seem like a bad idea; the muscle is already too contracted, so why would you want to contract it more? When a muscle is habitually tense, only a portion of it may be in this pattern. There is usually an area of this same muscle that is lacking muscle tone.

Also, muscles in a holding pattern are generally fuzzy areas in the sensory and motor cortices. I sum it up by saying, "Tension is a blurry map." When you do a full contraction of all parts of a muscle, it can improve the neural mapping of that area. Once the brain can feel the muscle again, tension in the area may dissipate. If you suspect that you have a chronically tight SCM, it's still worth doing the contraction drills, especially with the technique we are going to use.

We will work on creating SCM strength through *isometric* exercise. The definition I suggest for an isometric is "Tension but no motion." To feel the sensation of an isometric, press your palms together as hard as you can and maintain the pressure. Do you feel muscular energy in your body as you hold this position? An isometric is a low-threat way of building strength because the motor plan is so simple: contract a muscle and hold it. Isometrics have also been shown to reduce pain through the production of endocannabinoids (our inner "weed" system) when performed at an intensity level of 6–7 on a scale of 10.[38] They are a great way to build strength and reduce stress, and I use them regularly in my workouts.

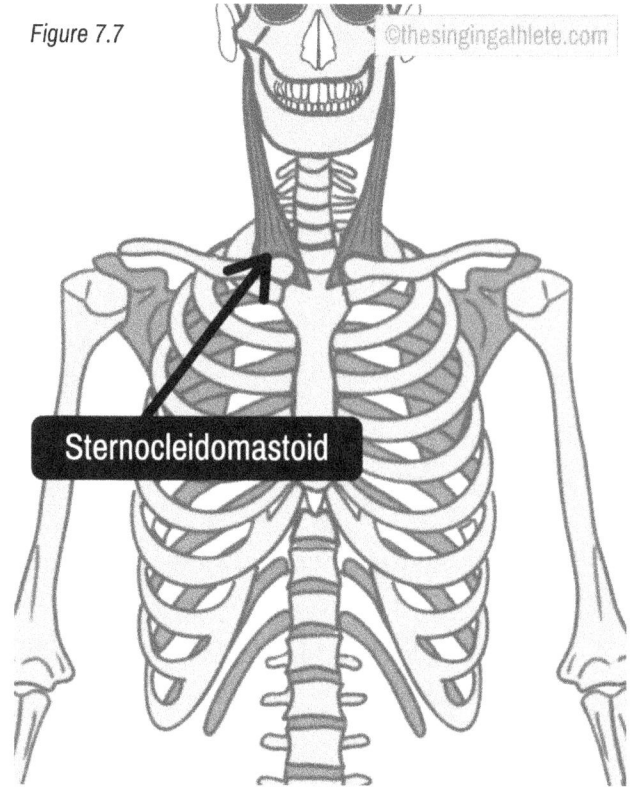

Figure 7.7

Strengthen your SCM *(Fig. 7.7)*

1. Assess your voice and body.

2. Place your right hand on the right side of your forehead.

3. Tilt your head to the right.

4. Rotate your head to the left.

5. Push the head down into the right hand on that angle.

6. Hold for 10–15 seconds. Try to pull the back of your right ear and your right collarbone and sternum together.

7. Reassess.

8. Repeat on the other side. Hand on the left forehead, tilt the head to the left, rotate right, push the head down, pull the back of your left ear and your left collarbone and sternum together for 10–15 seconds.

9. Reassess.

Stretch and Strengthen your Trapezius—Scapular Circles

Another useful way to improve strength is with slow, steady contractions throughout the muscle's path, known as a motor control exercise. The trapezius has three parts (upper/middle/lower), and you're going to strengthen all three by moving the scapula. These linear and circular motions will also create some stretch in the muscle at specific points.

1. Assess your voice and body.

2. Take your right arm directly out in front of you, parallel to the floor, with your thumb facing the ceiling.

3. Move the arm out toward the right until you are in about 45 degrees of abduction (away from the midline of the body).

4. Lift your right shoulder blade, keeping your fist still.

5. Now lower your right shoulder blade, keeping the fist still. Go up and down slowly, with steady control.

6. Now move your right shoulder blade in and out, sliding it forward and around your ribcage and then pulling it backward toward the center of your back.

7. Now play "connect the dots" and make a circle with your shoulder blade: up, out, down, and in. And then you reverse the circle: up, in, down, and out. After 3–5 reps in both directions, reassess.

To do an isometric version of a scapular circle, hold any point of the circle for 10–15 seconds with a firm, steady contraction.

THE SCALENES

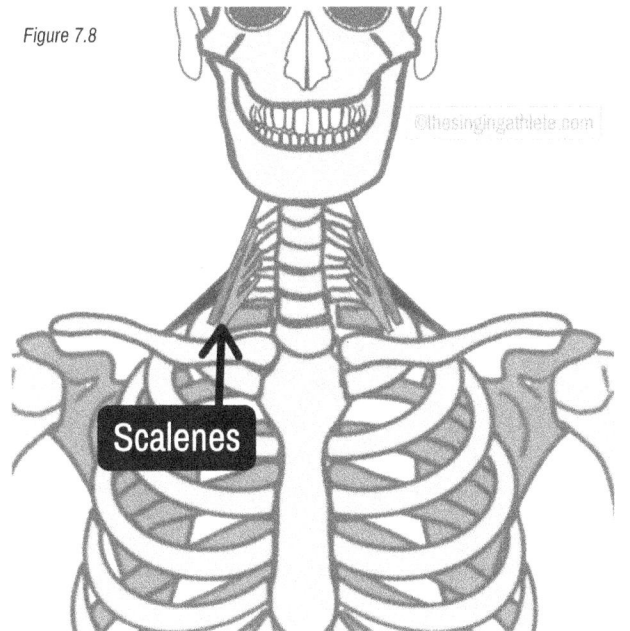

Figure 7.8

The *scalenes* (Fig. 7.8) attach the top two ribs to the sides of the cervical spine (C2-C7). When the diaphragm stops working, the scalenes tend to be the first muscles to take over the job of inhalation, contributing to a forward head posture.[39]

Stretch your Scalenes

Much like with the SCM Stretch, this drill should feel enjoyable; stop if you feel discomfort.

1. Assess your voice and body.

2. Reach your left hand across your body and curl your fingers back over the top edge of your right clavicle (collarbone). The goal is to press into this area until you make contact with your first rib. This area is tight and tender on many people, so if it's hurting, just press firmly enough to keep the top rib stable.

3. Pull your upper right ribs down toward the floor.

4. Let your head fall backward without lifting your right ribs.

5. Tilt your head to the left.

6. Rotate your head to the right.

7. Do some tiny nods/rotations at the top of your spine. Imagine you're wearing a turtleneck and a necklace (quite the look) and try to pull the upper back right edge of the turtleneck's collar apart from where the necklace drapes over your right collarbone.

8. Reassess.

9. Repeat on the other side. Right hand to the left clavicle, pull the left ribs to the ground, head falls back, tilts to the right and rotates left. Pull the upper-back-left edge of the turtleneck's collar apart from the necklace draping over the left collarbone. Do small nods and rotations.

10. Reassess.

Strengthen your Scalenes

1. Assess your voice and body.

2. Put your right hand on the right side of your forehead.

3. Drop your face a little bit down toward the ground.

4. Tilt your head to the right.

5. Turn your head to the left.

6. Push your head down and right on that angle. Try to bring your right upper neck and your right top two ribs together.

7. Hold for 10–15 seconds.

8. Reassess.

9. Repeat on the other side. Left hand on the left side of the forehead, drop the face, tilt the head left, rotate it right, push the head down on that angle for 10–15 seconds.

Blocked Inhalation

Even though almost all of the muscles we've just gone through have a respiratory function, one of the best ways to train them is without any air moving at all. In this blocked inhalation drill, you will close your airway off while making the motion of an inhalation. If breathing is a high-threat area for you, working the respiration muscles without airflow can reduce anxiety and improve performance.

1. Close your lips.

2. Close off your nose using your soft palate. If this is a new sensation for you, say "n-d" or "ng-g" several times. Focus on what happens in the back of the throat as you say the "d" or the "g." You will feel your palate lift and block off your nose.

3. Maintain this blocked position while relaxing the larynx. If you're doing this right, you should not feel any throat tension while performing the blocked inhalation. Now try to inhale; no air should enter, but you should feel an expansion of your torso.

Look back through these inhalation awareness drills and think about which one(s) felt the hardest to mobilize. Pick an area that felt challenging and focus on moving it in this drill.

1. Assess your voice and body.

2. Exhale about three-quarters of the air. Block your inhalation by closing your mouth and lifting your palate to close off your nose.

3. Make the motion of inhalation without actually taking in any air, focusing on moving and expanding the area that was weak in your testing.

4. Hold the blocked inhalation for a few seconds, letting a mild-to-moderate air hunger develop.

5. Repeat Steps 2–4 two more times.

6. Reassess.

This is the last breathing drill I'm presenting because it does two things at once. You are working the muscles of inhalation while allowing the blocked breath to make you more tolerant of building levels of CO^2. The best of both worlds, as far as I'm concerned.

Figure 8.1

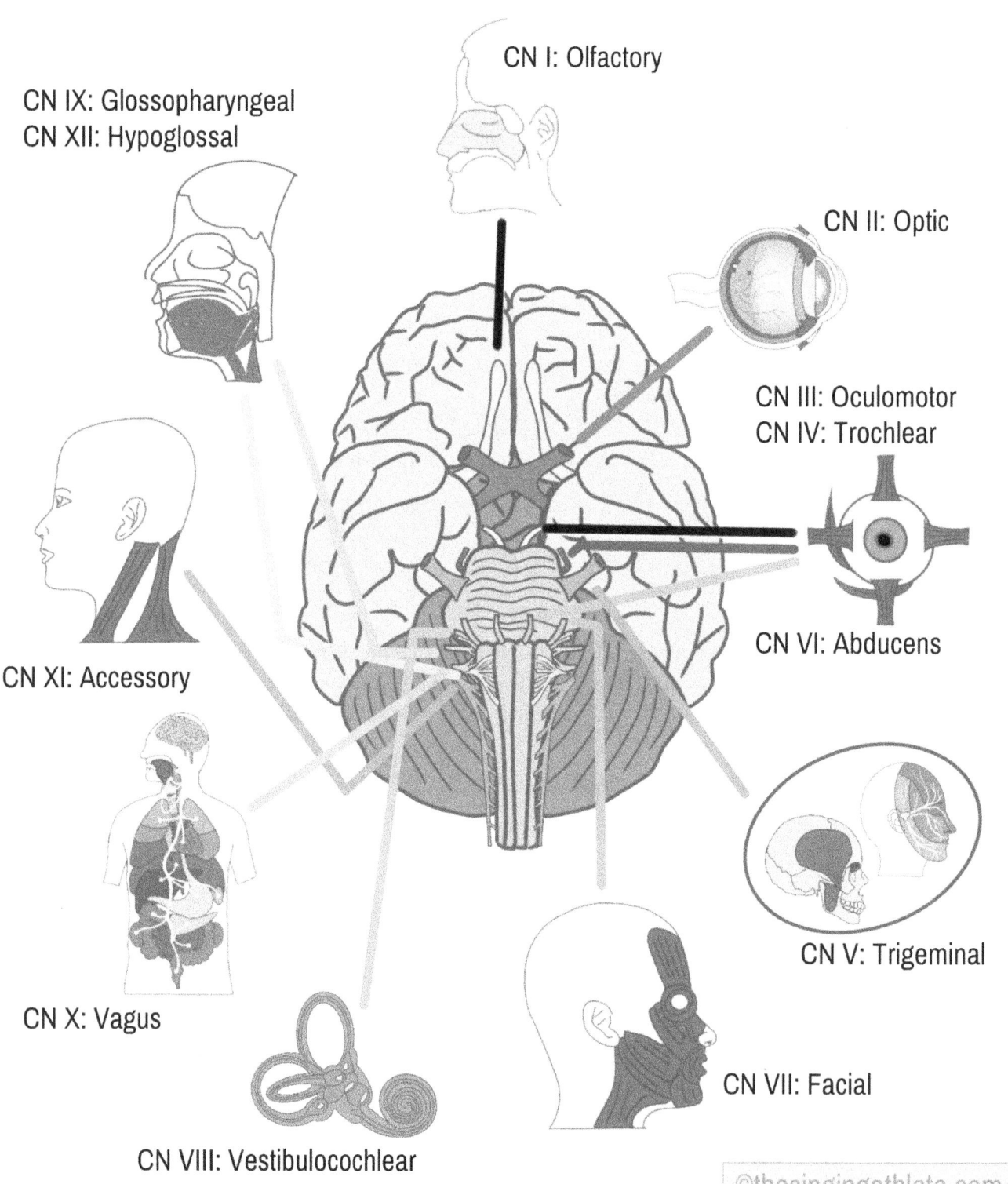

8. LARYNX AND PALATE

For a book that is intended for singers, I'm not going to spend much time talking about the internal anatomy of the larynx. While I, as a confirmed voice nerd, enjoy knowing about the different intricacies of the vocal folds, I'm not convinced this information is useful in making you a better singer. The laryngeal motor reflexes used in singing are built on those employed in speech, which are set up in infancy and occur mostly below your voluntary control.[40]

What I am going to discuss are practical ways you can improve laryngeal function. And since everything comes back to the brain, let's talk a bit about the fascinating bundle of nerves that gives you, among other things, your voice.

THE CRANIAL NERVES

The *cranial nerves (Fig. 8.1)* are called such because they originate in the brain itself, unlike the many nerves that emerge from the spinal cord. There are twelve of them, and they connect your brainstem to your sensory organs, face, skull, and the structures in your chest and abdomen. You have a left and a right set of each of the cranial nerves, but when I write them, I will list them singularly and use a Roman numeral (for example, "CN V"), which is the standard representation in neuroscience. The chart below shows the nerve's name, category (motor, sensory, and/or parasympathetic), and function. You can see that some nerves only do one thing, while others take on many roles. As you work through the next few chapters, it won't hurt to go back and review this information. (And if you prefer to learn the nerves in a catchy little song I wrote, you can hear it at thesingingathlete.com.)

Cranial Nerve	Name	Category	Function
I	Olfactory	Sensory	Smell
II	Optic	Sensory	Vision
III	Oculomotor	Motor Parasympathetic	Extraocular muscles (medial rectus, superior rectus, inferior rectus, inferior oblique)
			Eyelid (levator palpebrae superioris)
			Ciliary muscles (changing visual distance)
			Pupillary constriction
IV	Trochlear	Motor	Superior oblique muscle (Moves eye down and in)
V	Trigeminal	Sensory Motor	Sensation (touch, pain, temperature, vibration) for the face, anterior scalp, paranasal sinuses, teeth, nasal and oral cavities, front two-thirds of tongue, and anterior and middle cranial meninges.
			Muscles of mastication (chewing): masseter, temporalis, medial and lateral pterygoid
			Tensor tympani (tenses eardrum to dampen vibration)
			Tensor veli palatini (widens palate)
			Mylohyoid and anterior belly of digastric muscle (helps to depress jaw)

Cranial Nerve	Name	Category	Function
VI	Abducens	Motor	Lateral rectus muscle (moves eye out)
VII	Facial	Sensory Motor Parasympathetic	Sensation from ear, external auditory meatus and tympanic membrane
			Taste from anterior two-thirds of tongue
			All muscles of facial expression
			Parasympathetic to lacrimal glands, submandibular and sublingual glands, and oral and nasal mucosa
VIII	Vestibulocochlear	Sensory	Hearing Balance
IX	Glossopharyngeal	Sensory Motor Parasympathetic	Sensation from posterior one-third of tongue, tonsils, skin of external ear, internal surface of tympanic membrane, and pharnyx
			Sensation from the carotid body and sinus (monitors blood pressure)
			Taste from the posterior one-third of tongue
			Stylopharyngeus muscle
			Stimulates parotid gland
X	Vagus	Sensory Motor Parasympathetic	Sensation from the posterior cranial meninges, posterior ear canal, cymba conchae of the ear, pharynx, larynx, thoracic and abdominal viscera, aortic arch
			All muscles of the larynx
			Superior, middle and inferior pharyngeal constrictors, levator veli palatini, palatoglossus
			Smooth muscles and glands of the larynx, pharynx, thoracic and abdominal viscera, and cardiac muscle
XI	Accessory	Motor	Sternocleidomastoid and trapezius muscles
XII	Hypoglossal	Motor	Three of the four extrinsic tongue muscles (genioglossus, styloglossus, hyoglossus)
			All of the intrinsic tongue muscles

I don't understand why I wasn't taught the function of the cranial nerves in my voice degrees. This collection of nerves feeds the vast majority of the structures we use in singing. We use them every time we make a sound—but I had to go outside of the singing field to discover how to assess and train them. I think that learning to test and improve the function of the cranial nerves is mind-blowingly useful, and I hope you will feel the same.

THE LARYNX AND THE VAGUS NERVE

Figure 8.2 is a drawing of your larynx from the side. The main bony or cartilaginous structures of the larynx are:

- ***Cricoid Cartilage:*** The lowest cartilage in the larynx, the cricoid is the only complete circle in the airway. It's thinner in the front and thicker in the back.

- ***Thyroid Cartilage:*** The thyroid is the largest cartilage in the larynx, and its shield-like shape is accurate since it protects the airway. The anterior attachments of the vocal folds are found on the posterior surface of this cartilage. The thyroid cartilage is separate from the thyroid gland, which is lower down in the neck, surrounding the very bottom of the larynx and the upper trachea.

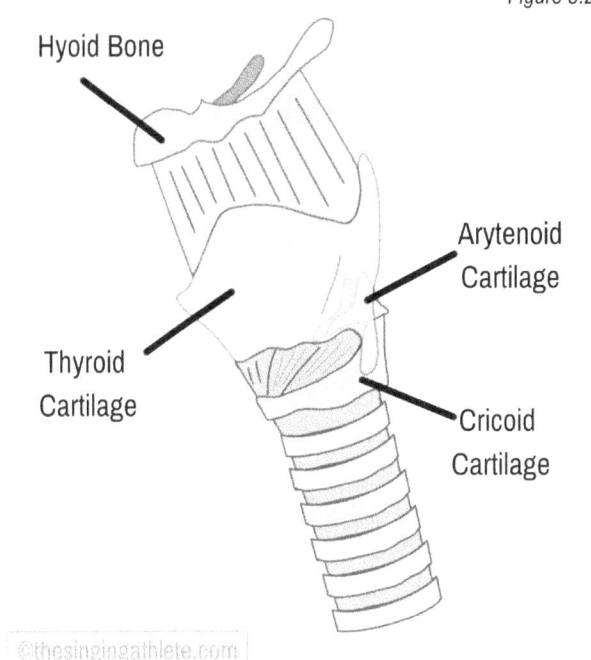

Figure 8.2

- **Arytenoid Cartilages:** The arytenoids are pyramid-shaped structures that sit on top of the cricoid and provide attachments for many laryngeal muscles, including the back of the vocal folds. They can pivot, rock, and slide in a variety of ways.

- **Hyoid Bone:** The horseshoe-shaped hyoid is the only bone in the body that doesn't connect directly to another bone, suspended instead by the muscles and ligaments that surround it. This gives it tremendous potential for flexibility and allows for the many types of vocal timbres that humans can create.

(Note: I've been using the term "vocal folds" in the book because it's more anatomically accurate than "vocal cords." And please don't ever call them "vocal chords," unless you possess the magical ability to produce more than one note at a time with your voice.)

Laryngeal muscles are attached to various points along these structures, and all of them are innervated by the ***vagus nerve*** *(Fig. 8.3)*. The vagus (pronounced like "Vegas [baby]") also has motor branches that go into most of the pharyngeal and soft-palate muscles (except the tensor veli palatini [CN V] and the stylopharyngeus [CN XII]). Branches of the vagus are also found in the very back of your tongue, your diaphragm, your heart, and the majority of your abdominal organs (including your esophagus, stomach, and most of the intestinal tract). It is the longest cranial nerve, running from the brain to the pelvic floor ("vagus" means "wanderer" in Latin).

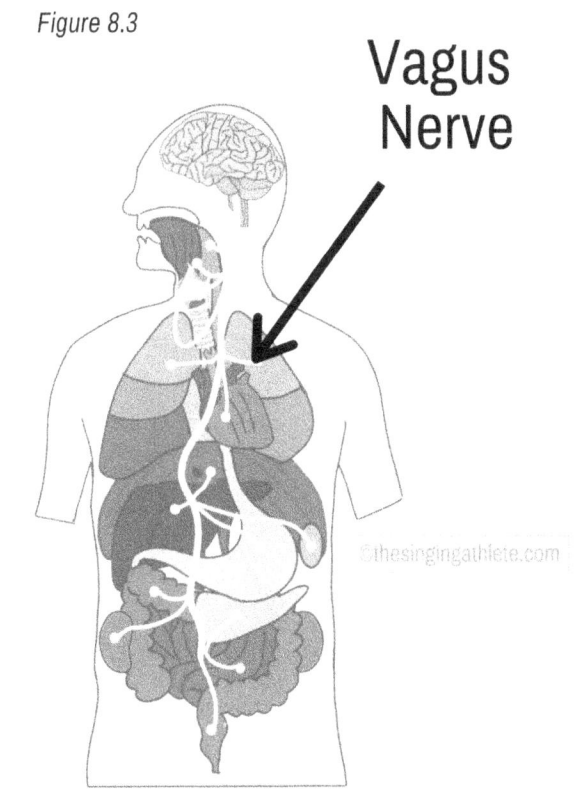

Figure 8.3

As the vagus leaves the skull through the jugular foramen, it travels briefly along the same sheath as the glossopharyngeal (CN IX) and the accessory nerves (CN XI). Some neuroanatomists feel that you can consider these three nerves as one unit. The accessory nerve controls your sternocleidomastoid (SCM) and trapezius muscles, which we looked at in the last chapter. The glossopharyngeal nerve (CN IX) is mostly sensory, receiving information from the pharynx, the tonsils, and the back third of the tongue. Its motor branch controls a muscle used in swallowing to elevate the larynx (stylopharyngeus), and it stimulates the parotid (salivary) gland. This nerve is also involved in the mechanism that controls blood pressure. (Remember this information when we get to tongue posture in the next chapter: a nerve in the back of your tongue affects your blood pressure.)

The vagus nerve is one of the major parasympathetic ("rest and digest") conduits in the body. If your vagus were cut, your heart rate would be around 100 beats per minute at rest. Research shows that many of the benefits from contemplative practices like meditation, tai chi, and gentle yoga may be attributed to signals sent along vagal pathways.[41] Vagal tone is suppressed during quicker inhalations and facilitated during exhalation and slow respiratory cycles.[42] If you feel calmer after doing the "In for Two, Out for Eight" exercise in Chapter 4, now you know why.

The vagus also reduces inflammation, producing molecules (known as anti-cytokines) that work similarly to a drug like Singulair. The anti-inflammatory properties of the vagus are so powerful that electrical stimulation of the nerve can reduce or replace pharmacologic interventions in autoimmune conditions such as rheumatoid arthritis and lupus.[43]

THE VAGUS AND THE VOCAL MUSCLES

Much like the glossopharyngeal nerve (CN IX), most of the vagus is devoted to sensory processing, not movement. Eighty percent of its fibers are designed to gather information about the well-being of the body (especially the throat and the visceral organs) and send that data to the brain. The breathing drills we've done all have a vagal component. Do you remember if any of them made you feel especially calm or focused?

Figure 8.4

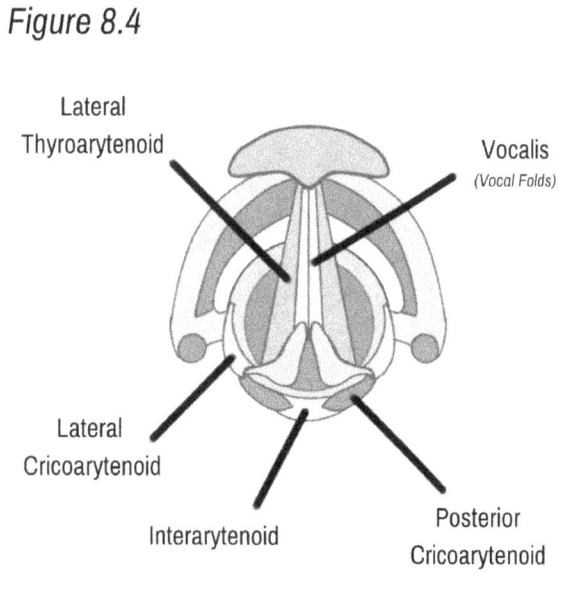
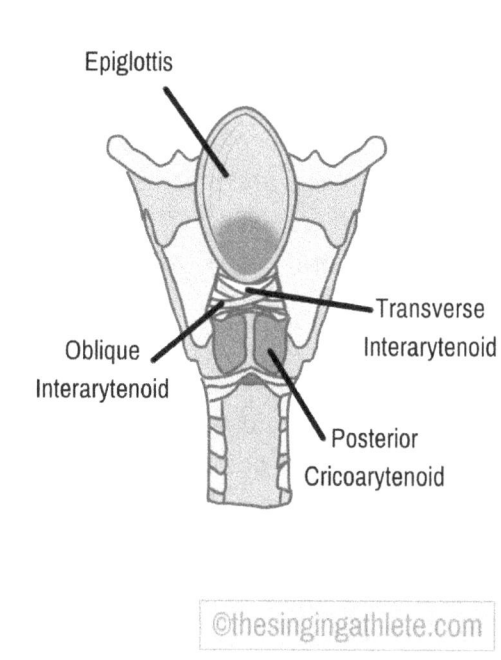

Some of the primary motor branches of the vagus are devoted to laryngeal control. The branch known as the ***recurrent laryngeal nerve*** guides the following muscles *(Fig. 8.4)*:

- ***Thyroarytenoid (TA):*** The TA muscle makes up the bulk of what we call the vocal folds. It can shorten and thicken the vocal fold mass, working in conjunction with the cricothyroid to coordinate pitch and volume. The vocalis muscle is a division of the TA.

- ***Posterior Crico-Arytenoid (PCA):*** The PCA is the only laryngeal muscle that abducts (or opens) the vocal folds. The glottis (opening between the vocal folds) widens when this muscle contracts.

- ***Lateral Crico-Arytenoid (LCA):*** The LCA muscle assists in closing the glottis.

- ***Transverse and Oblique Interarytenoids (IA):*** Also helping to close the glottis, the IA muscles are unpaired and may change the shape of the opening at the back of the larynx.

The fascinating thing about the recurrent laryngeal nerve is that it takes a different path on both sides *(Fig. 8.5)*. On the right side, the nerve hooks under the subclavian artery (right under your collarbone), whereas on the left side, it travels all the way under the aortic arch (between the ascending and descending aorta). The left side has a good distance longer to go, making it about 17 inches (50 cm) longer than the right.

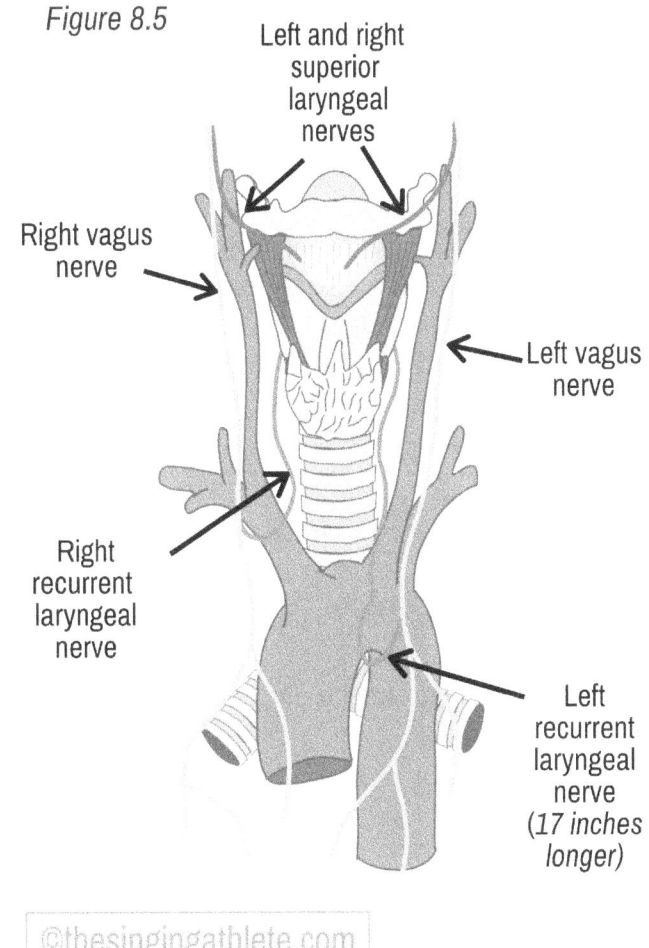

Figure 8.5

Although some authors feel that there is no difference in neural signaling between the left and right nerves, others find a time delay for neural impulses on the left of roughly 25 milliseconds, about the time it takes to pronounce a syllable.[44] When singers come to me with a diagnosis of vocal fold paresis (nerve weakness), I've noticed that it's usually the left side that has been identified as the weak one. And statistics show that a left-side recurrent laryngeal nerve issue is up to 2.5 times more common than the right.[45] More reason to remember those neck drills we did in the last chapter; maybe do a couple of extra reps on your left side.

The cricothyroid muscle (which thins and elongates the folds) is innervated by the ***superior laryngeal nerve***. This nerve takes a shorter path, and it is more symmetrical in how it enters the larynx. This neural structure may imply that elongated vocal folds are a high priority for the nervous system. Mammals require social cooperation for survival; hearing a gruff, monotonous voice puts us in a threatened state. Your first brain receives a gravelly vocal quality on the same wavelengths that stay alert for the growl of a predator. When you listen to a speaking voice that has varied pitch and a prosodic quality (i.e., a voice that uses the cricothyroid muscle), you instinctively relax and feel comfortable, allowing rapport and learning to develop.[46] Working on the softer and higher tones in your voice isn't optional; it's an essential tool for life.

THE VAGUS AND THE UPPER NECK

The vagus begins its descent into the body at your first cervical vertebra, or C1 (*Fig. 8.6*). When we address this suboccipital area, we can globally alter the vagal tone in the body. In this drill, you will use your hands and eyes to create more open space at the top of the spine.

<u>Chin Tuck</u>

1. Assess your voice and body.

2. Interlace your fingers and place them on the back of your skull. Using very slight pressure, tuck your chin until you feel a mild stretch at the upper back of your neck. You should not be rounding your neck forward but only tucking your chin from the space between your ears. Is the amount of saliva increasing or decreasing in your mouth?

3. Without moving your neck or hands, look at an object to your right. Hold your gaze here for fifteen seconds. Is the amount of saliva increasing or decreasing in your mouth?

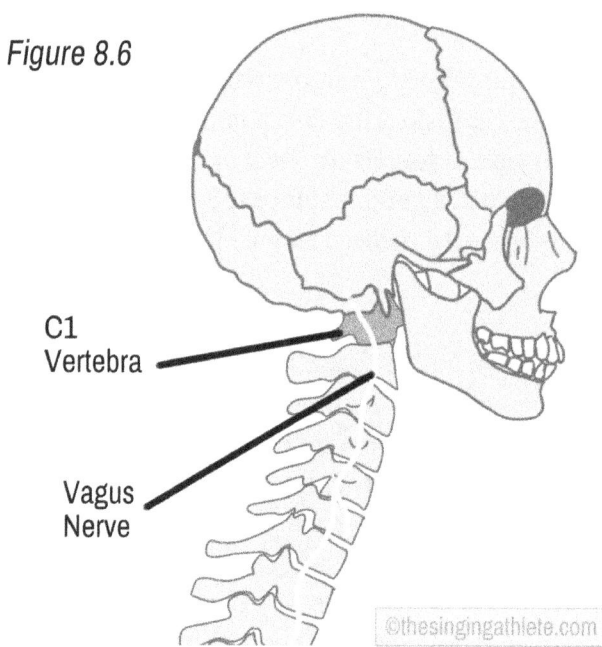

Figure 8.6

4. Look at an object to your left for fifteen seconds. How much saliva are you getting in your mouth now?

5. Look up for fifteen seconds. More or less saliva?

6. Look down for fifteen seconds. More or less saliva?

7. Finally, center your eyes and close them for fifteen seconds. More or less saliva?

8. Repeat a fifteen-second hold in the direction where you felt the most saliva in your mouth.

9. Reassess.

Since the vagus controls "rest and digest," a boost in saliva implies that the digestion process is kicking in and the body is calmer. If you start to feel a dry mouth, that is your "fight, flight, or freeze" activating. If you felt an increase in saliva when you looked in a particular direction, try looking there for a problematic vocal passage. It may calm you down and allow the note to come out more easily.

LARYNGEAL SYMMETRY TESTS

The larynx has separate right and left innervations, so it's a good idea to see if you're picking up on any noticeable differences from side to side. Touching these structures takes a little practice, and it may even feel "gross." These are going to be our laryngeal palpation rules:

1. Never move into pain.

2. If you start to feel nauseous or dizzy, stop and rest.

3. If you can't find the right points of contact, watch the videos on thesingingathlete.com.

Laryngeal Self-Palpation

Before we start moving the laryngeal structures, let's get acquainted with the landmarks. There are two ways to do this, so try both and see which is easier for you:

Version 1: Begin with your index finger on your Adam's apple (thyroid notch). Trace your finger down slowly until you feel an indentation into which you can get your finger; this is the cricothyroid space. If you keep going a tiny bit farther down, you will find the cricoid cartilage, which is the base of the larynx. Now return to the Adam's apple and go slightly up; you are now in the thyrohyoid space (the membrane and muscle between the thyroid cartilage and the hyoid bone). As you move up into the crook of your chin, you should be able to feel the hyoid bone.

Version 2: Begin with your finger on the bump that sticks out in the lower middle of your throat (not the Adam's apple). This is the cricoid cartilage. Bring your finger up just slightly; you are now in the cricothyroid space. If you keep going up, you're now on the thyroid cartilage, and you will eventually feel the thyroid notch (Adam's apple). Continue moving your finger up, and you are now in the thyrohyoid space. As you move up into the crook of your chin, you should be able to feel the hyoid bone.

Laryngeal Symmetry Test 1—Humming

We will now use a hum to test the evenness of your vocal folds.

1. Place your right and left index fingers on either side of your thyroid cartilage. You should feel a broad, flat surface on the sides of the larynx, slightly below the notch of the Adam's apple.

2. Hum a comfortable pitch. Are both sides of your larynx vibrating equally? If you can't tell, try touching the left and right side separately while humming and compare.

3. Vary the pitch higher and lower. Is the pattern consistent?

4. If you are finding a side that is vibrating less, can you leave that finger in place and consciously send vibration into that side of your larynx while humming?

This is one of the easier ways to assess the relative participation of both vocal folds in singing and speaking. Remember Davis' law—soft tissues (like vocal folds) reform along chronic lines of stress. If you're always favoring one side in the thousands of words you say in a day, one side of the larynx is eventually going to be the "strong" side.

Voice and Vibration

I prefer that you do this next drill with an external source of vibration, like an electric toothbrush or a Z-vibe. A Z-vibe is a vibrating oral motor device that comes with a rectangular rubber tip with different surfaces on each side. The reason I am such a fan of external vibration goes back to our discussion of internal vs. external focus. When our goal is fluidity and ease in performing, external targets often improve results. When you put a vibrating object on your larynx and think of sending the vibration out from your vocal folds to meet the intensity of the external vibration, you may enhance the flow of your voice.

Vibration signals are sent through the spinal cord in a tract known as the dorsal column. The dorsal column also conducts sensations like light touch (e.g., body brushing, gentle contact, scratching) and two-point discrimination (the ability to feel two distinct points on the skin). Stimulation of the dorsal column has also been shown to reduce pain[47] and improve proprioception.[48] The better your larynx vibrates, the more dorsal column stimulus you get, making you a happier human.

1. Assess your voice and body.

2. Place the vibration source on the weaker side that you found in the humming test. Leave it on for 10–15 seconds without making a sound.

3. Reassess.

4. Place the vibration source back on the same side and now hum or do a gentle siren through your range while the vibration continues. Attempt to send an equal vibration from inside your larynx out into the vibrating object.

5. Reassess.

6. Put the object back on a third time and sing your assessment scale or phrase with it on your larynx. Send your vocal vibration into the object.

You can also try the same protocol with an object that doesn't vibrate. I've used lots of things for this (a small squishy ball, the eraser of a pencil, etc.). Merely having an object on your larynx and sending vibrations into it can take you into an external focus and improve flow.

Laryngeal Symmetry Test 2—Cricothyroid

As I mentioned earlier, the cricothyroid is a small muscle that thins and elongates the vocal folds. In this drill, your fingertips will be in the cricothyroid space; you should be able to feel this space getting smaller in some way when the muscle is working.

1. Assess your voice and body.

2. Place the tips of your right and left pointer fingers in the cricothyroid space on both sides. As a reminder, this is the indentation between the thyroid cartilage and the cricoid cartilage. Your fingertips should be in the first crack you come to below the Adam's apple.

3. Move your fingers slightly out to the sides but stay in the "crack."

4. Lightly press your fingertips into this area. Is there any tenderness here? Is one side more sore than the other?

5. Close your lips and, on a hum, make a "whimpering/crying" sound in a middle-to-high range. You are trying to feel a small, subtle contraction under your fingertips that draws the top and bottom cartilages together and makes the crack smaller. This is a very small muscle, so it's not going to feel like a huge movement.

6. Once you're feeling the movement, ask yourself if both sides are moving at the same time, or is one side lagging?

7. If you do think you might have a sluggish side, keep whimpering and try to draw these two cartilages together to make the crack smaller on that side.

8. Reassess.

Laryngeal Mobilization—Thyroid Cartilage

The next two drills are designed to assess and improve flexibility in the laryngeal area. Here is another opportunity to explore internal vs. external focus; try both of these and see which works better.

Internal Focus

1. Assess your voice and body.

2. Find the sides of the thyroid cartilage with the thumb and the pointer/middle finger of your dominant hand.

3. With a relaxed throat, glide the larynx to either side with your fingers. Focus on feeling the cartilages move against each other. Repeat 3–5 times.

4. Reassess.

External Focus

1. Assess your voice and body.

2. Either put a glove on your hand or find a soft, stable object to put around your larynx, like a Theraband or a small towel.

3. Repeat the protocol from the exercise above; this time, focus on moving the object from side to side, not your larynx. For instance, if your gloved right hand is on your larynx and you're sliding it to the left, push the thumb of the glove toward the left wall.

4. Reassess.

If you are feeling clicks or pops as you move the larynx, it's nothing to be alarmed about, as long as the clicks are not painful. However, it may be a sign of some holding in that area; your body may have laid down some tissue to support the way you are habitually moving your throat. You can track over time if the clicks subside with more regular laryngeal mobilization.

Laryngeal Mobilization 2—Hyoid Bone

The hyoid bone is the main point of suspension for the laryngeal cartilages, and it also has an impact on your jaw, ears, and skull. As in the thyroid cartilage drill, we are going to try an internal and external focus to compare the effectiveness.

Internal Focus

1. Assess your voice and body.

2. Find the sides of your hyoid bone with the thumb and the pointer finger of your dominant hand. Your fingers should be above your Adam's apple and resting on the sides of the horseshoe-shaped hyoid.

3. With a relaxed throat, glide the hyoid to either side with your fingers. Focus on feeling the bone sliding. Repeat 3–5 times.

4. Reassess.

External Focus

1. Assess your voice and body.

2. Either put a glove on your hand or find a soft, stable object to put around your hyoid bone.

3. Repeat the protocol from the exercise above; this time, focus on moving the object from side to side, not your hyoid.

4. Reassess.

Variations for Laryngeal Mobilizations

If you identify that one side of your larynx generally feels less flexible (i.e., you can't slide your larynx as far to the right as you can to the left), you can try adding some variations to the stretch.

1. Assess your voice and body.

2. Using a glove or an external object, get a grip on either your thyroid cartilage or hyoid bone and slide it toward the stickier side. If it's comfortable, press your tongue to the roof of your mouth and maintain that position.

3. Once you are at a comfortable end range for the stretch, tilt your head the opposite way (if your larynx is pressed to the right, tilt your head to the left and vice versa).

4. Maintaining this lateral neck tilt, do a minimal upper neck rotation, shaking your head "no" (3–5 reps).

5. Then do a tiny upper neck nod, shaking your head "yes" (3–5 reps).

6. Release and reassess.

Once you're in the mobilization position, other things to try are:

- Lift and lower the same-side shoulder

- Lift and lower the opposite-side shoulder

- Do it on a strong exhalation

- Do it on a strong inhalation

- Take a different eye position (up/down/out the window and far away/close to your face)

- Close your eyes

- Do any of the tongue drills from the next chapter

- Smile

LARYNGEAL ELEVATORS AND DEPRESSORS

As I mentioned earlier in the chapter, the hyoid bone is the only bone in the body that is not directly secured to the skeleton. Its floating position makes it flexible but also unstable, which can be the source of vocal inconsistency. There are two sets of muscles (laryngeal elevators and depressors) that stabilize the hyoid. Let's look at the four main *laryngeal elevators (Fig. 8.7)*, which lie above the bone.

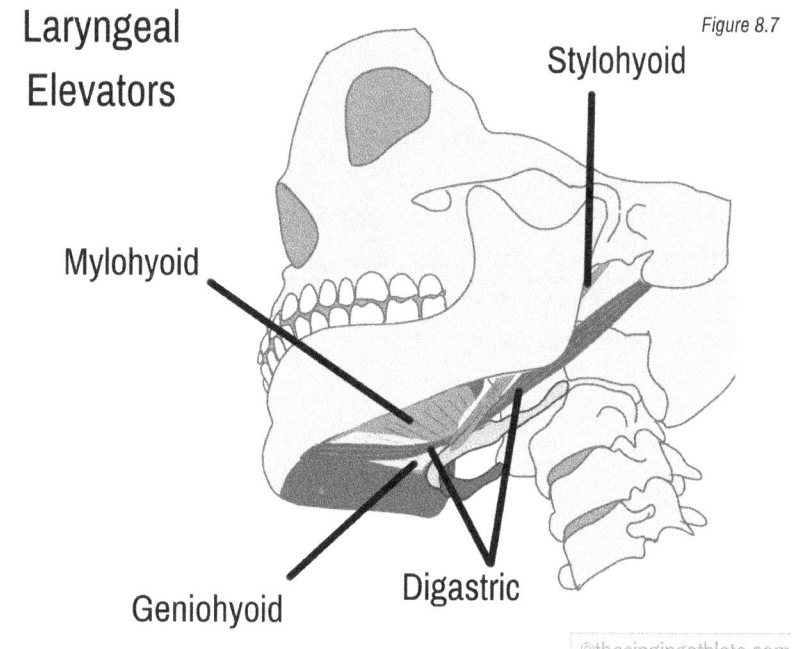

- *Mylohyoid (CN V):* Pulls the hyoid up. Also reinforces the floor of the mouth.

- *Geniohyoid (CN XII):* Pulls the hyoid forward and up to open the airway.

- *Digastric (anterior belly CN V/posterior belly CN VII):* Pulls the hyoid up. The posterior digastric can participate in upper neck extension.

- *Stylohyoid (CN VII):* Pulls the hyoid up and back.

In singing, these laryngeal elevators may be used for reaching high notes and for certain vocal styles (belting, country, pop, musical theatre, etc.).

Laryngeal Elevator Mapping 1

1. Place both thumbs under your chin.

2. Sing a phrase in a high range, using a "little kid" voice. (If you're stuck for an idea, you can use "We represent the Lollipop Guild" from *The Wizard of Oz*.)

3. Do you feel muscles contracting under your chin as you sing? Does it feel even on both sides? If not, can you work harder on the weak side?

Laryngeal Elevator Mapping 2

1. Place both pointer fingers and middle fingers underneath your ears, so the pointer fingers are touching the round bones behind your earlobes and your middle fingers are under your ears.

2. Do a vocal siren (slide) from your lowest comfortable pitch to your highest comfortable pitch. You can slide on a hum, an "ng" sound, a lip buzz (blowing air through your lips like a motorboat), or a vowel.

3. As you slide up, do you feel muscles contracting under your fingers? Is the work even on both sides? If not, can you work harder on the weak side?

Assess and reassess these two drills before belting or before singing high notes. If you've come from classical training, sometimes you've learned that the only way to stabilize the larynx is from below. I've found that anchoring from above can be equally effective, and this strategy is often more useful in contemporary singing styles.

Now, let's look at the *laryngeal depressors* (Fig. 8.8), which lie below the larynx and pull it down:

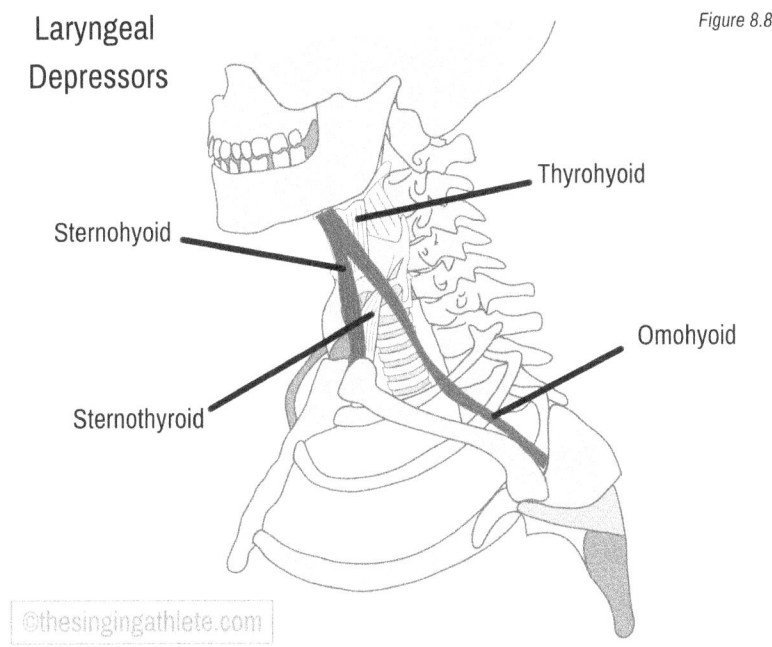

Figure 8.8

- **Sternohyoid** *(C1-3 vertebrae)*: Depresses the hyoid bone.

- **Sternothyroid** *(C1-3 vertebrae)*: Depresses the thyroid cartilage.

- **Omohyoid** *(C1-3 vertebrae)*: Depresses the hyoid bone and moves it backward.

- **Thyrohyoid** *(C1/CN XII)*: Depresses the hyoid bone and elevates the larynx.

In singing, these laryngeal depressors may be used for reaching low notes and for certain vocal styles (classical, gospel, R & B, soul).

Laryngeal Depressor Mapping

1. Place both pointer fingers in the notch of your sternum. Your fingertips should be as close to the midline of your body as possible.

2. Sing a low note in a "yawn" or "sob" quality. Do you feel muscles engaging under your fingers? Does one side feel like it's working less? If so, can you engage that side more?

Upper Neck Figure-8

If you struggle with low range or with depth in your voice, you have to develop excellent motor control in your upper three cervical vertebrae (C1-3). The nerves that control the lowering of your larynx all originate here. If you can't move well in this area of your spine, it will be hard to get your throat as low as you want it to be.

1. Assess your voice and body.

2. Place your pointer fingers right outside your ear canals. Do a very small nodding motion, moving on the axis created by your fingers.

3. Drop your fingers and do a small upper-neck rotation, shaking your head "no". Move only the very top part of your neck.

4. Now do a tiny lateral tilt, "bobbling" your head from side to side and rotating around the axis of your nose. Does your head move equally both ways?

5. Now combine these movements to draw a figure 8 (on its side) with your nose. Tuck your chin, tilt your head right, then rotate your head left on that angle. Tuck your chin, tilt your head left, then rotate your head right on that angle. (I've seen this motion be messy on a lot of people, so watch the video at thesingingathlete.com if you're not getting it.)

6. Reassess.

Another reason to perfect this drill is that the pharyngeal plexus of the vagus nerve is located right in front of these same upper-neck vertebrae. The pharyngeal plexus controls many muscles in your throat, including the palatoglossus (see next chapter) and the ***pharyngeal constrictors***. The constrictors participate in the reflexive portion of a swallow and may also contribute to vocal resonance and laryngeal posture. If the swallowing drills in the next chapter prove tricky for you, review the Upper-Neck Figure 8 and reassess.

THE SOFT PALATE

When I was a kid, I called my mom sick from school so she could come to take me home. I said, "Hi, Mom," but my stuffed-up nose made it sound like I was saying, "Hi, Bob." She responded, "There's no Bob here," and hung up. (Don't worry, she figured out her mistake and came and got me.) Nasal resonance makes an essential contribution to the clarity of language, and the ***soft palate*** controls it.

The soft palate (velum) is the rear portion of the structure that divides your mouth from your nose. It is composed of muscle fibers covered in a mucous membrane. On the sides, it intersects with two muscles to form arches: the ***palatoglossus*** in front and the ***palatopharyngeus*** in back. The tonsils lie between these arches.

In Figure 8.9, we see how a partially lowered palate produces a nasal vowel, and a fully lowered palate in contact with the tongue makes a nasal consonant like /ŋ/ ("ng"). A lifted palate makes the sound non-nasal. In the phone call I described above, my stuffed-up voice might have been erroneously described as "nasal," but I was actually speaking in a de-nasalized way. I couldn't access nasal resonance, so my /m/ sounded like a /b/.

Before we get to the palate muscles, let's do a quick check of your sensation in this area.

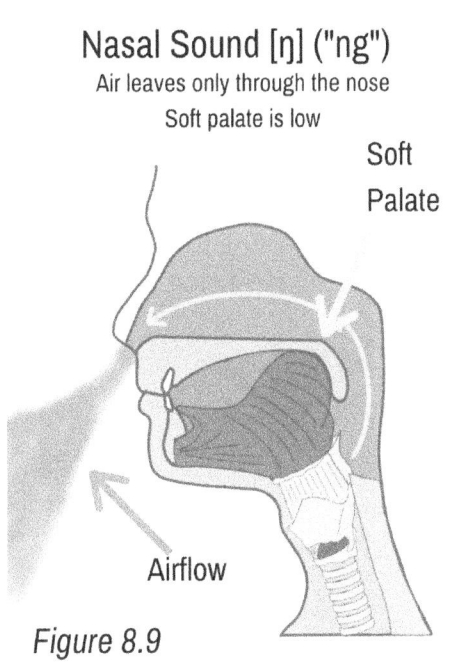 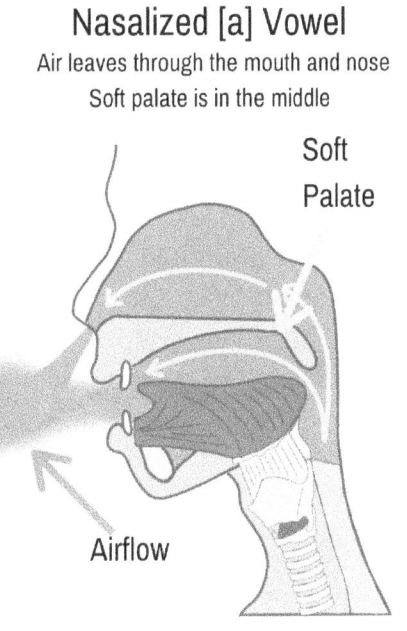 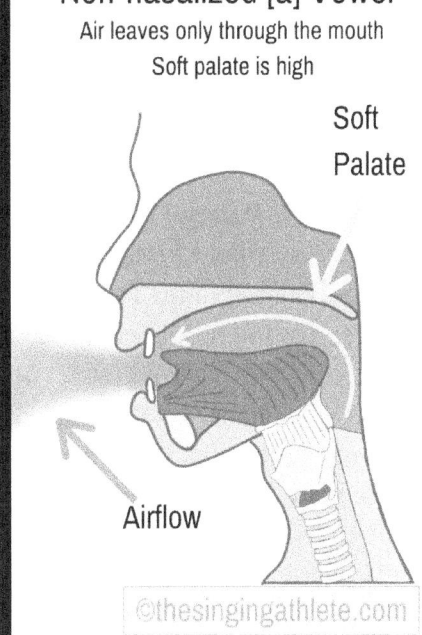

Figure 8.9

Soft Palate Gargle Test

1. Take a small amount of liquid into your mouth. It's interesting to use something that has a taste or bubbles (seltzer, juice, coffee, etc.), but water is fine, too.

2. Gargle for ten seconds. Try gargling both silently and with voice.

3. Did the sensation (temperature, taste) feel the same on the left and right sides of your palate? Did the movement of the gargle feel the same on both sides?

The muscular movement of the gargle is controlled by your vagus nerve (CN X). The sensation of taste and temperature is controlled by your glossopharyngeal nerve (CN IX). It's possible to feel the movement but not the sensation and vice versa.

If you felt that one side was weaker, try this:

1. Assess your voice and body.

2. Take a small amount of liquid in your mouth and start gargling.

3. Move your head around until you feel a more equal sensation in the gargle. You can try head rotation, lateral flexion (ear to shoulder), or letting your head drop farther forward or backward.

4. If you find an area where the sensation feels pretty equal, maintain the gargle there for fifteen seconds, breathing as you need to.

5. Reassess.

Another simple vagus drill is to gargle for a longer time. Try going for a minute, breathing as necessary.

The palate has several muscles that control its movement, but we will focus on two *(Fig. 8.10)*:

Tensor Veli Palatini (TVP): The TVP runs from the scaphoid fossa (part of the sphenoid bone) to the front area of soft palate; it is the primary muscle that lets you "pop your ears" when you get off a plane. The TVP helps to lift the palate, but because of its attachment angle, it pulls more horizontally, widening the palatal arch (a useful shape in belting). It is the only palate muscle innervated by the trigeminal nerve (CN V).

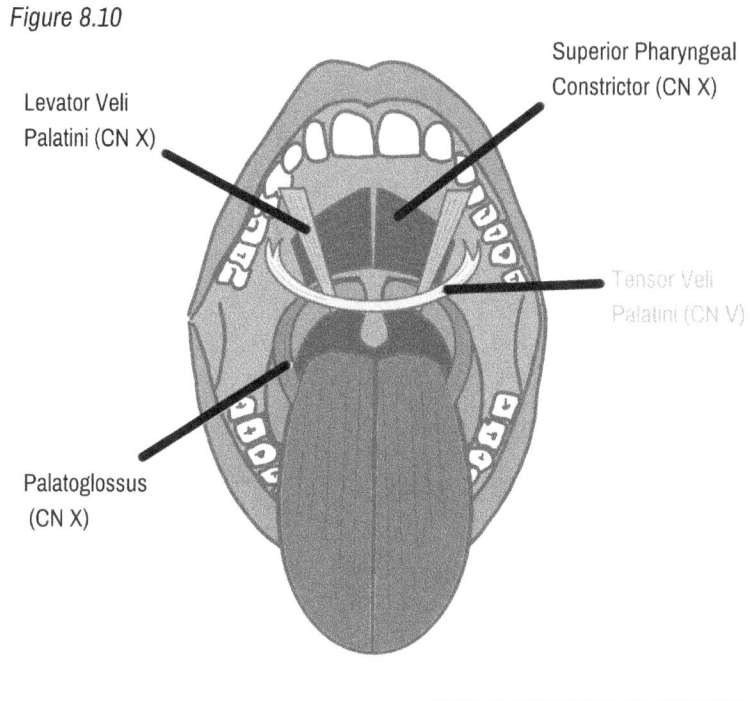

Figure 8.10

Levator Veli Palatini (LVP): The LVP is the main muscle that lifts the palate vertically; when you swallow, it contracts to seal it up against the back of your throat, making sure you don't get food in your nose. The LVP connects directly to your temporal bone (which covers your brain's temporal lobe) and your Eustachian tube. It assists the TVP in equalizing pressure in the inner ear. The LVP is innervated by the vagus nerve (CN X), which we'll take advantage of in the drill below.

Soft Palate Vagus Test

Since you have a right and a left branch of the vagus nerve, it's good to see how evenly they are working, using your levator veli palatini as a test *(Fig. 8.11)*:

1. Open your mouth and look in a mirror.

2. Look at your uvula (the small thing that hangs down in the center of the back of your throat). You may need a flashlight to see it clearly.

3. Say "ah-ah-ah" repeatedly; the sound should be staccato and crisp. Look for a symmetrical lift on both sides of the uvula.

If you observed that one side of your palate was not lifting as much, that less-active side is the sleepy vagus side. You can use this as a reassessment as you work through the rest of the book; if you see the palate activation evening out, you are doing the right drills.

Even more critical than the anatomical distinctions between the LVP and TVP are the two different nerves that control them *(refer back to Fig. 8.10)*. The brain is enveloped by membranes called ***cranial meninges***, which

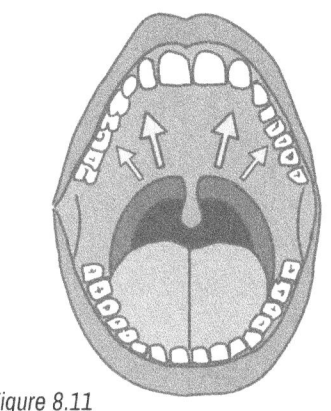
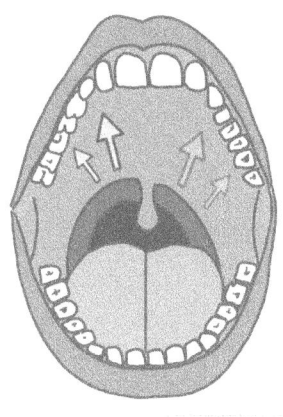

Normal Palate Lift *(Symmetrical Vagus Activation)*

Weak Palate Lift on Left *(Decreased Left Vagus Activation)*

Figure 8.11

protect it from injury and feed it with blood and cerebrospinal fluid. The anterior and middle sections are innervated by the trigeminal nerve (CN V), whereas the posterior branch is fed partially by the vagus nerve (CN X). When you focus on creating a tall soft palate, the LVP activates more, and that correlates with more sensation at the back of the skull; this may help to explain why opera singing is often felt "further back." Wider palatal shapes are mostly created by the trigeminally fed TVP muscle. When you stretch your palate out toward your ears, you may end up with more sensation in the middle and front of the skull. This correlates with the "frontal focus" that is often described in contemporary singing styles. (To be clear, I'm only talking about palate shape; the TVP creates an inside feeling of width, not necessarily a spread mouth.)

Let's try two different angles for stretching and activating the palate muscles *(Fig. 8.12)*:

Palate Stretch—LVP

Since the LVP is more vertically aligned, you'll push up on your upper back teeth to focus on a lift of the palate.

1. Assess your voice and body.

2. Place your thumbs onto your back upper molars. You can also try this with your thumbs on your wisdom teeth (or where they used to be).

3. Press vertically on the upper back teeth and hold for 5–10 seconds. You are trying to pull your palate up toward the center of your skull, using your thumbs to assist the movement. Does one side feel weaker? If so, push up harder on that side.

4. Reassess.

Palate Stretch—TVP

Since the TVP muscle controls the width of the palate, you'll use your thumbs to encourage a widening motion.

1. Assess your voice and body.

2. Hook your thumbs inside your back upper molars.

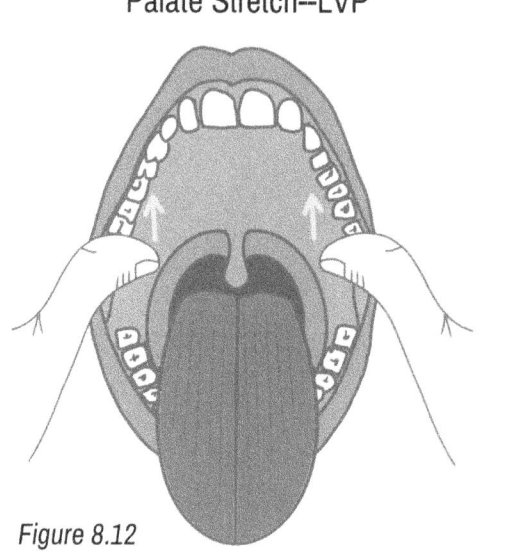

Figure 8.12

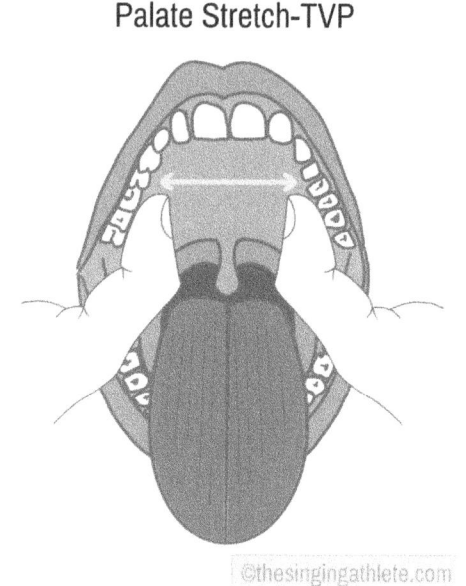

3. Pull out laterally with your thumbs and hold for 5–10 seconds. The attachment of the TVP is under the ears, so the action is to pull the palate out toward the earlobes, using your thumbs to guide the motion. Does one side feel weaker? If so, pull harder on that side.

4. Reassess.

You can also try singing with your thumbs in your mouth in either of these stretches (it will obviously affect your diction).

Some other palate-strengthening cues to try:

- Do vocal exercises that include /k/, /g/, or /ng/
- Make the motion of biting an apple
- Snort
- Pull up and out on your ears
- Pretend you are about to sneeze

9. TONGUE

In many ways, the tongue is more similar to a tentacle than to a trapezius muscle. Known as a muscular hydrostat, the tongue shares liquid properties with an octopus's appendages or an elephant's trunk, which use hydraulic elements to manipulate items like food. Most of the muscles in the body attach to bones, but half of the tongue muscles connect only to each other. Since muscle is mostly water and maintains a constant volume, when one part of the tongue decreases in dimension, there is an inevitable increase somewhere else, like squeezing a water balloon. Our mastery of this constant compression and decompression creates language. The tongue also gets a tremendous amount of space in both the sensory and motor homunculi. Its connection to many brain areas can make it one of the most high-payoff parts of the body to train.

TONGUE ANATOMY BASICS

The tip of the tongue (or apex) is the name for the very front area that can be made pointy for sensing or probing. The blade (or lamina) is a flexible, plane-like surface that creates a half-circle around the front. To find the blade, look in a mirror and form a cupped shape with your tongue, raising the edges and lowering the center; the edge of the "bowl" is the blade. The body of the tongue (or dorsum) makes up most of the rest of the tongue's mass and is further divided into front, middle, and back zones. You can move the body of the tongue from back to front by whistling from a low pitch (back of the dorsum is high) to a high pitch (front of the dorsum is high). The dorsum is less flexible than the tip or blade, but it performs several vital actions in forming vowels and swallowing. Finally, the tongue root (or radix) forms the very back area where it attaches to the hyoid bone and the larynx. The word "radix" has the same lexicological origin as my least-favorite root vegetable, the radish (gross).

The tongue has four extrinsic muscles *(Fig. 9.1)* that attach it to your skeleton:

- *Genioglossus*: The genioglossus arises from the mandible (jawbone); its inferior fibers are responsible for protrusion (sticking the tongue out), and its superior fibers retract the tongue, also bringing the tip down a bit. The genioglossus is the largest tongue muscle, making up over 20 percent of its mass. Some of its fibers work in sounds like /ð/ ("the") and /j/ ("you") *[Note: all the word examples used in this section assume a so-called "General American" accent.]* When the mandible is fixed, the genioglossus can elevate the hyoid bone, which can be useful in belting.

- *Hyoglossus:* The hyoglossus runs from the hyoid bone to the sides of the tongue. It depresses the tongue when the hyoid bone is fixed, like in a dark /ɑ/ ("calm"). If you place your fingers under your chin and push your tongue down against them, you can feel the hyoglossus working, bulging the tongue mass downward.

- *Styloglossus*: The styloglossus travels from the styloid process (a bony protrusion underneath your ears) to the tongue. It draws the tongue up and back, like in a /k/ ("cat"), /g/ ("God"), or /ŋ/ ("ring"). It also may work in vowels like /o/ ("go") and /u/ ("too"). The styloglossus attachment is deep inside the head, but if you place your fingers in the little space under your ears, you are close to it.

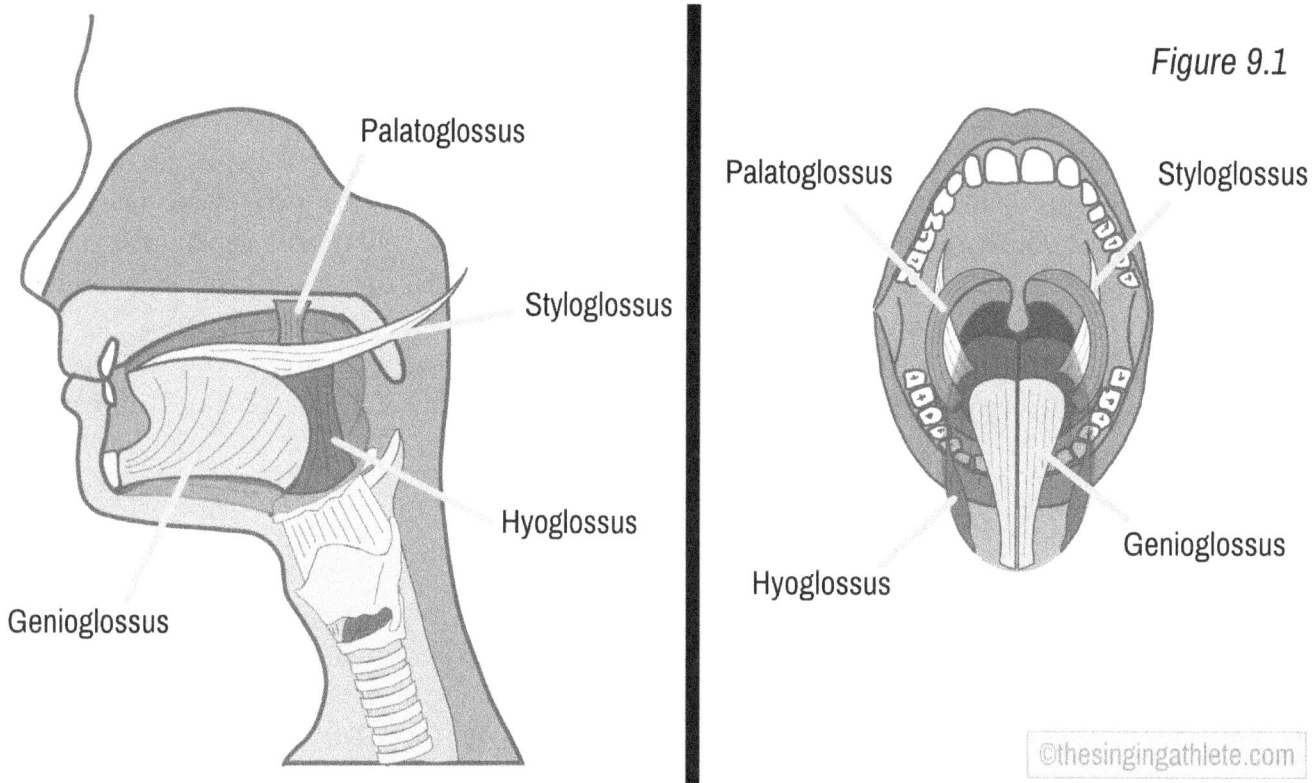

Figure 9.1

- **Palatoglossus**: The palatoglossus connects your palate and your tongue; it is the only tongue muscle innervated by your vagus nerve (CN X). If you look in your mouth, it's the muscle you see forming the front arch on the sides of your uvula. The palatoglossus assists the styloglossus in drawing the back of the tongue up, and it also has a big job in swallowing. This connection between the tongue and the palate is why some people will sound nasal on an /a/ vowel; as the tongue lowers, the palate may also lower, allowing air into the nasal passage.

The tongue also contains four intrinsic muscles *(Fig. 9.2)*, which lie inside it and change its shape from within:

- **Superior Longitudinal**: The superior longitudinal runs from front to back, along the top surface of the tongue. When you raise the tip of your tongue on an /n/ ("no") or a /d/ ("dog"), you're contracting this muscle.

- **Inferior Longitudinal**: The inferior longitudinal runs from front to back along the bottom surface of the tongue. Once you've said an /n/ or a /d/, this muscle brings the tip back down. It also helps in arching the tongue, so it assists in making sounds like /u/ and /g/. This muscle may partly achieve the raised tongue we see in lots of belters.

- **Vertical**: The vertical muscle runs from top to bottom in the tongue; its action is to widen and flatten it. If you bite your tongue between your molars, the spreading movement is controlled by the vertical muscle. It also helps in making vowels like /i/ ("see") and /e/ ("say"), and it makes a seal between your upper and lower teeth when you say an /s/; a leaky /s/ may be a vertical muscle that isn't functioning correctly.[49]

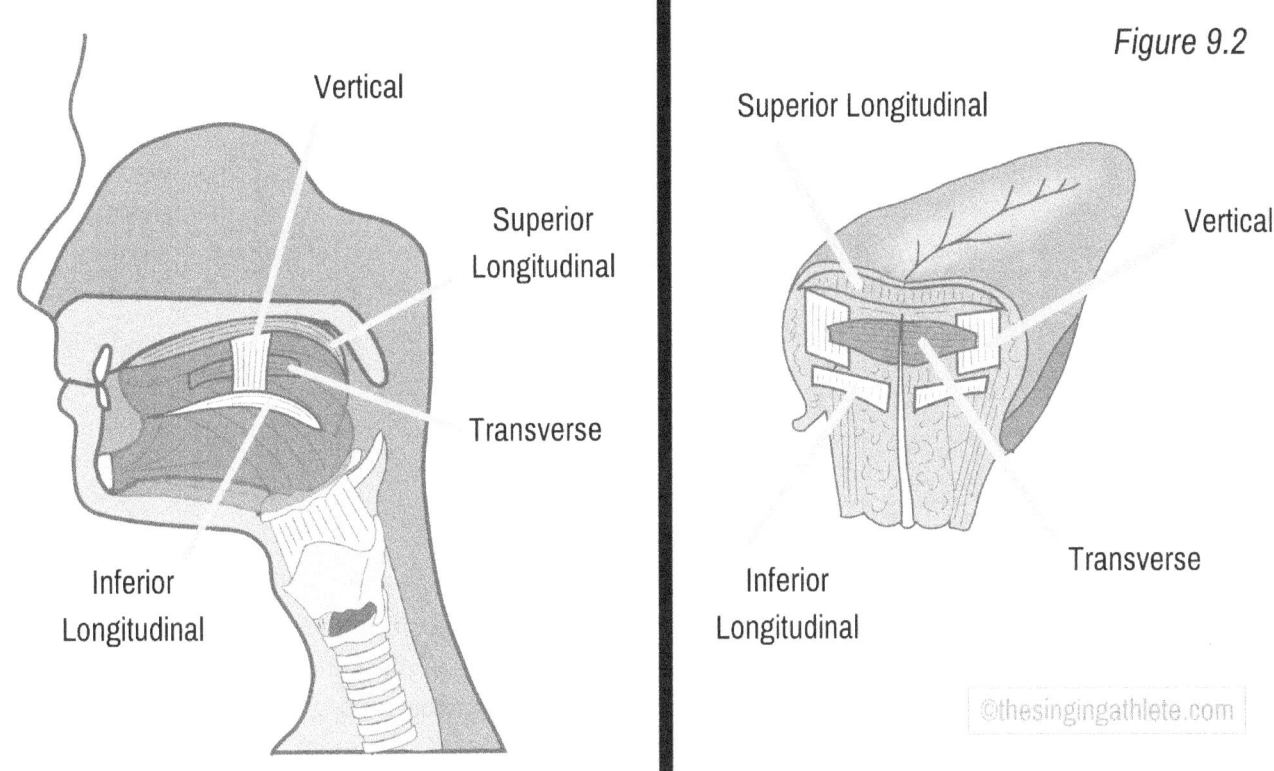

Figure 9.2

- **Transverse**: The transverse runs side to side; its action is to narrow, thicken, and elongate the tongue. This action is what creates fricative sounds like the /x/ in the German word "a<u>ch</u>."

THE TRANSVERSE MUSCLE AND AMERICAN /R/

In contemporary singing, one of the most problematic sounds for Americans is "r" (the phonetic symbol is [ɹ] because [r] refers to a rolled "r.") Part of the trickiness is that American-English speakers use two different strategies to make this sound:

- **Retroflex:** In a retroflex position, the tongue tip points toward the palate. You can feel this if you slowly say the word "learn"; the tip of your tongue will contact the area behind your upper teeth and then slide backward, no longer in contact but still pointing upward.

- **Bunched:** In this type of /ɹ/, the back of the tongue is bunched up and braced on the upper back teeth, with the tip pointed down. Feel this action by slowly saying the word "grade." Notice that the back of the tongue initially makes contact with the palate and then slides off, with the back staying high and contracted.

The transverse muscle participates in the bunched /ɹ/. It's surprisingly common to have poor muscle control in the tongue-narrowing action of this muscle. Grab a mirror and see if you have it mastered.

Transverse Muscle Strength

1. Place your tongue through your teeth.

2. Use the strength of your tongue to push your teeth apart. If you're doing this correctly, you will see your tongue bunch together and form an elongated tube, looking like a hot dog. If you see your lips trying to help, practice with a big cheesy smile.

Remember that the tongue is like a water balloon, so when a muscle engages, the whole shape is affected. As the transverse activates, some of the tongue "filling" may get squeezed back into the pharynx (throat). Since choking is one of the biggest threats to staying alive, the brain is very suspicious of anything entering the airway. If you have a poorly developed map of your tongue muscles, it can even interpret your own tongue as a foreign object, and the throat may start to close in protection when you sing /ɹ/. If you find yourself having vocal problems with words like "heart" or "more," practice the transverse drill above for better /ɹ/ control.

THE TONGUE AT REST

If there is one topic that singers seem understandably confused about, it's the resting position for the tongue. Some schools of thought have advocated that a low tongue position, with the tip touching the lower teeth, is considered "relaxed." I was told this often during my years of classical training. I tried for years to get a low tongue to feel right, but it always seemed like it wasn't meant to be there. When I started reading the work of orthodontists and dentists, I quickly saw they had a different opinion. They felt that the tongue should suction itself to the roof of the mouth, creating a high resting position *(Fig. 9.3)*.[50] I have muscle-tested these low and high tongue positions with at least a thousand people; in 100 percent of cases, the muscle tests are stronger in the version where the tongue connects to the roof of the mouth at rest. Strength in a muscle test implies that we are lowering threat, so I take that as evidence that the tongue should rest high in the mouth.

Correct Resting Tongue Position

1. Before you begin, run a finger along the alveolar ridge. You will find it along the roof of your mouth; it's the smooth edge where your palate meets your upper teeth. As you explore this with your fingertips, does anywhere feel dull? Does it feel ticklish? Is it the same left to right? It should be symmetrical and pleasantly sensitive everywhere.

2. Make an /n/ sound; feel the tip of the tongue just slightly behind the upper front teeth (on the alveolar ridge).

3. Now leave the tip in the /n/ and suction the rest of the tongue up as well.

4. If this feels impossible, try starting with an /ŋ/ ("ng") sound to get the back of the tongue up, and then bring the front section up in an /n/ while maintaining the /ŋ/.

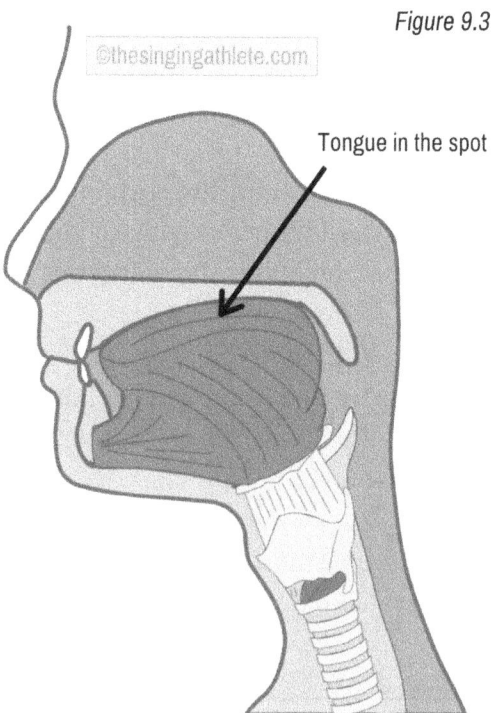

Figure 9.3

Tongue in the spot

We're going to call this tongue position "***the spot***," which is where it should be living 24/7 when you are not speaking or singing. Here are some of the benefits of keeping your tongue in the spot:

- You will be a nasal breather since your tongue blocks off your mouth.

- Keeping your tongue in the spot reduces stress on the jaw and can fix TMJ problems.

- The tongue serves as a natural palate expander. When the palate is broad, the airway is more open.

- Chronic sinus issues are often helped by maintaining the tongue in the spot.

One of the most common issues we see in singing is the head being too far forward. Generations of teachers have told students to "keep their head back" when going for high notes. One of the easiest ways to change this habit is through your tongue position. Any neck displacement usually points toward either proprioceptive or vestibular (balance) problems. It turns out that both neck muscle control and balance improve when the tongue rests in the spot.[51]

The change in strength from "tongue in the spot" can even reach muscles that are very far away from the head and neck. A 2013 study found that athletes were 30 percent stronger in their hip flexors when the tongue was in the spot.[52] If you are a dancer who struggles with "kicking your face," check out your tongue position when you are in class.

Why would there be these global changes in the body simply from the correct tongue position? If you remember from the previous chapter, the vagus nerve runs from the brain to the pelvic floor. The palatoglossus muscle is the only tongue muscle fed by the vagus nerve, and it is one of muscles that brings the tongue into the spot. It's possible that the simple action of bringing the tongue in contact with the palate can up-regulate your vagal tone and thereby affect myriad body systems.

Here are a few of the more common issues I run into as a singer searches for the spot:

- **The tongue wants to thrust.** For some people, the tip doesn't want to stay behind the upper front teeth but rather to touch the teeth or thrust through them. To fix this, I recommend the /n/ Push-up described later in this chapter.

- **The tongue wants to retract.** If the tongue is pulling back, try the Forward Roll exercise, found later in this chapter.

- **Confusion occurs as to how much of the tongue should be up.** The easiest way to answer this is to take your toothbrush and run it back along your tongue until you approach your gag reflex. Everything from the gag feeling forward should be able to rest comfortably on your palate (this will end up being about two-thirds of the tongue's entire surface).

- ***The tongue gets fatigued in the spot.*** As I said earlier, the tongue has both muscular and hydrostatic (water) properties. You may feel a bit of muscular effort at first, but the eventual goal is to let the tongue suction itself to the palate without a lot of muscle. If it feels tiring, do as much as you can and then rest.

If you're struggling to find the tongue in the spot, it could also be because the frenulum (the small strand of connective tissue you can see under the middle of your tongue) is too short and tight. The muscles above your hyoid bone may also be too tense, and placing the tongue in the spot can create too much stretch to be comfortable. Try the following adjustments with your tongue in the spot:

- Close your teeth lightly.

- Add a big, cheesy smile.

- Lift your eyebrows.

Once you've got the feel of it, you can relax your face and see if the tongue will stay put.

MUSCLE TESTING

I'm going to take you through one of the muscle tests I use for checking tongue position. There are two essential rules in muscle testing:

1. The athlete always initiates the test.

2. The coach never touches the muscle being tested.

I find that muscle-testing yourself is difficult. It's kind of like how you can't tickle yourself; it takes someone else's action to get the intended result. If you have someone in your life who will muscle-test with you, I recommend doing this with a partner. However, you may be able to pick up some difference in the muscle quality in the following drill if you want to try it alone. (If you're doing it alone, you will follow the instructions for both the coach and athlete):

Neck Flexor Muscle Test

1. The athlete rounds their neck forward, tucking their chin (cervical flexion).

2. The coach places their hand on the athlete's forehead; the coach's hand is going to try to undo the athlete's chin-tuck (they are trying to push the head into cervical extension). The athlete attempts to nod/tuck their chin harder against the pressure from the coach's hand.

3. For the first rep, the athlete lowers their tongue as far down their throat as possible. Now, the athlete presses their head down and tucks their chin into the resistance from the coach's hand.

4. For the second rep, the athlete presses their tongue into the spot. Repeat the muscle test and see which version made the neck stronger.

A strong muscle test means this physical position is lowering threat in the brain; a weak test means that threat increased in the position. If it were me, I would keep my tongue all day in whichever position tested stronger.

Separate the Tongue and the Throat

One of the biggest challenges for a singer is decoupling tongue and laryngeal movement. A great way to practice this is by using the spot as a tongue anchor:

1. Assess your voice and body.

2. Put the tongue in the spot.

3. Begin a yawning or sobbing motion, but do not let the tongue leave the roof of the mouth.

4. If you check yourself in a mirror and open your mouth, you should be able to see your larynx lowering (watch your thyroid or cricoid cartilage) while your tongue stays in the spot. You should feel a sensation of stretch in the hyoid area in the underside of your chin. Hold for ten seconds.

5. Reassess.

Returning to "the spot" for the inhalation before a big note can also be high-payoff. Try this:

1. Think of a phrase that gives you occasional vocal trouble.

2. Take a breath with a low/depressed tongue and sing the phrase.

3. Now, put the tongue in the spot and take a nose breath; sing the same phrase. Compare the result.

THE TONGUE AND SWALLOWING

Assuming you have now gotten your tongue comfortably in the spot, the next step is to look at how you are swallowing, which is a fascinating combination of conscious and subconscious actions *(Fig. 9.4)*. Swallowing begins with certain conscious muscles and points of contact in the mouth and then continues with automatic processes controlled in the brainstem that guide food and liquid down your pharynx and esophagus.

The surprising truth is that many adults don't swallow properly. A lot of us are still using a technique that is used by infants, never having fully "graduated" to an adult pattern. An infant swallows by widening the tongue and pushing it through the teeth while activating a suckling action with a muscle in the cheeks called the buccinator. You can feel your buccinator by making a "duck face" or sucking the skin of your

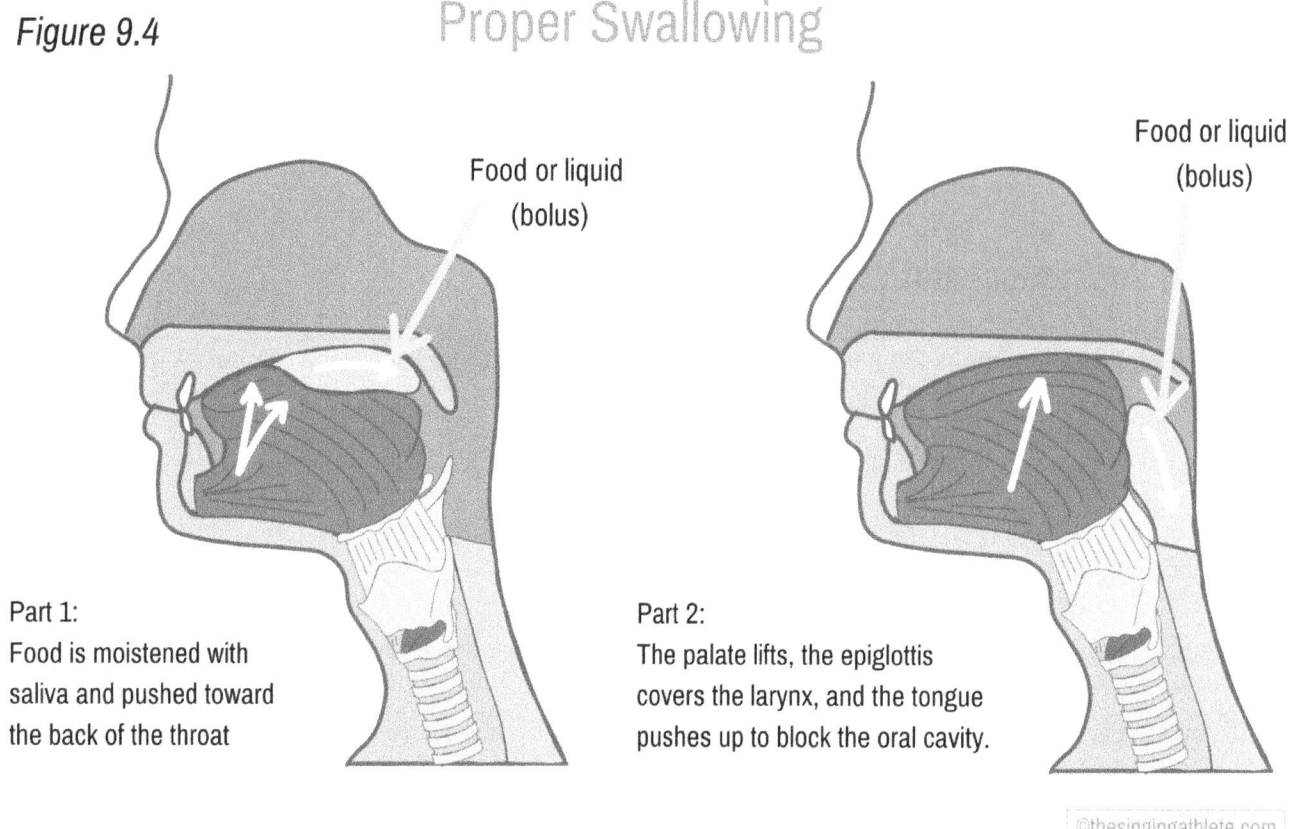

Figure 9.4 — Proper Swallowing

Part 1: Food is moistened with saliva and pushed toward the back of the throat

Part 2: The palate lifts, the epiglottis covers the larynx, and the tongue pushes up to block the oral cavity.

cheeks toward the midline between your teeth. By contrast, an adult is supposed to swallow with their tongue in the spot and the cheeks relaxed.

Swallow and see what your current habits are. Can you keep the tongue in the spot as the swallow happens? Can you do three in a row with minimal pauses in between? Can you do five?

A good swallow does several important things:[53]

- When the tongue is in the spot for a swallow, the eustachian tubes experience a change in internal pressure. The middle ear gets aerated and the tubes clear out. Anyone with a history of ear infections or hearing issues should investigate their swallowing pattern.

- Correct swallowing leads to fewer upper respiratory and viral infections.

- In a proper swallow, the palatoglossus muscle generates 6–8 pounds (around 3 kg) of force onto the palate. This pushes the palatine and vomer bones, which in turn creates movement in the sphenoid bone. The pituitary gland (sometimes called the "master gland") sits in a saddle-like depression in the sphenoid, so mobilizing it with your swallow can help regulate the many functions of the pituitary (growth hormone, thyroid, blood pressure, sex hormones, etc.).

- Singers tend to view the tongue primarily as a facilitator of speech and vowels. But it is also part of the digestive system, and the esophagus relies on proper tongue movement to work correctly. Dysfunctional swallowing relates to dysfunctional digestion.

Swallow Check

Like breathing, swallowing is a high-rep activity (around six hundred times a day).[54] You might as well do six hundred good reps every day. Here's how to check your habits; you'll need a mirror for this one:

1. Assess your voice and body.

2. Put your tongue in the spot as firmly as you can.

3. Close your teeth.

4. Do a cheesy smile (this is because you can't use your buccinator muscle while you are smiling).

5. Looking in a mirror, swallow three times, in as quick of succession as possible. If you can do that, try for five. You are watching to make sure your tongue does not thrust through your teeth as you swallow; it must stay in the spot.

6. Reassess.

Once you can do five swallows like this, progress to using liquid:

1. Assess your voice and body.

2. Take a tiny amount of liquid into your mouth and trap it between the roof of your mouth and your tongue.

3. Make a cheesy smile and do some neck circles, feeling the liquid running in a small circle along the surface of your palate.

4. Now level your head and swallow the liquid while pressing the tongue into the spot.

5. Reassess.

Once you can do the swallowing drills easily with the cheesy smile, do them again with a relaxed face. When you've mastered that, try one more variation where you engage a sweeping action of the tongue:

1. Take a sip of liquid and allow the tip of the tongue to lower while the rest of it stays up.

2. Now push the tip of the tongue up, creating a front-to-back wave motion that guides the liquid along the roof of your mouth and then down your throat.

From a brain-mapping perspective, swallowing and singing are very related. If you're in the market for quick vocal improvements, invest your energy in resting the tongue in the spot and learning to swallow correctly.

TONGUE NERVES

You have twelve cranial nerves, and six of them make their way into the tongue *(Fig. 9.5)*. One thing that all the cranial nerves have in common is their involvement in the search for, and processing of, food.[55] Since the tongue plays a major role in accessing calories from things you eat, it makes sense that it is a hotbed of cranial nerve action. All of these nerves have other functions, but this list shows how they interact with the tongue:

- ***Trigeminal Nerve (CN V):*** The trigeminal nerve controls sensation (vibration/light touch/pressure) on the front two-thirds of the tongue.

- ***Facial Nerve (CN VII):*** The facial nerve controls taste on the front two-thirds of the tongue.

- ***Glossopharyngeal Nerve (CN IX):*** The glossopharyngeal nerve controls sensation and taste on the back one-third of the tongue.

- ***Vagus Nerve (CN X):*** The vagus nerve controls the palatoglossus muscle in conjunction with the accessory nerve (CN XI). The vagus also has sensory fibers in the very back of the tongue and the epiglottis through the internal laryngeal nerve (a branch of the superior laryngeal nerve).

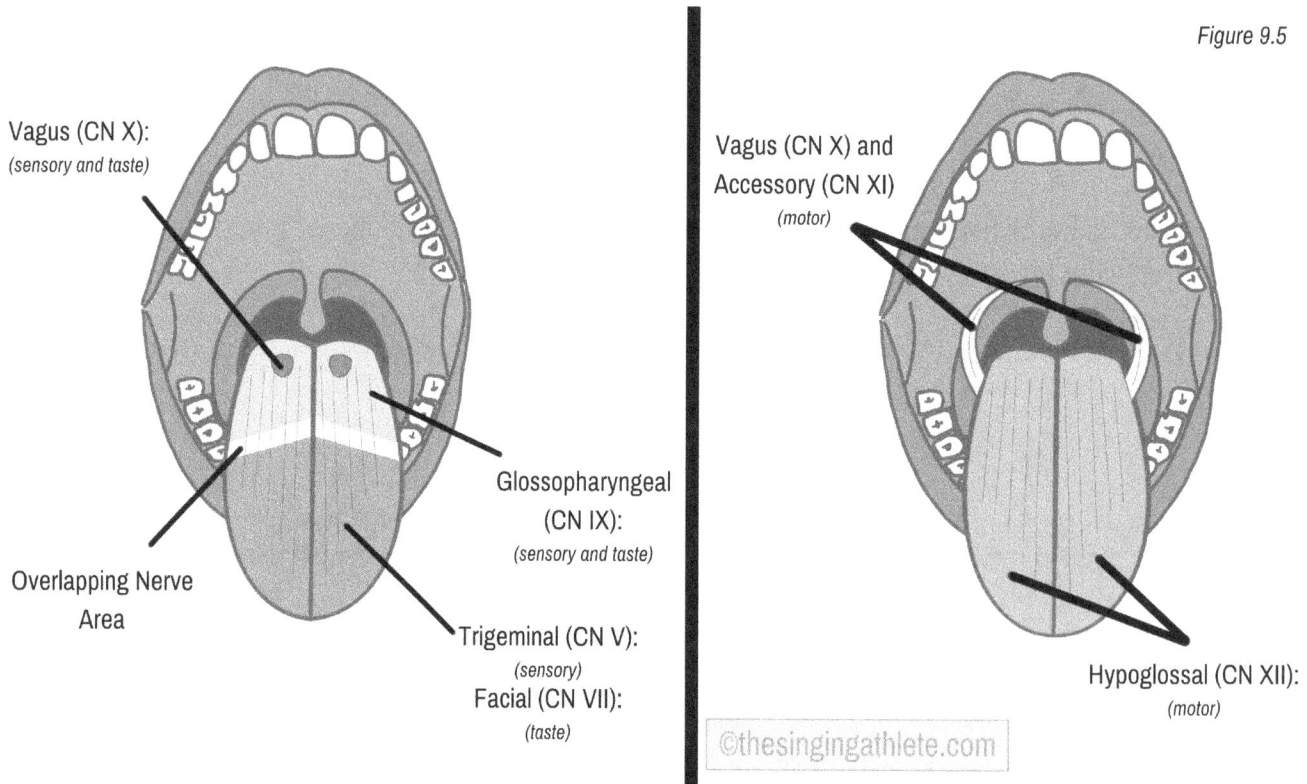

Figure 9.5

- *Accessory Nerve (CN XI):* Some sources indicate that the vagus nerve controls all of the palatoglossus muscle, but it seems in most dissections that the accessory nerve contributes some of its motor fibers.

- *Hypoglossal Nerve (CN XII):* Except for the palatoglossus, the hypoglossal nerve innervates motor function in all the other tongue muscles.

The tongue's nerves originate in two brainstem areas, called the **pons** and the **medulla**. The pons and medulla have many functions, but one of them is to facilitate flexion or extension in the body. Flexion means decreasing the angle of two bones as they meet at a joint, and extension means increasing the angle. For example, the rectus femoris (one of your four quadriceps muscles) is a hip flexor because it lifts the thigh out in front of you to decrease the angle between your pelvis and your femur. An example of an extensor would be your triceps, where one of its actions is to increase the angle between your upper and lower arm, thereby straightening the elbow.

In your brainstem, the pons, which contains cranial nerves V-VIII, facilitates extension. It is thought that the pons is one of the brain structures that took us from four legs (flexed) to two (extended). The medulla, meanwhile, is the source of nerves IX-XII; it inhibits extensors, which means that it essentially facilitates flexion.

The trigeminal (CN V) and the facial nerve (CN VII) originate in the pons, so stimulating sensation or taste on the front two-thirds of your tongue will engage these nerves, potentially improving your extensor tone. Meanwhile, the other four tongue nerves, which control all the aspects of tongue movement, are found in the medulla. That means that tongue movement drills can facilitate action in the flexors. Figure 9.6 states it simply:

Tongue sensation connects you to your back line.

Tongue movement connects you to your front line.

This information explains why there is no "one size fits all" training for singers. For someone like me, who tends to be overactive in my extensors, doing tongue sensation work never assesses particularly well, but when I do tongue movement drills and find my flexors, I sing better. You may have the exact opposite experience. In my Singing Athlete course, I've seen many occasions where the same drill gives one person a breakthrough while tightening up someone else. You have to assess and reassess. (I'll explain how to determine if you are flexor or extensor-dominant in Chapter 14.)

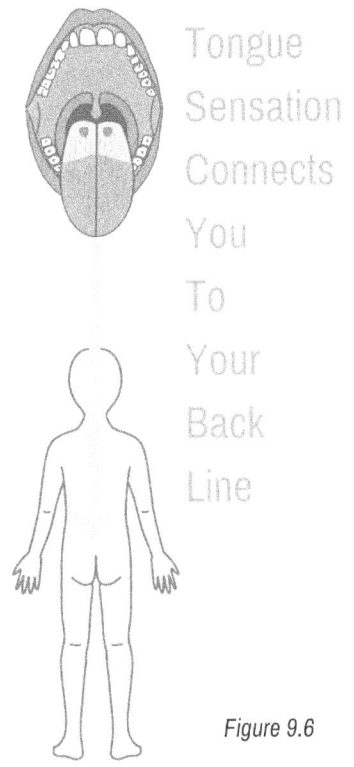
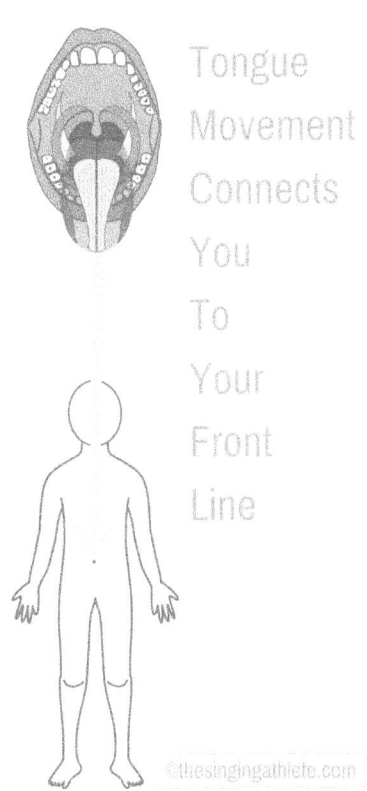

Figure 9.6

THE TONGUE AND CHANGING YOUR BRAIN

The fact that the tongue contains many different cranial nerves makes it a prime conduit for neuroplastic change. A fascinating example is the Brainport device, initially developed by Paul Bach-y-Rita to help with balance deficits. The Brainport consists of a group of accelerometers connected to a plate that sits on the tongue. As different parts of the tongue are stimulated, someone can learn to interpret these directional sensations to re-educate themselves on where they are in space. The Brainport has also been adapted to help visually impaired people "see." A camera digitizes the surroundings, which are then translated to the surface of the tongue, creating a picture of the world. White or bright colors are picked up as an intense tongue stimulation, grays as a medium stimulus, and dark colors not registering. With this oral information, a person can experience basic object recognition, essentially seeing with their tongue.[56]

Let's see how sensitive your tongue is. You can do this next drill with either a normal or (ideally) an electric toothbrush or Z-vibe.

Tongue Sensitivity

1. Assess your voice and body.

2. Without turning the toothbrush/Z-vibe on, place it on the right side of your tongue with the bristles/dots facing down and run it front to back, along the upper surface of the tongue.

3. Repeat on the left side of the tongue. Does it feel the same side to side?

4. Now turn it so that the bristles/dots are facing up to the ceiling. Place it under the right side of your tongue and run it from front to back, along the underside of the tongue. Can you feel this, or is it numb? If you feel your tongue pulling back, watch it in a mirror or hold it out of your mouth.

5. Repeat on the left side of the tongue. Does it feel the same?

6. Keep the bristles/dots facing up and run it front to back, along the hard and soft palate (roof of the mouth) on the right side. Does it feel the same front to back?

7. Repeat on the left side of the palate. Does it feel the same?

8. Reassess.

These light-touch sensors in the tongue are controlled by your trigeminal nerve. Next, if you have an electric toothbrush or Z-vibe, you're going to repeat the drill with vibration, which is another significant trigeminal stimulus.

1. Assess your voice and body.

2. Turn the toothbrush/Z-vibe on and with the bristles/dots facing down, run it front to back on the right side of your tongue while it is vibrating.

3. Repeat on the left side and compare the sensation. Also, notice if there are "dead spots" anywhere along the way on either side.

4. Turn the toothbrush/Z-vibe over so the bristles/dots face up and run it along the underside of the right side of your tongue.

5. Repeat on the left side and compare the sensation.

6. Keep the toothbrush/Z-vibe so the bristles/dots face up and run it along the right side of the roof of the mouth.

7. Repeat on the left side and compare the sensation.

8. Reassess.

If this all felt even and clear, great; if you found a spot that had less sensation, try brushing/vibrating that spot and then sing immediately afterward. You also may discover hypersensitive spots; see if the sensitivity decreases as you wake up the numb zones. Oral sensation is especially worth checking if you have any history of a speech impediment; tongues will innately avoid contact on areas that are uncomfortably sensitive.

If you had a good reassessment, use your daily dental routine to fix your sensory issues. Spend an extra few seconds brushing the dead spots with your toothbrush every day.

Shock Your Tongue

If you're ready to be hardcore, there's one more thing you can try, and it involves something you probably have lying around your house: a 9-volt battery *(Fig. 9.7)*. In addition to light touch and vibration, the tongue responds to electrical stimulus. A mild "shock" to the tongue is a direct route into the brainstem via the six cranial nerves mentioned earlier in the chapter. A team at the University of Wisconsin-Madison did a fourteen-week trial where they found that adding electrical tongue stimulation in rehab significantly improved scores on balance and fluidity of gait.[57]

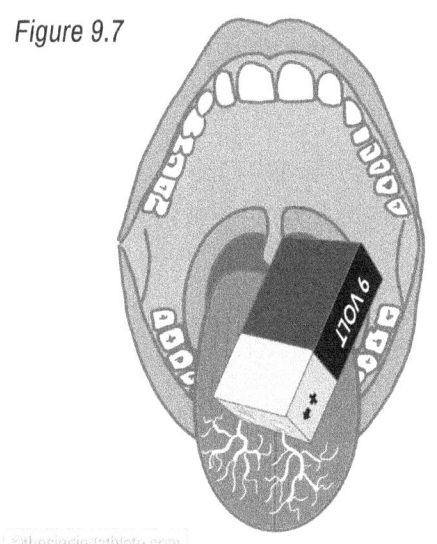

Figure 9.7

If you're feeling brave, give this a try:

1. Assess your voice and body.

2. Place the two electrodes on the top of the battery on the front right side of your tongue. You should only do this for a split-second and there should be a mild shock. It should not be excruciating, but it shouldn't be a dull sensation.

3. Repeat on the left side of the tongue. How is the symmetry of the sensation?

4. Repeat in the back right and back left areas of the tongue.

5. Reassess.

(Note: To be clear, this is just to be done for a split-second or two in each quadrant—you're not leaving a battery on your tongue for hours, as battery acid isn't a major food group.)

If you found a dead spot, try shocking the sleepy parts of your tongue into activation before you sing difficult music. We know that motor learning improves with sensory priming, which means waking up the sensation before we attempt new or challenging skills. Because of the tongue's prominence and location in the brain, it is a prime candidate for using sensory stimulation to improve motor function.

Taste and Singing

Many tongue sensations are controlled by the trigeminal nerve, but taste is the responsibility of the facial nerve (CN VII). This nerve is a big deal for singers because it participates in a portion of your hearing. CN VII innervates the stapedius, which is the smallest muscle in the body. The stapedius prevents excessive movement of the stapes, which helps to control the amplitude of sound waves as they reach the ear. A dysfunction in this muscle can result in hyperacusis, where average volumes sound very loud. If you know someone who gets easily overwhelmed in a noisy restaurant, they might have a facial nerve that's not pulling its weight. The facial nerve is also a player when it comes to judging the volume of your own singing voice.

You can test your facial nerve by using your tongue's sense of taste. You may have seen a map identifying where taste receptors were supposed to live on your tongue (sweet in the front, bitter in back, etc.). It turns out those maps were utterly wrong.[58] You are meant to perceive all the five primary tastes (e.g., sweet, salty, sour, bitter, umami) everywhere on your tongue.

In the front two-thirds of the tongue, the facial nerve (CN VII) controls taste. The back third is controlled by the glossopharyngeal nerve (CN IX). For this drill, you'll need a bit of sugar and salt, as well as clean hands.

1. Assess your voice and body.

2. Wet the tip of your finger and dip it in a bit of sugar.

3. Place your finger lightly on the front of the right side of your tongue. Can you taste the sugar easily?

4. Now place the sugar on the front of the left side of your tongue. Is the clarity of tastes the same as on the right?

5. Repeat with the back right and back left areas of the tongue. Reach as far back as you can without triggering a gag reflex.

6. Reassess.

7. Repeat Steps 2–6 with salt.

If your facial nerve is working the way it should, your left and right sides of the tongue should be equally sharp in perceiving taste, with the back portions of the tongue slightly duller. (We are designed to have more acute taste sensation in the front, in order to judge the freshness of food immediately.)

If you noticed a tongue area of less (or no) taste, this is worth fixing. Beyond the auditory reason already stated, the facial nerve controls several glands in the mouth that produce saliva. If you tend to get dry when you are nervous, improving your taste receptors may boost your salivary production under stress.

In this case, the test is the drill, meaning you should try putting something with a distinct taste on your weaker tongue areas when you practice. If sugar and salt aren't intense enough, try:

- Lemon juice
- Mint
- Fresh-ground pepper
- Any favorite spice
- Whatever else you can find in your kitchen—get creative

MOVING YOUR TONGUE

Before we get into tongue movement drills, take a moment to assess the balance in your hypoglossal nerve (CN XII), which controls most of the muscles we're about to train.

Hypoglossal Nerve Test

1. Sit or stand in front of a mirror.

2. Thrust the tongue directly out of the mouth. The tongue should be flat, with the tip not going up or down. The jaw should not be thrusting forward; you can hold the jaw if it's moving.

3. Relax and repeat the tongue thrust several times. Notice if the tip of the tongue is deviating to the left or the right as you stick it out. The tongue will drift toward the weaker side, so if you see the tip moving to the right, the right side is weaker vice versa. Most of the hypoglossal nerve is devoted to pushing the tongue forward. If one side is weak, it doesn't push as hard and the tongue falls off to that side.

4. Now thrust the tongue out and hold it for ten seconds. Does the tip move to the left or the right as you hold the position?

If you did see a weaker side, here's how to fix it:

Tongue Press

1. Assess your voice and body.

2. Push the tongue into the *opposite* cheek from the side that was weak. If your tongue was deviating to the left, push the tongue into your right cheek and vice versa. This asks the weak tongue side to have to push harder because it's moving farther across the mouth.

3. Hold the press for five seconds. If you want to make it harder, place your hand on the outside of your cheek and press back against the tongue, creating a more challenging isometric.

4. Repeat for four more reps.

5. Reassess.

If you didn't see a tongue deviation in the Hypoglossal Test, try the above drill while alternating sides. It often feels like a lot more work than you might be expecting.

Before we do more tongue strengthening, let's take two minutes to stretch it:

- **Two-Minute Tongue Stretch:** To do this passive stretch, you'll need a washcloth or towel. Using both hands, place the washcloth around the body of the tongue and guide the tongue directly out of your mouth. Find a comfortable but definite stretch and hold for two minutes. If you want to stretch with some music, I wrote a two-minute song called (creatively) "Two-Minute Tongue Stretch," which you can access at thesingingathlete.com.

For each of these movement drills, I want you to assess and reassess before and after you complete them. Use these exercises as a window into what kind of muscular training your tongue enjoys.

- **Forward Roll:** Place the tip of your tongue behind your lower teeth. Roll the tongue out of the mouth as far as possible, using the tip's position behind the lower teeth as an anchor. Hold for ten seconds; aim to feel a contraction on the underside of the tongue. Rest and repeat for five rounds total.

- **Tongue Circle:** Make five slow circles with your tongue in each direction. The tongue should be inside the cheeks/lips but outside the teeth, and the jaw should be still (hold the jaw if it's moving). With each progressive circle, reach the tongue farther back to every corner of the mouth. One circle should take about five seconds to complete; notice places where you speed up or slow down unintentionally.

- **Tongue Retraction**: Put the tongue in the spot and suck it up and back for ten seconds; it should feel a bit like you're trying to suck vigorously on a hard candy. Aim for engaging some muscle work near the palate and under the ears. Rest and repeat for five rounds total.

- **/n/ Push-up:** Make the shape of an /n/ consonant and press the tip up to the roof of the mouth, at the same time opening your jaw as wide as possible; hold for ten seconds. The goal here is not to roll the tongue under but to press the tongue tip straight up on the roof of the mouth. This trains the retroflex /ɹ/ motion we covered earlier in the chapter. Rest and repeat for five rounds total.

- **Blade Push-up:** This is similar to the /n/ Push-up, but now you're going to get the whole blade of the tongue on the palate. If you remember from the beginning of the chapter, the blade is the "bowl" that you see on the front and sides of the tongue when you lower the middle. You can think of it as a curve or semicircle around the front edge of the tongue. It should feel like you are pushing the semicircle up against the palate. Rest and repeat for five rounds total.

- **Backward Curl:** Curl the tip of your tongue backward until it touches the soft palate and press the underside of the tongue onto the palate for ten seconds. You should feel a strong curling action of the tongue and a stretch to the underside. Again, watch that the jaw doesn't help. Rest and repeat for five rounds total.

- **Blowfish:** Place the tongue in the spot, close your lips, and puff your cheeks out without moving your tongue. Now, move the air from the left to the right cheek without moving your tongue from the spot. Keeping the tongue in the spot, move the air from puffing out your upper lip to puffing out your lower lip.

For the following drills, you will need something flat, like a tongue depressor, popsicle stick, or butter knife.

- **Tongue Push-up—Center:** Place the tongue depressor on the center of your tongue. You want it in the traditional position used at the doctor's office when they look in your throat. Put the depressor as far back as possible on your tongue without triggering a gag reflex. Press the tongue up toward the roof of the mouth for ten seconds while pressing down with the tongue depressor; you are using the depressor to create an isometric exercise for your tongue elevators. Rest and repeat for five rounds total.

- **Tongue Push-up—Side:** Place the tongue depressor on the right side of your tongue; press the right side up toward the roof of the mouth. Switch to the left side, press up, and compare the strength. If you find a weaker side, train it by pressing that side up for ten seconds. Rest and repeat on the weak side for five rounds total.

- **Resisted Tongue Thrust:** Turn the depressor so it's parallel to the floor, with the flat side facing you. Put the tip of your tongue against it and push out against the depressor. You are trying to create an isometric where the tongue pushes forward and the depressor pushes back toward your face. Hold for ten seconds and repeat for five rounds total.

10. JAW AND TEETH

One way to conceive of the body is that you have a main trunk and five appendages: two legs, two arms, and a jaw. These connections between your midline and your peripheral structures are vulnerable areas, which makes hips, shoulders, and jaws easy areas to hold tension. Beyond its role in chewing, the jaw is also the gateway for letting vocal sounds leave your body.

JAW BASICS

The jaw *(Fig. 10.1)* consists of an upper portion fixed to the skull (***maxilla***) and a movable lower bone (***mandible***) that articulates at the ***temporomandibular joint (TMJ)***. The mandible is the largest and strongest bone in the face; it has a body, which forms the front of the jaw, and two rami, which form the back portions on either side. There are two protrusions, or processes, coming off each of the mandible's rami:

- ***Coronoid Process***: a thin, triangular point toward the front that provides attachment points for jaw muscles

- ***Condyloid Process:*** a thicker, rounded ridge toward the back that forms the lower portion of the jaw hinge

At the point where the condyloid process meets the temporal bone, there is some cushioning tissue called an articular disc. This area doesn't have nerves or blood vessels, so it can't feel pain. That's a good thing because the jaw has to slide forward when you open your mouth wide, and you need a buffer to prevent damage to the bones. Right behind this disc is what is called retrodiscal tissue; unlike the articular disc, this tissue is fully innervated and vascular. If you experience pain when opening the mouth, it can be because the articular disc has been displaced forward, and the retrodiscal tissue is being squeezed between the skull and the condyle. Remapping jaw movement can be the solution to this issue.

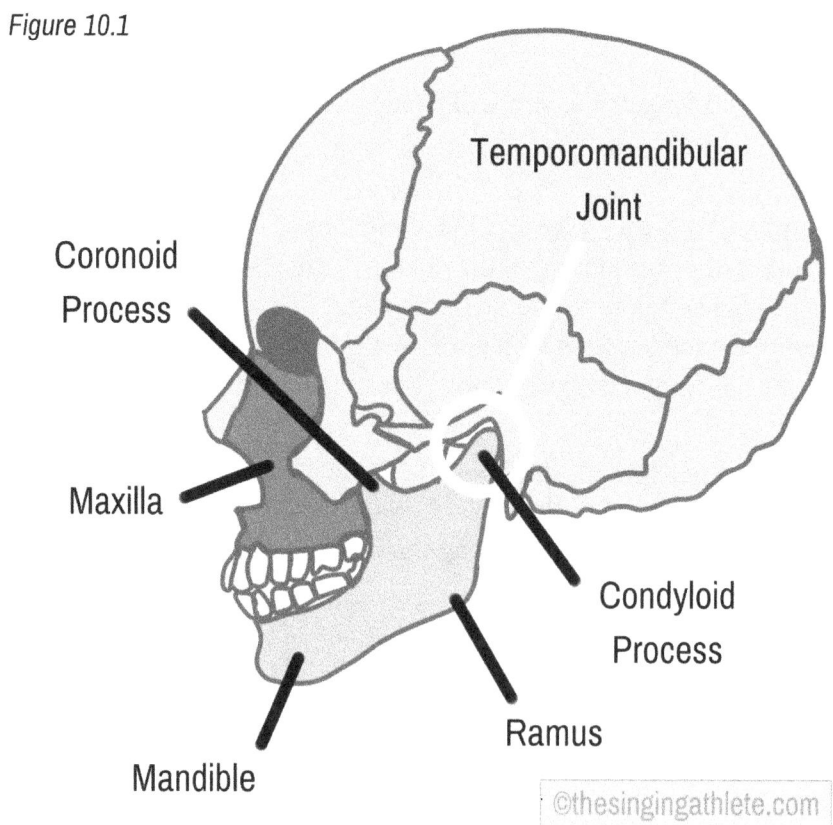

Figure 10.1

JAW MUSCLES

There are four primary muscles of mastication, or chewing *(Fig. 10.2)*. All of these muscles are innervated by the trigeminal nerve (CN V):

- *Masseter:* The masseter is the most powerful and prominent of the jaw muscles. It has a superficial part (connecting to the zygomatic bone) and a deep part (connecting to the temporal bone). The masseter's primary function is to help you bite down.

- *Temporalis:* The temporalis is a broad muscle fanning out along either side of your skull, attaching to the mandible at the coronoid process. It assists in closing the mouth, but it also retracts (pulls back) the jaw.

- *Medial Pterygoid (the "p" is silent, like "pterodactyl"):* The medial pterygoid also lies on the inside of the jaw, and its main function is to help in closing the mouth, mirroring the action of the masseter.

- *Lateral Pterygoid:* The lateral pterygoid is the only muscle in the skull that has two heads (superior and inferior), and both attach the jaw to the sphenoid bone (more on the sphenoid later). When both the left and right lateral pterygoids activate, the jaw is pulled forward (protraction). When the muscles act unilaterally, they contribute to a side-to-side motion. The lateral pterygoid is also the only mastication muscle that can participate in opening the jaw instead of closing it.

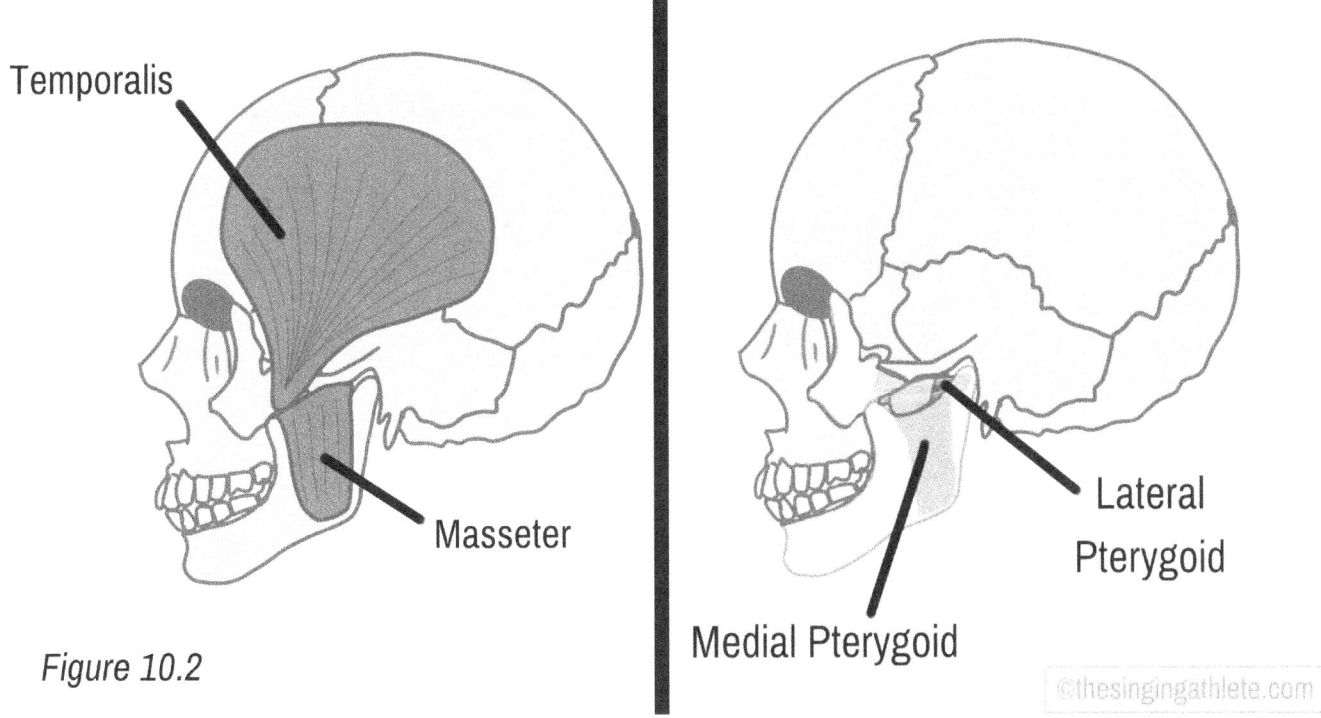

Figure 10.2

Three other muscles can assist in opening the mouth; we already looked at these muscles briefly in Chapter 8:

- *Digastric:* The digastric is a two-bellied muscle; the posterior branch is longer and attaches to the mastoid process (the rounded bony area behind your ear). The anterior branch attaches to the mandible, and they meet at an intermediate tendon that loops onto the hyoid bone. The anterior belly is innervated by the trigeminal nerve (CN V), but the posterior belly gets its nerve input from the facial nerve (CN VII).

- *Mylohyoid:* The mylohyoid is a broad, triangular muscle that forms the floor of the oral cavity; it is innervated by the trigeminal nerve (CN V).

- *Geniohyoid:* The geniohyoid is a narrow muscle that connects the chin and the hyoid bone. Unlike the other jaw muscles, the geniohyoid is fed by a branch of the hypoglossal nerve (CN XII), making it more neurally related to tongue motion.

The primary function of these three muscles is to elevate the hyoid bone in swallowing. However, if the hyoid is fixed in place, they can assist in opening the jaw by pulling it toward the hyoid.

THE JAW AND THE EARS

Place your fingers inside your ear canals and push your fingers toward the front of the canals. Slowly open and close your mouth. Do you feel the mandible rolling as you open and close? Does one side move first, or move more? The jaw and the ear are intimately acquainted; the name "temporomandibular joint" implies a joining of the temporal bone/lobe of the brain ("temporo-") with the jaw ("-mandibular"). The temporal lobe is where hearing is processed; every time the jaw moves, the movement registers in a bone that connects you to your auditory world. The back of your jaw is the front of your ears.

There are two ligaments (oto-mandibular ligaments) that attach the malleus of the inner ear to the jaw. There are studies showing a correlation between tinnitus (ringing in the ear) and TMJ dysfunction on the same side.[59] I've found jaw work to be a reliable helper for many singers who experience tinnitus issues.

The trigeminal nerve (CN V) controls the muscles of chewing as well as the tensor tympani muscle of the eardrum. The tensor tympani controls the volume of the sound of chewing (it makes sense that the action and the sound are in branches of the same nerve). If you are bothered by your own eating sounds, that can point toward a trigeminal nerve problem.

When the tensor tympani contracts, it tightens the tympanic membrane, dampening the vibrations in the ear ossicles. This tympanic reflex may have developed to help us deal with the rumbling of loud thunder. It responds in forty milliseconds, quick enough to dampen thunder but not fast enough to protect from the sounds of gunshots or explosions (or loud concerts—don't forget your earplugs). The tensor tympani also works to soften the internal volume when you shout. If you don't like to belt or sing big high notes, jaw work may help.

WHAT IS TEETH-GRINDING ABOUT?

Bruxism, or grinding your teeth, is a commonly diagnosed issue in which repetitive jaw clenching causes a wearing down of the teeth, headaches, etc. This pattern can either happen during sleep or while awake. The question is, why does your brain think you need to tighten the jaw so much? The most likely reason is that you are mouth breathing and your tongue is not in the spot. The brain knows that the nose is the preferred breathing path and that you have to retain some carbon dioxide in your tissues. If you are mouth breathing with a low tongue, the body's supply of CO^2 gets depleted. To prevent further loss, your brain decides to clamp your jaw shut. The problem is, the masseter is extremely strong; the muscle can quickly go past its mark, leading to unhappy teeth.

If you grind your teeth at night, wearing a night guard is one possible solution. If a student uses one, I have them bring it to a lesson and we muscle-test with it in and out. I've seen brains that love a night guard (stronger muscle test with it in) and others that hate it (weaker muscle test with it in). If you use one and want to test it, it's simple; all you need is your thumb and a friend.

1. Put your thumb up in a traditional "thumbs up!" gesture.

2. Have your friend try to bend your thumb down and forward while you try to keep it straight and extended.

3. Now put in your night guard.

4. Repeat the muscle test.

If you were stronger with the guard in, it's probably working for you. Another valid (and much cheaper) option is mouth taping, which many students have told me has helped to resolve their TMJ issues. Mouth taping can also help with:

- Sleep Apnea
- Snoring
- Poor sleep quality
- Anxiety
- Frequent throat infections
- Blocked sinuses

Here's how it works:

Mouth Taping

1. Go to a pharmacy and get what's called "paper tape"; it's usually in the first aid section.

2. Before bed, tear off a piece that will cover your mouth when placed horizontally (about three inches or seven cm)

3. Blot it several times on the back of your hand to make it less sticky.

4. Put the tape over your mouth.

5. Go to bed.

Some mouth-taping tips:

- Try it for a few minutes before you go to bed to see how you react. Some people love this feeling, and some don't.

- If your lips don't like the sensation of the tape on your mouth, try applying a little coconut oil or lip balm before putting it on.

- This is probably obvious, but mouth taping is for adults, not children.

You can assess the effectiveness of mouth taping by timing your Air Hunger Test first thing in the morning (see Chapter 4). If you are maintaining proper CO_2 levels throughout the night, you should have a longer time in your Air Hunger Test when you wake up.

THE CHRONIC PAIN CYCLE AND THE JAW

If you have a history of TMJ discomfort, work through these upcoming jaw exercises slowly, letting your body tell you when it's time to stop. That being said, if you are never fully moving your TMJ, your jaw issues may only become more pronounced. When students come to me with jaw pain, they often also have weak muscles of mastication. In an effort to not make their jaw problems worse, a process called the Chronic Pain Cycle *(Fig. 10.3)* may have been taking place.

Here is an example of how the Chronic Pain Cycle can go:

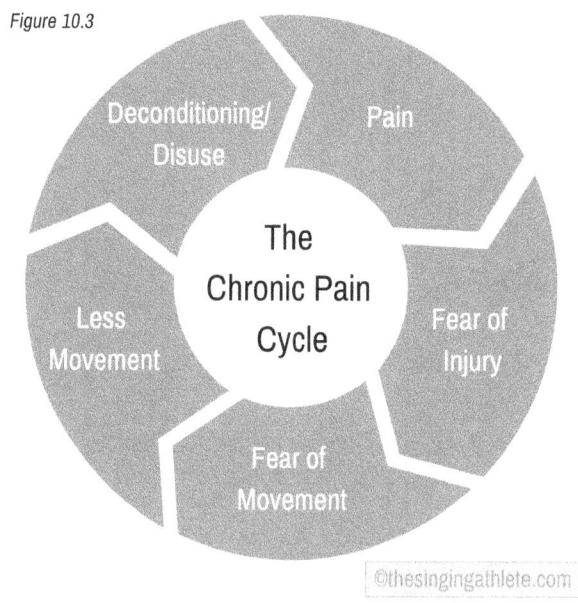

Figure 10.3

You wake up in the morning and your jaw aches, like usual. You tentatively open your mouth; the pain is worse, so you decide that if you move your jaw, you must be damaging the joint. You go through weeks of never opening your mouth. The next time you have to open wide (say, singing an "ah" vowel on a high note), it feels scary; you break into a full-body sweat and your heart races. As soon as you close your mouth, the pain returns. You conclude more firmly that you should never stretch your jaw; after all, who wants to feel that much discomfort? Your jaw muscles continue to weaken, and you may beat yourself up emotionally.

Remember that acute pain (e.g., stepping on a nail) is an essential part of staying alive. But chronic situations, where the brain has become hyper-excitable around certain body areas over a long period, are different. If your jaw isn't moving well, vascular tissue can get trapped in the hinge, potentially causing nociceptive signals to travel to the brain. For some brains, these signals will be received gratefully, and the movement error will be corrected. For others, these nociceptive messages can get overanalyzed by the brain; it's like you typed "A" into your phone and "AAAA" appeared on your screen instead. The information from your jaw receptors is over-interpreted, and the brain creates a much larger response than necessary, limiting your movement and causing constant pain.

So, how to do you reduce this sensitivity? Remember that pain does not equal injury. In chronic situations, the increase of pain you may feel in movement is probably the result of neural habit, not further tissue damage. Neuroplasticity isn't good or bad; it just is. If you've had chronic pain for a while, the complex loop of threat signals firing around your brain has become quite efficient at communication. The most likely case is that exploring movement in a sensitized jaw isn't causing any further problems in the joint; in fact, it is probably helping. Deliberate, well-coordinated movement can lower the water in the threat bucket, helping nociceptors to calm down. Go slow and small, making the motion a little bigger and faster every day.

Opening the Mouth

For something we do all day long, opening the mouth is a complex process. The muscles I mentioned earlier in the chapter (e.g., lateral pterygoid, digastric, mylohyoid, geniohyoid) help to create this action. It is also assisted by eccentric contraction (lengthening under load) from the other muscles of mastication. Gravity also plays a part.

The motion of jaw opening is really two movements. For the first inch (2–3 cm), the jaw rotates open; as you open farther, the mandible slides forward, in what's known as translation. Let's see if you can feel the moment when the movement shifts:

1. Assess your voice and body.

2. Place your fingers on the tragus of your ears, which is the small triangular point in front of the ear canals. Now move your fingers slightly forward until you are in the jaw hinge; you are looking for a "hole" into which you can get your fingers. As you start to open your mouth, you should feel movement in the jawbone. Your fingers are now on or near the condyloid process of the mandible.

3. Open and close your mouth very slowly; become aware of the movement of the condyloid processes, which will feel like a rolling motion. Does this rolling happen at the same time on both sides?

4. As you open wider, can you feel the moment when the jaw changes from a rotation pattern to a translation pattern (i.e., the condyloid processes slide forward)?

5. Drop your fingers and go through a few full open/close cycles, paying attention to the quality of the movement.

6. Reassess.

Also, remember external targets; if you start getting stressed by this movement, pick up an object and place it on the front of your jaw. Focus on moving the object up and down, not your jaw.

Jaw Lateral Glides

Moving the jaw smoothly from side to side requires unilateral control of the muscles of mastication. This movement is also part of chewing, so it's important to get right. (Remember that chewing and vocalization are neighbors in the motor cortex.) It's trickier than it seems, so you may want to do this one in a mirror.

1. Assess your voice and body.

2. Close your teeth lightly and begin a small slide of your jaw from side to side, trying to touch your lower canine tooth on each side to the upper canine tooth (the canines are the ones that look like fangs). This motion should be minimal and slow, done with control; focus on the sensation of your teeth sliding against each other. Do five reps.

3. If this feels alright, open the mouth slightly more vertically and make the motion a little bigger. The goal is to keep your face and cheeks relaxed as the jaw slides. Is it going smoothly and evenly to both sides? Do five reps.

4. Now try it even more slowly; take five seconds to slide to the left and five to slide to the right. Do five reps.

5. Reassess.

If this feels stressful, try these things:

- Put your hands on the sides of your jaw while you glide.

- Place your fingers or two pencils out a half-inch (1 cm) from the sides of the jaw. Slide the jaw toward your fingers/pencils on both sides.

- Do it seated, on the floor with your back against a wall, or lying down.

- Exhale while doing the movement.

Jaw Front-to-Back Glides

For most of us, sliding the jaw forward is more accessible than sliding it backward, so again, a mirror is probably your friend here.

1. Assess your voice and body.

2. Slowly slide your jaw forward. Does it move smoothly and evenly? Do both sides move forward at the same tempo?

3. Slowly slide your jaw backward. Does it move smoothly and evenly? Do both sides move back at the same tempo?

4. Repeat for five reps.

5. Now make the same motion even more slowly; take five seconds to move the jaw forward and five seconds to move it backward. Repeat for five reps.

6. Reassess.

If you're struggling with this one, try it leaning forward using a desk or table, with your head resting on your folded arms like you're taking a nap at school. This way, you can use gravity to assist you in making the movements cleanly.

Jaw Circles

The coordination required for circular motions is greater, and it upregulates an integral part of your first brain called the cerebellum, which we'll be studying in Chapter 15.

1. Assess your voice and body.

2. Stand or sit with a tall posture.

3. Use your jaw to draw a vertical circle in the air, taking it to the right, down, left, and up. Repeat for five reps.

4. Reverse the circle (jaw to the left, down, right, up) for five reps.

5. Now, make a horizontal circle by taking the jaw to the right, forward, left, and back. Repeat for five reps.

6. Reverse the circle (jaw to the left, forward, right, and back) for five reps.

7. Now, make a front-to-back circle by taking the jaw forward, down, back, and up. Repeat for five reps.

8. Reverse the circle (jaw to the back, down, forward, and up) for five reps.

9. Reassess.

These are the most common errors for all of these jaw drills:

- Trying to achieve the jaw movements by moving the lips
- Trying to achieve the jaw movements by moving the neck
- Not breathing
- Moving the jaw too fast
- Missing part of the movement
- Tightening other facial muscles (eyebrows, cheeks)

Also, try these jaw motions while pulling down on your earlobes. These drills open the eustachian tubes, so they can be useful on planes or when getting over a clogged ear or sinus infection.

MUSCLE STRENGTH FOR THE JAW

Because eating is so important to the first brain, the jaw is an amazingly powerful area. A human should be able to create around 150–200 lbs. of force just by closing their molars. The Guinness World Record belongs to Richard Hofmann, who recorded a bite strength of 975 lbs. for two seconds in 1986.[60] Let's check out how strong your jaw is.

Masseter *(Fig. 10.4)*

1. Assess your voice and body.

2. Place your fingers on the sides of your face about an inch in front of your ears.

3. Close your jaw firmly; if you are in the right place, you should feel a symmetrical bulge of muscle outward against your fingers. Is this muscle easy to feel? Does one side feel stronger, or does one side move out farther than the other?

4. If there was a weaker side, put something (Z-vibe, cork, or rubber object) between the molars on the weak side and bite down. Palpate the weak masseter muscle now and try to get it to bulge out against your fingers. Hold for fifteen seconds.

5. Reassess.

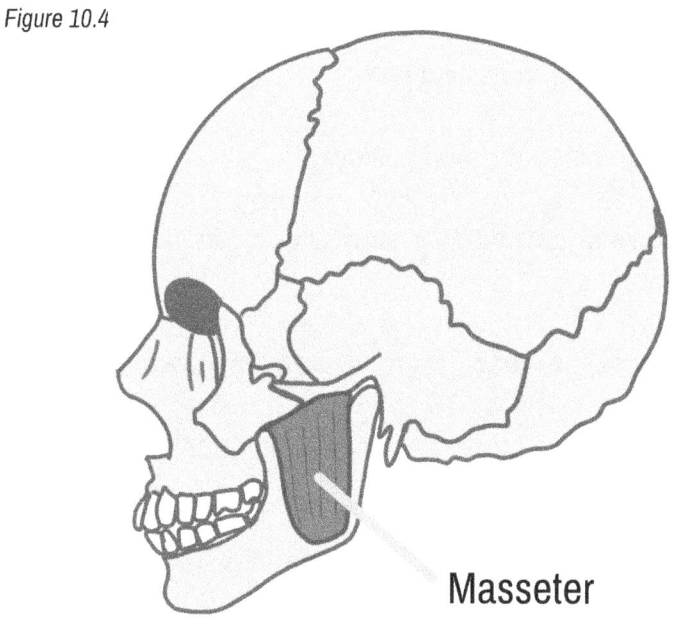

Figure 10.4

Temporalis *(Fig. 10.5)*

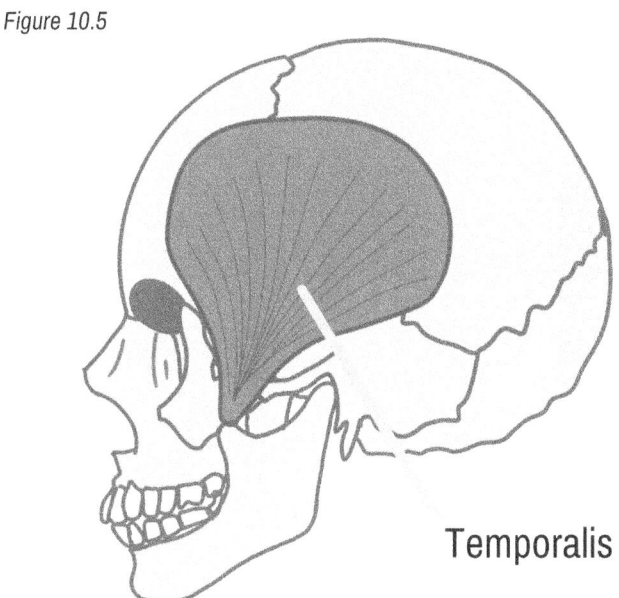

Figure 10.5

1. Assess your voice and body.

2. Place your fingers on the sides of your head. Your pointer fingers should be above your ears, and your pinkies should be on your temples.

3. Close your jaw firmly; if you are in the right place, you should feel a symmetrical bulge of muscle against your fingers when you clench. Does one side feel stronger/bulge out farther than the other?

4. With your fingers still on the sides of your head, slide your jaw forward and backward, as we did in the front-to-back glides. Do you feel a symmetrical muscle bulge on both sides as you slide backward?

5. If there was a weaker side, put something (pencil, tongue depressor, Z-vibe) between the molars on the weak side and bite down. Palpate the weak temporalis muscle and try to get it to bulge out against your fingers. Hold for fifteen seconds.

6. Reassess.

Medial Pterygoid

The more internal position of the pterygoids *(Fig. 10.6)* makes them easiest to access from within the mouth. These are tricky to describe, so I'd recommend watching the videos on thesingingathlete.com.

1. Assess your voice and body.

2. Using your right hand, reach across your mouth and place the pad of your right thumb between your upper and lower left molars. Slide backward until you feel the front edge of the ramus of the mandible (refer back to Figure 10.1 if needed). If you keep going further back with your thumb on the inside of the bone, you will find the medial pterygoid. (You may also feel the pterygomandibular raphe, which is a ligamentous band that attaches the sphenoid bone to the mandible.)

3. Press into the muscle at a three on a scale of ten in terms of pressure. Is there any tenderness here?

4. Take the pointer and middle fingers of your left hand and press the same spot from the outside.

5. Moving very slowly, slide both your right thumb and your left fingers forward. As this happens, let your jaw hang.

6. Reassess.

7. Repeat Steps 2–5 on the other side.

8. Reassess.

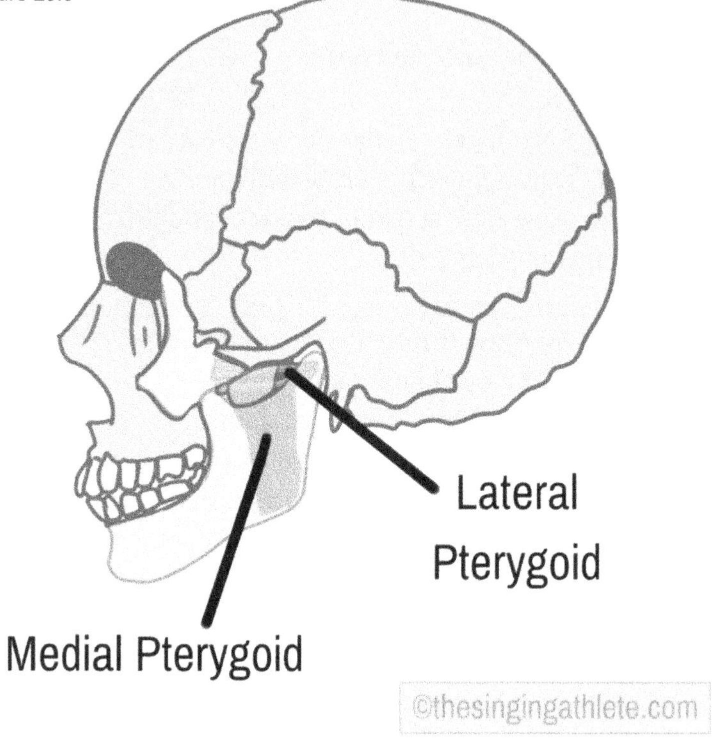

Lateral Pterygoid

1. Assess your voice and body.

2. Take your right pointer finger and put it on the outside of your upper left gums (across your mouth), with the pad of the finger pointing out toward the cheek. Slide your finger backward along the gums; you'll eventually come to a pocket of space in the upper back inside corner of the mouth (if you can't find it, slide your jaw a little bit to the left). You are now on (or close to) the lateral pterygoid.

Figure 10.6

3. Press backward into the muscle lightly to assess for any tenderness.

4. Take the pointer and middle fingers of your left hand and press the same spot from the outside.

5. As you press up and out with your right pointer finger (from the inside), draw the fingers of your left hand down the outside of the cheek. Hold for 10-15 seconds.

6. Reassess.

7. Repeat Steps 2–5 on the other side.

8. Reassess.

Jaw Isometrics

Isometrics are the lowest-threat form of strength training, and they have been shown to decrease pain, making them an excellent option for a sensitive area like the jaw. As a review, an isometric is an exercise where there is muscle tension but no movement. These are static positions, but they should feel pleasantly active in your muscles. In each variation, the goal is to keep the tongue in the spot. Remember your minimal effective dose (it's easy to overdo these) and reassess after each direction.

Opening

- Place both thumbs under the front edge of your chin and open your mouth slightly (.75 inches/2 cm). As you push up with your thumbs, push your jaw down into your fingers and hold for fifteen seconds. You should feel muscular work under your chin and possibly in or near your jaw hinge.

Closing

- Hook your pointer fingers over your lower front teeth. Close your mouth and pull down with your fingers (experiment until you find a place that this doesn't hurt your fingers). Continue closing against the resistance from your fingers and hold for fifteen seconds.

To the right

- Place your right hand on the right side of your jaw. Press your jaw to the right, meeting the pressure by pushing your right hand to the left. Hold for fifteen seconds.

To the left

- Place your left hand on the left side of your jaw. Press your jaw to the left, meeting the pressure by pushing your left hand to the right. Hold for fifteen seconds.

Forward

- Place your pointer fingers on either side of the front of your chin. Press your jaw forward, pushing backward with your fingers. Continue sliding the jaw forward into the resistance from your fingers and hold for fifteen seconds.

Back

- Hook your pointer fingers behind the bottom of the jawbone (in front of your earlobes). Slide the jaw back and pull forward with your fingers. This spot can be quite sensitive (there are a bunch of lymph nodes here), so experiment until you find a point of resistance that feels comfortable. Continue sliding back into the resistance from your fingers and hold for fifteen seconds.

TEETH AND YOUR VOICE

I find that most singers have never considered their dental past as relevant to their voice training *(Fig. 10.7)*. And yet the teeth are very close to many structures we think about all the time in singing. If you have a complicated dental history, the nerve connections in your teeth may be impacting your ability to control your tongue, jaw, and resonance. Additionally, neural input from your teeth can cause reflexive neck muscle overactivation and can affect postural stability in your entire body.[61]

Reach into your mouth and grasp one of your molars (the broad, flat teeth toward the back). Move it around a bit (side to side, front to back, in a circle, in a twisting motion). Can you feel the slight movements that are possible? Your teeth are more mobile than you may think. Each one is innervated by a branch of the trigeminal nerve (CN V), which also controls facial vibration, all the chewing muscles, and the sensation in the front of your tongue. When you think about it, it makes good sense to have the same nerve controlling your teeth and your tongue, so you don't bite your tongue off when you're eating.

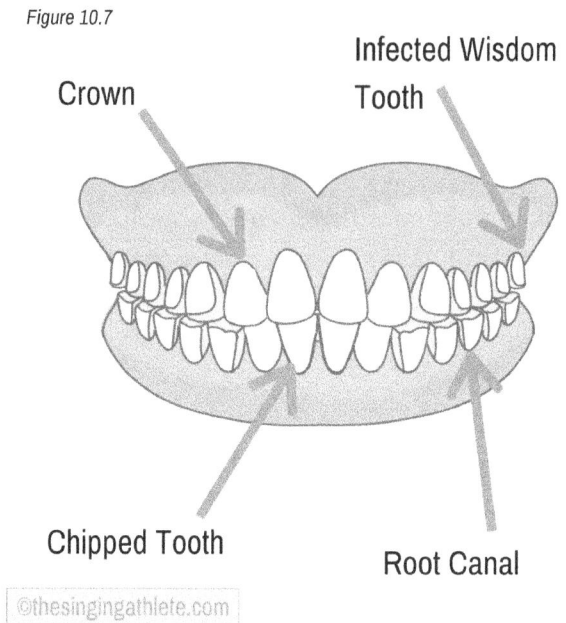

Figure 10.7

Let's use the teeth to learn how to pressure-check a body part.

Pressure-Checking your Teeth

Pressure checking is a simple concept, but its application can be profound. When you pressure-check, you are asking the first brain whether a certain kind of physical contact, direction, and pressure is either raising or lowering threat. You will be using your fingers to move a body part. If the direction and force applied results in an improved range of motion and freer singing, you've lowered threat. If the reassessment is negative, either the threat is too high in that area, or you didn't find the right direction and pressure. Pressure checking can be especially useful after a surgery or injury; you can "ask" the brain if the body area in question is ready to be handled. I'll address this more in Chapter 12.

You can pressure-check any body part (e.g., skin, fascia, nerves, joints, skull), but this section will explain how to do it with a tooth. If you've had a filling, crown, or any other work done on a specific tooth, use that tooth for this drill. If you haven't had any dental work, choose a tooth on the side of your jaw that was more problematic in the earlier drills.

1. Before making contact with the tooth, find a range of motion that feels at least somewhat limited and do the movement a few times to get a sense of how the body is moving. Make sure whatever motion you're using isn't going to be hard to repeat while touching the tooth. Some good options are: neck rotation/tilting, shoulder flexion/abduction/internal rotation/external rotation, hip flexion/extension.

2. Place your thumb and pointer finger lightly on the tooth.

3. While keeping the contact on the tooth, reassess your range of motion.

4. If that was a neutral or positive reassessment (your range of motion stayed the same or increased), begin to move the tooth around, looking for directions that don't want to move easily. Try rotating the tooth as well.

5. Move the tooth toward a sticky area and, while holding that pressure, reassess.

6. If that went well, hold the pressure for a few more seconds. If that didn't go well, try pulling the tooth in the opposite direction. For example, if the tooth doesn't want to spin to the left, turn it to the right.

7. While keeping a hold in that direction, reassess.

8. If neither of those reassesses well, try some other directions and repeat.

9. Keep reassessing as you check different directions.

When you've had any dental surgeries more serious than filling a cavity, you probably have some rehab left to do in that area of your mouth. This is especially true in the case of a root canal, which is essentially a nerve ablation, where sensory fibers that carry signals to the brain are destroyed.

You can rehab teeth by repeating your high-payoff pressure-check directions; hold your good direction a little bit longer each time you practice. If you're also open to getting a tool to help you with dental sensation, a good option is a Z-vibe, which has a textured biting surface that vibrates, allowing you to regain sensation in teeth and gums. An electric toothbrush can also work for this drill.

1. Assess your voice and body.

2. Turn the Z-vibe/toothbrush on and place it on the tooth in question.

3. Reassess.

4. If the reassessment was negative, stop. If it was positive or neutral, try biting down on the Z-vibe/toothbrush, trapping it between the tooth you are testing and its upper or lower opposite.

5. Reassess.

If this went well, spend a little time in each practice session with the Z-vibe on the affected tooth.

Tooth vibration is useful for rehab, but even if you have no history of dental problems, it can be a game-changer. There is an area of the brain called the ***supplementary motor area (SMA)***, which is involved in coordinated bilateral stability. Musicians have a higher gray-matter concentration in the SMA, and this area of the brain is active during any musical performance or vocal activity.[62, 63] The SMA helps to activate any bilateral midline structure, such as the larynx, the diaphragm, and the pelvic floor.[64][65]

Here's the cool thing: the SMA responds to tooth vibration.[66] If you're looking for a way to directly improve vocal coordination, stick a Z-vibe or electric toothbrush between your teeth when you sing. I've seen tons of people drastically improve their physical and vocal ranges when they bite a Z-vibe, and this connection to the SMA may be why.

11. NOSE AND SKULL

Before we look at how nifty the nose is, let's take a moment to remember why breathing through it is a good idea:

- Nasal breathing warms and humidifies the incoming air, which vocal folds strongly prefer.

- The nose provides a filtering system. If you're in a city like NYC, a nose breath catches more of the crap in the environment before it reaches your lungs.

- Nasal breathing slows your rate of respiration. The simplest way to reduce any tendency toward anxiety and hyperventilation is to breathe through your nose.

NOSE BASICS

The inside of your nose is made up of two nasal cavities, divided in the middle by a septum, which is both cartilage and bone *(Fig. 11.1)*. A deviated septum is a condition in which the cartilage becomes crooked, either through direct trauma to the face or a more subtle, long-term process. This deviation can make nasal inhalation difficult and lead to problems where the sinuses cannot drain correctly. If you have chronic issues with breathing through both nostrils equally, it's worth seeing an ENT to confirm if there is a deviation and how significant it is. I generally see surgery as a last resort, but if I had a strongly deviated septum, I would have it corrected; that is how important I believe nasal breathing is.

In the interior of each side of the nose, you have three long, narrow shelves of bone called **nasal turbinates**. The superior turbinates are the smallest and the inferior are the biggest (about the size of your index finger). The turbinates are comprised mostly of mucosal tissue that is connected to your trigeminal nerve (CN V). The erectile tissue in the turbinates can cause congestion due to environmental, immunological, or neurological reasons.

The inferior turbinates also can go through a usually unnoticed process called the **nasal cycle**, where alternate sides of the nose will become partially congested for a period of time (somewhere between fifteen minutes and several hours). Not all adults experience a nasal cycle, so take a moment to individually assess your nostrils.

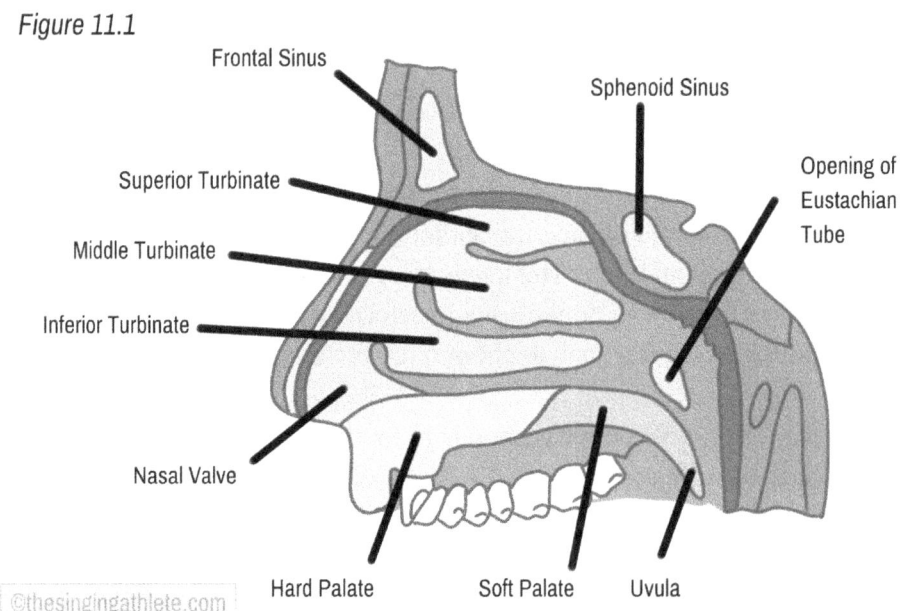

Figure 11.1

Nostril Check

1. Plug your left nostril and breathe in and out through the right. Keep your lips closed. How easily does the air come in and out on this side?

2. In a modest range, keep your left nostril plugged and hum a note through the right nostril only. How much sound is leaving?

3. Switch to plugging your right nostril and breathe in and out through the left. Keep your lips closed. Is the breathing easier or harder on this side?

4. Hum the same note through your left nostril with your right nostril plugged. How much sound leaves on this side?

If you noticed a sizable difference, keep checking this for a few days. If the congestion is slight and it keeps switching, this is probably just the nasal cycle doing its thing, which is perfectly normal. If it's always more plugged on one side, there may be either a deviation or a difference in hemispheric brain activation. If you notice that one side is usually more open than the other, the opposite side of your brain may be the dominant one (i.e., if your left nostril is generally more open, your right brain may be more active).

Yogic practices have employed one-nostril breathing techniques for millennia, and current research is backing up the validity of these regimens. If you remember from the larynx chapter, the vagus nerve is involved in parasympathetic (calming) responses. The left vagus is more parasympathetic and the right more sympathetic (activating). Breathing through the left nostril communicates with the left vagus, resulting in a calmer autonomic system.[67] Conversely, right-nostril breathing can be associated with an increase in blood pressure and heart rate. If you're trying to chill out, breathe through your left nostril; if you're trying to gear up, breathe through your right nostril.

Think back on what I said about fixing a deviated septum; now it might make more sense why this is a big deal. If you're always getting more air in one nostril, it may be globally affecting your energy and stress levels.

Nasal Valve Test

When you inhale, air passes through an area known as the ***nasal valve*** *(Fig. 11.2)*, which is the narrowest passageway in the nostril. The triangular borders of the nasal valve are the inferior turbinate, the septum, and the side of the nostril. If your nasal valve has a tendency to collapse, it can cause breathing problems and congestion. Here's how to test yours:

1. Take a breath through both nostrils. How easily does the air enter?

2. Hum a note. How easily does the sound come out?

3. Place your right and left pointer and middle fingers on both sides of your nose and pull outward *(Fig. 11.2)*. Take a breath; is it easier to inhale now? Hum again; how easily does the sound leave?

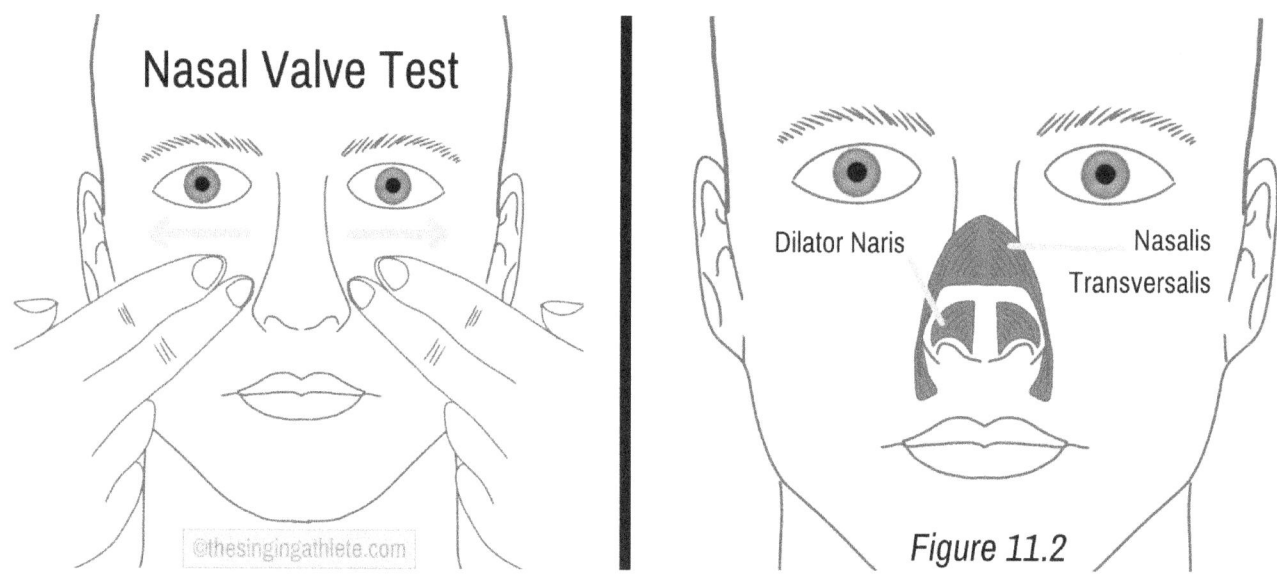

Figure 11.2

If you noticed an improvement with the fingers pulling the sides of the nose out, add that maneuver to your practice. You can also try using Breathe-Right strips, which you can get at any drug store.

Another great drill is practice opening your nostrils actively. The **dilator naris** and **nasalis transversalis** muscles are both supposed to be active during inhalation. Studies have shown that these muscles are usually underdeveloped in people with collapsed nasal valves.[68] When someone has a deviated septum, these same muscles often don't fire on the side toward which the deviation goes. By actively widening your nostrils and the bridge of your nose, you can improve muscle tone, resulting in easier nasal breathing.

OLFACTORY NERVE

Your olfactory (smell) nerve (CN I) is one of the two cranial nerves not found in your brainstem, the other being your optic nerve (CN II). Unlike the other senses, which travel through the thalamus (the "gatekeeper" of the brain), the olfactory nerve connects directly with the limbic (emotional) brain areas. This path explains why certain smells transport you powerfully back to distant memories. Your olfactory nerve also has a direct line to your hypothalamus, which regulates your hormones. CN I also sends signals to your brainstem, helping with postural control and pain inhibition.

One of the most common early signs of dementia and Alzheimer's disease is a loss of olfaction, so it pays to keep this sense up.[69] Additionally, because of the direct connection of the nose to the sinuses, a singer needs to make sure that their olfactory nerve is functioning well.

We're about to do some smell testing, so let's take a moment to talk about essential oils. While many performers swear by them, there is also some evidence of their toxicity,[70] and it's my opinion that they should not be ingested. I think they are fine for olfactory use, but if you have any concerns about them, the test below can be done with anything that has a smell you enjoy.

Smell Test

1. Find two things with an identifiable and pleasant smell.

2. Close your eyes and block your left nostril. Slowly move the first item you've chosen toward your right nostril. Stop when you can identify the smell; notice how far away the object is from your nostril.

3. Switch to closing your right nostril and slowly bring the same item toward your left nostril with your eyes closed. Stop when you can identify the smell, comparing the distance you had to get to before you could identify it with the left nostril.

4. Repeat Steps 2–3 with the second item, but this time start with the right nostril closed.

5. When looking at both tests, was there a nostril that you had to get closer to before you could smell the item? If so, that's the weak olfactory side.

If you identified a weaker side, try the drill below.

Olfactory Nerve Stimulus

1. Assess your voice and body.

2. Close the stronger nostril and put one of the items from the Smell Test right in front of your weaker nostril.

3. Take 3–5 deep, full inhalations, trying to get as much of the smell into that nostril as possible.

4. Reassess.

It's also smart to do the Smell Test with ammonia. The smell of ammonia is processed in the trigeminal nerve, not the olfactory nerve. Since it's a different and very important nerve, the results of testing with ammonia can be quite illuminating. If you find a weak ammonia side, take a whiff on the weak side and reassess your voice. A quick sniff of ammonia is also worth trying for sinus problems.

SINUSES

The *sinuses (Fig. 11.3)* are air-filled chambers extending from the nasal cavity. Since they are outgrowths of the nose (their full name is the paranasal sinuses), they are all designed to drain back into the nose. There are openings on the top and outside of your nasal cavity that connect to each of your four sinuses:

- The *frontal sinuses* are found in the forehead, right above the middle portion of the eyebrows.

- The *sphenoid sinuses* lie farther back, nearer the center of the skull. The sphenoid sinuses are only separated from the pituitary gland by a thin layer of bone.[71] When the sphenoid sinuses vibrate in singing, it's possible there could be a resultant stimulus to the pituitary gland (another reason to practice).

- The *ethmoid sinuses* are in front of the sphenoid sinuses, behind the eyes and bridge of the nose.

- The *maxillary sinuses* are the biggest of the four and lie under your cheekbones, at the sides of your nose. Fluid can drain from the other sinuses into the maxillary sinuses, making them more prone to infection.

No one is sure why we have sinuses.[72] Some theories are:

- They lighten the weight of the skull.

- They help with facial growth.

- They moisten and warm inhaled air.

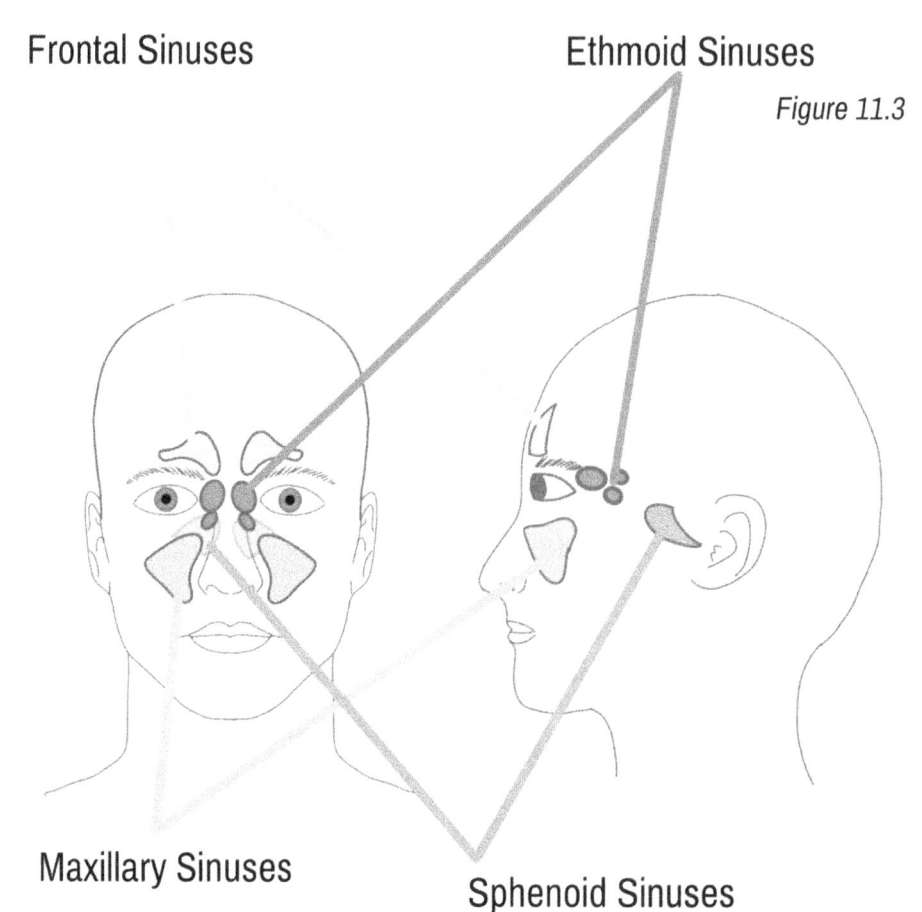

Figure 11.3

Whatever the reason you have them, improving sinus resonance can help singing feel less effortful. All the sinuses are innervated by the trigeminal nerve (CN V). If there is chronic congestion here, the nerve signals are reduced and you cannot feel where the sound should go. (Remember, CN V also controls facial and skull vibration.) To sing with a clear resonance, you need clear sinuses.

These are my favorite sinus drills:

Sinus Drill 1—Plug 'n' Shake

The Plug 'n' Shake works by trapping CO^2 in your nose, which is a vasodilator (i.e., it opens blood vessels up). By pushing the CO^2 into every corner of your nose and sinuses through head movement, you will reduce congestion and open the airway.

1. Take a breath in through your nose, noticing how clear your nose and sinuses currently feel.

2. Exhale through your nose until you are 80 percent out of air.

3. Plug your nose with one hand and close your mouth.

4. While holding your breath, perform a few reps of the following motions:

    - Shake your head "no"

    - Shake your head "yes"

    - Tilt your head from side to side

    - Make a circle with your head in both directions

    - Do some free-form shaking

5. Keep going until you feel a moderate desire to inhale. Take a new breath and repeat Steps 2–4 three more times.

6. Reassess by breathing in again through your nose, seeing if it feels clearer.

Sinus Drill 2—Vibration

1. Assess your voice and body.

2. Place your fingers on your maxillary sinuses (on either side of your nose), pressing in lightly.

3. Hum on a siren up and down, trying to find a pitch and volume that produces the most vibration in your fingertips.

4. Once you've found the optimal pitch, maintain it for twenty seconds (breathing when you need to).

5. Reassess.

You can also do this drill with the fingertips on the bridge of your nose/under your eye socket (ethmoid sinus), on either side of the center area right above your eyebrows (frontal sinus), and the temples (sphenoid bone/sinus).

If you need more stimulus, you can use a Z-vibe, a face massager, or anything else that vibrates. Hum and match the internal vibration intensity (not necessarily the pitch) to the external one. You can also put any object on the sinuses and send the vibration into the object.

My other favorite sinus drills are:

- *Air Hunger Drills:* Builds CO^2 systemically, which opens all tissues up, including sinuses (see Chapter 4).

- *Any of the drills in Chapter 10:* The jaw and the sinuses are both controlled by the trigeminal nerve.

- *Trigeminal/Facial Nerve Glide:* Stretches the nerve that controls your sinuses (we'll learn this one later in the chapter).

- *Sphenoid Mobilization:* Moves the bone that contains the sphenoid sinus and is close to the other sinuses (we'll learn this one later in the chapter).

NASAL BREATHING AND EXERCISE

Let's take a moment to define the three energy systems used by the body:

- *Alactic:* The fastest energy-producing system. It can create maximal effort for about 10–12 seconds. It can be trained through sprints, jump squats, or other explosive movements.

- *Glycolytic*: Produces energy of moderate-to-high intensity for 90–120 seconds by burning glucose (blood sugar) or glycogen (stored sugar). It can be trained with any speed-intensive general exercise.

- *Aerobic:* A stable, efficient system that utilizes fats and oxygen. Because it relies on respiration to drive the oxygen exchange in the cells, it cannot produce explosive power. It can be trained through activities such as jogging/brisk walking, hiking, swimming, biking, etc.

One of the main reasons to train these systems is to improve your respiratory and cardiovascular health. Cardiac output, which is the amount of blood that the heart pumps through the circulatory system over a given time, is a big part of staying alive. I like to train my alactic/glycolytic systems with things like hill sprints, push-ups, squats, etc., and I practice them all hypoxically (see Chapter 4). Here's a sprint drill for alactic and glycolytic training:

Sprinting Drill

1. Exhale 80 percent of your air and hold your breath at the end of the exhalation.

2. Sprint for as many strides as possible on this exhaled breath-hold.

3. When you can go no more, stop and take your first inhalation as a nasal breath. Get your breath back under control in one cycle of inhale/exhale.

4. Once you have recovered, repeat for ten reps.

Breathing Pattern for Aerobic Exercise

Nasal breathing provides more resistance to inhalation than mouth breathing; the air comes in more slowly. Knowing this, it would seem to make sense to switch to mouth breathing when you are taxing your lung during aerobic exercise. However, even under load, nasal breathing creates a stronger vacuum in the lungs, which increases total lung volume and improves arterial oxygen concentration.[73] Also, when you nose-breathe, you experience more efficient oxygen extraction on inhalation and more steady CO_2 excretion on exhalation. From a psychological standpoint, nose breathing makes the demands of exercise less threatening. Your brain knows that mouth breathing is a last resort, so it thinks, "Well, if you're breathing through the nose, this jog can't be all that bad." For your next workout, give this a try:

1. Breathe in and out through your nose as you exercise (at dance class, running, brisk walking, biking, hiking, interval training, cardio workouts, flow yoga, etc.).

2. If you come to a challenging section of the workout, nose-breathe until you can't anymore, then switch to an inhalation through your nose and an exhalation through your mouth.

3. If you can't maintain the "nose in/mouth out" breathing pattern, walk or slow down for a bit until you can resume nasal breathing.

In a northern climate, the weather isn't always so conducive to outdoor running, but I'd rather bundle up than run on a treadmill. There are a couple of reasons why I don't use them:

- When your proprioceptive and your visual systems aren't getting the same information, that is called sensory mismatch (see Chapter 13). Sensory mismatch can cause a lot of nasty things, like pain, vertigo, and spinal problems. When you run on a treadmill, your eyes are telling your brain that you are stationary, but your feet are contradicting that information. This conflict has been shown to lead to visual disturbances and could contribute to other maladaptive postural processes.[74]

- The constant backward motion of a treadmill means that your gait is not the same as walking or running on solid ground, which affects the activation of your posterior-chain muscles.[75] Elliptical machines also do not do a good job of mirroring reflexive gait mechanics.

If you are in a bad-weather situation, try these training options:

- Take a dance class
- Take a workout class
- Use a rower or stationary bike (these don't mess with your primal gait patterns)
- Find an indoor track
- Do yoga or Pilates
- Use an online workout video
- Bundle up and run through the crappy weather (C'mon! You can do it!).

NASAL BREATHING AND MEMORIZATION

A 2016 study found that nasal breathing helps you memorize information.[76] The way that the nose regulates airflow seems to be related to coordination in your brain's neural networks. Here are the key findings:

- Memory was more accurate during inhalation.

- Memory was better with nose breathing.

One of the common "audition disaster" stories I hear is forgetting lyrics in the room. And yet, most of us have never paid attention to our breathing when we are encoding (memorizing) our text. Try this the next time you are throwing a patter song into your voice for a callback:

- Consciously inhale slowly and diaphragmatically through your nose as you learn the lyrics of the song.

- If you're stressed by memorization, close your right nostril and breathe in through your left while memorizing. This will calm you down.

- If you're bored by memorization, close your left nostril and breathe in through your right while memorizing. This will get your energy up.

FACIAL SENSATION AND SINGING

As I've said previously, the nose and sinuses are fed by your all-important trigeminal nerve *(Fig. 11.4)*. You have three branches of this nerve:

- **Ophthalmic Branch (V1):** This uppermost branch of the nerve supplies sensation to your upper eyelid, your forehead, and the front/middle portion of your scalp, as well as three of your sinuses (e.g., frontal, ethmoid, sphenoid). If your eyes water a lot, this is a branch worth addressing.

- **Maxillary Branch (V2):** The middle branch of the nerve controls your lower eyelid, your cheekbones, and your biggest sinuses

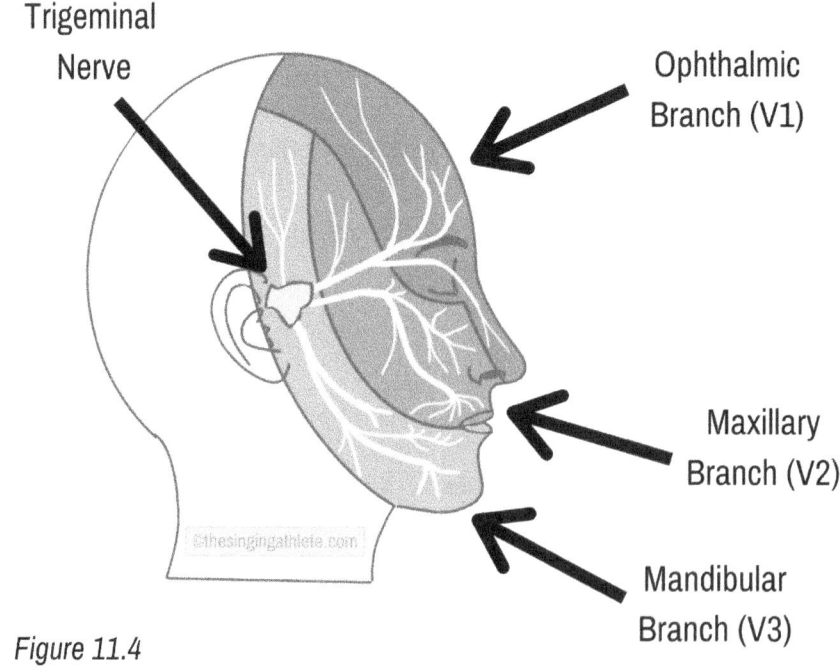

Figure 11.4

(maxillary). It also provides sensation to your upper teeth and lip, your palate, and most of your nose.

- *Mandibular Branch (V3):* The lowest branch is the only one to have motor functions, controlling all the muscles of mastication as well as the tensor tympani in your ears and the tensor veli palatini in your palate. It also provides sensation to your chin, lower lip, bottom row of teeth, and the front two-thirds of your tongue.

You are looking to have equal feeling in all of these branches on both sides. Let's do a test to see how your sensation symmetry is:

Facial Sensation Test 1—Light Touch

1. Twist the end of a tissue until it makes a point.

2. Run the tip of the tissue along the left side of your forehead, then the right. Is the sensitivity the same on both sides?

3. Run the tip of the tissue along the left side of your cheekbone, then the right. Is the sensitivity the same on both sides?

4. Run the tip of the tissue along the left side of your jawbone, then the right. Is the sensitivity the same on both sides?

5. Did any part of the face feel particularly dull or hypersensitive?

Another critical trigeminal assessment for a singer is vibration. To do this one, you need either a tuning fork, a Z-vibe, or a gentle massager. I prefer to use either a C-128 or a C-256 tuning fork, so that's how I'll describe it here.

Facial Sensation Test 2—Vibration

1. Hold the rounded end of the tuning fork in your dominant hand, making sure not to touch the flat part. Start the tuning fork vibrating by tapping the circular ends together. I usually tap it on the outside of the heel of my hand on the pinky side.

2. While it's still vibrating, place the handle of the tuning fork (the small rounded end) on the left side of your forehead. Retap the tuning fork, then do it on the right. Did it feel the same on both sides?

3. Retap the fork and place the handle on the left cheekbone. Retap, then do it on the right. Did it feel the same on both sides?

4. Retap the fork and place the handle on the left side of your jawbone. Retap, then do it on the right. Did it feel the same on both sides?

5. Did all three branches feel the same up and down?

When we discuss "placement" in singing, we are really talking about our ability to feel vibration in our bones. The term for this sense is **bone conduction**, which I will discuss in more detail in Chapter 13. I've tested the bone conduction of these three trigeminal branches on a whole lot of singers. Experientially, this is the trend I've seen:

- Singers who struggle to find chest voice (thick folds) often have a reduced sense of vibration in V3 (this is often paired with a lack of sensation on the collarbones and sternum).

- Singers who struggle with mixing and high belting often have a reduced sense of vibration in V2.

- Singers who struggle with head voice (thin folds) often have a reduced sense of vibration in V1.

One of the biggest causes of phonotrauma (pushing your voice until you hurt yourself) is an inability to feel vibration. A reduction in vibratory sensation can cause you to increase air pressure on the vocal folds in an effort to project. If you train yourself to feel vibration better in your face, you may stop adding needless strain to your voice.

If you found sensory issues in any of these facial areas, the test is the drill. By this I mean, if you had a reduced vibration in your right forehead, put a vibrator or tuning fork on your right forehead when you practice. Sing in a way that matches from the inside what the external vibration feels like on the outside. The nerves are still there; they just need to be told to wake up.

FACIAL STRUCTURE AND SINGING

The human eye is designed to see facial symmetry as aesthetically pleasing. The celebrities that we think are the most beautiful generally have precisely symmetrical features. We respond favorably to this because our first brains perceive symmetry as representing health. As we age or become ill, facial features tend to become less balanced, and so we view an even face as representing a vital brain and body.[77]

> Let's talk for a moment about cosmetic treatments like Botox, Restalyne, etc. Botox is a neurotoxin that works by preventing nerve signals from reaching muscles. It has certain medical applications but is also used to change appearance. When it is injected into the face, it reduces fine lines and wrinkles through paralysis of the underlying muscles.
>
> Humans are designed to mirror emotions; if you see someone in pain, you mimic their facial expressions. This lets them know that you understand them and allows you to work through the feeling in your own body. When you remove your face's ability to mirror emotion, it can cause problems in processing emotion and relating to others. Beyond these emotional consequences, as a singer, you need to be able to feel your face. It's my opinion that no one should mess with that type of sensory awareness.

In the chapter on the tongue, we talked about how the facial nerve (CN VII) controls most of your taste and a portion of your hearing. CN VII also innervates all the muscles of facial expression. If one of your facial nerves is sleepy, it will affect the evenness of your appearance. Let's check where your facial symmetry currently is.

Facial Symmetry Test

1. Look in a mirror.

2. Smile as big as you can and hold it for ten seconds. Is one side not lifting as high as the other?

3. Relax the smile and raise your eyebrows as high as you can for ten seconds. Does one side start to sink as you maintain the lift?

4. Relax your eyebrows and puff your cheeks out and hold for ten seconds. Does one cheek not puff out as much?

If you noticed a difference, the side that is lifting/expanding less is the weak facial nerve. The following nerve stretch can fix the imbalance.

Facial/Trigeminal Nerve Glide

In this nerve glide, you are looking to feel a stretch sensation in front of the ear on the side that ends up facing toward the ceiling.

1. Assess your voice and body.

2. Tuck your chin as firmly as possible from the very top of your spine. Think of starting the tuck from between your ears; you should begin to feel a sensation of stretch in the skin on your scalp.

3. Without losing the chin tuck, slightly tilt your head AWAY from the weak facial-nerve side.

4. Without losing the tuck/tilt, begin to slightly round your whole neck forward (take your nose toward the ground). As this happens, the stretch sensation should increase, not decrease. If you are getting less stretch, you are probably not tucking your chin enough.

5. Open your mouth and glide your jaw AWAY from the weak side.

6. Perform several small nods/head shakes in this position.

7. Relax and reassess by looking at your smile/forehead-raise/cheek-puff again. Is it more symmetrical?

Because the facial and trigeminal nerves share a similar path, you can use this stretch for either nerve. For instance, if you felt a reduced sensation in the vibration on one side of your head, you could also use this stretch to wake up the trigeminal nerve and then reassess.

SINGING AND THE SKULL

In addition to the fourteen bones that make up the face, there are eight that form the housing for the skull *(Fig. 11.5)*:

- *Occipital (1)*
- *Parietal (2)*
- *Temporal (2)*
- *Frontal (1)*
- *Sphenoid (1)*
- *Ethmoid (1)*

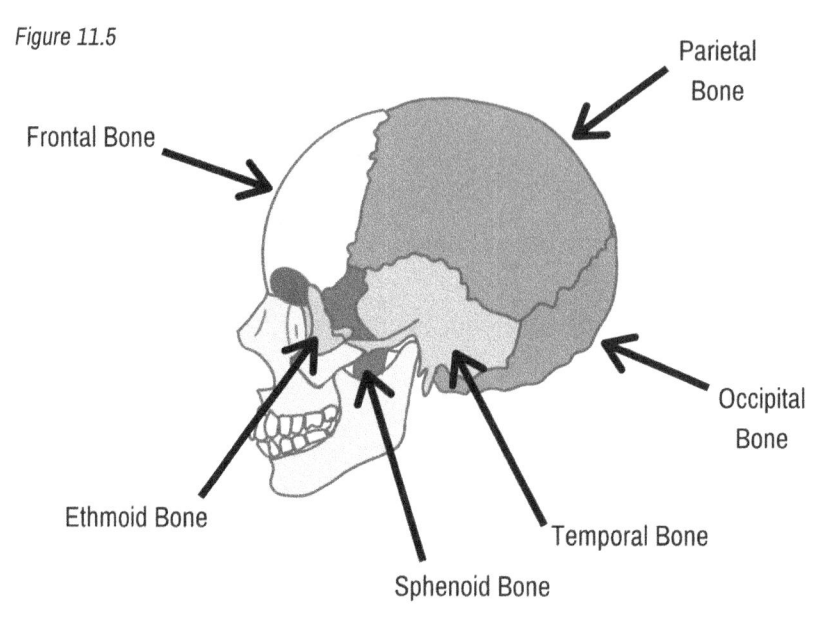

Figure 11.5

The joints that bring these bones together are called **cranial sutures**, which are fibrous seams found only in the skull. It was classically taught that the jaw is the only genuinely mobile joint in the cranial system. However, modern research and the effectiveness of skull-based bodywork suggest something else; these other cranial joints do seem to matter. There is a great deal of variety in how much movement is available in cranial joints among different people.[78] (As we go through the following mobilizations, bear that in mind; depending on your particular skull, it may or may not be easy to feel movement here.)

Regardless of mobility, we all have important nerve connections in this area. As your voice vibrates your skull, the sensations in the front and middle portions are processed by the trigeminal nerve (CN V). The back of the skull is taken care of by a combination of nerves, including the vagus (CN X). This means that the receptors in the skull have a direct connection into the brain itself.

Skull Exploration

1. Place your fingertips on either side of the skull above your ears.

2. Move the skin on both sides, looking for sticky directions or places that feel tender. Do both sides move equally?

3. Move your fingers up higher, so they are about equidistant between the tops of your ears and the center line of your skull. Repeat the exploration of the scalp here.

4. Move your fingers up, so they are on either side of the midline of the top of your skull. Is there any tenderness here?

5. Try some other places (forehead, back of the head) as well.

If you found a tender spot or an area that had less motion, let's work with it.

Skull Pressure-Checking

1. Assess your voice and body.

2. Find the tender/sticky spot and pull the skin of the scalp in the direction that feels the most stuck.

3. Hold it in that direction as you reassess.

4. If that didn't go well, try pulling it away from the direction that feels the most stuck.

5. Hold it in that direction as you reassess.

If you have a positive reassessment in a certain direction, hold this good angle when you are practicing tricky passages. If you've got the hair for it, you could even explore "neural braiding," where you pull or braid your hair in the scalp direction that gives you the best result. (Plus, think how fashionable you'll look.)

Sagittal Suture Mobility

There are many joints in the skull, but we are going to focus on two that tend to be most important for singers. The first is the *sagittal suture (Fig. 11.6)*, which joins the two parietal bones of the skull. Singing is highly activating to the somatosensory cortex, which lies right under this joint, so you want excellent mobility here.

Assessment

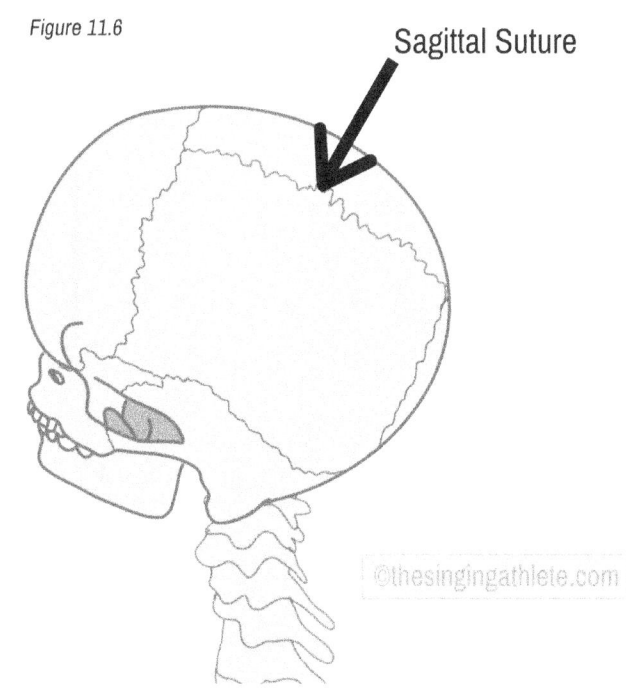

Figure 11.6

1. Place your fingers on either side of the top midline of the skull. You are trying to feel for a slightly raised ridge right down the middle. Once you've found it, settle all your fingers on either side of this ridge.

2. Inhale slowly and deeply. You are looking to feel a very slight, subtle widening of this joint on inhalation and a subtle contraction on exhalation.

3. Do both sides move equally? Does one side feel more stuck? Try to identify a side that feels tighter.

4. Now hum in a comfortable range. Do you feel symmetrical vibration in the skull here?

Mobility

1. Assess your voice and body.

2. With your hands by your side, tuck your chin from the very top of your upper neck as strongly as you can.

3. Without losing this upper-cervical flexion, tilt your head away from the tighter side of your skull.

4. Now, slowly round your neck slightly forward, being sure to keep your chin tucked.

5. Once you feel a stretch on the top of your skull, begin a slow, small nodding motion from the very top of your spine. Do 5–10 reps.

6. Reassess.

Sphenoid Bone Mobility

The ***sphenoid bone*** *(Fig. 11.7)* is a butterfly-shaped structure that attaches the face to the skull. It forms a portion of your eye sockets as well as serving as the anchor point for several muscles that move your jaw. The sphenoid houses the pituitary gland, so moving this bone can be important for lots of hormonal reasons. Proper sphenoid mobilization can even help astigmatism in your eye.[79]

You can palpate the sphenoid on the sides of your head; when you're touching your temples, you're on your sphenoid bone.

Assessment

1. Place your pointer fingers on both outer edges of your eye sockets.

2. Move your fingers about 2–3 finger-widths back and slightly up until you feel a broad, flat surface in your temple area. Your fingers are now on your sphenoid bone. Press into both

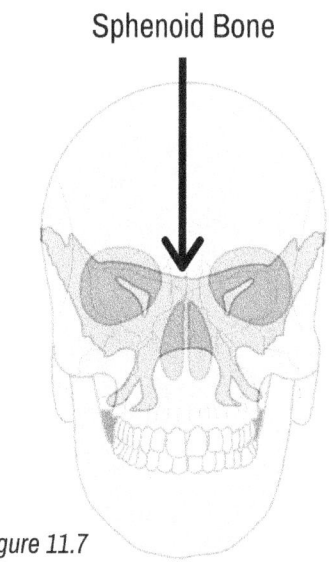

Figure 11.7

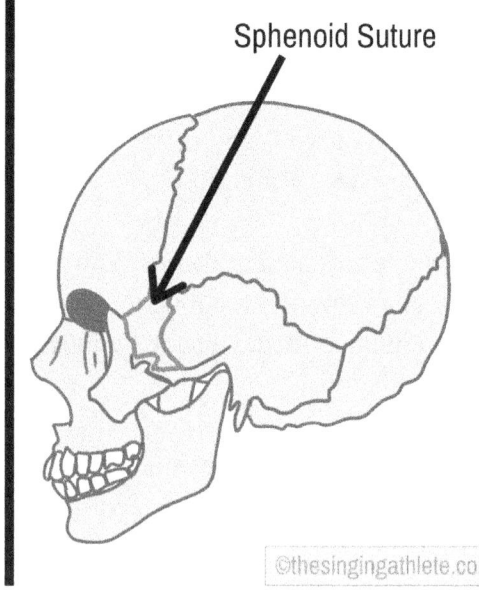

sides. Is there any soreness here?

3. Take several deep inhalations with your fingers lightly resting on the bone; you should feel a very slight expansion of this bone on both sides during inhalation. Is one side moving more than the other?

4. Hum a comfortable pitch. Do both sides of the sphenoid vibrate equally?

Mobility

1. Assess your voice and body.

2. Like in the sagittal suture exercise, tuck your chin down as strongly as you can, trying to initiate this movement from the very top of your spine, between your ears.

3. Without losing the chin tuck, turn your head 20–30 degrees TOWARD the side that feels stuck.

4. Without losing the head rotation, tilt your head slightly AWAY from the side on which you're working. This motion should be coming from the very top of your spine, not your whole neck.

5. Open your jaw a bit and glide the jaw AWAY from the side on which you're working.

6. Perform 5–10 small, slow nodding motions from the top of your spine. The goal is to feel the stretch/movement in the temple area of the side that is tilted up toward the ceiling. If you're not feeling a stretch, try tilting your head farther.

7. Reassess.

These mobilizers can be subtle, and they require some control of the upper neck that can be challenging. If you're having trouble with feeling these drills in the right place, here are some things to try:

- Place your fingers on the skull joint you are trying to move

- Put some vibration on the skull joint you are trying to move

- Perform the drill with your tongue in the spot

- Look up at the ceiling

- Take deep, slow breaths once you're in the full stretch position

- Do three swallows in the full stretch position.

12. SCARS

A scar is an area of prolonged threat.

Scars are mostly described as something that heals and then we move on. We tend to forget about them, particularly because they may bring up memories of traumatic events. The truth is, the skin in a scar will never be the same as it once was, and there needs to be a rehabilitation process on the scar itself and the area surrounding it.

I have a large scar on my left pelvic area from my childhood hernia surgery. As an adult, I hadn't given it much thought until I started rehabbing my elbow problems at the piano. As I worked through various methods to heal my arm, I found that my left abs were considerably weaker than my right. Whenever I did a core-focused yoga pose or Pilates exercise, my left side would shake. It had never occurred to me until Z-Health to check if my hernia scar was affecting my abdominal strength.

The prolonged-threat concept hit home for me when one of my coaches pressure-checked my scar and I broke into a full-body sweat. Just having it touched raised my threat level off the charts. I realized this was an area that needed attention, so I did some sensory work on and around it for several weeks.

After a couple of months of work, the pressure check went better, so I had my coach tape the scar with Kinesio Tape. That night I headed out the door to a concert gig. On my walk there, I passed a Thai restaurant and the smell caused a giant wave of nausea. I ducked into an alley, thinking I was going to hurl right then and there. I thought I had picked up some horrible stomach bug. Then I remembered the tape on my scar; I reached down and removed it, and the nausea immediately went away. Whoops. Definitely violated that "minimal effective dose" thing. I also noticed that I had broken out in a rash where the tape was, even though I had used this same tape in many other areas of my body with no problem. I was "allergic" to the tape in this one specific high-threat zone.

I left the scar alone for a bit; the next time I taped above it, not in contact with it. No nausea, good reassessment, so I kept up that version of taping for awhile. At a certain point, I redid the original "Pad Thai puke" taping pattern, and there was no longer a nausea or rash problem. I had reduced the threat enough to begin reintegrating the scar into my nervous system. My abdominal strength assessments started to improve: my plank-hold times got longer, and the shaking in my abs under high effort became more even.

Think through your history. Are there scars that you've not thought about recently? Have you had a C-section? Had your tonsils out? Do you have tattoos or piercings? A scar may be holding you back from getting to that next vocal level.

WHAT EXACTLY IS A SCAR?

A scar is tissue that grows in the place of skin after an injury or surgery. Organs can also produce scarring (a heart attack scars the cardiac muscles). Dermal scars are made up of collagen, just like normal skin, but it grows in a way that results in lower tissue quality and a more random arrangement of fibers *(Fig. 12.1)*. When it comes to movement, a scar has less elasticity than the skin around it.

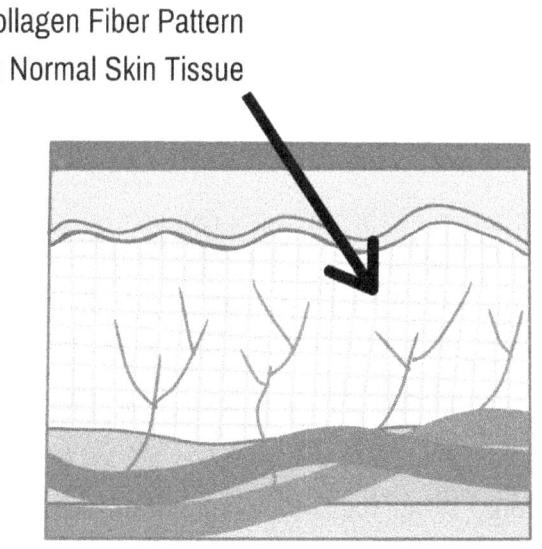
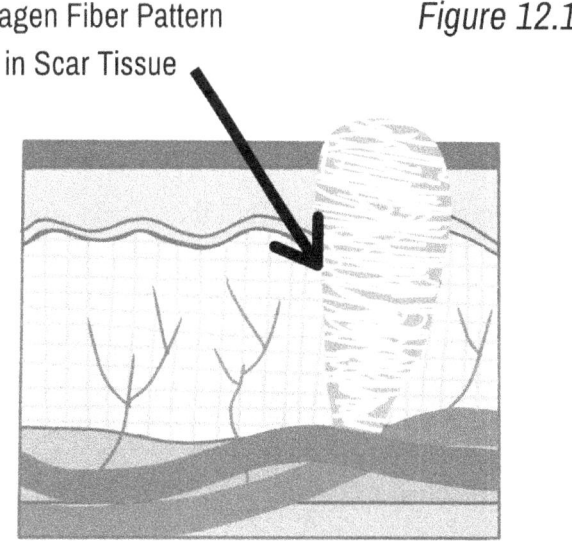

Figure 12.1

Collagen Fiber Pattern in Normal Skin Tissue

Collagen Fiber Pattern in Scar Tissue

If we accept that scars are areas of prolonged threat, it makes sense that they experience a lot of nociceptive activity even after they've "healed." The weird thing is, even though nociceptors are probably firing right now around any scars you have, you may not be experiencing pain in the area. And yet, your brain may be altering your movement based on these continuous threat signals.

This is why pressure checking is such a great tool for rehabbing scars. As a review, pressure checking is a way to determine if a certain kind of contact or movement is raising or lowering the threat level in the brain. When you touch and move a scar, you wake up the mechanoreceptors in the local tissue. Through a process called lateral inhibition, the receptors in the skin around the scar become suppressed, allowing more neural focus on the scar itself.

When your range of motion increases during a pressure check, we take that to be a lowering of threat. Global muscle tone is set by the brainstem, cerebellum, and vestibular systems (see Chapters 13 and 15). If you give your scar a stimulus that improves cortical activity by finding the right pressure and direction, these reflexive brain areas will "take the brakes off" and give you more fluid movement.

Pressure-Checking a Scar

If you have a scar you'd like to work with, identify it and make sure you can reach it easily. If it's somewhere hard for you to access, have a friend do the pressure check.

1. Before making contact with the scar, find a range of motion that feels at least somewhat limited and do the movement a few times to get a sense of how the joint is moving. Make sure whatever motion you're using isn't going to be hard to repeat while touching the scar. Some good options are: neck rotation/tilting, shoulder flexion/abduction/internal rotation/external rotation, hip flexion/extension.

2. Place your fingers lightly on the scar.

3. While keeping contact on the scar, reassess your range of motion.

4. If that was at least a neutral if not positive reassessment (your range of motion stayed the same or increased), begin to move the scar around, going through the eight compass points, including diagonals. Look for places that don't want to move easily.

5. Try gently pushing toward the "stuck" area and, while maintaining the pressure, reassess.

6. If that went well, hold it for a few more seconds. If that didn't go well, try pulling the scar in the opposite direction of the stuck area. For example, if the scar doesn't want to move down, pull it up.

7. While keeping a hold in that direction, reassess.

8. If neither of those reassesses well, try some other directions, or touch different parts of the scar and repeat.

9. Keep reassessing as you check different directions.

There are a few other things you can try:

- Pulling the scar apart (two fingers spread it apart)

- Pinching the scar together (two fingers pinch it together)

- Rotating the scar in both directions (especially good in arthroscopic surgeries or abdominal scars)

- Pressing deeper into the tissue and repeating the compass points

Let's say you had a good reassessment with one of these directions. If so, you might want to try taping the scar in that direction with Kinesio Tape. This kind of thing is more of a "watch and learn" experience, so watch the videos on thesingingathlete.com if you want to try this out.

Sensory Work for Scars

As I said, the skin around a scar is different, so there usually needs to be some rehab done on the dermal sensation:

- Put something cold on the scar, then on another area of skin nearby. Does the temperature feel the same?

- Repeat with something warm.

- Repeat with something like a toothbrush that can provide a light touch.

- Repeat with something that vibrates.

- Repeat with something that can alternate between sharp and dull. (I use a retracted mechanical pencil, alternating between the pencil end and the eraser end.)

If you found any of these sensations lacking, do 15–20 seconds of that type of stimulus and reassess your singing and movement. I can do a cleaner pull-up with a cold pack on my hernia scar; be curious about what limitations you could overcome if you had better sensation in a scarred area.

TATTOOS AND PIERCINGS

Tattoos and piercings are voluntary scars. If you love being inked and having a ring in your navel, that's cool. Just make sure you understand how to rehab a scar. I've seen several pianists get out of pain by pressure-checking and taping arm tattoos. I've also found many belters who find their facial resonance improves once they take a ring out of their nose.

You can pressure-check a tattoo using the same process detailed above. If you remember what part of it hurt the most when you got the ink, start your pressure-checking there. You can also pressure-check any red ink because that seems to be the most neurologically problematic color.[80] If it's really big (like a sleeve covering your arm), try a few different spots. You can also look up the ***motor points*** for that part of the body and pressure-check those areas. (Used in acupuncture, motor points are locations where the motor nerves of muscles come closest to the skin.)

As for a piercing, if you're set on keeping it in, try pulling it in different directions and go through the same assess/reassess process. See if your voice and body respond best to a particular direction of pull. If you're willing to consider taking it out, do this:

1. Assess your voice and body.

2. Take the piercing out.

3. Reassess.

I'm especially concerned about midline piercings (e.g., nose, lip, tongue, navel, genitals). A piercing can reduce your sensory awareness of an area, and singing is a midline activity coming out of the main trunk of your body. If you're serious about high-level performance, either do the work to rehab the piercing or get rid of it.

SCARRING IN THE MOUTH AND THROAT

If a singer has their tonsils out, there is understandable concern over whether the surgery will affect vocal production. In addition to getting used to a new space in the throat, part of the rehab process is addressing the resulting scarring.

Once the surgical sites have had time to heal, try to go through a pressure-check process, depending on how strong your gag reflex is. If you can identify a side where the throat infections usually started, begin the pressure check on that side. If not, try both sides.

1. Assess lateral neck flexion (ear to shoulder) on both sides.

2. Place your finger(s) on or near where the tonsils were removed.

3. Reassess lateral neck flexion.

4. If that went okay, move that area of the throat in several directions, looking for what feels sticky. Hold in that direction and reassess.

5. If the range of motion improved, hold the direction for a few more seconds and then take the fingers out and try singing. If it was a negative or neutral reassessment, move the tissue away from the "stuck" spot, spreading it out.

6. Reassess.

Another way to rehab tonsil scars is through vibration around the scar. The same rules that apply to rehabbing dental surgeries with a Z-vibe or electric toothbrush can be applied here. Also, the drills in the section on the soft palate are essential for rehabbing tonsil surgeries.

EMOTIONAL AND CREATIVE SCARRING

The definition of a scar as an area of prolonged threat can apply to emotional and creative matters as well. Much like the disorganized collagen that regrows around a surgical incision, negative experiences can create a plastic change where neural pathways become altered and fire in less-than-ideal directions when certain situations arise. If you've had episodes in your history where there has been a pattern of emotional abuse, or if someone stomped on your creative impulses, it's worth thinking about rehabbing these scars. The drills that could be useful are:

- VOR (Chapter 13)

- VOR-C (Chapter 13)

- Smooth Pursuits (Chapter 14)

- Saccades (Chapter 14)

- Pencil Push-up (Chapter 14)

- Any of the drills in Chapter 17

This is how you would test them:

Creativity Scar Rehab

1. Think about a time when something happened that caused an emotional or creative scar. Give it a numerical rating on a scale of ten as to how upset it makes you to think about this.

2. Do several reps of one of the drills listed above.

3. Reassess by thinking about the event again. If the emotional number is lower (you feel less upset after the drill), you have found a high-payoff drill. Do this drill regularly for several weeks and reassess by checking in with how you are feeling.

13. EARS

Think about the typical equipment found at a playground. There are things that spin you (merry-go-round), drop you (slides and poles), arc you (swings), and slide you forward and back (zip-line, if you have a really cool playground). As a culture, we inherently understand that kids need to move regularly in a great variety of directions. What about adults? Don't we still need that type of stimulation?

One of the culturally approved ways that grownups seek this type of inner-ear excitement is through listening to music and moving along with it. (When an '80s classic comes on, I often find myself bopping my noggin along.) Music engenders movement, and some authors believe that music itself developed out of our physical selves. Studies have shown that we gravitate toward musical tempi that are consistent with the speed of our walking gait.[81] Moving the body can also enhance listening. In training methods like Dalcroze Eurythmics, concepts of rhythm and musical expression seem to be retained better when taught through movement exploration.[82]

There is one cranial nerve that is most responsible for your ability to appreciate and make music; it's called the **vestibulocochlear nerve (CN VIII)**. This one nerve controls both your **vestibular system** (the official name for the sensory organs in your inner ears that provide the sense of balance) and the majority of your hearing, which is processed in the **cochlea.** CN VIII is the first nerve in the body to be myelinated (insulated), around five months in-utero. This fact seems to argue for the primal importance of acoustic and balance skills.[83]

The rhythmic aspects of music intertwine with the vestibular system. A lack of proper vestibular input can alter your perception of the metrical structure of rhythm.[84] In other words, if your balance sucks, you can't feel the beat. If you are someone who has trouble being rhythmically "in the pocket" when you sing, the balance drills in this chapter will be great for you to explore.

Figure 13.1

Meanwhile, the melodic aspects of music are more the domain of the cochlea, which we will study later in the chapter. The more rhythmic a musical genre is, the more vestibularly focused it is, with melodically driven music being more cochlear. Figure 13.1 is an over-simplified chart of how musical styles intersect with CN VIII. (There are obviously many exceptions within these genres.) Do you gravitate more to vestibular or cochlear music? In your singing, do you have more trouble with intonation or with staying in rhythm?

VESTIBULAR SYSTEM BASICS

The inner ear is one of the first things to form and to become bone in the body, beginning to take shape around twenty-one days after conception, with full development by five months.[85] Even before we're born, understanding our orientation to gravity is essential. (This prenatal vestibular connection can make balance training a potent tool for actors who are looking to find more visceral instinct in their work.)

You know how, when you rotate your phone, the screen changes orientation? That function is controlled by an accelerometer, which is a good analogy for how your vestibular system works. It is always answering the following two questions:

1. Which way is up?

2. Which way am I going?

The vestibular system also performs these functions:

- *Provides visual clarity:* The greatest threat to being able to see clearly is the disturbance created by your own movement. The vestibular system allows for a clear view as you meander through the world. Later in the chapter, we'll learn how to train this reflex.

- *Stabilizes your posture:* Through a pathway called the vestibulospinal tract, the system sends information down your spinal cord to create reflexive adjustments that keep your musculature balanced.

- *Boosts your immune system:* CN VIII fires into the vagus nerve (CN X), which, among its many other functions, prevents you from getting sick. If you challenge your balance, you raise your vagal tone and may be able to fight off viruses better.[86]

- *Regulates your autonomics:* Your heart rate and blood pressure are influenced by your vestibular system's connection to the vagus nerve.

There are also cognitive and emotional benefits to training this vital system:

- A dysfunctional vestibular system leads to deficits in spatial navigation and learning (e.g., remembering your blocking onstage).

- Vestibular problems adversely affect attention and the ability to stay focused.

- Bilateral vestibular damage can cause atrophy of the hippocampus, where long-term memories are encoded.[87] If you can't remember your lines, do some balance work.

- A lack of proper balance function is directly linked to panic attacks[88] and to issues like diabetes[89] and high blood pressure.[90]

A 2016 study done among college students found that vestibular training also had a positive impact on depression, anxiety, and stress. The stimulus was simple; the subjects were asked to use a swing every day for as long as they wanted. After 150 days, the students who used it more often showed markedly improved resilience to anxious and depressive feelings.[91] Adults need playgrounds, too.

VESTIBULAR ANATOMY

The vestibular organs lie deep in your skull, a few centimeters in from the outer part of your ear; they are located almost directly behind the eye sockets. The system is composed of five paired structures on either side of the head:

- *Three semicircular canals* (horizontal, anterior, posterior) that perceive rotational movement

- *Two otolith organs* called the *utricle* and *saccule* that perceive linear movement

SEMICIRCULAR CANALS

The *semicircular canals* orient at 90 degrees to one another *(Fig. 13.2)*. Each canal is a loop formed with bone that contains a jelly-like substance called endolymph. At the end of each loop is an enlarged area

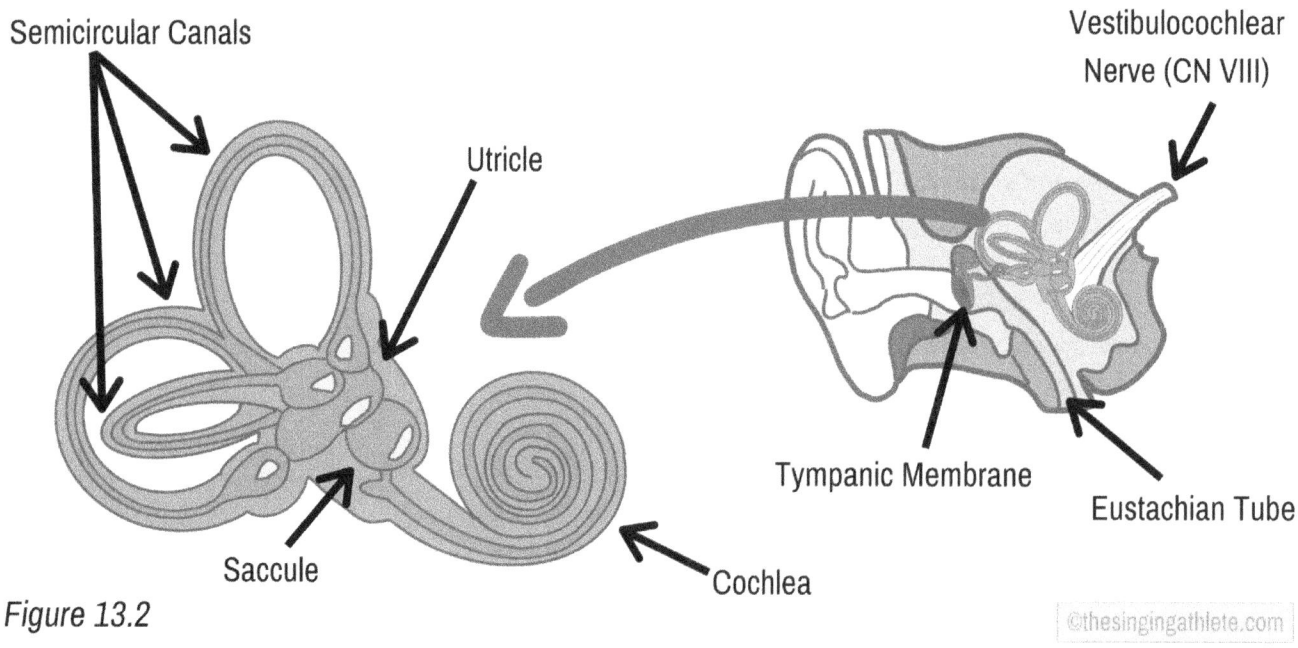

Figure 13.2

(ampulla) with a sail-like structure (cupula). Depending on which way you turn your head, the cupula will bend, signaling the nerves in your ear to fire either more or less intensely.

Turn your head to the right. As you do this, the firing rate in your right ear increases and your left ear decreases, telling your brain about the rightward turn. Now turn your head to the left. The opposite happens, with the left ear increasing and the right ear lowering its signals.

Now imagine that you experience an injury in your right ear. Perhaps a bad infection happens on that side, or a pressure change in a rough plane ride causes a ruptured right tympanic membrane. At this point, the firing rate of the nerves in your right ear may be constantly lowered. The brain may now think that you're perpetually turning your head to your left. This could result in an altered head position at rest, with postural distortions in your neck and throughout your body.

One of the most common habits I see in singers is unconscious head rotations and tilts when performing. When you watch a video of yourself singing, see if you notice that happening in big vocal moments. Over time, if you keep turning your head the same way, the brain goes through a plastic change and starts to lay down tissue to support this postural habit. This can lead to uneven neck and laryngeal musculature and possible vocal problems down the line. To fix this pattern, muscle work is not enough; you need to assess and train your vestibular system as well.

SENSORY MISMATCH

Every time the nerves in your vestibular system fire, the brain compares the information with input from your proprioceptive and visual systems. It is imperative that all three of these systems tell the same story to the brain at all times. You can think of this process like a GPS, which triangulates your location based on information from three satellites *(Fig. 13.3)*.

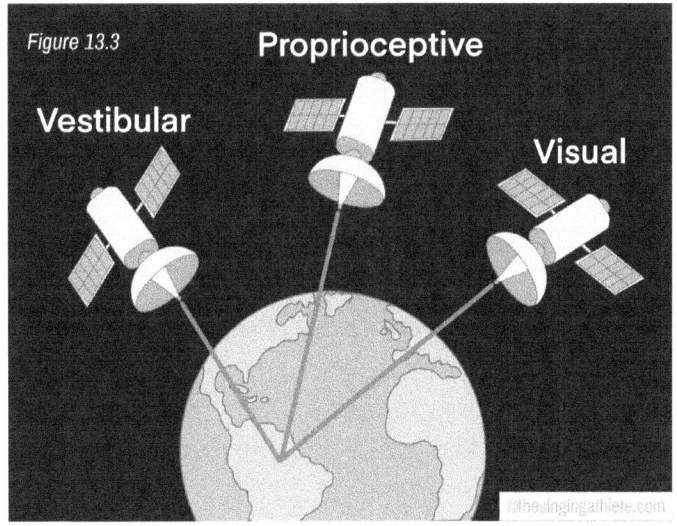

What would happen if you were using a map on your phone to navigate to a new location, and each of the three GPS satellites started sending conflicting information? The dot would be bouncing all over the screen, and it would be challenging to know how to proceed. You would be very confused and have to move slowly, with a lot of false starts and backtracking. There would probably be an emotional reaction as well, with frustration and anger increasing with each unreliable signal.

This analogy gives us a window into how we react when one of our sensory systems is messed up. This occurrence is known as ***sensory mismatch***, and it can result in many undesirable outputs. The most well-known of these is motion sickness. When the ears and eyes are sending different information to the brain, threat goes up and the brain takes action (producing nausea or vomiting) in an attempt to get your behavior to change.

Here are some other possible effects of sensory mismatch:

- Pain
- Poor coordination
- ADHD
- Muscle tension
- Anxiety/depression
- Vertigo

Another outcome that is more specific to the vestibular system is scoliosis. There is a well-established correlation between idiopathic (i.e., not caused by a known illness) scoliosis and vestibular dysfunction.[92] If you have a history of irregular spinal curvatures, something may be going on with your balance.

So, how do you avoid or fix sensory mismatch? You need to start by making sure that your vestibular system is working as it should.

BALANCE QUESTIONS

Before we get started with balance, here are a few questions to ask yourself about how well your vestibular system is currently working:

1. Have you ever had an episode of vertigo?

2. Do you ever get lightheaded after standing or sitting up quickly?

3. Do you get motion-sick?

4. Do you have a hard time with IMAX movies?

5. Do you find yourself standing in a wide stance or with your feet turned out?

Standing wide or in turnout can be a subconscious attempt to provide a broader base of support for the body. Stand up and put your feet in parallel at hip width; does this feel awkward or unstable to you?

As you progress through these drills, here are a few things to keep in mind:

- Choose a challenging but safe stance. If the drill is too easy, nothing will change in your brain. However, if you feel too wobbly, your first brain will not feel safe enough to allow improvements.

- Monitor your surroundings. Some of these drills will require you to balance and close your eyes, so remove anything you might stumble into by accident.

- Feel free to set yourself up near a wall, counter, etc., that you can grab onto if necessary.

- Do these drills without shoes. Depending on their structure, footwear can create false support that may skew your results.

Vestibular Screening 1—Feet-Together Balance

1. Stand tall with your feet touching and parallel, arms hanging by your side.

2. Close your eyes.

3. Notice if you are swaying and, if so, toward which direction (the first sway is usually the most telling). Also, notice in which joints the swaying is occurring (ankles, knees, hips, etc.).

4. Maintain the pose for thirty seconds.

A little swaying in this feet-together balance pose is not a cause for concern, but if you are falling over, I'd ask you to contact your doctor. This can be a sign of issues that might require further testing.

If that felt okay to you, this is the next progression:

Vestibular Screening 2—Balance Beam

1. Begin in a neutral stance, with your arms hanging by your side.

2. Bring your feet into a parallel line, with your back toes touching your front heel. If you can align yourself along a line on the floor, that is great. You want to be sure you are keeping a perfectly straight line with no turnout of your feet.

3. Keep your arms relaxed at your side and close your eyes.

4. Maintain the position for thirty seconds.

5. Repeat the test with the opposite foot behind.

Did you notice if you were consistently wobbling/falling to one side? You can use this stance as a reassessment to see if your balance is improving as you do the drills. (And, to be clear, you don't need to contact your doctor if you're falling out of this pose; it's quite common to find this one challenging.)

Vestibular Screening 3—One-Leg Balance

1. Begin in a neutral stance, with your arms at your side. Look down and make sure your feet are parallel and hip-width apart.

2. Lift your left foot off the ground; keep it out to the side, so it doesn't touch your right leg.

3. Close your eyes. Hold your balance on this leg for thirty seconds.

4. Switch sides, with your left foot down and your right foot up. Close your eyes and hold for thirty seconds.

5. Was one side easier than the other? Does the musculature feel the same in both legs?

The goal is to eventually be able to do each of these drills for one minute without falling.

MOVING YOUR HEAD

Up to this point in the chapter, the drills we've done have been mostly proprioceptive in nature (i.e., determining how well you can feel the floor). Now, we're going to start to train the vestibular system in earnest. In traditional balance training (wobble boards, BOSU, etc.), the focus is often on using unstable surfaces. We are going to concentrate instead on performing head movements on solid ground. This is for a simple reason; the vestibular organs are located in your skull. If you don't move your head, you're not moving your balance system, either. People who have excellent balance in static yoga poses (like tree or eagle) may find that they have significant deficits once head movements enter the mix.

Let's talk about the use of BOSU and physio balls for a moment. I have both in my studio, and I employ them for specific purposes (see the section on the saccule). I am not, however, an advocate for using these as your primary mode of vestibular training. This is for two reasons:

- If we think back to the SAID Principle, we remember that the specificity of training matters. Unless you are planning to sing in a trampoline act, you will probably be performing on a stage that is hopefully pretty stable. There will be more carryover from your vestibular training to your performance if you work on solid ground.

- Think about how you react when you step on an icy or slick surface; do you feel relaxed and open, or are you tense, guarding against a fall? You are looking to avoid a startle reflex in your voice practice. Even if you spend a lot of time on a BOSU, you will never have the speed, fluidity, and power that you can generate when you train in contact with the earth.[93]

Head Movements

1. Stand tall with your feet together and your eyes open (easier) or closed (harder).

2. Nod your head "yes," going as far as you can comfortably go in both directions.

3. Shake your head "no," going to an end-range rotation on both sides.

4. Tilt your head laterally both ways, so that each ear travels toward the shoulder as far as it comfortably can.

5. Take your nose on a diagonal line, bringing it up and over your right shoulder and then down toward your left armpit. If this motion is confusing, get the starting position by turning your head to the right and then lifting your chin.

6. Reverse the diagonal, bringing your nose up and over your left shoulder and then down toward your right armpit.

Were there directions that felt more difficult? If it felt too hard, open your eyes, widen your stance, or sit. If that felt pretty easy, do the drill again in one of these more challenging positions:

- Standing on one leg *(hardest)*

- Balance beam—feet in a line, no turnout, back toes touching the front heel *(a little easier)*

- Split stance—same as above but the back big toe touches inside of the front heel, creating a slightly wider but still parallel position *(easiest)*

COORDINATING BALANCE AND VISION

One of your vestibular system's most important jobs is maintaining visual clarity on a target as your head moves. The name for this is the ***vestibulo-ocular reflex (VOR)***, which is one of the fastest in the human body; the brain path that controls the VOR is only three neurons long. Gaze stabilization during head motion is a complex process that requires finely tuned coordination between the eye and neck muscles. The six semicircular canals (three on each side) are paired to individual eye muscles to keep your vision fixed on a target while your head is moving *(Fig. 13.4)*. An example is spotting in dance; when you look forward, but your head and body start to turn, that is your VOR in action.

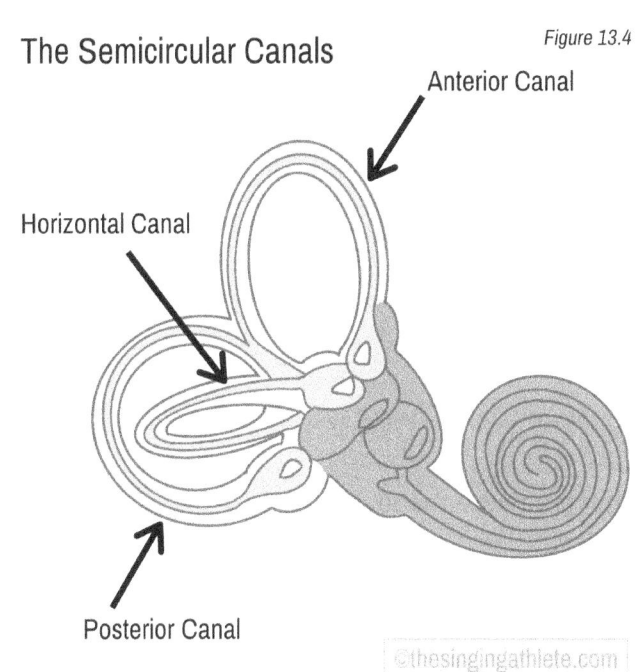

Figure 13.4

From a threat-bucket perspective, think of how urgent visual clarity during movement is. If you're trying to run away from a predator, you need to keep a clear focus. This drill may seem like no big deal, but I've seen it be pretty intense for some people. If you have a history of motion sickness, monitor your own experience and take a break if needed.

(Note: In some of the drills coming up, you will find a letter to look at while you do the exercise; the goal is to keep the letter clear. Your head will sometimes be moving, so the letter may look like it's also shifting a

bit, and that's not as big of a deal. What you're most interested in is clarity. In other words, do the edges of the letter become blurry as you move?)

Test Your VOR

1. Find something with letters on it (a sign, spine of a book, etc.) and stand 3–4 feet away. Choose a letter small enough that it is right at the edge of visual clarity.

2. Perform a head rotation from right to left (shake your head "no") while you keep looking at the target. The rotation tempo you are looking for is quarter note=120 on a metronome, or two shakes per second. Is there any loss of visual clarity as you turn your head laterally?

3. At the same tempo, perform a head nod from top to bottom (shake your head "yes") while you keep looking at the target. Is there any loss of visual clarity as you move your head vertically?

4. Perform a head rotation on a diagonal, taking your nose up over your right shoulder and then down toward your left armpit. Is there any loss of visual clarity when you move your head on this diagonal?

5. Perform a head rotation on the opposite diagonal, taking your nose up over your left shoulder and then down toward your right armpit. Is there any loss of visual clarity when you move your head on this diagonal?

Take note of any directions where you felt the following:

- Lack of clarity on the target

- Swaying in the body

- Choppy or uncoordinated neck movement.

The diagonal movements are the hardest to do cleanly, so watch them on thesingingathlete.com. At the website, you can also download a VOR chart that you can print and hang at eye level to learn the movements.

Train Your VOR

1. Assess your voice and body.

2. Get a metronome app for your phone and set it to 120 bpm.

3. Stand tall and look at the same target as in the drill above.

4. Nod your head vertically in the rhythm of the metronome, up for one click and down for the next. If the pace is too fast, take the speed down until you can maintain clarity while moving.

5. Maintain the head-nodding motion to the beat for thirty seconds.

6. Reassess.

7. Repeat Steps 4–6 with head rotations (shake your head "no") and diagonals (nose over the right shoulder and down to the left armpit; nose over the left shoulder and down to the right armpit). The goal is to maintain clarity of the letter at which you are looking. Remember to reassess after each movement.

If you have something more specific going on with your vestibular system, you may need to break the movement down to an individual ear canal. If you notice that you lose clarity or balance every time you turn your head a certain way (e.g., "It always looks blurry when I turn my head to the left"), that is a clue that you need to be more targeted. If you have a history of vertigo, think about which direction the world tends to spin. If you have dysfunction in the left vestibular organs, the vertigo sensation will be one of rotating to the right and vice versa.

Here's how you train a specific direction:

1. Assess your voice and body.

2. Look at the same target you used in the previous exercise.

3. Perform a head rotation in a challenging direction. Move your head at a pace that is quick but keeps the target clear. Once you've reached your end range, close your eyes and return to the center.

4. Reopen your eyes and repeat Step 3 four more times.

5. Reassess.

6. Choose a different head motion that was challenging and repeat Steps 3–5.

If you're finding the VOR movements hard or if they are reassessing poorly, try these things:

- Look at a target that is farther away or closer.

- Look at a bigger target.

- Reduce the range of motion and speed.

- Do it seated, sitting with your back against a wall, or lying down.

- Do them on an exhalation.

- Keep your tongue in the spot.

You can also do VOR training while walking. Pick a sign in the distance and walk toward it while shaking your head yes/no and taking it on the diagonals. Can you keep the letters on the sign clear as you move? What about when you move backward or sideways?

VOR Cancellation:

While the VOR is an essential reflex, there are times when you may need to track an object by moving your head and your eyes concurrently. This inhibition, or cancellation, of the VOR involves your frontal lobe, making it a more complex process in your brain.

VOR-C Version 1

1. Assess your voice and body.

2. Recheck your balance by briefly standing on your right foot, then switch to your left, keeping your eyes closed. Which side felt more wobbly?

3. Find a pencil or something with a letter on it and hold it out in front of you at arm's length.

4. While looking at the letter, begin to spin toward your weaker balance side. If you felt more unsteady on your left foot, you'll turn to the left (vice versa for the right side). If you have access to an office chair that spins, you can also try rotating yourself that way.

5. While looking at the letter, do 3–5 rotations at a speed that is challenging but safe. Notice if the letter is staying clear as you spin.

6. Stop and once you've steadied yourself, reassess.

VOR-C Version 2

1. Find an object with some writing on it and hold it out in front of you at arm's length.

2. Slowly begin to move your arm and your eyes horizontally off to the right as a unit; your arm, eyes, and head should all be moving in the same direction at the same time. You want to imagine a line between your eyeballs and the pencil that doesn't change as you move. Once you've gone out about 30 degrees, bring everything back to the center.

3. Try the same process to the left, up, and down. If that feels okay, try diagonals (up/right, up/left, down/right, and down/left).

If you're struggling with this, tie a piece of dental floss to the pencil and bite the other end between your teeth. This will give you a line to look at as you move your head and the pencil in coordination.

These VOR and VOR-C drills can also be useful for dance training; dancers who "don't like to turn" often have unresolved problems with their inner ears.

TRAINING YOUR OTOLITHS

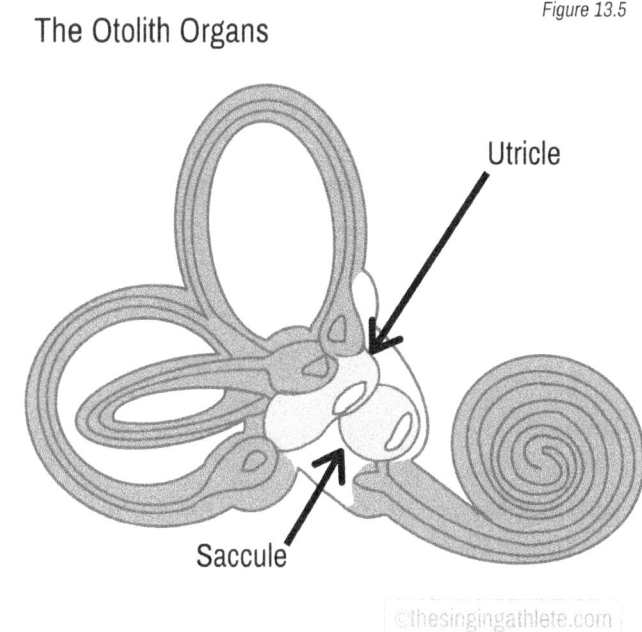

Whereas the semicircular canals control angular movement in your head and neck, the *otolith organs* (Fig. 13.5) control linear movement. The *utricle* is involved with horizontal movement (like on a train) and the *saccule* with vertical movement (like on an elevator). The two otoliths lie at 90 degrees to one another. The word otolith means "ear stone," and you can think of these organs as full of stones with tentacles that reach down into a gelatin-like substance. Any head movement will cause some of the "ear stones" to shift, letting your brain understand if you're standing, lying down, etc.

Neck Lateral Glide

The utricle senses horizontal linear movement in all directions, including laterally. This motion is hard for many people, so I recommend watching this one in a mirror.

1. Assess your voice and body.

2. Place the tips of both pointer fingers on either cheekbone.

3. Move your fingers out one inch (2.5 cm) laterally away from your face on both sides.

4. Glide your right cheekbone toward your right finger and then your left cheekbone toward your left finger. The motion should be a glide and not a tilt or rotation, like your chin is sliding along an imaginary horizontal shelf. You should see your ears sliding toward each opposite wall.

5. Do five reps.

6. Reassess.

If this felt hard to coordinate, your utricle might be under-performing.

Sustained Head-Tilt

When the head tilts, different parts of the ear can activate based on the tempo of the movement. In a quick lateral tilt, the semicircular canals wake up. However, in a slow and sustained tilt, the canals quiet down but the utricle fires.

1. Assess your voice and body.

2. Find a letter you can see at eye level. Stand at a distance where it is clear but still a slight acuity challenge.

3. Slowly tilt your head to the left (ear to shoulder) as you look at the letter. Hold this position for fifteen seconds. Does the letter blur as you hold the position? Is your body stable or wobbling?

4. Reassess.

5. Slowly tilt your head to the right as you look at the letter. Hold this position for fifteen seconds. Does the letter blur as you hold the position? Are you stable or wobbling?

6. Reassess.

Walking

The utricle is also involved in visual convergence, which means keeping an object clear as you move toward it or as it moves toward you.

1. Assess your voice and body.

2. Rotate your head to the left and walk forward for a few paces, looking at an object in the distance in front of you. Is the object you are looking at staying clear? Reset and repeat two more times.

3. Bring your head back to center and tilt your head to the left. Repeat the walking pattern. Is the object you're looking at staying clear?

4. Reassess.

5. Rotate your head to the right and walk forward for a few paces, looking at an object in the distance in front of you. Reset and repeat two more times.

6. Bring your head back to center and tilt your head to the right. Repeat the walking pattern. Is the object you're looking at staying clear?

7. Reassess.

You can also train your utricle in the following exercises:

- Push-ups against a wall.

- Lunges in different directions (e.g., in front, to the side, behind).

- Sliding your head forward and back or side to side in any of the VOR positions.

Train Your Saccule

Since the saccule is involved in vertical motion, you can train it by jumping rope or bouncing. This is how I use the BOSU trainer in my studio; I have students bounce on a flat surface, but I also test them bouncing on the BOSU.

To do your saccule training, we'll again use visual acuity:

1. Assess your voice and body.

2. Find a target you can see that is just at the edge of clarity.

3. Do quick standing calf raises (pop up onto your tiptoes) while looking at the target—is it staying clear?

4. Now do quick standing knee drops or mini-squats. How is the clarity now?

5. If that's easy for you, increase the tempo and amplitude of the movements. Is the target still clear?

6. Continue for thirty seconds.

7. Reassess.

Other saccule training ideas:

- Take a walk and pause every few steps to bounce or do some small squats.

- Do squats at varying speeds while looking at a visual target and noticing any loss of clarity.

- Do squats with your eyes closed.

Visual Vertical

Another way to test and train otolith function is with an app called Visual Vertical. This program shows you a solid line on your phone for a period of time (ten seconds or more). You are challenged to hold your phone at an exact vertical; at the end of the time period, you'll see how close you were to straight. A deviation of more than 2.5 degrees from vertical can be indicative of otolith problems, with the top of the line moving toward the side of dysfunction. You can also test horizontal (the number that comes up should be either 90 or 270 when testing sideways). If you have correctly functioning otoliths, you should be able to get within 1.5 degrees of horizontal, with the line tipping downward on the side of dysfunction. You can use the app for training as well.

HEARING AND YOUR VOICE

Have you ever noticed the tendency to speak louder when you're wearing headphones? This is known as the Lombard effect; vocal amplitude increases when the auditory signal is reduced. This effect is but one example of a simple fact: your hearing controls your voice. Although vocal production also has complex sensory and motor elements, it doesn't happen correctly without the auditory system. Individuals with hearing impairment show a lack of coordination in both intrinsic and extrinsic laryngeal musculature.[94] Even in professional-level singers, pitch accuracy degrades when auditory signals are disrupted.[95]

The auditory system provides both feedback and feed-forward control over your voice. Feedback helps you correct your phonation by processing sensory information from the larynx while speaking or singing. It is also the basis of pitch-matching. Furthermore, feedback causes an automatic spike in vocal volume when you are in noisy environments, which is why good vocal monitors are so essential in amplified singing. Feed-forward control lets you rely on previously learned commands without needing continuous auditory feedback. The better your practice regimen is, the better the feed-forward oversight is when hearing is disturbed.

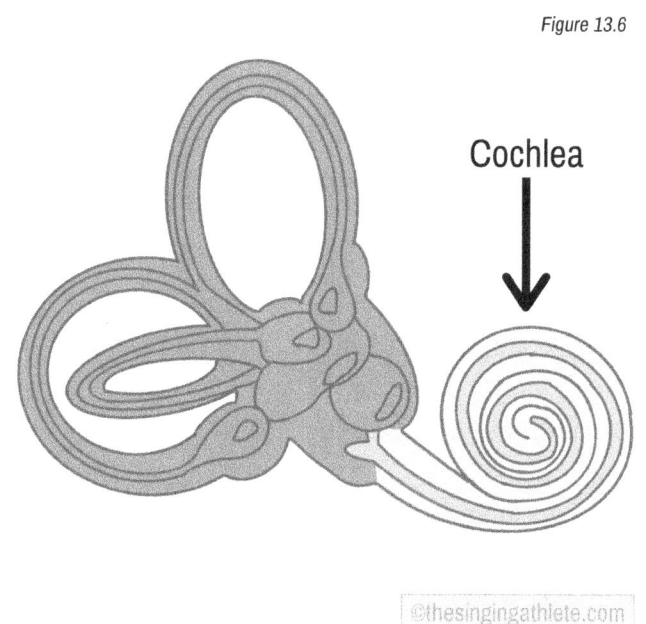

Figure 13.6

Sounds are processed in the ***cochlea*** *(Fig. 13.6)*, a snail-shaped structure in the inner ear that spirals up, making two-and-a-half turns along the way. The cochlea contains thousands of hair cells, which move as sound waves enter it. Through a process called mechanotransduction, the hair cells convert this movement into neural impulses that the brain interprets as sound. The distribution of the hair cells is not even; they are more numerous in the range that detects high frequencies. By sheer numbers, it appears that high-frequency receptors have the potential to engage more acoustic energy than low-frequency ones. This could be one of the reasons we love to listen to live singing. As the overtones grow more complex with greater vocal range and volume, high-frequency receptors wake up, energizing the listeners.[96]

Here's how to test your enjoyment of high-range frequencies; you'll need some headphones, preferably in an over-the-ear style, connected to a source of music. You should use a song that has a lot of high-frequency overtones with some volume contrasts. The piece that I suggest is the first movement of "Spring" from *The Four Seasons* by Vivaldi.

High-Frequency Test

1. Assess your voice and body.

2. Place the right headphone over your right ear and listen to thirty seconds of the Vivaldi.

3. Reassess.

4. Place the left headphone over your left ear and listen to thirty more seconds. Does it sound the same on this side?

5. Reassess.

6. Now try with the headphones on both ears; listen for thirty more seconds.

7. Reassess.

Let's talk about headphones for a moment. A 2016 study showed that chronically listening to loud music using in-ear headphones caused problems in the subjects' neck posture and balance, as well as their hearing. The average in-ear headphones can now produce up to 120 decibels of sound; anything above 85 decibels can be harmful to your cochlea with long-term use. This is what I do for myself:

- Instead of in-ear models, I use over-the-ear headphones when I can. In-ear models increase the volume by about nine decibels simply by being closer to the tympanic membrane of the ear.

- I use headphones with a noise-canceling function, which give an added layer of protection.

- I follow the rule of 60; not more than 60 minutes of headphone use at a time, with the volume not above 60 percent.

If you are interested in musical frequencies and their effect on the brain, it is worth looking into different tunings. The standard tuning for the musical note A^4 (the A above middle C) is 440 Hz, which was adopted for the tuning of musical instruments by the International Organization for Standardization in 1955 and reconfirmed in 1975.[97] Scientifically speaking, though, the tuning for A^4 should be 432 Hz, where middle C is 256 Hz, the 8th power of 2. This is the way A^4 used to be tuned, and there is a movement to return instrumental tuning to the A^4 432-Hz standard.

When I do the High-Frequency Test, I have a noticeably stronger reaction and better reassessment from the 432-Hz tuning for the Vivaldi. (You can try this test for yourself on thesingingathlete.com.) An experiment was recently done where two twenty-minute music sessions were conducted, with the same piece played first at 440 Hz and then at 432 Hz, without the audience knowing which was which. The 432-Hz tuning created a reduced blood pressure, reduced heart rate, and slower breathing compared to the 440-Hz version. Additionally, the subjects self-reported more musical enjoyment at the 432-Hz tuning.[98]

Here's another way to test high-frequency listening:

Finger-Rub Test

1. Using your dominant hand, lightly rub your thumb and forefinger together in front of your right ear.

2. Using the same hand, reach around your head and rub the same fingers together in front of your left ear.

3. Are the volume and quality the same on both sides?

If you noticed a muddier side, try listening to some high-frequency music in the weaker ear more regularly.

HEARING MAPS

If you sing in auditions frequently, you may have noticed that certain songs are inconsistent. This may be caused by faulty hearing maps in the brain. In a singing audition, you rarely have control over where the accompanying music is being played. If you can't easily perceive from where sounds are originating, your brain may get freaked out and not allow your voice to open up.

In a part of your brainstem called your midbrain, you have something called the *inferior colliculus*. The inferior colliculus is one of the main players in sound localization; it creates the map of your auditory world. When you sing to an accompaniment, the inferior colliculus is charged with discerning where that music is occurring.

The inferior colliculus is also involved in perceiving pitch frequency, so waking it up can improve intonation.[99] Additionally, this part of your brainstem is the start of your IML (intermediolateral) nucleus, which is the top of the chain that makes up the sympathetic nervous system. If you don't know where sounds are coming from, your stress levels will be elevated. Imagine how scary it would be if you were crossing a busy street and you heard the sound of a car's engine roaring toward you, but you couldn't tell from which direction it was coming.

Let's test how good your hearing map is; the results of this test may surprise you. You'll need a friend for this drill.

Hearing Map Test

1. Stand in a comfortable position and plug your left ear.

2. Close your eyes.

3. Have your friend snap their fingers once somewhere on your right side and hold their hand precisely in the place where they snapped.

4. Without opening your eyes, point to where you think the sound occurred.

5. Open your eyes and see how close you were.

6. If you were off, point to the correct spot. (You want to re-map this hearing area, so it's essential to take a moment to point to the exact location of the snap.)

7. Repeat Steps 2–6 in a few more spots on the right side.

8. Switch to the other side (you plug your right ear and your friend snaps on your left side) and do a few reps there.

If you found some mapping issues, they are fixable. Let's say you had trouble knowing where sounds were in the lower quadrant of your right side. Take your phone and put on a favorite song. With your eyes closed, hold it on your lower right side for a few seconds. Listen hard and move your phone around a bit on the lower right; even though your hand is moving the phone, it will still improve your mapping.

You can also try setting a speaker up on a shelf and move your body around while music plays. Spend a few seconds in each quadrant, noticing any areas where things feel different. I also like to practice my hearing maps outside in a park. I close my eyes and try to locate the sounds of the environment, both natural and human-made. After I think I've pinpointed something, I open my eyes and see how accurate I was.

TINNITUS AND WHAT TO DO ABOUT IT

Neurons are fascinating; much like organisms as a whole, they have strategies to avoid decay and death. If there starts to be a problem in a brain area, neurons in that troubled zone may begin to go through a process called ***transneuronal degeneration (TND).*** Before the neuron dies, it will become very excitable, resulting in a hyper-sensitive and constant firing pattern. An example of this process is tinnitus, or ringing in the ears when no external sound is present.

When tinnitus occurs, we can surmise there is an area in the brain that is being under-used. As a consequence of this neglect, some of the neurons associated with hearing begin to lose function. In a bid to prevent further degeneration, the neurons force you to notice them by creating a piercing, ringing tone. It's like they're screaming, "Pay attention to me!"

If we remember that pain is an action signal, we must provide a stimulus to engage the under-performing systems. If you currently have tinnitus, try this:

1. Get an app that produces a steady pitch; I use Tone Generator or Function Generator Pro.

2. Slide the pitch control on the app until it matches the pitch that is ringing in your ear. Hold your phone in front of the ringing ear for a few seconds.

3. Did the pitch ringing in your ear change? If so, use the app to match the new pitch and hold it again in front of the ear.

After doing this, turn the pitch off and see if the volume of the ringing has decreased or disappeared. If no change happened, here are some other things to try:

- Lie on your side, with the ear that is ringing facing up to the ceiling. Pour a small amount of cold water into the ear canal and rest for thirty seconds.

- Try the same exercise with warm/hot water.

- Do the jaw-mobility drills in Chapter 10 while tugging/pulling on the ringing ear in a few directions.

- Use the OKN Strips or Optodrum app, as described in Chapter 16. If the ringing is on the right, the stripes should move from the left to the right. If the ringing is on the left, the stripes should move from the right to the left.

- Smell something that you like in the same-side nostril as the ringing ear, plugging the other nostril closed.

- Take a quick whiff of ammonia in the same-side nostril as the ringing ear, plugging the other nostril closed. Ammonia, unlike other smells, is processed in the trigeminal nerve, which lives closer to the nerve that's causing the tinnitus.

BONE CONDUCTION

When Beethoven began to experience hearing loss in his twenties, he came up with an ingenious solution. He placed one end of a metal rod between his teeth, with the other end resting inside his piano. As he played the instrument, the vibrations traveled through his teeth and jaw, eventually reaching his cochlea. This technique allowed him to hear enough to continue composing. I, for one, am glad he was able to keep going. (I can't hear the last movement of the *Ninth Symphony* without sobbing.)

Beethoven took advantage of the duality of hearing in the human body. The two strategies *(Fig. 13.7)* are:

- ***Air Conduction:*** Sound waves enter the ear canal and travel until they reach the tympanic membrane (eardrum) and the ossicles. The ossicles are three small bones that send vibrations to the vestibulocochlear nerve (CN VIII) in the inner ear. CN VIII transmits this information to the temporal lobe of the brain, where it is processed as sound.

- ***Bone Conduction:*** Sound waves bypass the eardrum and travel directly through the bones of the body. Much like the sound waves entering the outer ear, vibrations can enter the bones themselves. CN VIII and the temporal lobe can convert these vibrations into the perception of sound.

Figure 13.7

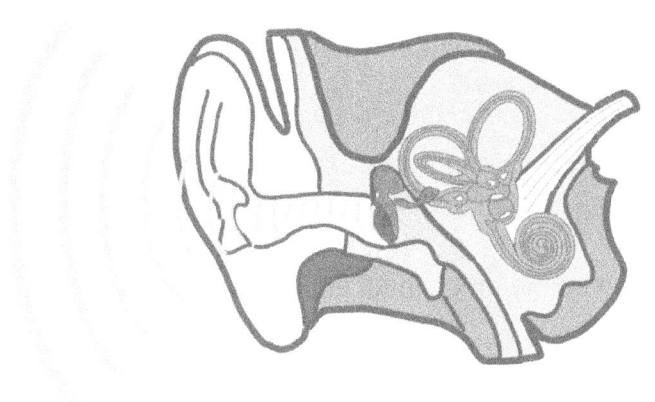
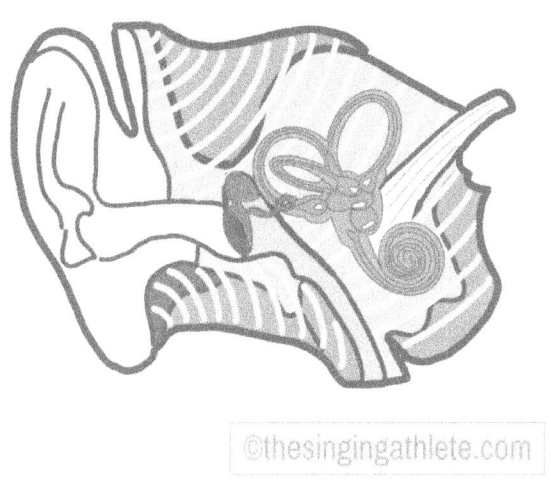

Bone conduction is also widely used in the animal kingdom. Whales use it for hearing, and elephant mating calls are performed with a female stomping the ground so a male can feel her message in the bones of his feet. The tone of bone conduction sounds lower than air conduction because the skull conducts lower frequencies better than the air. This explains why your voice may sound higher to you on a recording; when you speak, you usually hear your voice partially through bone conduction.

As a singer, the reason you want excellent bone conduction is that it helps you judge the necessary effort to make sound. If you "hear" your voice properly in your bones, your reflexive use of air pressure will be more economical and precise, and your voice won't get as tired.

Bone Conduction Test

1. Hum a pitch in a comfortable range.

2. Keep humming and plug your right ear by pushing in the tragus (the pointy triangle shape in front of your ear canal). Did the hum get louder, softer, or stay at the same volume when you plugged your ear?

3. As you keep humming, now plug the left ear by pushing in the tragus and again note any volume change. Is it the same as the right side?

When air conduction is turned off by plugging the ear, bone conduction should take over, resulting in a louder internal perception of sound with the ear plugged. If you want to do a more thorough test, use a tuning fork. I prefer to test with a C-128hz or C-256hz tuning fork since bone conduction tends to be easy to hear in that range of frequencies.

Tuning Fork Test

1. Start the tuning fork vibrating by tapping the circular ends together. I usually tap it on the outside of the heel of my hand on the pinky side.

2. Using your right hand, place the handle of the tuning fork (the small rounded end) behind your right ear on the mastoid process (the bone you feel right behind your ear).

3. While the tuning fork is still vibrating, plug your right ear again, pushing in the tragus (you'll need to reach across with the left hand). Did the sound get louder, softer, or stay the same when you plugged?

4. Repeat the setup on the left side (left hand holding the tuning fork behind the left ear, right hand reaching across to plug the tragus).

If the sound was symmetrically louder on both sides when you plugged your ear, your bone conduction is probably working well. If the sound didn't get louder, or both sides weren't equal, here's how you train it:

1. Assess your voice and body.

2. Repeat the setup from the Tuning Fork Test on the weaker side. With your ear plugged, try to "listen hard" when the fork is on your mastoid. Encourage the vibration to travel into the bone.

3. Repeat 3–5 times, each time striking the tuning fork so the vibration remains strong.

4. Reassess.

Rinne and Weber Tests

Once you have a tuning fork, you can perform two other self-tests for your bone and air conduction. They are called the Rinne and the Weber tests, named after the German physicians who came up with them. The Rinne test is done like this:

1. Start the tuning fork vibrating, like above.

2. Place the handle of the tuning fork against the right mastoid bone, similar to the Tuning Fork Test.

3. Once you can no longer hear the sound through the mastoid, place the two large circles of the (still-vibrating) tuning fork directly in front of your ear canal.

4. Repeat the setup on the left side.

You should still be able to hear the sound of the tuning fork when it's right in front of your ear canal. Although bone conduction is essential, air conduction should have more sensitivity overall, so it should last longer.

The Weber test is done like this:

1. Start the tuning fork vibrating.

2. Place the handle in the dead-center of the top of your skull. (You may want to look in a mirror to be sure you are accurate.) Do you hear the sound equally on both sides of your head?

The Rinne and Weber tests are quick screens for hearing. I'm presenting them here because big things come from small things, and as musicians, we need to be vigilant about our ears. If I had any results from these tests that were confusing or concerning, I would make an appointment with an audiologist for a professional opinion.

Bone Conduction Headphones

One of the best ways to improve your bone conduction is through the use of specialized headphones. I use Aftershokz headphones paired with an app called Function Generator Pro. Here's how to test which frequency is best for you:

1. Stand in the Feet-Together Balance position (e.g., feet together, arms by your side, eyes closed). How stable do you feel? With your eyes still closed, turn your head slowly to the right and left. Recenter your head and then lift and lower your chin.

2. Put on the bone conduction headphones and use the Function Generator Pro app to start a beat at 60 BPM, 100 Hz. The sound should be in both ears.

3. Reassess your head movements (eyes closed) while the beat is going. Can you rotate farther or less far? Are you more or less steady?

4. Move the beat to the left ear only. Reassess your head movements.

5. Move the beat to the right ear only. Reassess your head movements.

6. Try some other frequencies.

You can also try this test in the more challenging balance drills in the earlier part of the chapter. If the bone-conduction headphones test well for you, you can leave the beat going for up to an hour each day; I do this often while exercising. In addition to improving bone conduction, this is an excellent drill for training the utricle and saccule; try using the beat more on your weaker ear side.

14. EYES

In my eleventh-grade chemistry class, I remember sitting in the back and suddenly not being able to read the equation on the board. My chem teacher was not my favorite; he didn't know the subject matter, and he compensated by being rude and condescending. The frustration I felt in his class coincided with the first moment that I can remember my vision becoming myopic, or near-sighted.

Shortly after that, I got glasses and contacts, which I wore for over twenty years. As I understood it, this was how vision worked; when you stopped seeing clearly, you corrected it with apparatus. Sure, I noticed that my prescription kept having to get stronger, but from all the examples I saw around me, it seemed that eyesight was supposed to degrade. Middle-aged people used reading glasses to see the menu at a restaurant. Older people got cataracts. That was the "normal" visual progression, as far as I could tell.

My opinions about all this changed in an instant when I attended a Z-Health course that involved vision training. We were reading a typical Snellen chart that you see at the eye doctors (the ones with the big "E" on top). I was struggling to make out any more than the first line or two without my glasses (at the time, my prescription was -3.75 in my right eye and -3.25 in my left). A coach gave me a pair of <u>pinhole glasses</u> to try. I went back to the chart and I could read the whole thing, top to bottom. With these pinhole glasses on, my vision was better than 20/20. How was this possible? The only "lenses" in the pinhole glasses were two pieces of black plastic with holes in them. No prescription. No correction. And yet I could see perfectly.

When I first put the pinholes on, I also remember feeling my tailbone drop to the ground. I had worked for years in Alexander Technique lessons to reduce anterior tilt (swayback) in my pelvis. With these glasses on, my alignment was correcting itself without any conscious thought. When I learned that vision controls up to 70 percent of reflexive posture, my spinal reaction started to make sense. I thought about students who I had told a million times that their head was creeping forward when they sang, but the physical correction never stuck. Was it possible they had a visual issue that was causing this postural habit?

From that class forward, I committed to living without visual correction as much as possible. As I began to navigate this new, slightly blurry world, I quickly learned how vision, like everything, is very responsive to threat. When I was in relaxed situations, my eyes began to clear up; when I was under stress, everything would fuzz out. But slowly, using the exercises in this chapter along with help from my coaches, my visual resolution improved. I recently played an orchestral program in Switzerland in a fifteen-hundred-seat house with no corrective lenses; I could see the conductor fine. Before I started training my eyes, that would have been unimaginable for me.

My journey with vision helped me understand that it is a dynamic, multidimensional process. When you see, over thirty different areas of the brain can get involved. Your eyes are having a constant conversation with your inner ear, your cerebellum, your neck muscles, and your limbic (emotional) centers. The chem teacher I hated? My limbic and visual systems made a joint decision to "protect" me by blurring the images in the distance. Remember, your brain can produce any output imaginable, including a degrading of your visual resolution, in an attempt to keep you safe. If you wear corrective lenses or are having visual issues, it is worth thinking about when you first realized there was a problem. Eyes hold on to emotion.

WHY SHOULD SINGERS WORK ON VISION?

In your brain, cranial nerves II, III, IV, and VI control your vision and eye movements. Nerve V is the trigeminal nerve, which we've been looking at in the previous chapters. These nerves surround one another in the brainstem. Neurons that fire together, wire together, so a great way to fix chronic TMJ problems can be working with the eyes. And since vision controls such a large percentage of your posture, alignment and vocal support can be significantly affected by eye training.

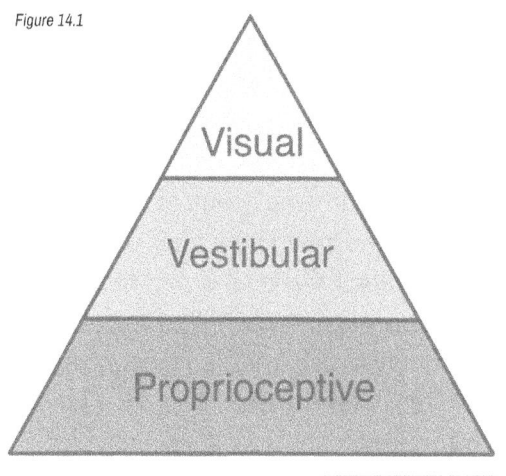

Figure 14.1

Your brain has a neural hierarchy *(Fig. 14.1)* when it comes to a motor output like singing. It goes like this:

1. Visual system

2. Vestibular system

3. Proprioceptive system

Input is prioritized based on how useful it is for making predictions. When it comes to threat, you're going to see the grizzly across the mountain before you hear it rustling the leaves (and hopefully before you feel its paws on you). Therefore, the visual system gets the highest authority to control your movement patterns. If you work with skeletal muscles but ignore these higher-order systems, you may be missing a big piece of the puzzle.

To be an elite-level singer, you should have high-level function in the visual, vestibular, and proprioceptive systems. Since the visual system is the most important, an estimated breakdown of the percentage of contribution might look something like this:

Visual: 42%   *Vestibular: 34%*   *Proprioceptive: 24%*

Total: 100%

Now, let's say you're an average adult and you've accumulated some dysfunctions in all of these systems (astigmatism in the right eye, a history of chronic ear infections, lack of complete rehab from a torn ACL, etc.). As you start a training program, your numbers might be:

Visual: 34% (out of 42%)   *Vestibular: 25% (out of 34%)*   *Proprioceptive: 17% (out of 24%)*

Total: 76%

If your training focuses only on the proprioceptive system and it is wildly successful, your numbers might now be:

Visual: 34% (out of 42%)   *Vestibular: 25% (out of 34%)*   *Proprioceptive: 24% (out of 24%)*

Total: 83%

Well, you've done an excellent job of improving your proprioception. However, you're still only earning a low B. If you can start to improve the predictive capabilities of your vision and your balance, you are much more likely to get yourself to 100 percent.

EYE BASICS

We'll start with what you see as you look in the mirror. The whites of your eyes are called the ***sclera***, and the colored part is the ***iris*** *(Fig. 14.2)*. The black circle in the middle is the ***pupil***. If you have a mirror handy, take a look at your pupils; are they the same size? If you see that one is larger, that same side of your brain may be less active.

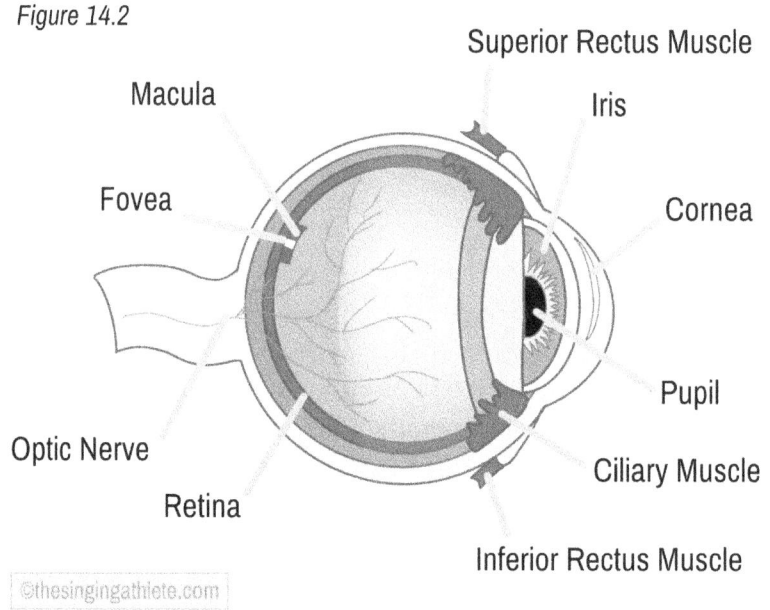

Figure 14.2

The protective covering over the front of your eyes is called the ***cornea***. Each eye has around 1 million nociceptors (threat receptors), whereas the lumbar spine only has a few thousand. Your brain has decided that vision is vital, and anything that comes in contact with the cornea is a big deal. The reason dry eyes are so miserable is that, as moisture decreases, the cornea becomes scratchy and a ton of nociceptors start firing.

The back of the eye is known as the ***retina***; this is like a canvas for the images coming into the eyeball. Each retina has about 130 million photoreceptors, known as rods and cones, which communicate with approximately 1 million neurons per side. There are also roughly 1 million neurons that control all voluntary movement of the skeletal muscles. Two million nerves for vision, 1 million for every dance move imaginable: eyes definitely matter.

In the back of the retina is a small area called the ***macula*** (you may have heard of macular degeneration, which is exactly what it sounds like) and, within that, an even smaller space called the ***fovea***, which is made up mostly of cones. This is where clear, focused vision and bright light conditions are processed in the eye; it makes up around 1.5–2 degrees of your visual field. The rest of the retina is mostly made up of rods, which respond to low light conditions and peripheral (ambient) vision.

Rods outnumber cones by about 20:1, which tells us that peripheral vision is critical. The rods are supposed to "tune" your proprioception and joint motion. If a lion jumps out at you from the bushes, you better be able to see it out of the corner of your eye and run for the hills. The way that glasses or contacts work is by focusing a beam of light at a certain angle onto your fovea, which solves the problem of acuity but creates a major peripheral vision issue. As light burns onto the fovea, the ambient visual system begins to degrade. The cones are bombarded with light, but rods are starved. This can lead to a lack of peripheral awareness, which in turn can cause postural distortions and a blurry body map.

EYE NERVES

Your *optic nerve (CN II)* controls your vision. Let's do a quick test *(Fig. 14.3)* to determine how active your optic nerve is.

Eye Cover Test

1. Sit, ideally at a table where you can rest your elbows.

2. Close your eyes.

3. Cover your closed eyes with your palms as shown. Make sure you are not pressing on your eyeballs but cupping your hands slightly, with your fingers sealed together to block out all light.

4. Do you see black? Or are colors showing up?

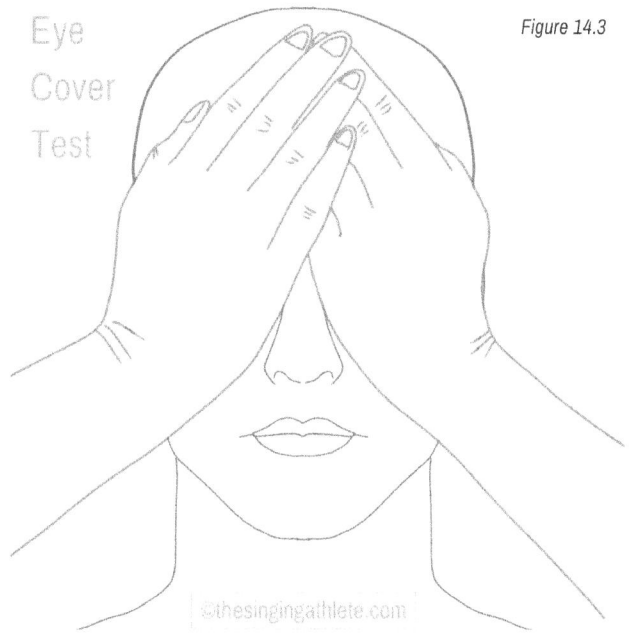

Figure 14.3

When there is no light coming into the eyes, the optic nerve should be quiet, which means you should see all black. If you see colors, stay in this position for a bit, taking slow, diaphragmatic breaths and focusing on seeing black. See how calm this makes you feel.

Six extraocular muscles move your eyeballs; they are innervated by cranial nerves III, IV, and VI *(Fig. 14.4)*. A full 25 percent of your cranial nerves are devoted to moving the eyes; again, it seems like your brain thinks this action is vital. Other than your optic nerve, the most indispensable visual nerve is your *oculomotor nerve (CN III)*, which controls four of the six extraocular muscles. CN III also controls the ciliary muscles, which change the shape of the lens for visual accommodation, or shifting from near to far vision.

The oculomotor nerve also controls your eyelid; a droopy lid is a CN III problem. Look at your eyes in a mirror or photo and see if you notice one or both lids drooping. A useful singing drill for CN III is to open your eyes as wide as possible, like a creepy doll. The goal is to lift the eyelids, not the eyebrows (lifting the eyebrows is a facial nerve drill). Try this "surprised" look on a tough phrase of music and see if it helps.

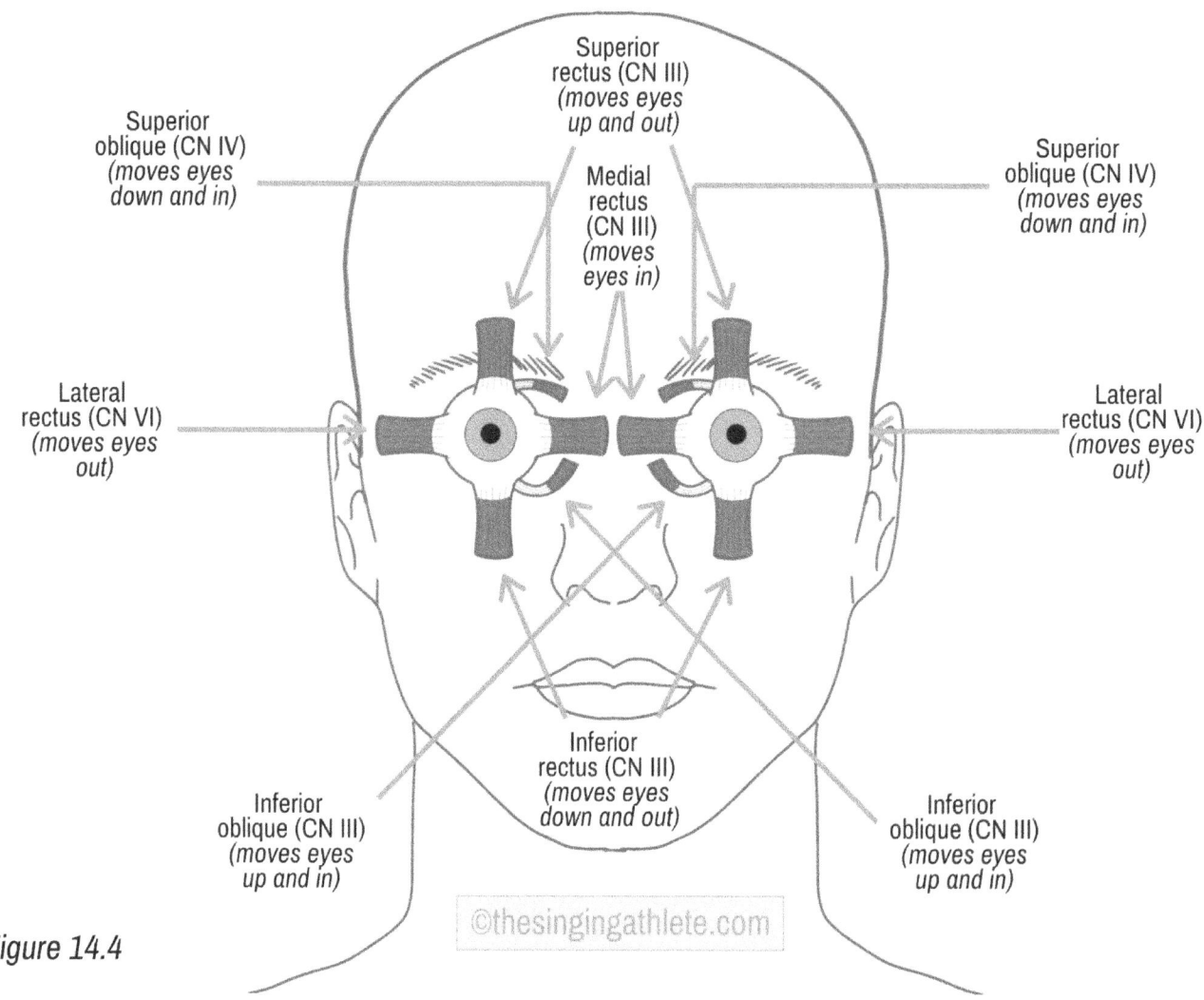

Figure 14.4

Your ***trochlear nerve (CN IV)*** controls looking down and in; most of us get a lot of trochlear practice looking at our phones all day. Your ***abducens nerve (CN VI)*** moves the eyeballs out laterally to help with distance vision.

FOUR VISUAL SKILLS

Here are the four areas of vision training we'll be exploring in this chapter.

Visual Resolution: Visual acuity is the ability to see objects clearly at any distance, with the head still or in motion. Along with acuity, visual resolution also includes contrast sensitivity (day vs. night vision) and your ability to perceive color. The way that your optometrist measures your eyes is not the whole story. Vision changes with stress. Do you feel relaxed when you're standing there, trying desperately to make out a line of letters on a doctor's chart? Also, in this kind of test, you are standing still and the chart is not moving. You might lose the ability to "see 20/20" after movement gets involved. In a show, are you generally standing completely still while nothing and no one moves onstage? We have to train visual resolution dynamically.

You can use your visual resolution as a reassessment for the drills in this chapter. You can download a Snellen chart (for working on far vision) and multisize font chart (for working on close vision) at thesingingathlete.com.

Eye Movements: The extraocular muscles are responsible for turning your eyeballs in various directions. They can get weak due to habit or disuse. Humans also tend to avoid certain eye movements for subconscious emotional reasons. If someone gets in a car accident where they are rear-ended, the last thing the driver might see before impact would be the other car zooming at them in the rearview mirror. If you're driving in the U.S., that would mean the driver probably would have looked up and right on impact (up and left in the United Kingdom, Australia, etc.). Depending on how that incident was processed, that person's brain may have decided that looking up and right is permanently a bad idea. After all, something awful happened there. They may now never be looking in that direction, or they might be compensating by turning their head so the eyeball can stay centered. Any avoidance of an eye position can have enormous brain consequences.

Depth Judgment: The primary reason you have two eyes is to be able to perceive how far away an object is. If one eye is doing more of the work, your head may tilt or turn when you sing, in an attempt to put the sharper eye to the center.

Peripheral Awareness: The question to ask yourself with peripheral awareness is, "How well can I see what I'm not looking at?" Look straight out in front of you and notice how wide your peripheral vision goes. Does it feel equal from left to right? Up and down? In addition to the fact that peripheral vision improves proprioception, it is also involved in reducing stress. When the peripheral system degrades, a sub-cortical belief in safety fails and anxiety will occur.

RULES FOR VISION TRAINING

1. *Train in a safe environment*: There is an outside chance that one of these drills will make you dizzy, so if you have concerns about that, do them seated or lying down. When standing, move anything out of the way that might be a tripping hazard.

2. *Use feedback*: Visual training is an area where it's beneficial to have someone watch you. If you try to rely on your internal sense of what's happening, you're bound to miss things. Do them with a friend or take a video of yourself. (It may just be me, but I think it's pretty fun to watch these drills back on video and see what my eyes are doing.)

3. *Relax and breathe*: Stack these drills with your favorite exercises from the breathing chapters.

4. *Correction or not?:* I would prefer that you do these drills without your glasses or contacts unless the blurriness is too intense for you. If it's too threatening, try them with correction, but make it your goal to wean yourself from them after a couple of weeks of practice.

These are some errors to watch out for as you go through the exercises:

- Are you breathing?

- Are you moving your head/neck and not your eyes?

- Are you swaying?

- Is your forehead staying relaxed?

- Are you frowning or tightening your mouth and jaw?

Vision training is very metabolically demanding, so do these drills when you've eaten well and are rested. If your eyes start to get tired or you experience threat, below are some visual resets.

Visual Reset Drills

- *Eye Cover:* We did this one earlier in the chapter. Close your eyes, cover your eyes with your palms, and breathe; wait for it to turn black.

- *Rapid blinking:* Blink your eyes as fast as you can for 5–10 seconds.

- *Eyeball press*: Close your eyes. Take the pointer and middle fingers on each hand and very lightly press the fingertips onto your eyelids. Hold for 2–4 breaths.

- *Eye socket massage*: Walk your fingertips around the edge of the bony ridge of your eye sockets. Make a complete circle and spend some extra time in any areas that feel tender.

If you're serious about seeing improvement in your eyes, you have to do about ten minutes of practice at least 4–5 times a week. That doesn't mean ten minutes all at once. I use subway time to get my vision practice in; instead of staring at my phone, I work on my eyes.

Eye Mobility

Before we start using the eye muscles, let's take a moment for self-assessing your ocular mobility.

1. With your eyes closed, take your fingers and alternately press each eyeball lightly toward the back of your head. Does one side move in less?

2. With the eyes still closed, lightly grasp the right eyeball with your fingertips and manually move it up, down, left, right, in diagonals, and in a tilting motion. Repeat with the left eye. Are there motions where you feel your eye resisting, or do you notice small muscle spasms in any planes of motion?

3. Redo one of the motions that felt sticky. Then tuck your chin and tilt your head away from the side you're pressing on. Does this make the eyeball more willing to move?

Whenever you do upper-cervical flexion (tucking the chin) and lateral flexion away (tilt the head away from the side you're working), you stretch the brainstem. This is where the extraocular nerves live, so opening this neck area can improve visual mobility and acuity.

Gaze Stabilization

A huge portion of your brain is devoted to stabilizing your gaze, and yet the pace of our culture is making it harder to focus visual attention. The next time you are in a movie, notice how frequently the cuts between shots occur. In 1930, the average length of a shot was twelve seconds; by 2010, it had decreased to 2.5 seconds.[100]

This gaze stabilization drill *(Fig. 14.5)* is a great way to reclaim your ability to focus your eyes steadily on a target. Fixating your gaze is the foundation of the visual system and must be mastered before you work on more complex movements, so take your time with this one. For the drill, you need a pencil with some writing on it.

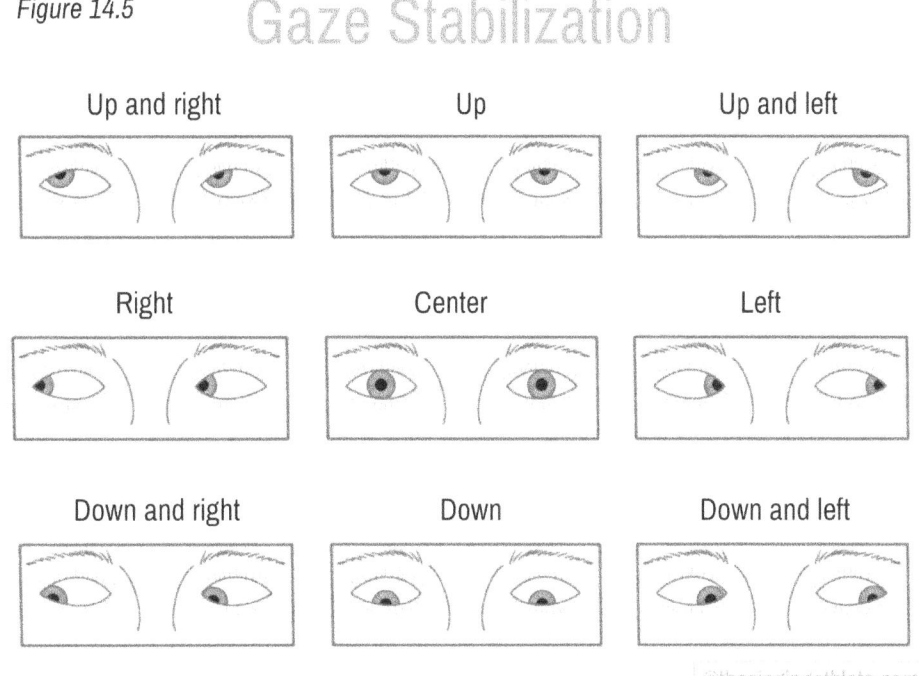

Figure 14.5

1. Assess your voice and body.

2. Sit or stand in a comfortable position.

3. Hold the pencil out in front of you at arm's length and focus on a letter for ten seconds. You can blink when needed, but notice if you're blinking a lot; that can be a sign of threat.

4. Reassess.

5. Repeat this drill with the pencil out at arm's length in the following quadrants, switching your pencil-holding hand whenever necessary. Reassess after each one of the following positions:

    - Pencil up and center

    - Pencil up and right (diagonal)

    - Pencil right

    - Pencil down and right (diagonal)

- Pencil down and center

- Pencil down and left (diagonal—switch the pencil to your left hand).

- Pencil left

- Pencil up and left (diagonal)

In each of these positions, your goal is to look intently at the letter you've chosen. When you get off to the sides, your nose can get in the way of binocular vision. Test this by opening and closing each eye, making sure you can see the letter on both sides. If your nose is blocking it, move the pencil in a bit until you see it with both eyes.

Smooth Pursuits

Another essential visual skill is the ability to track an object as it's moving, which is known as a smooth pursuit *(Fig. 14.6)*. Smooth pursuits are there to keep you focused on predators or prey that are in motion. The visual receptors activated in a smooth pursuit are especially attuned to objects that are either small and close or farther away, thereby appearing small on the horizon. It is a visual skill mostly processed in your parietal lobe (see Chapter 16). These are called smooth pursuits because the eyes should be moving fluidly; notice any areas where the visual movement becomes choppy or you lose focus.

1. Assess your voice and body.

2. Sit or stand in a comfortable position.

3. Hold the pencil out in front of you at arm's length and focus on a letter.

4. Center your head. While holding your head as still as possible, move the pencil up while following it with only your eyes.

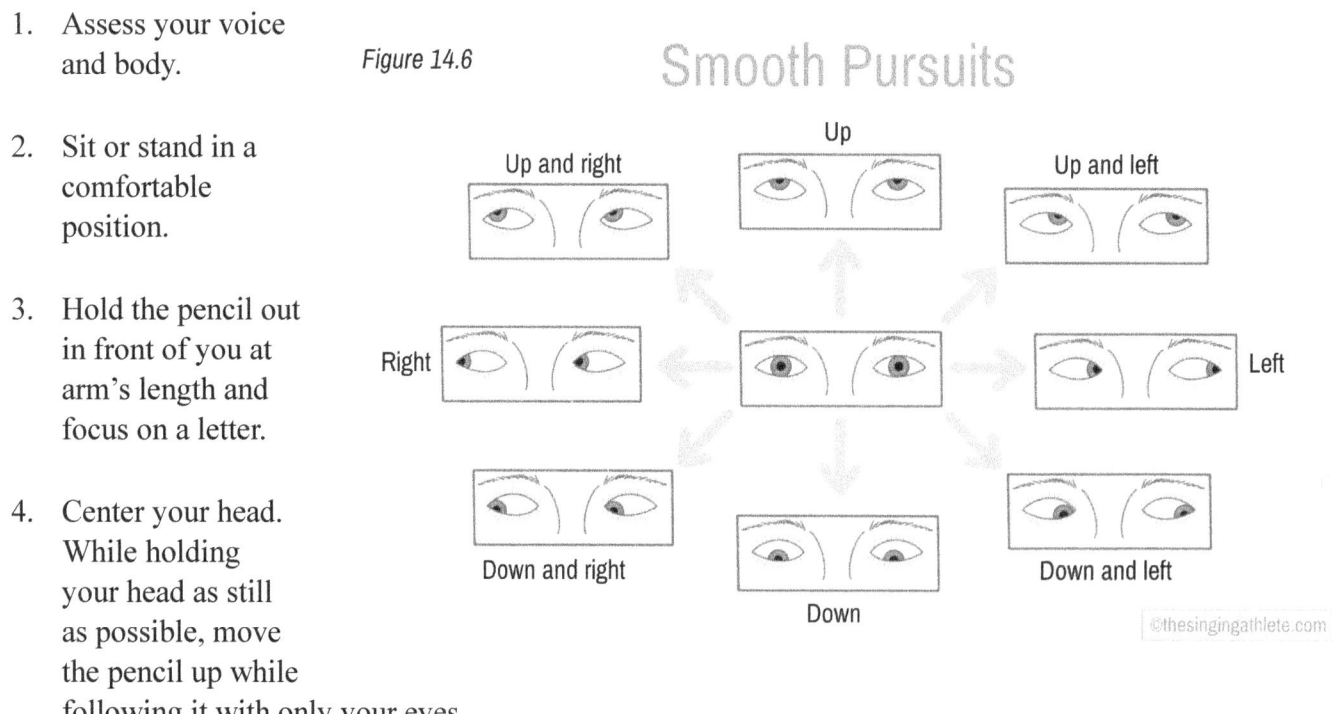

Figure 14.6

5. When you reach the maximum comfortable distance, stop and close your eyes. With your eyes closed, bring both your eyes and the pencil back to the center. Reopen your eyes and refocus on the letter.

6. Repeat Steps 4–5 two more times in the same direction.

7. Reassess.

8. Repeat Steps 4–7 in the following directions, reassessing after each one. In each of these, your eyes and the pencil will start in the center, then move out in the various directions. Your head is always meant to stay still. Switch the pencil-holding hand whenever necessary:

    - Eyes and pencil up and right (diagonal)

    - Eyes and pencil right

    - Eyes and pencil down and right (diagonal)

    - Eyes and pencil down and center

    - Eyes and pencil down and left (diagonal)

    - Eyes and pencil left

    - Eyes and pencil up and left (diagonal)

Once you know which eye positions assess the best for you, you can make more specific visual choices onstage. If you reassess well when you look up and left, why not shift your focus to that corner for the big note? Or if you know that you're stronger with a rightward gaze, maybe you should put your imaginary scene partner slightly off to the right.

Saccades

A saccade is a shift between visual targets without a change of focal length *(Fig. 14.7)*. A saccade can go side to side, up and down, or on a diagonal, but the two objects you're looking at are going to be relatively at the same distance from your eyes. Reading this passage is a series of saccades.

A saccadic eye movement is motivated by assessing threat (sensing a theme yet?). If you're lying out in the park and a dog

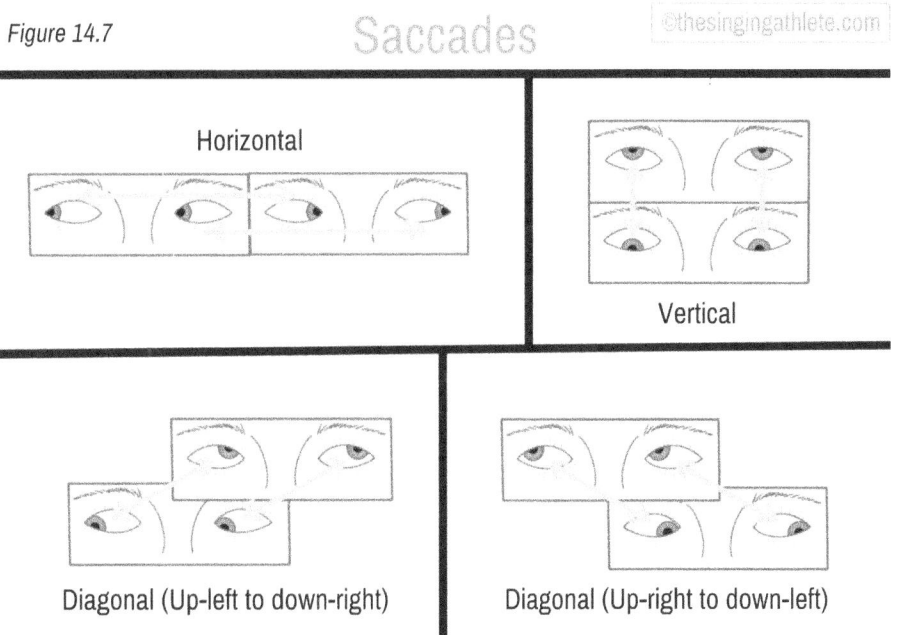

Figure 14.7

runs into your peripheral field, your first brain needs to decide whether this is a friendly labradoodle or a hungry wolf. Your eyes will reflexively saccade to the target, your brain will assess the threat level, and decisions will be made (hopefully to pet that adorable labradoodle…here, boy!).

Training saccades may also slow down the perception of time passing. Older people generally have a longer latency (delay) is performing saccades; the slower the eye movements become, the more quickly time is perceived to slip by.[101] Saccadic training can be a visual fountain of youth.

1. Assess your voice and body.

2. Hold two pencils, one in each hand, at arm's length in front of you with the tips up. The pencil tips should be about shoulder width.

3. Quickly switch your eyes between each pencil tip twenty times (ten on each side).

4. Reassess.

5. Realign the pencils so they are parallel to the ground, with the tips pointing into the center line of the body. Position one pencil at your forehead and the other at your sternum. Repeat the twenty eye switches.

6. Move the pencils away from the midline until they form a diagonal. Repeat the twenty switches on this angle. Then reverse the diagonal by bringing the higher pencil down and the lower one up. Repeat the twenty switches here.

VISION AND YOUR MUSCLES

Where you look has a massive impact on strength and flexibility in your skeletal muscles, and the visual ***vergence*** system is one of the big players. Vergence is the term for simultaneous movement of the eyes in opposite directions to maintain binocular vision at different distances. ***Convergence*** is a coordinated and simultaneous movement of both eyes inward for a close focus; taken to an extreme, convergence is a "cross-eyed" look. ***Divergence*** is the opposing motion, when your eyes move out to look at far objects. Depending on what angle your head is in and where an object is coming from, different eye muscles may be involved in convergence and divergence. If your head is in neutral and the object you are looking at is in front of you, your medial rectus (CN III) controls convergence and your lateral rectus (CN VI) controls divergence.

Through the neural hierarchy, the extraocular muscles send signals down to your spinal cord and out into the body. Here are the rules to remember *(Fig. 14.8)*:

- *Looking close facilitates your **flexors** (pectoralis major, biceps brachii, psoas, rectus abdominis, rectus femoris [flexor of the hip]).*

- *Looking far facilitates your **extensors** (latissimus dorsi, posterior deltoid, triceps brachii, gluteus maximus, hamstrings [extensor of the hip]).*

The nerve that controls convergence (CN III) lives in the midbrain, which is responsible for facilitating flexion in the body. The nerve that controls divergence (CN VI) is found in the pons, which facilitates extension. If you are flexor-dominant (e.g., head pulled forward, tight chest and stomach, "hunched" posture), try looking far away when you sing your big notes. If you are extensor-dominant (e.g., swayback, tight hamstrings, overly puffed-out chest), try looking close.

Figure 14.8

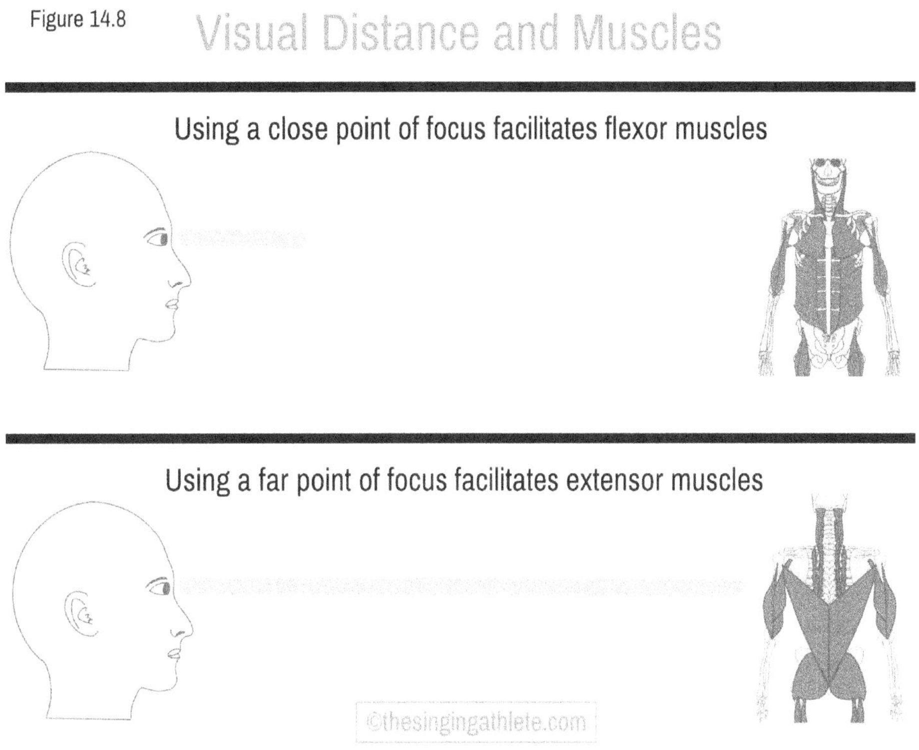

Visual Distance and Muscles

Using a close point of focus facilitates flexor muscles

Using a far point of focus facilitates extensor muscles

©thesingingathlete.com

If you're not sure whether your flexors or extensors are more dominant, here's how to figure it out:

Flexor/Extensor Dominance Test

1. Set up a video so that you're facing sideways to the camera (in profile), with your whole body visible.

2. Keep your feet wider than hip-width apart.

3. Side-bend your torso to a comfortable end-range of motion, both toward and away from the camera.

When you watch the video back, this is what you're looking for:

- In a flexor-dominant pattern, you'll see a tip forward and tightening of the abs at the end range of torso motion. It will look like you're slightly falling forward.

- In an extensor-dominant pattern, you'll see a leaning back at the end range of torso motion. It will look like a bit of a backbend.

If you still can't tell, sing a phrase looking close and far and see which assesses better for you.

TROPIAS AND PHORIAS

Much like the tone between flexors and extensors can be uneven, it's also possible that your extraocular muscles are in a pattern where one is too dominant and the eye rests in an off-center position. The name for this is a ***tropia***, which can be present in one or both eyes *(Fig. 14.9)*. A milder version of a tropia is a ***phoria***, where the dominance only shows up when the eye is covered. There are several types of phorias, but the two we are concerned with are:

- ***Exophoria***: The muscles that pull the eyes out are stronger than the muscles that pull them in.

- ***Esophoria***: The muscles that pull the eyes in are stronger than the muscles that pull them out.

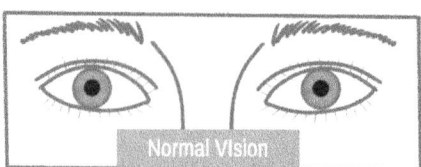
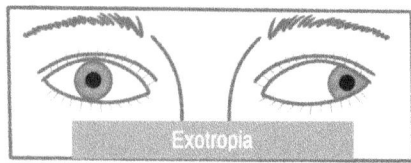
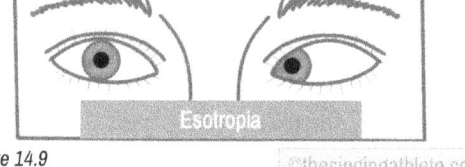

Figure 14.9

For an exophore, converging the eyes takes extra effort, which may result in quick fatigue when reading. If you always fall asleep when you're studying, you might be exophoric. Also, exophoria is common in people diagnosed with ADHD.[102] Exophorics see the world as farther away than it actually is; a twenty-foot room may look like twenty-five feet. Esophoria is the opposite issue, with the muscle pattern causing the eyeballs to turn in. This can result in a feeling of being overwhelmed in large social situations. The same twenty-foot room that looks huge to an exophore may look like fifteen feet to an esophore.

With phorias, the implications for voice are huge. If you tend to push your voice, you may be exophoric. Performance and audition spaces will look bigger to you than they are; in an effort to "fill the space," you may overshoot your energetic needs and strain your voice. Conversely, if you're an esophore, you may struggle with vocal energy and belting. Large vocal sounds can feel uncomfortable since you won't want to overwhelm what looks to you like a small space. Many singers who've come to me and said something like "I'm afraid to belt," have turned out to be esophoric.

Here's how to test yourself for a phoria *(Fig. 14.10)*:

1. Set up a camera directly in front of you at eye level. Start recording.

2. Look directly at the camera and cover your right eye with your hand (the eyes should stay open). Hold for ten seconds.

3. Quickly pull your hand away to the side.

4. Repeat Steps 2–3 with the left eye and left hand.

5. Repeat twice more on both sides, each time holding the eye cover for ten seconds.

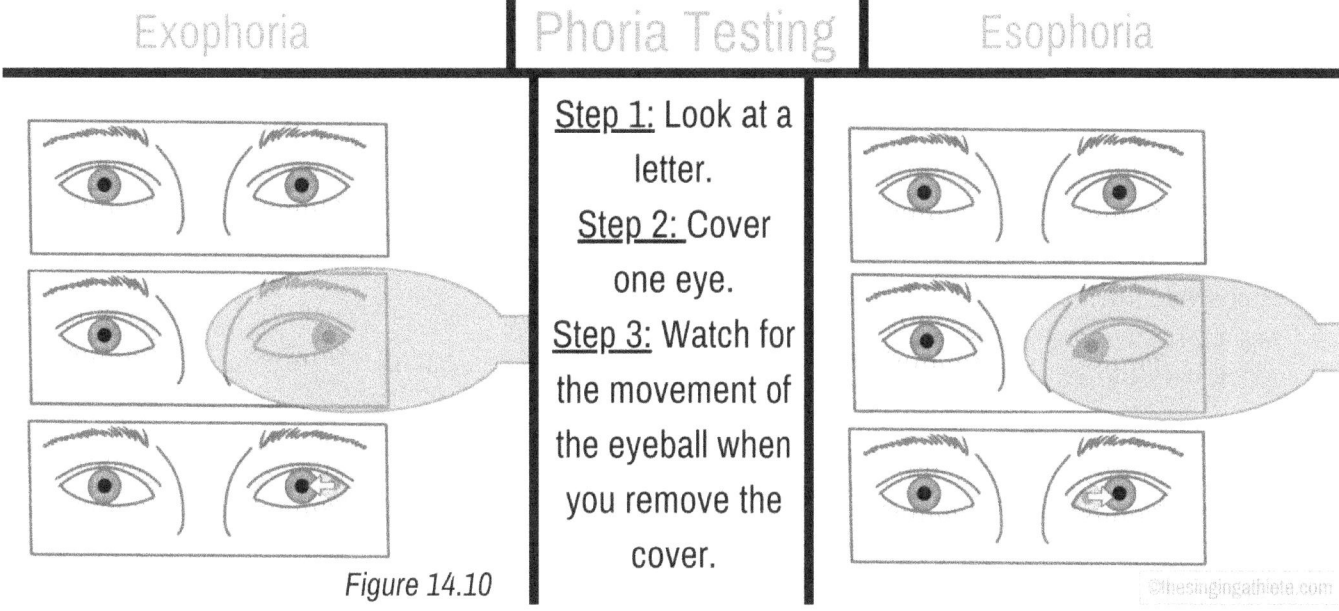

Figure 14.10

Watch the video back; here's what you're looking for:

- If you're exophoric, you'll see your eye snap back in toward your nose when you remove your hand. When the eye is covered, the muscle dominance activates and the eyeball starts to drift out. When the hand is removed, the eyeball snaps back into place, in this case, moving back toward the center.

- If you're esophoric, you'll see your eye snap back out toward your temple when you remove your hand. When the eye is covered, the muscle dominance activates and the eyeball starts to drift in. When the hand is removed, the eyeball snaps back into place, in this case, moving out away from the center.

If you see exophoria, do the Pencil Push-up and Stereogram drills below to correct it. If you see esophoria, do the Near/Far Switches drill coming up, focusing more on the distant target.

Pencil Push-ups and "The Mask"

A typical voice instruction is to feel the resonance in "the mask." The structures that are in the dead-center of "the mask" are the eyes. Correct visual vergence helps to direct vibration to this area of the face. When a singer is asked to "collect the sound in the front," or "imagine a small forward point for the tone," these instructions can be ineffective if someone has an undiagnosed phoria. If you can't converge your eyes, you can't converge your voice.

The Pencil Push-up *(Fig. 14.11)* is a drill that works on the convergence of your eyes. Depending on the angle at which you do the push-up, you will be working either CN III or CN IV.

Version 1

1. Assess your voice and body.

2. Hold a pencil out in front of you at arm's length, with the tip facing up.

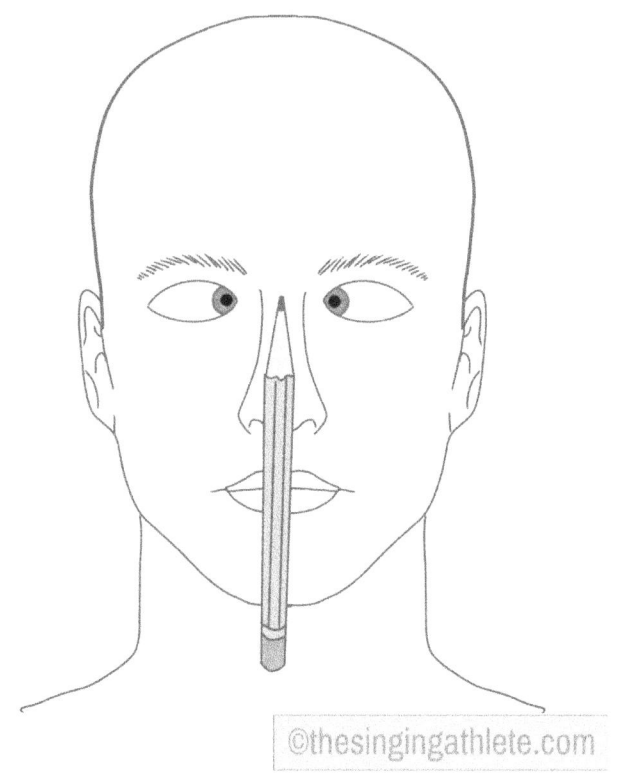

Figure 14.11

3. Focus on the pencil tip and slowly bring it in toward the bridge of your nose.

4. The goal is to bring the tip of the pencil as close as possible; the tip should be one image all the way in. If the image splits into two, take the pencil back out away from your face.

5. Repeat 3–5 times. Also try holding the converged position to see how your endurance is.

6. Reassess.

Version 2

In Version 2, we will add visual acuity to the drill:

1. Assess your voice and body.

2. Hold a pencil with writing on it out in front of you at arm's length.

3. Focus on a letter and slowly bring the pencil in toward your nose.

4. Stop when the letter becomes blurry.

5. Bring the pencil back out and repeat 3–5 times, each time approaching the edge of blurriness.

6. Reassess.

Variation 1: Do the Pencil Push-up from a different angle. Start with the pencil below eye level and track the object coming up and in (tip of the pencil to the tip of your nose). This version trains a different cranial nerve—your trochlear nerve (CN IV). If you are struggling with the original Pencil Push-up, this version may feel easier.

Variation 2: Do the Pencil Push-up starting with it above eye level and track the object coming down and in.

Variation 3: Perform the Pencil Push-ups from different angles while singing a challenging phrase. Sing it once with the pencil coming toward you and once with it going away from you. See which feels better vocally.

If you're struggling with the Pencil Push-up, you may have one eye that is not converging. The best way to tell what's going on is to video yourself as you do the drill. You should see both eyes moving in symmetrically as the pencil tip approaches your eyes. If you see one eye moving in while the other moves late, moves less, or shakes on the way in, that lagging eye is the one that needs training. Do 2–3 Pencil Push-ups with the "good" eye covered and only the "bad" eye doing the convergence. For instance, if you saw your left eye lagging in the video, cover your right eye and do the push-ups with only the left eye. *[Note: if you use the front-facing camera on your phone, it will probably flip the image when you watch it back, so make sure you keep track of which side you're looking at.]*

You have to be careful that you don't cheat when doing a monocular Pencil Push-up:

- *Cheat #1: Missing the center of your nose.* The tendency is to make it easier on yourself by moving the pencil off to your left if you're working your left eye and vice versa. It's better to overcorrect than under-correct. If you're targeting the left eye, move the pencil farther to your right and then bring it toward your face, aiming for the outside of your right nostril. For the right eye, move the pencil to your left and then bring it in, aiming for the outside of your left nostril.

- *Cheat #2: Turning your head to avoid convergence.* You have to keep your head still during a Pencil Push-up. If you're working on your left eye and you turn your head to the right, you avoid the converged position and negate the exercise. This can be tough to feel. Video yourself or press your head against the back of a chair/wall/car seat to make sure you're not moving the head at all.

Once you've done three reps with the non-converging eye, uncover the stronger eye and do 2–3 Pencil Push-ups with both eyes. This is both to notice improvement and to reconnect to binocular vision.

Proper vocal energy requires an accurate visual assessment of the size of the acoustic space into which you are singing. This is especially problematic in "dead" spaces, where the auditory feedback is reduced and you rely more on your vision to judge vocal effort. A good Pencil Push-up can be all you need to reduce or eliminate vocal strain.

Stereogram

As a kid, you might remember doing a "Magic Eye" puzzle, where you have to cross your eyes to see a hidden image. The term for this is a ***stereogram*** and it's another excellent convergence drill; I've created a simplified version here *(Fig. 14.12)*.

1. Hold Figure 14.12 about two feet away from your eyes and look at the bottom set of circles; if it's blurry, move it in or out until the letters are clear.

2. Hold a pencil in front of the chart with the tip up and fixate on the tip.

3. As you keep fixating on the pencil tip, move it toward your eyes until you see the bottom circles converge into a third circle in the middle. If you're reading a black-and-white edition of the book, download the color version of the stereogram at thesingingathlete.com. With the color version, you

should see a green circle on the left, a red circle on the right, and a dark circle in the middle. If the middle circle is green, you're favoring your left eye; if it's red, you're favoring your right eye. Try to get the middle circle dark, with the letters looking a little three-dimensional.

4. If you've got the lower middle circle stable, move up a line and repeat Steps 2–3. The greater distance makes convergence more challenging. I've also left out a few letters; you should be able to fully read "Singing is a sport" when your eyes are converged. See if you can go all the way to the top line.

5. Once you've got the middle circles dark and stable, use the VOR drill from the previous chapter (shaking your head "no," shaking your head "yes," tilting your head, moving your head on diagonals). You should be able to move your head in all of those angles without losing the clear middle circle.

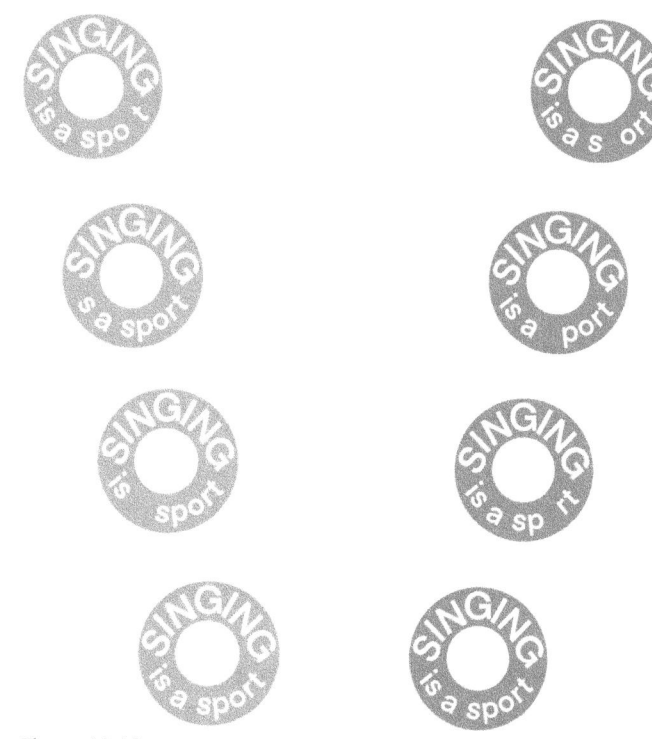

Figure 14.12

6. If you've got the hang of the stereogram, sing a phrase of music while keeping the middle circle present. Many of us think we know what we're looking at when we sing, but we're not truly focused. The stereogram will keep you honest as to how good your visual targeting is.

Near/Far Switches

So what if you are not exophoric but esophoric? If you need more vocal energy, or need to connect more to your extensor muscles, try these Near/Far Switches *(Fig. 14.13)*:

1. Assess your voice and body.

2. Stand in a comfortable position, looking at an object as far away as you can; forty meters or more is an ideal distance.

3. Hold a pencil in your hand with the tip up. Bring it in, so it is close but not blurry.

4. Quickly switch your focus back and forth from the near pencil tip to the far visual target.

5. Repeat for ten rounds of near-and-far switches.

Figure 14.13

6. Reassess.

Like in the Pencil Push-up, one eye may be doing this better than the other. Video yourself; if you see an eye that is lagging, repeat the near/far drill, this time covering the stronger eye. Switch ten times with only the weaker eye, then reassess. Follow this with ten switches with both eyes.

You can also try a "far/far" version of the exercise. Pick two objects of different distances that are both fairly far away from you. Do ten switches between these distant objects and reassess.

EYES AND BELTING

Since looking far facilitates extension in the body, it can be especially useful in belting. When you sing, your vocal folds go through a vibratory cycle of closed phases (when the folds touch) and open phases (when they don't). In a belt quality, the closed phase of the vocal folds is longer. In each cycle of vibration, the folds spend more time touching, with less air passing through them. Therefore, when you belt, you don't want to use a lot of air.

In Chapter 2, we discussed the startle reflex, which recruits flexors like your abs and chest muscles. These muscles are good at creating quick, explosive contractions to protect the body. When they activate, they can also send a quick puff of air at the folds. This puff is not helpful for belting; when the folds are closed, there's nowhere for this air to go and it can result in a squeezed vocal quality.

When belting, you may instead want to create a reflexive activation of your extensor muscles. Unlike the flexor muscles that create the quick movement of a startle reflex, extensor muscles are better at slow, controlled contractions. This measured activation is useful for the needs of belt singing. A simple way to activate your extensors is to look farther away when you belt. These visual reflexes don't last forever, so it's best to "save" the far focus for the big notes. Look at a close or medium distance for most of the song, and shift your vision farther out when it counts.

Eye Dominance

If you are noticing an eye that is slow on these drills, it is a good idea to check your eye dominance *(Fig. 14.14)*. Here's how to test yours:

1. Put your arms out in front of you and make a small triangle with the thumbs and the first knuckles—the whole triangle should be about an inch (2.5 cm) or so on each side.

2. Find a small object in the distance and put it in the center of the triangle.

3. Close your left eye. If the object remains in your view, you are right-eye dominant. If your hands move off the target to the left, you're left-eye dominant.

4. To check your results, recenter the target with both eyes open and then close your right eye. If the object remains in your view, you are left-eye dominant. If your hands move off the target to the right, you're right-eye dominant.

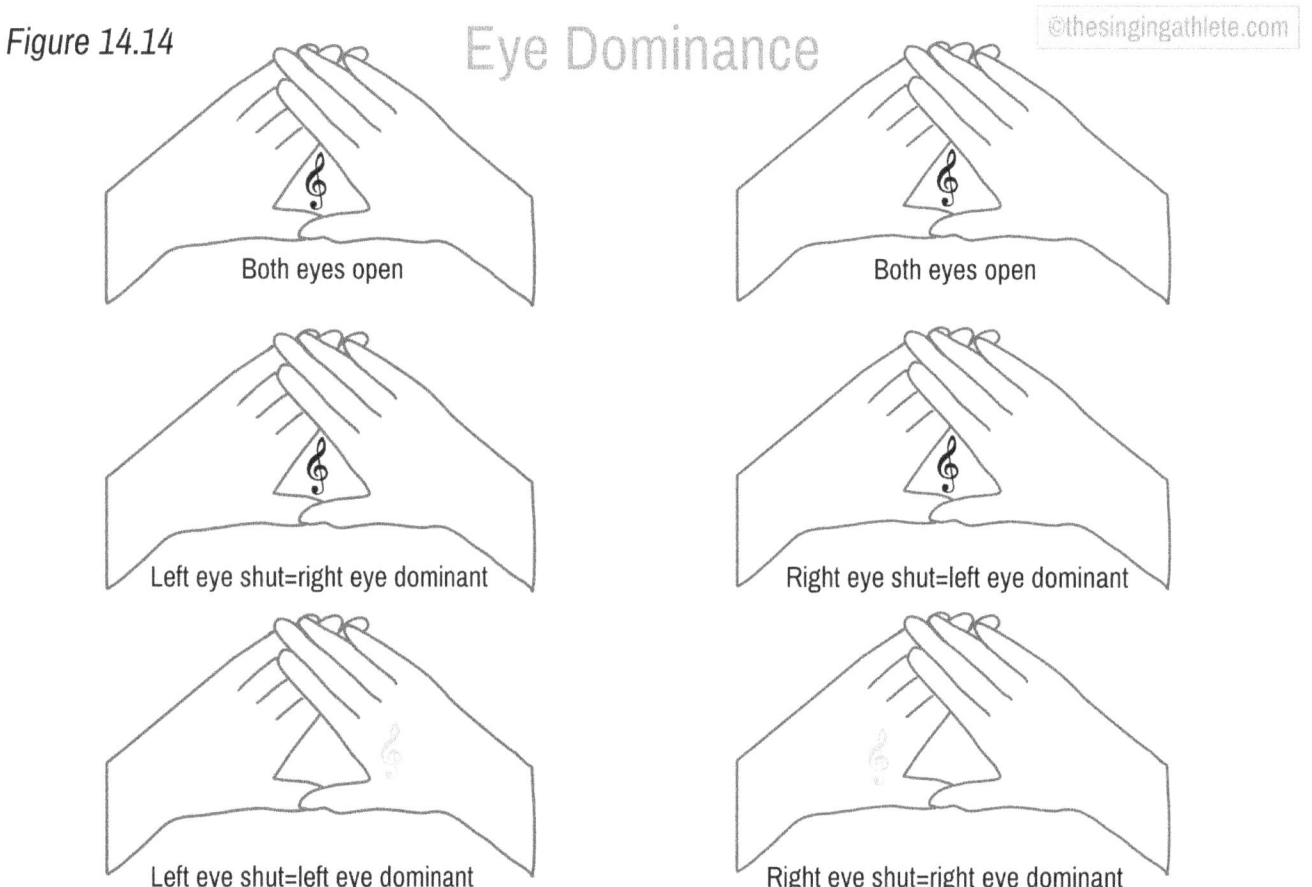

Figure 14.14

It's normal to have a stronger eye, and you will probably always have a slightly faster reaction time (14–21 milliseconds) in your strong eye. There are two situations where eye dominance may matter:

- ***Eye dominance vs. hand dominance:*** About 20 percent of the population has a different dominant hand than their dominant eye. If that's you (e.g., you're right-handed but left-eye dominant), neck mapping is essential. Your visual system controls your suboccipital muscles (under your skull) and your hand dominance affects your brachial plexus (bottom of your neck). If your left eye is working overtime at the same time you're using your right hand to get through the day, the cross-wiring in the neck can leave it very confused and tight. Review the SCM, trapezius, and scalene exercises in Chapter 7.

- ***Switching eye dominance***: Some people switch their dominance at different distances. Test yourself by repeating the eye-dominance drill at closer and farther points. If you're relying on one eye for close objects and the other for far ones, the constant switching can get exhausting. This fatigue can also be an issue with monovision contacts and surgeries (where one eye is corrected for close vision and the other for distance vision). Because visual accommodation (focusing at different distances) is so crucial to the brain, I wouldn't use any products that made my eyes uneven in this way.

Peripheral Awareness

When you are experiencing stress, your visual field closes in. A 2005 study found that peripheral visual fields were more open in athletes during a typical practice day than in a high-intensity game. They lost part of their visual field when anxiety increased.[103] And as with everything, peripheral skills are SAID-specific. When you live in New York, every day is an assault of people wanting your attention. It's often best to keep your eyes straight ahead and tune everything out, but that comes at a cost to your eyes and brain.

Let's see how good your peripheral vision currently is *(Fig. 14.15)*. It is most responsive to movement, so these drills will involve flicking your fingers.

1. Stand in a comfortable position with your hands directly in front of you

2. Begin to flick your pointer fingers up and down. Focus your eyes on an object directly in front of you.

3. Move your arms out slowly toward the side, stopping when you can barely see the wiggling of your fingers. Don't move your eyes; keep them looking straight ahead.

4. Once you reach the end-range of your peripheral vision, stop flicking your fingers but leave your hands where they are. Now, turn your head and take a look at how far out your peripheral field went. Is it even on both sides?

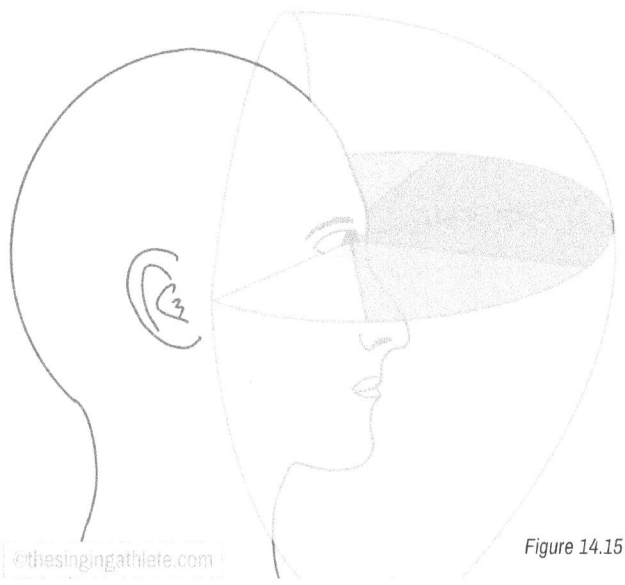

Figure 14.15

5. Repeat, with your flicking fingers going up and out on a diagonal.

6. Repeat, with your flicking fingers going down and out on a diagonal.

This drill assesses your lateral peripheral vision, where you should be able to get to 100–110 degrees (slightly past your ears). Now, close each eye individually and look at an object directly in front of you. Keep looking at the object you've chosen and see how far across your nose your peripheral field extends medially; you should be able to get to 60 degrees across the midline. With both eyes open and your focus directly in front of you, become aware of your vertical field. In the superior direction, you should be able to see about 60 degrees because the forehead blocks some of the view. Your inferior peripheral field should go farther, and you should be able to see about twelve inches (thirty cm) in front of your feet as your eyes look directly forward. A loss of peripheral vision in the down direction is a hazard when it comes to falling, so if you trip a lot, this might be worth checking.

One of my favorite drills in my Singing Athlete course is to have two people stand at the edge of the performer's peripheral visual field and make crazy shapes while the performer sings (I love creative people). Often, this peripheral stimulus will lower the threat of difficult vocal skills. When the rods in the eyes get activated through movement, the proprioceptive ability of the brain goes up. Suddenly, coordination that seemed difficult happens fluidly and efficiently. We can thus infer a direct correlation between peripheral vision and the throat. If you are trying to actively "open the throat," that may be difficult if your peripheral field is shut down. When vision expands, the throat can expand with it.

Improving your peripheral awareness is simple; situate yourself so that something with movement is in your periphery while you practice. You can play an online video with the sound muted or use an app like OKN Strips or Optodrum on your phone. Based on your assessments, you can situate the movement so it's creating stimulus in your weaker peripheral quadrants. You can also practice becoming more aware of colors, shapes, and movement in your periphery as you walk around throughout the day.

Training peripheral vision is also an excellent investment in your personal safety. I got a mild concussion in a show when I was in grad school; a cue was miscalled, a set piece got stuck, and a painting fell on my head. If I had been training my peripheral vision back then, I wonder if I could have gotten out of the way in time.

COLOR, THE EYES, AND THE BRAIN

When you play Elphaba, you are lit in green the entire show. Depending on how your brain responds to that color, that's either going to be awesome or terrible news for you. Let's take a look at how color and the brain intersect.

(Note: In my studio, I use colored glasses for testing. If you want to try this at home without buying glasses, you can download a PDF at thesingingathlete.com that will allow you to test yourself.)

Green

Although it may not be easy being green, it is certainly relaxing; the cortex calms down in the presence of verdant colors. This response may be because humans have evolved into seeing trees and leaves as non-threatening things. In migraine research, green glasses have been shown to reduce the spike in cortical activation that follows the start of the migraine. If a migraine sufferer puts green glasses on when they feel the first signs of a migraine coming on, it can reduce the severity of the symptoms.[104] This fact can be extrapolated to use in any chronic-pain or anxiety situation. In these states, there is too much cortical activation going on; if you slap some green glasses on, the stress and pain may reduce. If you feel that your brain is always in overdrive, try wearing green glasses while you practice.

Blue

While green calms the cortex, blue wakes it up. You've probably heard the (very good) advice to reduce blue-light exposure at night. But just because you shouldn't stare at your phone at 1 a.m. doesn't mean blue light is inherently detrimental. It can be a great way to get geared up. In my case, I can sing higher and longer with blue glasses on.

Let me explain why, using myself as an example. I've had two minor concussions; in neither case did I lose consciousness, and I was declared fine by the medical folks I saw. But with the hindsight of what I know now, I think they both left me with some minor cortical-activation problems. When you take a hit to your head, the area where the impact happens goes through a threat response, possibly reducing neural activation there.

One reason why I feel great wearing blue glasses is that the color might be waking up neurons that are dormant. If you have anything in your history that sounds like a reduction of brain activation (e.g., concussions, visual issues, hearing issues, lack of smell or taste, numbness or tingling in your limbs), blue glasses are worth a try.

> This is a good time to expand a bit on what is known as a mild TBI (traumatic brain injury) or concussion. You don't have to have a background as a football linebacker to consider this in your history. If you've ever taken a blow to the head, even if it didn't result in a loss of consciousness, there may have been changes in your brain afterward. Visual and vestibular symptoms are some of the most common long-term results from a mild TBI. It's highly unlikely that a thorough neurological exam was done after a bump to the head, so you may notice some peculiar things while doing the vision exercises in this chapter. Wearing a pair of colored glasses that assess well for you can be a great way to reduce visual threat as you train your eyes. You can also review the Visual Reset Drills we did earlier in the chapter; use them if you start to get tired.

Red

Red light is perceived differently throughout the day. In a phenomenon known as Rayleigh scattering, the sky looks red at sunrise and sunset while appearing blue at midday; your eyes perceive these daily color shifts to entrain your circadian rhythms. If you wear red glasses in the morning, they are cortically activating; they mimic the sunrise, when your body energy is supposed to kick in. If you wear them in the evening, red glasses are calming; they replicate the feeling of winding down for the night. This is why your phone turns red every night when you use a program like Night Shift on iOs.

The shift in light wavelengths that occurs throughout the day is why it's important to get outside more. If the weather is nice, I often work out in the park instead of spending time under the fluorescent lights of the gym. Since my job as a teacher requires me to be inside a lot, I try to maximize my exposure to daylight. I also situate my studio so that I sit by the window.

Exposure to red light can raise metabolic efficiency and provide benefits such as improved thyroid function,[105] better jaw movement,[106] and reduced pain after surgery.[107] I use red light frequently; it makes me feel great. I get my supplies from redlightman.com.

Yellow

Yellow improves visual clarity. Many singers who have acuity issues sing better in yellow glasses. If you are trying to wean yourself off corrective lenses, a pair of yellow glasses can be smart to keep around.

TEMPORAL AND NASAL VISUAL FIELDS

Each of your eyes divides into a temporal (outside) and a nasal (inside) field *(Fig. 14.16)*. The visual information taken in from the temporal field of your left eye and the nasal field of your right eye goes to the right hemisphere of the brain for processing. The information taken in from the temporal field of your right eye and the nasal field of your left eye goes to your left hemisphere. Here's a quick experiment you can do to see if you have a side of your brain that needs more activation.

<u>Brain Hemisphere Test</u>

1. Assess your voice and body.

2. Use the flashlight on your phone to shine a light into the outside area (temporal field) of your left eye for ten seconds. Move the light around a bit on the left side while you look straight forward. You are stimulating your right hemisphere.

3. Reassess.

4. Now shine the light in the outside area of your right eye for ten seconds. Move the light around and keep looking forward. You are now stimulating your left hemisphere.

5. Reassess.

If you had a better result on one side, shine the light outside the good eye before performing.

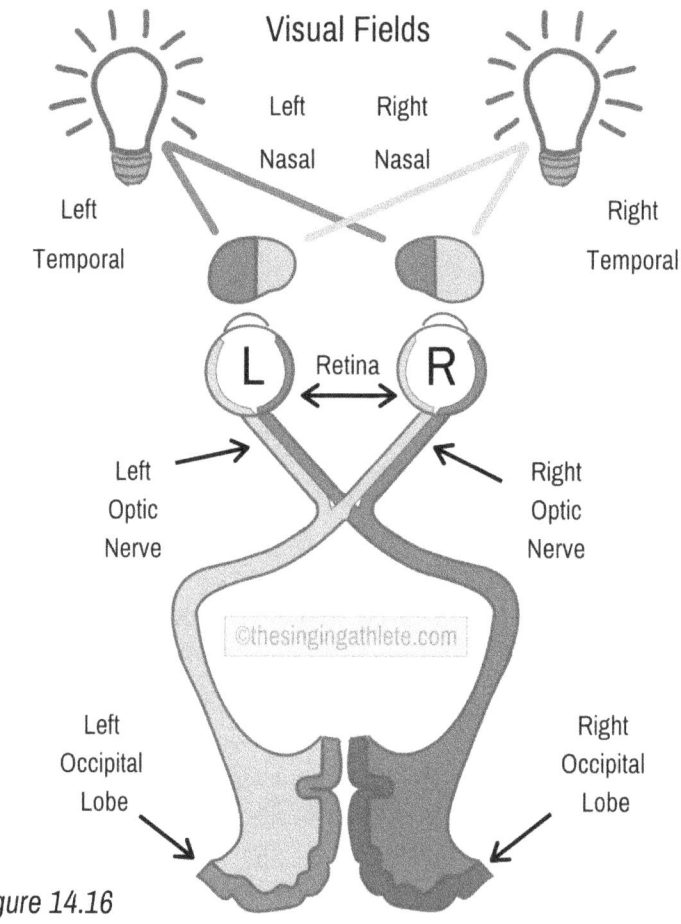

Figure 14.16

Pinhole Glasses

I talked about pinhole glasses at the start of the chapter; if you wear corrective lenses, here's a home experiment:

1. Remove your glasses/contacts.

2. Look at some writing that looks blurry without correction; it can be close to you or far away.

3. Form your hand into a tube shape, so your fingers touch your palm and you can see a little daylight through the curl of your fingers.

4. Hold the "hand tube" up to your eye. Look at the writing through this tube, with the other eye closed. Is it easier to read?

5. If you have a comb handy, look at the writing through the teeth of the comb and see if that improves clarity.

For many of us, our brains have trouble making sense of the light entering the eyes. When you look at an object through a small hole or the teeth of a comb, the visual information becomes easier to interpret, thus potentially improving acuity. Pinhole glasses utilize this concept to train vision; they are frames containing two black pieces of plastic with small holes in them. They can boost either close or far vision, and if you noticed an improvement in the drill above, they might be beneficial. They can be worn watching TV, reading, or (with practice) walking around; I use mine instead of sunglasses. The only main contraindication is you shouldn't wear them while driving.

Prescription lenses are designed to provide a clear image at a fixed distance. Pinhole glasses allow your eyes to use their natural process of accommodation, providing clarity at all distances. Their black color also stimulates the low-light-sensitive rods in the retina, toning up your peripheral visual receptors. When you are starting with pinholes, 5–10 minutes at a time is a good beginning session.

15. FIRST BRAIN

A hefty amount of the brain is devoted to automatic processes. You're probably not consciously aware of pumping blood through your arteries, moving food through your digestive tract, or dilating your pupils—and yet you do all of these things constantly. Singing is an activity that takes place along similar reflexive pathways. The vocal folds come together anywhere between 50 and 1,500 times a second; does that sound like a tempo that you can consciously control?

The first brain is the originator of these reflexive pathways, and we've already been training it for most of the book. When you do conscious breathing work, activate your cranial nerves, or learn new movement patterns, there is an effect in your first brain. In this chapter, we will learn more about the brainstem and cerebellum, two of the main structures that form this vital area.

THE BRAINSTEM

The brainstem *(Fig. 15.1)* is responsible for maintaining the systems that keep you alive. It has a powerful role in inhibiting pain, stabilizing your body for athletic movement, and regulating your stress levels. The brainstem is active in any reflexive vocalization (e.g., laughing, crying, screaming). It is also the origin point for ten of your twelve cranial nerves (all except CN I and II).

How would you know if you have issues in your brainstem? Some history questions to consider are:

1. Do you have a history of high blood pressure or hypertension?

2. Do you tend to sweat a lot? On one side more than the other?

3. Do your feet or hands get cold?

4. Do you have issues with your gut (reflux/IBS/Crohn's/constipation/chronic diarrhea)?

5. Do you have a history of injuries that are more focused on one side of the body?

6. Are you sensitive to light and sound? Do you avoid bright light and noisy places?

Figure 15.1

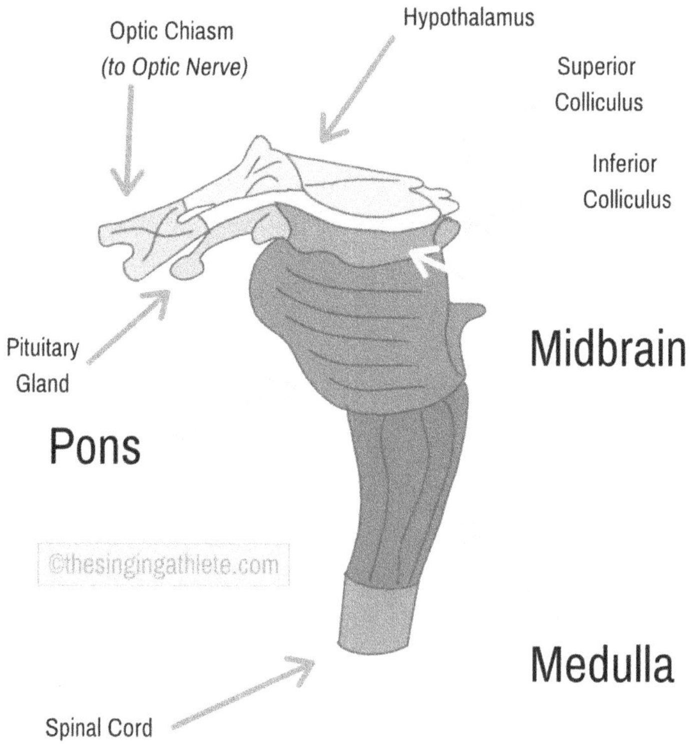

The brainstem consists of three anatomical parts:

- *Midbrain*

- *Pons*

- *Medulla*

The *midbrain* is the smallest area of the brainstem (about .75 inches/2 cm long) and is an area that receives input from all lobes of the cortex. The midbrain functions like an association zone, taking in neural information and deciding whether a sympathetic response (increase in blood flow, heart rate, breathing rate) is necessary. Any brain injury, like a concussion, can leave you with a midbrain that won't relax, causing a chronically stressed state.

Think of it this way: if you reached out several times to a friend and never heard back from them, your subsequent communications would be more insistent. Eventually, you might get concerned about their well-being due to their lack of responsiveness. The midbrain is continuously asking for information from its "friends" (i.e., different locations in the brain). A neural zone can become dormant due to concussion, sensory issues, or lack of movement. When an area stops responding, the midbrain becomes more and more agitated by the absence of data, potentially leaving it in a hyperactive state.

You can train your midbrain by doing most of the drills in the last chapter. Cranial nerves III and IV live here, so moving the eyes provides a strong midbrain stimulus. Exercises like Pencil Push-ups and Saccades can be especially helpful. The midbrain also contains the **superior and inferior colliculi**, which are brain areas that map your visual and auditory worlds. The Hearing Map Test (Chapter 13), which helps you locate where a sound is coming from, is therefore also a midbrain drill.

Sometimes, the midbrain needs to be inhibited instead of activated; if you answered yes to any of the history questions earlier in the chapter, you might have an overactive midbrain. Try these things to quiet it down:

- Dark glasses
- Green glasses
- Pinhole glasses
- Earplugs

THE BRAINSTEM AND YOUR MUSCLES

The midbrain facilitates flexor muscles *(Fig 15.2)*. The other two parts of the brainstem are the *pons* and the *medulla*, which we've talked about along the way. As a review, the pons contains cranial nerves V-VIII, and it facilitates your extensor muscles. The medulla forms a bridge between your pons and your spinal cord. It contains cranial nerves IX-XII, and it inhibits extension (so it, in effect, promotes flexion).

In the Flexor/Extensor Dominance Test we did in Chapter 14, you were looking for a pattern of favoring either the front or back line muscles of your body. The mild stress of a side bend gives you a clue into how your brain reacts under the load of performance. If you tip forward doing an end-range lateral movement, you probably also rely more on your flexors when you're nervous. If you tip back, you may over-contract your extensors under pressure.

Review the Flexor/Extensor Dominance Test (Chapter 14) before you read on. If you're still not sure which one you are, here are a few clues:

- *Flexor-dominant:* head too far forward, chest caved in, abs tight, neck in a "hump" shape.

- *Extensor-dominant*: lower back in a swayback, hamstrings tight, chest pushed forward, back muscles shortened (can't do a good forward bend).

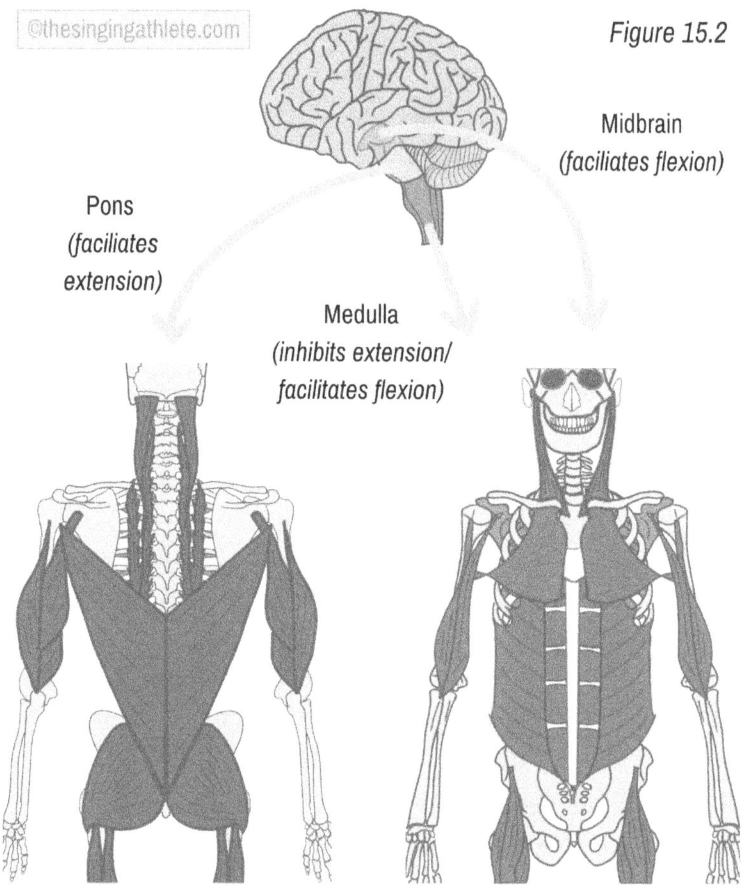

Figure 15.2

Pons *(faciliates extension)*

Midbrain *(faciliates flexion)*

Medulla *(inhibits extension/ facilitates flexion)*

If you're too flexed, you're looking for more extensor tone; that would mean doing drills that wake up your pons. Since cranial nerves V-VIII live there, any exercise that rouses these nerves could improve your muscular balance. Conversely, if you are too extended, you may need to upregulate your midbrain and medulla. Doing drills for CN III-IV (midbrain) and IX-XII (medulla) will awaken your flexors and potentially create a high-payoff result. Use the following chart to provide a framework for applying the exercises we've already done (and a few that are coming up.)

Flexor vs. Extensor Dominance and the Brainstem

If you are flexor-dominant, you need to wake up your pons, which contains cranial nerves V-VIII. Assess and reassess these exercises:	If you are extensor-dominant, you need to wake up your midbrain and medulla, which contain cranial nerves III-IV and IX-XII. Assess and reassess these exercises:
Trigeminal Nerve (CN V):	Oculomotor Nerve (C III)/Trochlear Nerve (CN IV):
Palate Stretch—TVP *(Chapter 8)*	Gaze Stabilization *(Chapter 14)*
Tongue Sensitivity *(Chapter 9)*	Smooth Pursuits *(Chapter 14)*
Shock Your Tongue—front 2/3 of tongue *(Chapter 9)*	Saccades *(Chapter 14)*
Opening the Mouth *(Chapter 10)*	Pencil Push-ups *(Chapter 14)*
Jaw Lateral Glides *(Chapter 10)*	Stereogram *(Chapter 14)*
Jaw Front-to-Back Glides *(Chapter 10)*	
Jaw Circles *(Chapter 10)*	Glossopharyngeal Nerve (C IX):

If you are flexor-dominant, you need to wake up your pons, which contains cranial nerves V-VIII. **Assess and reassess these exercises:**	**If you are extensor-dominant, you need to wake up your midbrain and medulla, which contain cranial nerves III-IV and IX-XII.** **Assess and reassess these exercises:**
Masseter *(Chapter 10)*	Soft Palate Gargle Test *(Chapter 8)*
Temporalis *(Chapter 10)*	Tongue Sensitivity-back 1/3 of tongue *(Chapter 9)*
Pterygoids *(Chapter 10)*	Shock Your Tongue—back 1/3 of tongue *(Chapter 9)*
Jaw Isometrics (Opening) *(Chapter 10)*	Taste and Singing—back 1/3 of tongue *(Chapter 9)*
Jaw Isometrics (Closing) *(Chapter 10)*	
Jaw Isometrics (To the right) *(Chapter 10)*	**Vagus Nerve (CN X):**
Jaw Isometrics (To the left) *(Chapter 10)*	Chin Tuck *(Chapter 8)*
Jaw Isometrics (Forward) *(Chapter 10)*	Laryngeal Symmetry Test 1—Humming *(Chapter 8)*
Jaw Isometrics (Back) *(Chapter 10)*	Voice and Vibration *(Chapter 8)*
Teeth Pressure-Checking *(Chapter 10)*	Laryngeal Symmetry Test 2—Cricothyroid *(Chapter 8)*
Sinus Drill 1—Plug 'n' Shake *(Chapter 11)*	Laryngeal Mobilization—Thyroid Cartilage *(Chapter 8)*
Sinus Drill 2—Vibration *(Chapter 11)*	Laryngeal Mobilization 2—Hyoid Bone *(Chapter 8)*
Facial Sensation Test 1—Light Touch *(Chapter 11)*	Soft Palate Gargle Test *(Chapter 8)*
Facial Sensation Test 2—Vibration *(Chapter 11)*	Soft Palate Vagus Test *(Chapter 8)*
Facial/Trigeminal Nerve Glide *(Chapter 11)*	Palate Stretch—LVP *(Chapter 8)*
Skull Pressure-Checking *(Chapter 11)*	Skull Pressure-Checking—back of head *(Chapter 11)*
Sagittal Suture Mobility *(Chapter 11)*	Vagus Ear Stim *(Chapter 17)*
Trigeminal Nerve *(cont.)* (CN V):	Trunk Palpations *(Chapter 17)*
Sphenoid Bone Mobility *(Chapter 11)*	Inversions *(Chapter 17)*
	Insular Belt/Weighted Blanket *(Chapter 17)*
Abducens Nerve (CN VI):	**Accessory Nerve (CN XI):**
Gaze Stabilization *(Chapter 14)*	SCM Stretch *(Chapter 7)*
Smooth Pursuits *(Chapter 14)*	SCM Strength *(Chapter 7)*
Saccades *(Chapter 14)*	Scapular Circles *(Chapter 7)*
Near/Far Switches *(Chapter 14)*	
Facial Nerve (CN VII):	**Hypoglossal Nerve (CN XII):**

If you are flexor-dominant, you need to wake up your pons, which contains cranial nerves V-VIII. Assess and reassess these exercises:	If you are extensor-dominant, you need to wake up your midbrain and medulla, which contain cranial nerves III-IV and IX-XII. Assess and reassess these exercises:
Taste and Singing—front two-thirds of tongue *(Chapter 9)*	Tongue Press *(Chapter 9)*
Blowfish *(Chapter 9)*	Two-Minute Tongue Stretch *(Chapter 9)*
Facial/Trigeminal Nerve Glide *(Chapter 11)*	Forward Roll *(Chapter 9)*
	Tongue Protrusion *(Chapter 9)*
Vestibulocochlear Nerve (CN VIII):	Tongue Circle *(Chapter 9)*
Train your VOR *(Chapter 13)*	Tongue Retraction *(Chapter 9)*
VOR-C Version 1 *(Chapter 13)*	/n/ Push-up *(Chapter 9)*
VOR-C Version 2 *(Chapter 13)*	Blade Push-up *(Chapter 9)*
Neck Lateral Glide *(Chapter 13)*	Backward Curl *(Chapter 9)*
Sustained Head-Tilt *(Chapter 13)*	Tongue Push-up—Center *(Chapter 9)*
Walking *(Chapter 13)*	Tongue Push-up—Side *(Chapter 9)*
Train Your Saccule *(Chapter 13)*	Assisted Tongue Thrust *(Chapter 9)*
Finger-Rub Test *(Chapter 13)*	
Hearing Map Test *(Chapter 13)*	
Bone Conduction Test *(Chapter 13)*	
Tuning Fork Test *(Chapter 13)*	

The chart is intended to give you a framework for exploration, not to be definitive. Remember that you have trillions of possible connections in your brain. If you think you need extensor tone but the related drills aren't testing well, try some things from the other list. Be curious and open to surprises.

The following drills can do good things for everyone's brainstem:

- ***Long spine*** *(Chapter 3)*

- ***All breathing drills*** *(Chapters 4–7)*

- ***Tongue in the spot/proper swallowing*** *(Chapter 9)*

- ***Scar rehab*** *(Chapter 12)*

THE PMRF

The next time you're out and about, take a look at some folks walking around. Do you notice people walking with their feet turned out? If you watch their swinging arms from behind as they walk, do you see their lower arms rotated in (with the palms facing you)? This gait pattern is so common that you might think this is the way things are supposed to be. Most likely, though, people who walk like this have a sleepy brainstem.

There is a part of your brainstem called the ***pontomedullary reticular formation***, or ***PMRF*** *(Fig. 15.3)*. The PMRF is a set of interconnected nuclei that run through your pons and medulla. It controls reflexive actions like walking gait and is also a big player in all things vocal. In 2007, Jürgens and Hage wrote:

"The reticular formation of the pons and medulla *(PMRF)* has direct connections to the motor neurons for all phonatory muscles and thus may coordinate phonatory muscle groups to generate complete vocal patterns."[108]

You have a right PMRF and a left PMRF. Besides the vocal aspects, each PMRF does other indispensable things on each individual side of the body:

- Inhibits pain

- Controls your autonomics (e.g., heart rate, blood pressure)

- Provides reflexive stability (in conjunction with your cerebellum)

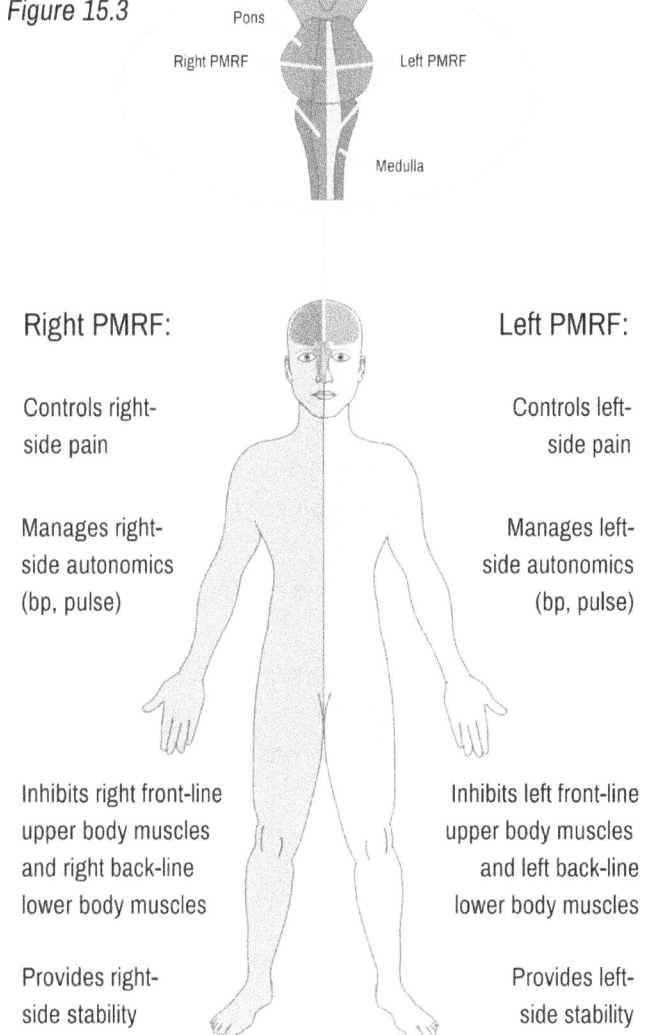

Figure 15.3

If you've had a history of more pain on one side of your body, that could be your weak-PMRF side. You can also use autonomic testing as a confirmation. This is what we would expect to see:

- Higher blood pressure on the weak-PMRF side

- A higher heart rate on the weak-PMRF side

- A lower perfusion index on the weak-PMRF side

You can test these things with a pulse oximeter; refer back to Chapter 4 to review how to do it.

Another great PMRF test is to shoot a video of yourself walking. In terms of gait, the PMRF is supposed to inhibit the front-line upper-body muscles (pecs, biceps) and inhibit the back-line lower-body muscles (glutes, hamstrings). If the PMRF isn't working, the upper-body front line becomes too active, and the lower arms start to turn in (pronate). In the lower body, a weak PMRF lets the back line become too active, and the lower legs begin to turn out, creating a "duck walk."

Start a video on your phone and walk away from the camera. When you watch it back, look for two things *(Fig. 15.4)*:

- When you walk away from the camera, are your feet turning out or tracking straight?

- When you walk away, do you see your palms facing the camera or do you see the sides of your hands?

- Is it happening more on one side?

PMRF Gait Pattern

Figure 15.4

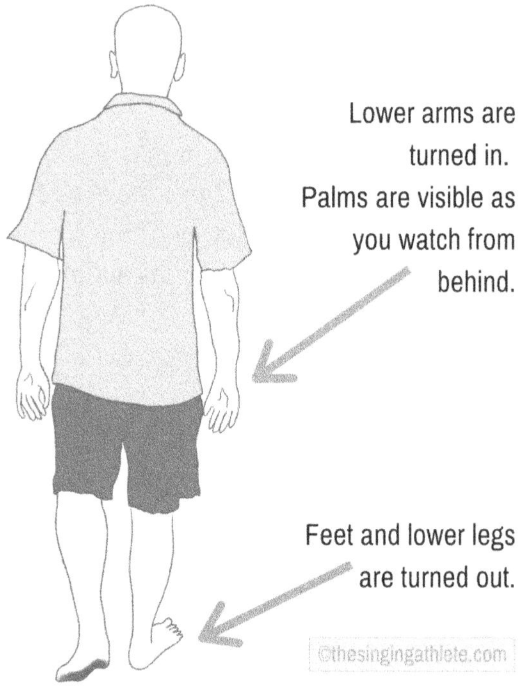

Lower arms are turned in. Palms are visible as you watch from behind.

Feet and lower legs are turned out.

In proper gait reflexes, the feet should track straight and the sides of the hands should be visible as you walk away, not the palms. If you see your feet turning out and your palms facing the camera, your PMRF needs some love. If the pattern is more visible on one side, that is the side on which you need to concentrate.

FIXING A PMRF ISSUE

So, let's say you've determined that you do have a weak-PMRF side. How do you fix it? Because the cranial nerves intertwine with the PMRF, any of the drills found on the flexor/extensor chart earlier in this chapter might help. Do a drill that tested well for you, and then re-record your gait as a reassessment. If you see less turnout and a straighter arm swing, you are helping your PMRF and should keep that drill in your rotation.

Because of how the PMRF affects posture, there are certain muscles that tend to be weak when it's not working properly. Here is a list of a few muscles you can work out on your weak-PMRF side (if you need help finding exercises to target these muscles, do a quick online search):

- Triceps
- Latissimus Dorsi
- Rhomboid
- Rectus femoris (quad)
- Tibialis anterior

So, if you see your right foot turning out more when you walk, do reps of exercises that target these muscles on your right side. For example, maybe you do ten reps of a triceps kickback on your right, then reassess your gait.

THE CEREBELLUM

The cerebellum, or little brain, is tucked under the back side of the cortex *(Fig. 15.5)*. Traditionally, it was thought to be mostly a motor structure because damage to the cerebellum results in problems with movement and posture. However, current research seems to show that it also plays a vital role in sensory integration from different brain areas. The cerebellum makes up about 10 percent of the brain's weight but contains around 50 percent of the total number of neurons.

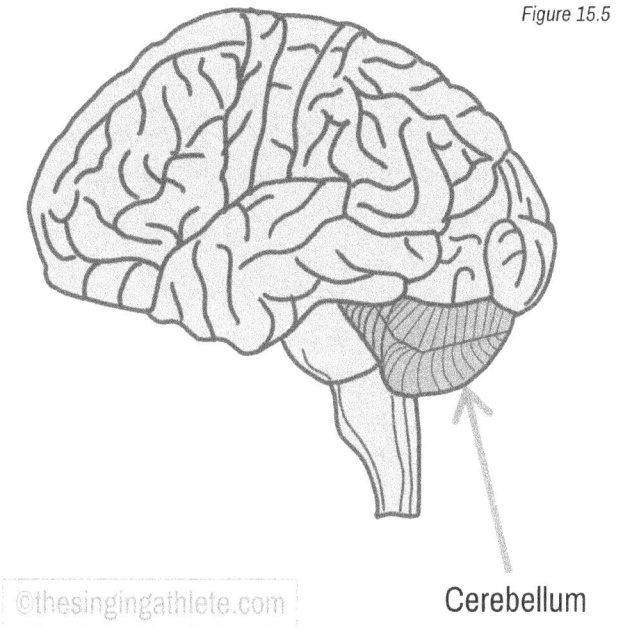

Figure 15.5

Cerebellum

These are the three key points to remember about the cerebellum:

The cerebellum is about integration: The cerebellum is tasked with taking in a lot of disparate information and producing one output. Let's say you're in rehearsal for a show. The director asks you to hit a certain mark at the last word of your song. The music director wants to change your cutoff. The choreographer is after you about the angle of your left arm. It is the cerebellum's job to take in all these instructions and give everybody what they want, all at once.

The cerebellum controls the ABCs: The cerebellum is responsible for accuracy, balance, and coordination (the ABCs). It controls the accuracy of a movement, the coordination of all necessary body parts, and the balance and stability needed while the movement is performed. A 2004 study showed that a damaged cerebellum produced inaccurate speech articulation and rhythm, along with trouble controlling vocal volume, pitch, and duration.[109] Music processing is also hindered by an under-performing cerebellum.[110] In another study published in 2009, it was found that the greater the level of vocal training, the greater the amount of cerebellar activation. Opera singers had more bilateral cerebellar activation than university voice students, and the voice students had more than laypeople.[111] If you think of all the possible challenges that a stage performer faces, it makes sense why high-level performers have robust cerebellums.

The cerebellum stops all unwanted movement (including unwanted thoughts). Reach for a (real or imaginary) glass of water with your right hand and bring it up to your lips. As you do this, your left motor cortex confers with your **basal ganglia** (a part of the brain that helps create the timing of movement) to make a plan for how to do this. It then sends the necessary signals down your right arm to produce the muscle tone needed to complete the task. As you do this, there are sensory receptors that go back up to the cerebellum to compare the motor plan with how accurately you hit the target.

Now, let's imagine that, as you reach for the glass, someone slaps your arm out of the way ("How DARE you drink that water!"). If your cerebellum weren't there, your arm would keep traveling in the direction you got hit, away from the intended target. Luckily, you do have a cerebellum, so the sensory receptors in your arm stop the unwanted movement, correcting your course back toward the cup (so you can throw it in that rude person's face!).

Your cerebellum is there to fix the inevitable mistakes that come up in movement plans. Going out of tune is a movement error. Getting behind the beat is a movement error. Pushing your voice is a movement error. A cerebellum that is healthy and awake can correct these mistakes.

Possibly the coolest thing the cerebellum does is to stop unwanted thoughts. At a neural level, thoughts are movement, and many of us have gotten into poor habits when it comes to the way we think about singing. You may have gotten into a comparison habit, always judging your voice against "better" singers. You may get anxious every time you think about getting onstage. You may have become depressed about a lack of vocal progress. If you're lying awake in bed at night, turning something over again and again in your head, doing any of the following drills can interrupt this negative thought loop.

CEREBELLAR TESTS

Have you ever noticed a difference in your side-to-side coordination? As a left-handed person, I was always perplexed that I struggled so much more with left-hand scales on the piano. When I was assigned a new piece, my heart would sink if I saw a bunch of running sixteenth-notes in the bass clef. Once I figured out that I had a deficiency in my left cerebellum, it all made sense.

You have a right and a left cerebellum. Both sides are active in vocalization, but the left cerebellum is more active in singing and the right more active in speech. When we discuss the brain lobes in the next chapter, we'll see that it is a mirror image there, with the right cortex and left cerebellum guiding music, and the left cortex and right cerebellum guiding language.[112]

Remember that the cerebellum contains 50 percent of your brain's neurons. Its metabolic demands are high, and you should do the following tests when you are rested, fed, and breathing well. The cerebellum's high metabolic needs also make it very sensitive to alcohol. It contains **Purkinje cells**, which are some of the largest and most influential neurons in the brain. Ingesting alcohol inhibits these cells, and chronic drinking can kill them. As you go through the cerebellar drills, a couple of them may remind you of sobriety tests, and now you know why. Alcohol use is generally discouraged in voice circles for its drying and reflux effects. To me, the much bigger deal is its effect on the cerebellum. As you age, falling is one of the biggest threats you will face, and Purkinje cells help to keep you on your feet. If these cells die, they don't come back, leaving you at a higher risk for a serious accident.

I don't drink anymore, except on very rare occasions (like maybe five alcoholic drinks a year). I used to drink socially, but the more I've learned about the brain, it seemed like a good idea to stop, so I did. If you can reduce or cease your alcohol consumption, do it. If you are going to drink, here are three guidelines to make it less harmful:

Andrew's Alcohol Rules:

- Hard liquor is better than wine or beer. Beer is high in estrogen-producing compounds that mess with your metabolism, and wine is high in histamines (allergy-producing substances).

- Adding fruit juice to hard liquor makes it metabolize more efficiently.

- It's best to consume alcohol with food but not with foods high in polyunsaturated fatty acids (PUFA). PUFAs are found in most processed cooking oils (except coconut oil), nuts, and seeds. This means the classic "fried food and alcohol" combo is bad news unless they'll cook it for you in coconut oil or butter. You can find complete lists of PUFA-heavy foods online.

Okay, let's do some cerebellar testing. You have a right and left cerebellum. The left cerebellum is more responsible for movement on the left side, and the right cerebellum deals with the right side. As we get into testing, we are looking for a pattern. Does it seem like you have more trouble on the right or left?

Cerebellar Test 1—Foot Tapping

1. Stand tall and put your right foot out in front of you.

2. Lift the ball of your right foot while keeping your heel on the ground.

3. Begin to rapidly tap the ball of your right foot for a minimum of five seconds (your heel stays on the floor). You are looking for a steady, rhythmic movement with no stuttering or change of tempo.

4. Repeat with your left foot out in front.

Other than steadiness of rhythm, a feeling of more tension in the shin on one side points toward that being the weaker cerebellar side for you.

Cerebellar Test 2—Heel to Shin

If your balance isn't great, perform this drill while holding onto something.

1. Stand tall and lift your right foot off the ground.

2. Place the heel of your right foot directly below the kneecap on your left leg.

3. Run your right heel down your left shin and out along your left big toe.

4. Without putting your right foot down, repeat the motion four more times. Your right heel begins touching under the left kneecap, down the left shin, and out the left big toe. Pay attention to how accurately you can touch the underside of the kneecap with your heel.

5. Repeat with the left heel touching under the right kneecap, down the right shin, and out the right big toe (five reps)

We are testing the cerebellum on the side with the active leg—so if it's harder to find the right kneecap with the left heel, it's the left cerebellum that is weaker here.

Cerebellar Test 3—Finger Tapping

1. Put your hands out in front of you. Touch your pointer finger to your thumb, with the fingers as straight as possible.

2. Begin to tap the pointer finger and thumb together rapidly. Make sure you are moving both pointer fingers and thumbs and continue for 10–15 seconds.

3. Look at your hands and see if one side is slowing down. Also notice if one hand starts to feel fatigued.

The weaker cerebellar side is the hand that starts to lag or get tired.

Cerebellar Test 4—Hand Tapping

1. Bring the fingers of your right hand (including your thumb) together with your fingers straight, like a seal's flipper.

2. Put your left hand out in front of you, palm up.

3. Place the back of your right hand on top of your left hand.

4. Alternately tap the back of your right hand and the palm of your right hand on your left palm as rapidly and accurately as possible. Notice if your right fingers are staying together. The rotation for this movement should be happening from your elbow; your upper arm and shoulder shouldn't be involved.

5. Continue for 10–15 seconds.

6. Switch to the other side.

We are testing the hand that is doing the tapping, so whichever side was less accurate is the weaker cerebellar side.

Cerebellar Test 5—Shoulder Rotation

1. Bring your arms out directly in front of you with your fingers together (like a Frankenstein walk).

2. Start to rotate your upper arms (biceps) as rapidly as you can.

3. Notice if one arm gets tired, slows down, or loses accuracy of movement.

The more tired/less accurate arm is the weak cerebellar side.

Cerebellar Test 6—Finger to Nose

1. Stand tall with your feet together.

2. Bring your arms out in front of you, slightly wider than shoulder-width.

3. Close your eyes.

4. Starting with your right pointer finger, bring your fingertip to your nose as quickly and accurately as possible and then take it directly back out to the starting point.

5. Repeat with your left pointer finger, keeping the eyes closed.

6. Repeat with all other fingers.

You're trying to notice if you're more accurate on one side. Could you find the tip of your nose, or were you hitting yourself in the face? Did you find yourself slowing down as your finger approached your nose? Maybe your finger was shaking as you got close to your nose?

With these tests, you may find a side that is clearly weaker. You may also have mixed results, or maybe a split between your lower body and upper body. There are different parts of the cerebellum, so varied outcomes are not uncommon. Either way, everything we just did is both a test and a drill, so you can use these movements to train and wake up your cerebellum when you're singing. Can't get that high note to work? If your left foot tap was weak, do it for five seconds and try the note again. If that didn't work, try the hand tapping for five seconds and reassess.

Remember that practice is like a drug, and we're always looking for that minimal effective dose. There is not a magic length of time for which everyone should practice; one person might finally feel warmed up after forty-five minutes while another is starting to fatigue. So when I get asked the question, "How long should my practice session be?" my answer is, "Do a cerebellar test." Because this part of the brain is so metabolic, it will clearly show you how your resources are at the moment. If you reach a point in a practice session where you think, "Should I keep going? It's feeling good, but I don't want to overdo it," a cerebellar test can answer your question. Choose a test that is hard for you and repeat it. If it's less coordinated than usual, it might be time to stop practicing. If the test is at least as good as usual or better, it's probably fine to keep going.

Here are three other ways to upregulate your cerebellum:

- All the vestibular drills we did in Chapter 13 have a cerebellar component to them.

- The cerebellum partners with your vestibular system to facilitate the posterior chain muscles. If you have a weak cerebellar side, try these exercises unilaterally on the weak side:

  - Lat pulldown
  - Row
  - Triceps kickback
  - Single-leg deadlift

- The cerebellum responds more to complex, non-linear movements. If you have a weight in your hand for a triceps kickback, make it a circular motion as you extend the elbow, instead of a straight line.

16. SECOND BRAIN

Since we've been talking about the brain throughout the book, here are a few "fast facts" about this fascinating structure:

- The human brain weighs around 3 lbs. (1.3 kg) and is about 75 percent water.

- There are around 100 billion neurons in the brain, covering approximately 125,000 miles.

- Your brain uses 20 percent of the oxygen in your body.

- There are 100,000 miles of blood vessels in your brain.

- Neurons develop at the rate of 250,000 per minute during early gestation.

- A newborn baby's brain triples in size in the first year of life.

- When you're awake, your brain generates between 10 and 23 watts of power, which is enough to illuminate a light bulb.

- The average number of conscious thoughts a human is believed to experience each day is around 70,000.[113]

In the last chapter, we took a look at the brainstem and the cerebellum, two first-brain structures that are essential for reflexive control of your voice. Now we're going to discuss how to train the lobes of the cerebral cortex, or second brain. Whereas the first brain structures are non-rational and below your consciousness, the lobes of the second brain control decision-making, sensory processing, and creativity. Although the first brain activates your vocal folds, it's the commands that come from the second brain that form sounds into music.

There are four recognized lobes of the second brain (e.g., frontal, parietal, temporal, and occipital) and a fifth that we will consider as separate in the next chapter (insular). Although we will be looking at each lobe individually, the enormous amount of connections between these areas mean they really work together. When I mention the frontal lobe, I'm talking about the frontal lobes; you have a left and a right of each of these areas, and they are not necessarily symmetrical. And if you're a lefty like me, the maps are pretty much the same as for a right-handed person; hand dominance doesn't seem to make a big difference in cortical mapping.

FRONTAL LOBE

The *frontal lobe (Fig. 16.1)* is the neural home of higher-order thinking and voluntary movement. It is the largest part of the cortex, making up around 33 percent of the surface area. Its blood is supplied by two arteries that branch off the carotid (heart and brain health go together).

How would you know that you need frontal lobe training? Here are some things to look for in your history:

- Difficulty with focus and attention/ADHD

- Poor modulation of emotions

- Poor movement control due to lack of core stability

- Bladder control issues

- Difficulty reading

- Rhythmic issues in music

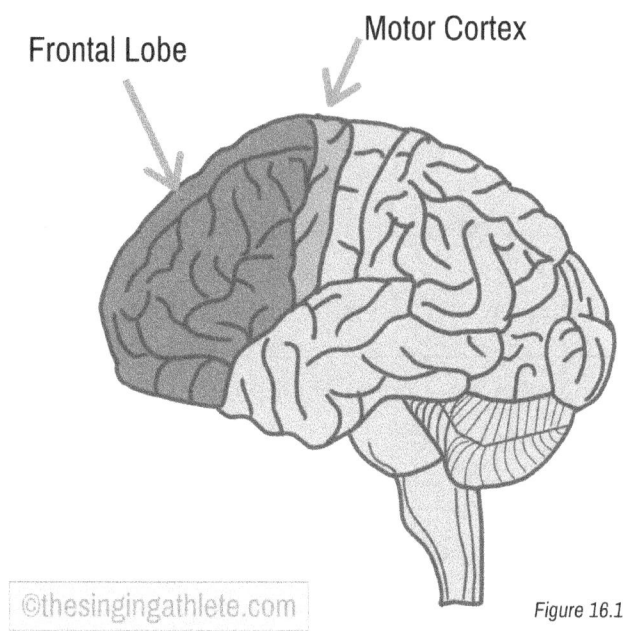

Figure 16.1

There are a few areas of the frontal lobe that are more active when you sing, including:

Motor Cortex (Precentral Gyrus): This is where the force and speed of a movement are encoded. In other words, do you really need to push your abdominals so hard to hit that high note? When singing, the right motor cortex is more active; the left is more associated with language and the right more with melodic elements. Since language is already practiced throughout every day, lyrics probably provide less novel brain stimulus than melody. This may be why singers are more likely to forget words than music when they perform; the right motor cortex may be more awake.

Dorsolateral Prefrontal Cortex (DLPFC): The DLPFC is the home of executive function, goal-setting, and planning. This is also a brain area that guides attention management and task switching. There is usually decreased activity in the left DLPFC in cases of chronic pain and depression. Remember my chronic pain story from the beginning of the book? My DLPFC gave me pain, and when that didn't work, it gave me depression. The right DLPFC is involved in pitch memory, so this is an area you want to target if intonation is an issue; try all the drills I list at the end of this section.[114] Also, because the DLPFC controls switching between tasks, you can energize it by adding more variety to your warm-up. Try singing a head-voice and a belt exercise back to back, or alternate quickly between musical styles and vocal ranges.

Supplementary Motor Area (SMA): The SMA integrates midline stability into coordinated movement, including any vocalization. We discussed in the jaw chapter that tooth vibration activates the SMA. It also responds to the visualization of movements that have already been done. When you mentally think through your performance, you activate your SMA, potentially improving midline stability.

In Chapter 2, I said that an essential function of the frontal lobe is inhibiting the first brain and its primal emotions. From a training perspective, though, any time you have to inhibit a reflexive action, you are engaging the frontal lobe. Two drills we've already done that train this inhibitory pathway are:

- ***Hypoxic Training*** *(Chapter 4):* Stopping the inhalation reflex boosts the frontal lobe.

- ***VOR-C*** *(Chapter 13):* The normal VOR stays fixated on an object when the head moves. To "cancel" that reflex requires intervention from your frontal lobe.

Here are some other training ideas:

- ***Saccades*** *(Chapter 14):* The part of your visual system that controls saccades lives in the frontal lobe. When you quickly move your eyes to a target to your right, that eye movement is driven by your left frontal lobe, and vice versa. If you want to prioritize getting out of chronic pain or depression, focus on doing saccades to the right. Start with your eyes in the center, switch your gaze to an object to your right and close your eyes to bring them back to center, repeating ten times.

- ***Identifying Smells:*** The ability to smell something comes from your temporal lobe, but identifying the smells is a function of your frontal lobe.

- ***Rhythm:*** Adding a rhythmic element to any drill upregulates the frontal lobe. An example would be doing lateral jaw glides but adding a metronome and moving to the beat.

- *Stroop Test:* Named after American psychologist John Ridley Stroop, the Stroop Test shows how interference with brain processing can affect your reaction time. You see a card with a color on it, except the name is printed in a different color (e.g., the word "purple" is written in red ink). You name the color you see, not the word; the temptation is to say "purple," even though the color on the card is red. There are several apps that perform this test (search for "Stroop Test"), so put one on your phone and do a round while practicing.

- ***Optokinetic Reflex (OKN):*** The optokinetic reflex is an eye movement that combines a smooth pursuit and a saccade. Because of the combined action, this drill activates both the frontal and parietal lobes. Test this with an app; I use either Optodrum or OKN Strips. You will see a series of moving stripes. To do the test, hold your phone horizontally (so the moving lines are aligned vertically) in front of your eyes. Start the stripes moving at a comfortable speed and hold the phone directly in front of your visual field. The goal is to keep your eyes on the middle of the screen (don't follow a stripe all the way to the edge of the screen). Try it with the stripes going to both the left and the right and reassess each direction. If you're working on chronic pain or depression, the stripes should move toward the left. You can also track the lines vertically and on diagonals.

PARIETAL LOBE

The ***parietal lobe*** *(Fig. 16.2)* forms about 20 percent of the cortex. It is the home of sensory processing, with the somatosensory cortex lying within its boundaries. When we look at the brains of singers, we see a strong association between voice training and increased activity in the somatosensory brain area. Although we do also see changes in the frontal lobe's motor cortex, the sensory changes seem to be more dramatic for vocalists. This points toward the essential inclusion of sensory training in your voice practice. If you can't feel it, you can't fix it.

Some history findings that might indicate issues with the parietal lobe are:

- Chronic pain

- Sensory loss (if the loss is on the left side, that means the right parietal lobe needs training and vice versa)

- Speech difficulties

- Dyslexia

- Difficulty understanding language

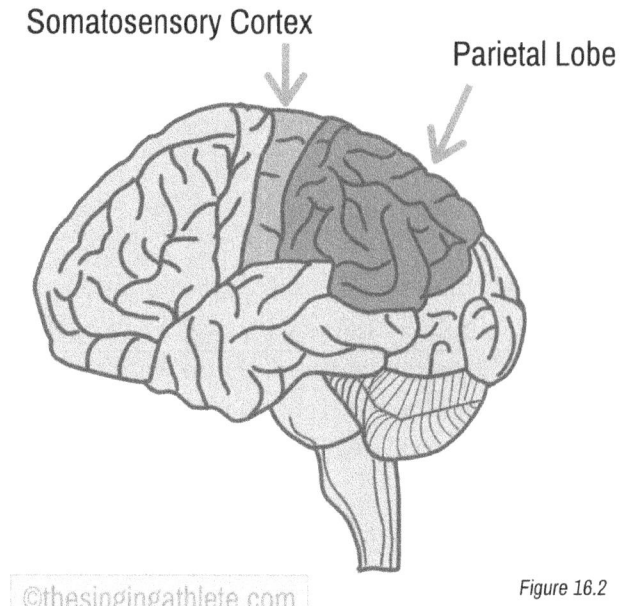

Figure 16.2

Let's highlight a couple of music-specific areas of the parietal lobe:

Somatosensory Cortex (Postcentral Gyrus): As I mentioned above, this area is strongly involved in singing, especially in the area that controls the larynx and orofacial muscles. Any complicated mouth or tongue activation engages this area, which is why it's great for singers to study new accents. I study accent training with Knight-Thompson Speechwork.

This area is also involved in volitional swallowing. As I detailed in the tongue chapter, proper swallowing has notable implications for singers. Can you put your tongue in the spot and complete 3–5 volitional swallows in relatively rapid succession?

Inferior Parietal Lobule (IPL): The IPL is one of the areas of the brain where there is a distinct side-to-side difference. The left side is involved in calculations and math, whereas the right side helps you pay attention and choose what's worthy of your time.[115] The right side also has a role in pitch discrimination.[116] This is yet another reason to include music in educational models; being able to hear a note correlates with being able to decide what's essential in life.

When we look at younger singers, they show increased IPL activation on both sides compared to untrained singers. As singers become more experienced, there is a shift toward a right-dominant IPL pattern. My theory is that, as singers get more experienced, the "math" elements of keeping in time with the music become more manageable, and the brain shifts toward a finely graded appreciation of pitch and musical elements.

Some of the drills we've already done that are good for the parietal lobe are:

- ***Diaphragm Push-up—Visceral*** *(Chapter 5)*

- ***Light Touch Test/Vibration Test*** *(Chapter 11)*

- ***Skull Exploration*** *(Chapter 11)*

- ***Sagittal Suture Mobility*** *(Chapter 11)*

- ***Pressure-Checking and Sensory Work for Scars*** *(Chapter 12)*

- ***Auditory Mapping*** *(Chapter 13)*

- ***Smooth Pursuits*** *(Chapter 14)*

- ***Optokinetic Reflex*** *(described earlier in this chapter)*

Here are some other parietally focused exercises:

- *Mindfulness:* Whether this takes the form of an official meditation practice, or merely means that you become more aware of your movement throughout the day, mindfulness activates your parietal and insular lobes. For instance, when you do "in for two, out for eight" breathing, you become more mindful of respiration. Really, almost any drill in this book can provide a focus that could be considered meditative. You can also look into an app like Headspace if you want a more guided mindfulness experience.

- *Ear Training:* Pitch discrimination can be trained by any number of apps, or by playing some chords on the piano and singing every note in the chord.

- *Math and Word Games:* Sudoku, Scrabble, or crossword puzzles are all valuable options. If you're a crossword fan, writing the answer in backward (from right to left or bottom to top) can create a stronger parietal activation.

- *Body Brushing:* Get a brush that feels good on your skin and brush yourself all over for 2–3 minutes after your shower. If you have any issues with either your bladder or your bowels, you should focus on body brushing in the feet and legs. The paracentral lobule of the parietal lobe is involved in regulating these body systems, and it responds uniquely to lower-extremity skin stimulation.

TEMPORAL LOBE

The ***temporal lobe*** *(Fig. 16.3)* takes up about 17 percent of the cortex; primates are the only mammals that have a temporal lobe. This lobe is involved in many functions, including auditory processing, balance, vision, smell, and language. Some neuroanatomists also include brain structures like the hippocampus, amygdala, and hypothalamus in the temporal lobe. Your left temporal lobe is focused on speech processing, while your right looks after body language and gestures. When it comes to singing, the left temporal lobe controls lyrics and the right controls melody. Is one of these musical elements harder to learn and maintain?

Some history findings for temporal lobe consideration are:

- Tinnitus/hearing loss

- A tendency to avoid loud or confusing sound environments

- Long-term memory issues

- Difficulty recognizing objects, faces, and scenes

- Motion sickness

All the drills from Chapter 13 target the temporal lobe. Other ideas are:

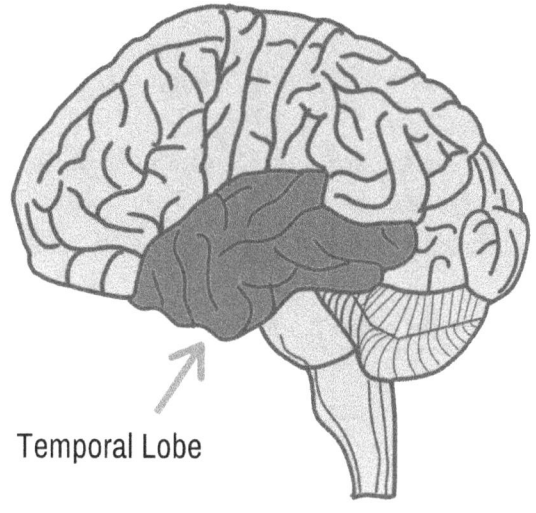

Temporal Lobe

Figure 16.3

- **Memory Drills:** The hippocampus is responsible for encoding long-term memories of both facts and experiences. You can upregulate it by giving yourself more memory tasks in your day. Let's try one. Memorize these five words: shovel, palace, numerous, bring, river. Keep reading, and I'll ask in a little bit if you remember them.

- **Performing Lyrics and Melodies Separately:** Lyrics are stored in the left temporal lobe and music in the right. Take a familiar song and do the following:

  - Sing it on a single vowel.
  - Sing it on gibberish words.
  - Recite the lyrics in tempo but without music.
  - Recite the lyrics as quickly as you can.

- **One-Sided Movement:** If you keep forgetting the words of your song, try some right-sided movement drills before singing (this wakes up the left cortex). If you have trouble staying in tune, try some left-sided movement drills before singing (this wakes up the right cortex).

- **Music vs. Podcasts:** When you're out and about, do you prefer to listen to music or podcasts? Music is more of a right temporal stimulation, whereas podcasts are more left. This preference might be a clue into which side of your brain needs activation. I'm a music listener, and I wonder if part of my inclination is related to the fact that I have more movement issues on my left side. (Remember, the right cortex controls voluntary movement on the left.)

- **Working on a 2nd/3rd/4th Language:** Having to create new neural pathways for additional languages is a strong temporal-lobe stimulus.

Before we move on, do you remember the five words I gave you earlier in this section?

OCCIPITAL LOBE

The *occipital lobe (Fig. 16.4)* is the main center of visual processing. This lobe makes up about 12 percent of the cortex, although vision as a broader process makes up around 25 percent since it also involves other lobes. The foveal area of your vision (where you see most clearly) makes up a tiny fraction of your entire visual field, and yet 50 percent of the five billion neurons in your occipital lobe are devoted to getting information from this minuscule area. The brain desperately wants to understand what it's seeing.

All the drills in the vision chapter target the occipital lobe. One additional exercise we will do involves lines in different orientations. You have neurons in your occipital lobe that only turn on when you see a vertical, horizontal, diagonal, or curved line. Part of being a singer is to be able to get lyrics into your head quickly, and certain letters are harder than others for your brain. A letter like "b," with its combination of curved and vertical lines, is more challenging than a letter like "l." These line-recognition receptors can also be part of the reason that long hours on a computer can be tiring. Let's test your eyes:

Eye Line Test

1. Assess your voice and body.

2. Look steadily at the horizontal lines in Figure 16.5 for ten seconds.

3. Reassess.

4. Repeat with the vertical, diagonal, and curved lines, reassessing after each one.

There are specific receptors in the eyes that are designed to perceive long horizontal lines (i.e., the horizon). This is one of the reasons why going to the beach or other open spaces is so rejuvenating; if you live in a city, remember to make some time for nature.

Figure 16.5

17. FEELING

Pause for a moment and attempt to become aware of your heartbeat without touching a pulse point. Can you feel it easily? Your ability to sense your heart rate is a quick test of your *interoception*, which is your intrinsic sense of the physiological state of your own body. Interoception can be both conscious and unconscious, and it covers a wide range of systems, including digestion, breathing, pain, temperature regulation, and certain types of touch. Interoception is also a big player in performance anxiety.

The brain is always trying to make predictions, and the same holds true for your interoceptive system. Your brain is trying to guess the internal needs of your performance. How much blood flow will it take to engage your abdominals to support that high note? How does your breathing rate need to adjust to keep in time with the music? The better your interoception works, the less scary it is to sing.

Let's imagine two performers walking onstage together, one with interoceptive deficits and one without them. As the stage lights hit them, both singers will feel their sympathetic nervous systems kick in. Their pupils will constrict, their heart rates will increase, and their breathing rates will increase. The singer whose interoception is working properly will feel these changes and calmly monitor them. They will understand that the increased activation of their internal systems matches the external event. The singer who has faulty interoception may have a different experience. To them, the heightened signals arriving in their brain may be misinterpreted, causing a shift into survival mode for the duration of the performance.

In the chapter on ears, I shared the analogy of the visual, vestibular, and proprioceptive systems functioning like a GPS, triangulating to keep you safe. Another GPS-style trio is the sensory triad, which we first looked at in Chapter 2. When you are performing, what you see (exteroception), where you physically are (proprioception), and what you feel inside (interoception) must all be consistent. If any part of that equation is off, anxiety and a degraded performance will result.

INTEROCEPTIVE ANATOMY

These are the three main interoceptive structures *(Fig. 17.1)*:

- ***Insula (insular lobe) of the brain***

- ***Vagus nerve***

- ***Unmyelinated free nerve endings (C-fibers)***

INSULA

The *insula* is now considered by some neuroanatomists to be the fifth lobe of the brain, and it is involved with an extensive amount of body processes. It is tucked deep into a central

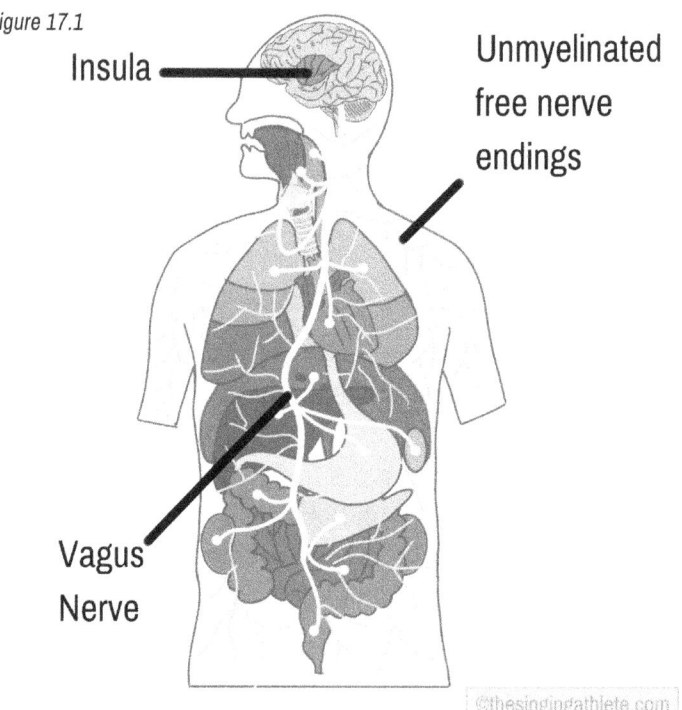

Figure 17.1

area of the cortex known as the lateral sulcus, being "insulated" by the frontal, temporal, and parietal lobes. Most research is pointing to the insula serving as a multifunctional brain area, taking a role in integrating perception, emotion, cognition, and sensation. When viewed on fMRI, the insula is usually the most active region of the brain, no matter what task is happening.

Based on current research, here is a partial list of sensory inputs that are processed in the insula *(Fig. 17.2)*:

- Temperature (Warm/cool)
- Itch
- Tickle
- Hunger/Thirst
- Sexual Arousal
- Air Hunger
- Heartbeat
- Vasomotor Activity (actions on a blood vessel that alter its diameter)
- Distension of Organs (bladder, stomach, rectum, esophagus)
- Taste
- Sensual/Pleasurable Touch

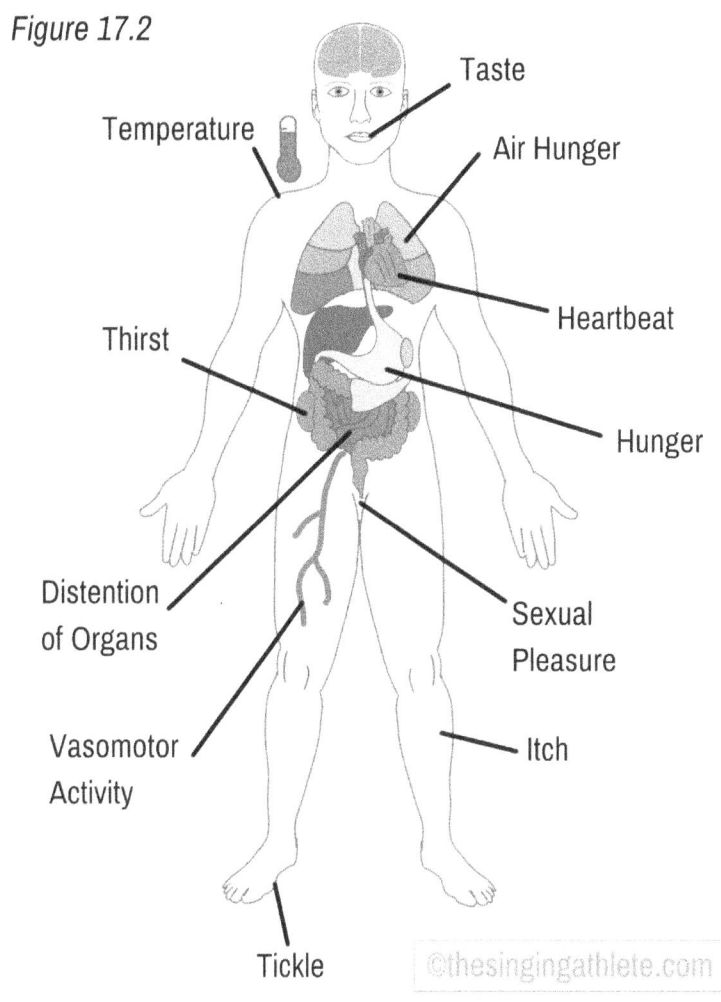

Figure 17.2

The insula helps control your breathing, heart rate, and gut function. Any digestive issue is, to some degree, an insular issue.
The **enteric nervous system**, or "belly brain," is a mesh-like arrangement of neurons that governs the function of the gastrointestinal tract. Many of the 100 million neurons found in this system are connected directly with the insula. And because the insula is also involved with emotion, this is why you may "feel" gut problems more than, say, a torn rotator cuff.

The insula processes emotional experiences related to body ownership; if it's not working, you can end up feeling like your body is not your own. It also plays a role in social connections and to your "why" (i.e., your larger purpose in life). In terms of singing, a damaged insula results in a loss of emotion in the vocal tone. A dysfunctional insula can make you completely lose the desire to sing.[117] You can think of it as the connection zone between music and emotion.

There is an area in the right anterior insula that seems to play a curiously direct role in singing. There was an experiment done in which the sensory feedback in the vocal folds was anesthetized in trained vocalists. In these numbed singers, the right anterior insula showed reduced activity. This may be one of the brain areas where associations are made to create a complete, emotionally resonant vocal performance.[118]

One sign of insular problems is taking a long time to warm up. The insula is involved with shunting blood to body tissues; if you have to vocalize for forty-five minutes before you're ready to sing, it is probably underperforming.

Some other findings in your history that may point to a need for insular training are:

- Irritable bowel syndrome
- Reflux
- Bloating/not being able to tell when you're full
- Eating disorders
- Anxiety/Depression
- PTSD

- Poor cardiac/respiratory response to exercise (e.g., "I hate cardio.")
- Difficulty judging degree of pain and sensation
- Chronic immune-system issues
- Pelvic floor dysfunction
- Alexithymia (emotional blindness)

VAGUS NERVE

As you may remember from other chapters, the **vagus nerve** is a significant player in the world of singing. It is also the main communication pathway for information to and from the insula. Here is a reminder list of its functions:

- Provides motor innervation of all muscles of the pharynx and larynx as well as most of the soft palate muscles
- Innervates the smooth muscle of the trachea (an open throat is basically a well-functioning vagus nerve)
- Provides sensation to the abdominal viscera
- Increases the rate of stomach emptying and stimulates acid production (a key to preventing reflux)
- Regulates heart rhythm
- Provides innervation of the crura (pillars) of the diaphragm
- Provides the foundation of your parasympathetic ("rest and digest") system

- Serves as a major anti-inflammatory pathway in the body (you can think of the vagus as the "recovery nerve")

UNMYELINATED FREE NERVE ENDINGS

Myelin is a sheath of tissue that surrounds a nerve to make its communication faster and smoother, like the insulation around a wire. There are free nerve endings that talk to the vagus nerve and insula, and they are mostly unmyelinated. The type-C tactile fibers are of particular importance here. They are found in fascia and hairy skin, and a newly discovered correlate has also been discovered in smooth skin, like the palms and the soles of the feet.[119]

The type-C fibers are different from the receptors that normally activate when you move your body. If you lift your arm, various mechanoreceptors (e.g., muscle spindles, Golgi tendon organs, Pacinian corpuscles, Ruffini endings) may feel the movement and send signals to your somatosensory cortex. C-fibers, meanwhile, are more responsive to light touch, stroking, or deep pressure. Instead of sending their information to the somatosensory cortex, they communicate directly with the insula through the vagus nerve.

The improvement you may feel after certain forms of bodywork can be due to C-fiber activation. For every mechanoreceptor, there are seven nerve endings that could be considered interoceptive.[120] A large percentage of the nervous system is devoted to being able to tell how you feel inside.

TRAINING YOUR INTEROCEPTION

Many of the drills we've already done in the book have a sizable interoceptive component:

- ***Breathing*** *(Chapters 4–7)*: Both the insula and the vagus nerve are involved with respiration.

- ***Abdominals/Pelvic Floor*** *(Chapter 6)*: The vagus runs through this entire area.

- ***Tongue*** *(Chapter 9)*: In the homunculus, the tongue is located very near to the insula, so all tongue drills can be interoceptive.

- ***Teeth*** *(Chapter 10)*: Vibrating your teeth activates both sides of the insula.

- ***Balance*** *(Chapter 13)*: Balance is an internal predictive and sensory process, and the insula has direct connections to the vestibular system.

Let's learn some other ways to access your interoceptive system.

THE VAGUS AND THE EAR

Although the vagus is a very long nerve, there is only one branch that finds its way to the skin, in a small portion of the ear and ear canals *(Fig. 17.3)*. Stimulating the skin here can affect vagal tone and interoception.

Vagus Ear Stim

1. Assess your voice and body.

2. Take your right pointer finger and turn your hand so you are looking at the pad of your finger, with the fingernail away from you.

3. Put your finger in your ear canal, with the fingernail facing forward. Press lightly into the back of your right ear canal.

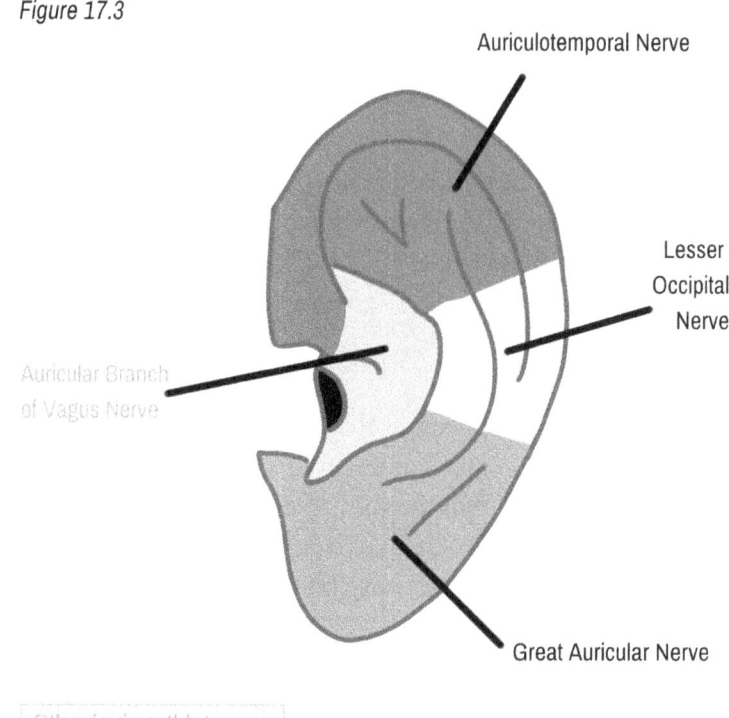

Figure 17.3

4. What does this tissue feel like here? Springy? Sore? Boggy?

5. Make a circle with your finger, pressing into the posterior wall of the ear canal with a pressure that feels good.

6. Reassess.

7. Do the same setup on your left ear. Does the sensation feel the same when you make a circle on the left side?

8. Reassess.

Another excellent target for the vagus is the *cymba conchae (Fig. 17.4)*. Try the above process with that location as well.

Here are some other things to try, using the assess/reassess protocol:

• Grab the posterior part of the ear and pull back and out.

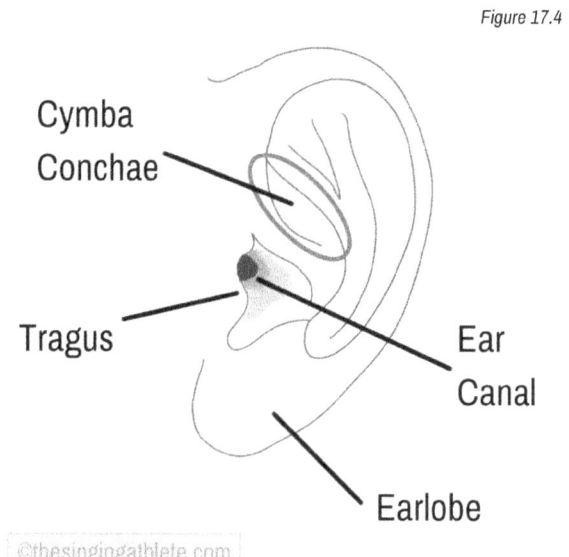

Figure 17.4

222

- Grab an earlobe and pull down and out.

- Dip a Q-tip in warm water and move it around the back of the ear canal and the cymba conchae.

- Put a Z-vibe or an electric toothbrush in the ear and press it toward the back of the canal and against the cymba conchae.

Trunk Palpations

Since the vagus runs through the chest and abdomen, moving the fascia in the trunk can train interoception. In this drill, you'll experiment with using your hands to stimulate C-fibers by shifting the fascia and the skin while you sing.

1. Place your right hand across the center line of your body until your hand is resting on the area underneath your left ribcage.

2. Press in a little bit until you feel like you are right below the skin level but not creating any discomfort in the abdomen.

3. Move the skin/fascia under your hand, looking for directions that feel sticky.

4. Slide and hold the fascia in one of the sticky directions while you sing a phrase of music.

5. Depending on how that went, you can also try moving directly away from the sticky area, spreading out the stuck area.

6. Sing the same phrase.

7. Repeat Steps 1–6 on the left.

Use the same process in your lower abdominal area (left hand across to the lower right and vice versa), with a hand flat on your sternum, and on either side of your upper chest.

Inversions

Inversions *(Fig. 17.5)* are a great way to experience novel sensations in visceral ligaments, which can give your insula lots of fresh information. You know your own body, so stay within the realm of what is safe for you. Some yoga options are:

Figure 17.5-- Me practicing inversions

- Headstands
- Handstands
- Shoulder stand
- Plow
- Crow

If these are too advanced for you, you can hang off the edge of a bed/table or lie backward over a physio ball. Get creative.

Insular Belt/Weighted Blanket

Another great insular drill is wearing a neoprene belt. Because C-fibers respond to deep pressure, a belt like this wakes up a ton of activation in these nerve endings. If you think you have interoceptive issues, I highly recommend you try this, starting with a session of about ten minutes or so and working up to longer and longer times. You can even wear one below your audition outfit, as they lie quite flat to the body.

A weighted blanket can be used for this same purpose; if it feels good, you can sleep under one. You should get one that is around 10 percent of your body weight and start with a brief session (again, around ten minutes or so). See how it makes you feel.

18. NEXT STEPS

You made it! Congratulations! I hope you will think of yourself from now on as a Singing Athlete. Now, let's talk about a game plan. Here are the next steps I suggest you take:

- *Pick a few high-payoff drills to boost performance:* Flip back through the book and choose a few drills that gave you a good reassessment. Use these in your practice for a few weeks and, if you have a performance coming up, do them beforehand.

- *Choose one or two rehab drills to work on resolving threats:* Determine a couple of exercises that you found very challenging or maybe caused a threat response (e.g., sweating, dizziness, muscle tension, startle, etc.). Work slowly on these drills for a few weeks, using the regressions I went over in Chapter 3. See if you can reduce threat signals with a few weeks of diligent practice. Don't do these drills before a performance; practice them at other times during the day, preferably when you're feeling good and have enough fuel.

- *Reread the book:* This book is no joke; reading it is like drinking from a fire hose. You absorbed some of the material, but there is a lot that you probably couldn't process the first time around. You will discover new things in subsequent passes, I promise.

In the end, this book is about making you a more awesome version of yourself. And this new awesomeness will only stick if you create good practice habits. Here are ten concluding thoughts to help you follow through on what you found:

1. Take the "What's My Performing Personality?" quiz at thesingingathete.com to learn more about how you respond to expectations, both from within and from others.

2. Set up your space to remind yourself that you like to sing. Visual cues are crucial in keeping practice commitments. Keep your music in a location where you can easily see it.

3. Habits live on a calendar. It's too easy to break promises to yourself if you don't see them written down. If you're committing to doing vestibular drills for two minutes after work, put those two minutes in your calendar.

4. Any change process you are undertaking needs to be able to happen on your worst day. Make the instructions easy, tangible, and clear. Something like "I'm going to do my gaze stabilization drills once a day on the train" or "I'm going to do three jaw glides every night before bed," are good options. If you make it easy enough, you'll actually do it, even when your life is chaos.

5. Figure out what time of day is best for you to train. If you're a morning person, get up a few minutes early and do your drills. If you're a night owl, set some time aside each evening.

6. Ask yourself whether you have a "prevent loss" or a "promote growth" mindset. Do you avoid investing in your career? Do you stop yourself from going to an audition because that new song hasn't

been perfected yet? Elite athletes live from a "promote growth" place. They take risks financially, physically, and emotionally; basically, they bet on themselves winning.

7. A brain in a habit-change process consumes 25 percent more calories than a brain watching a screen. Keep your fuel up. Eat foods that make you feel energized, moderate/eliminate alcohol, and get enough sleep.

8. Motor learning research shows that the more results-focused you are ("I've got to book this job!"), the more likely you are to choke in performance. When you're singing, put your attention on communicating the text and on your sensory experience (what you see, hear, smell, feel, etc.).

9. Start today. One of the most insidious human avoidance tactics is "the better-future fallacy." We tell ourselves, "I'll start practicing next week when I'm less stressed," or, "Once I get my (fill-in-the-blank) out of the way, I'll start performing again." Do it now. The change can be embarrassingly easy; practice your singing for one minute. One minute is way better than zero minutes.

10. Whatever you want to achieve with your voice and your life, don't give up. There is a ton of hope, and that hope is backed up by science. All it takes for a breakthrough is accurate information and a willingness to keep exploring.

If you want to connect with me for more information or training, here's how:

Main website: andrewbyrne.com

Access the videos and additional content that accompany this book: thesingingathlete.com

I teach The Singing Athlete™ all over the world, so drop me a line if you're interested in hosting a course. You'll find my contact information at either website.

Thank you!

ABOUT THE AUTHOR

Andrew Byrne is the founder of The Singing Athlete™, a training program that brings sports performance and neuroscience into the voice studio. He is based in New York City, and his students have appeared in leading roles in over seventy-five Broadway shows. In 2016, Andrew was the first arts envoy appointed by the U.S. State Department to the nation of Belarus, where he was the vocal coach on a Russian-language production of *Next to Normal*.

Guest Faculty in Musical Theatre: The University of Michigan, The Banff Centre, Shanghai Theatre Academy, The Danish Musical Theater Academy, The Danish Actors Association, American Musical Theatre Live! Paris, Collectif Sondheim (Lausanne, Switzerland) and four residencies at the Victorian College of the Arts in Melbourne, Australia.

Photo by Thomas Overend

Regional Theatre: Sundance Theatre Lab, Yale Repertory Theatre, North Shore Music Theatre, Weston Playhouse. Television: *Penny Dreadful: City of Angels*, *America's Got Talent*. Film: *Waiting in the Wings: The Movie Musical*.

Learn more at andrewbyrne.com

DRILL WORKSHEET

If you want to keep track of which drills create the best results for you, here is a chart of all the exercises in the book. Do your high-payoff drills right before performance and work on fixing your rehab drills at other times in your day.

Drill	High Payoff	Rehab	Neutral
Chapter 3—Practice			
Finger Circles			
Long Spine			
Chapter 4—Breathing			
In for 2, Out for 8			
Hypoxic Drill 1: Reduced Breathing			
Hypoxic Drill 2: Walk and Hold			
Hypoxic Drill 3: Squats			
Hypoxic Drill 4: Push-ups			
Bag Breathing			
Chapter 5—Diaphragm			
Diaphragm Stretch 1			
Diaphragm Stretch 2			
Diaphragm Stretch 3			
Diaphragm Strength—Respiratory			
Diaphragm Strength—Visceral			
Breathing Wave			
Phrenic Nerve Glide			
Chapter 6—Exhalation			
Exhalation Awareness Drill 1: Rectus Abdominis			
Exhalation Awareness Drill 2: External Oblique			

Drill	High Payoff	Rehab	Neutral
Exhalation Awareness Drill 3: Internal Oblique			
Exhalation Awareness Drill 4: Transversus Abdominis			
Exhalation Awareness Drill 5: Internal Intercostals			
Exhalation Awareness Drill 6: Transversus Thoracis			
Exhalation Awareness Drill 7: QL/Serratus Posterior Inferior			
Exhalation Awareness Drill 8: Pelvic Floor			
Chapter 7—Inhalation			
Inhalation Awareness Drill 1: Pectoralis Minor			
Inhalation Awareness Drill 2: Pectoralis Major			
Inhalation Awareness Drill 3: Serratus Anterior			
Inhalation Awareness Drill 4: External Intercostals			
Inhalation Awareness Drill 5: Serratus Posterior Superior			
SCM Stretch			
SCM Strength			
Scapular Circles			
Scalene Stretch			
Scalene Strength			
Blocked Inhalation			
Chapter 8—Larynx and Palate			
Chin Tuck			
Humming			
Voice and Vibration			
Cricothyroid			
Thyroid Cartilage Mobilization			
Hyoid Bone Mobilization			
Laryngeal Elevator Mapping 1			
Laryngeal Elevator Mapping 2			

Drill	High Payoff	Rehab	Neutral
Laryngeal Depressor Mapping 1			
Upper Neck Figure 8			
Soft Palate Gargle Test			
Soft Palate Vagus Test			
Palate Stretch—LVP			
Palate Stretch—TVP			
Chapter 9—Tongue			
Transverse Muscle Strength			
Correct Resting Tongue Position			
Separate the Tongue and the Throat			
Swallow Check			
Tongue Sensitivity			
Shock Your Tongue			
Taste and Singing			
Hypoglossal Nerve Test/Tongue Press			
Two-Minute Tongue Stretch			
Forward Roll			
Tongue Circle			
Tongue Retraction			
/n/ Push-up			
Blade Push-up			
Backward Curl			
Blowfish			
Tongue Push-up (Center)			
Tongue Push-up (Side)			
Resisted Tongue Thrust			
Chapter 10—Jaw and Teeth			

Drill	High Payoff	Rehab	Neutral
Mouth Taping			
Opening the Mouth			
Jaw Lateral Glides			
Jaw Front-to-Back Glides			
Jaw Circles			
Masseter			
Temporalis			
Medial Pterygoid			
Lateral Pterygoid			
Jaw Isometrics (Opening)			
Jaw Isometrics (Closing)			
Jaw Isometrics (To the right)			
Jaw Isometrics (To the left)			
Jaw Isometrics (Forward)			
Jaw Isometrics (Back)			
Pressure-Checking Your Teeth			
Chapter 11—Nose and Skull			
Smell Test			
Sinus Drill 1: Plug 'n' Shake			
Sinus Drill 2: Vibration			
Facial Sensation Test 1: Light Touch			
Facial Sensation Test 2: Vibration			
Facial/Trigeminal Nerve Glide			
Skull Pressure-Checking			
Sagittal Suture Mobility			
Sphenoid Bone Mobility			
Chapter 12—Scars			

	Drill	High Payoff	Rehab	Neutral
Pressure-Checking				
Sensory Work for Scars				
Tattoos and Piercings				
Scarring in the Mouth and Throat				
Creativity Scar Rehab				

Chapter 13—Ears				
Train your VOR				
VOR Cancellation Version 1				
VOR Cancellation Version 2				
Neck Lateral Glide				
Sustained Head-Tilt				
Train Your Utricle: Walking				
Train Your Saccule				
Visual Vertical				
High Frequency Test				
Finger-Rub Test				
Hearing Map Test				
Bone Conduction Test				
Tuning Fork Test				
Rinne and Weber Tests				

Chapter 14—Eyes				
Eye Mobility				
Gaze Stabilization				
Smooth Pursuits				
Saccades				
Pencil Push-ups				
Stereogram				

Drill	High Payoff	Rehab	Neutral
Near/Far Switches			
Peripheral Awareness			
Color, Eyes and the Brain: Green			
Color, Eyes and the Brain: Blue			
Color, Eyes and the Brain: Red			
Color, Eyes and the Brain: Yellow			
Brain Hemisphere Test			
Pinhole Glasses			
Chapter 15—First Brain			
Cerebellar Test 1: Foot Tapping			
Cerebellar Test 2: Heel to Shin			
Cerebellar Test 3: Finger Tapping			
Cerebellar Test 4: Hand Tapping			
Cerebellar Test 5: Shoulder Rotation			
Cerebellar Test 6: Finger to Nose			
Chapter 16—Second Brain			
Stroop Test			
Optokinetic Reflex			
Body Brushing			
Performing Lyrics and Melodies Separately			
Eye Line Test			
Chapter 17—Feeling			
Vagus Ear Stim			
Trunk Palpations			
Inversions			
Insular Belt/Weighted Blanket			

REFERENCES

[1] Chavan, Sangeeta S., Valentin A. Pavlov, and Kevin J. Tracey. "Mechanisms and therapeutic relevance of neuro-immune communication." *Immunity* 46.6 (2017): 927-942.

[2] de Gobbi Porto, Fábio Henrique, et al. "In vivo evidence for neuroplasticity in older adults." *Brain Research Bulletin* 114 (2015): 56-61.

[3] Flegal, Kristin E., and Michael C. Anderson. "Overthinking skilled motor performance: Or why those who teach can't do." *Psychonomic Bulletin & Review* 15.5 (2008): 927-932

[4] Wyke BD. Laryngeal neuromuscular control systems in singing. A review of current concepts, *Folia Phoniatrica et Logopaedica (Basel)*, 1974, vol. 26 (pg. 295-306)

[5] Parker, Stephen. "The Happiness Hypothesis: Putting Ancient Wisdom and Philosophy to the Test of Modern Science [Book Review]." *Australian Journal of Adult Learning* 50.1 (2010): 199.

[6] Buckner, Randy L. "The Cerebellum and Cognitive Function: 25 Years of Insight from Anatomy and Neuroimaging." *Neuron* 80.3 (2013): 807-815.

[7] Simonyan, Kristina. "The laryngeal motor cortex: its organization and connectivity." *Current Opinion in Neurobiology* 28 (2014): 15-21.

[8] Wyke, B. D. (1974). Laryngeal neuromuscular control systems in singing. A review of current concepts. *Folia Phoniatr. (Basel)* 26, 295–306.)

[9] Lotze, Martin, et al. "The musician's brain: functional imaging of amateurs and professionals during performance and imagery." *Neuroimage* 20.3 (2003): 1817-1829.

[10] Hund-Georgiadis, Margret, and D. Yves Von Cramon. "Motor-learning-related changes in piano players and non-musicians revealed by functional magnetic-resonance signals." *Experimental Brain Research* 125.4 (1999): 417-425.

[11] B. Kleber, R. Veit, N. Birbaumer, J. Gruzelier, M. Lotze, The Brain of Opera Singers: Experience-Dependent Changes in Functional Activation, *Cerebral Cortex*, Volume 20, Issue 5, May 2010, Pages 1144–1152

[12] Merzenich, Michael M., et al. "Somatosensory cortical map changes following digit amputation in adult monkeys." *Journal of Comparative Neurology* 224.4 (1984): 591-605.

[13] Stavrinou, Maria L., et al. "Temporal dynamics of plastic changes in human primary somatosensory cortex after finger webbing." *Cerebral Cortex* 17.9 (2006): 2134-2142.

[14] Hanna, Thomas. "Clinical somatic education." *A new discipline in the field of health care* (1990).

[15] Wayne, Peter M., and Mark Fuerst. The Harvard Medical School guide to Tai Chi: 12 weeks to a healthy body, strong heart, and sharp mind. Shambhala Publications, 2013.

[16] Wulf, Gabriele, Markus Höß, and Wolfgang Prinz. "Instructions for motor learning: Differential effects of internal versus external focus of attention." *Journal of Motor Behavior* 30.2 (1998): 169-179.

[17] Freedman, Skott E., et al. "Internal versus external: Oral-motor performance as a function of attentional focus." *Journal of Speech, Language, and Hearing Research* (2007)

[18] Atkins, Rebecca L. "Effects of focus of attention on tone production in trained singers." *Journal of Research in Music Education* 64.4 (2017): 421-434.

[19] Maurer, H. E. I. K. O., and K. A. R. E. N. Zentgraf. "On the how and why of the external focus learning advantage." Gabriele Wulf on attentional focus and motor learning. Eds: Hossner, EJ and Wenderoth, N. E-Journal Bewegung und Training 1 (2007): 31-32.

[20] Edwards, William H. Motor learning and control: From theory to practice. Cengage Learning, 2010.

[21] Rendic, Slobodan. "Summary of information on human CYP enzymes: human P450 metabolism data." *Drug Metabolism Reviews* 34.1-2 (2002): 83-448.

[22] Lin, I-Mei, and Erik Peper. "Psychophysiological patterns during cell phone text messaging: A preliminary study." *Applied Psychophysiology and Biofeedback* 34.1 (2009): 53-57.

[23] Newhouse, Michael T. "Tennis anyone? The lungs as a new court for systemic therapy." *Cmaj* 161.10 (1999): 1287-1288.

[24] Roberts D, Smith DJ, Donnelly S, Simard S. Plasma-volume contraction and exercise-induced hypoxaemia modulate erythropoietin production in healthy humans. *Clin Sci*. 2000 Jan;98(1):39–45.

[25] Bordoni, Bruno, and Emiliano Zanier. "Anatomic connections of the diaphragm: influence of respiration on the body system." *Journal of Multidisciplinary Healthcare* 6 (2013): 281.

[26] [26] Dooley, Dr. Kathy and Folckomer, Anna "Immaculate Dissection: Core Concepts" New York, NY

[27] Masaoka, Tatsuhiro, Hidekazu Suzuki, and Toshifumi Hibi. "Pleotropic Effects of Proton Pump Inhibitors Guest Editor: Yuji Naito Gastric Epithelial Cell Modality and Proton Pump Inhibitor." *Journal of Clinical Biochemistry and Nutrition* 42.3 (2008): 191-196.

[28] Reimer, Christina. "Safety of long-term PPI therapy." *Best Practice & Research Clinical Gastroenterology* 27.3 (2013): 443-454.

[29] Cheung KS, Chan EW, Wong AYS, et al Long-term proton pump inhibitors and risk of gastric cancer development after treatment for Helicobacter pylori: a population-based study *Gut* 2018;67:28-35.

[30] Gomm, Willy, et al. "Association of proton pump inhibitors with risk of dementia: a pharmacoepidemiological claims data analysis." *JAMA Neurology* 73.4 (2016): 410-416.

[31] Casale, M., et al. "Breathing training on lower esophageal sphincter as a complementary treatment of gastroesophageal reflux disease (GERD): a systematic review." *Eur Rev Med Pharmacol Sci* 20.21 (2016): 4547-4552.

[32] Martin, Ruth E., et al. "Cerebral cortical representation of automatic and volitional swallowing in humans." *Journal of Neurophysiology* 85.2 (2001): 938-950.

[33] Lee, Sangsoo, Chang Jin Oh, and Jeong Won Seong. "Sympathetic Nerve Entrapment Point Injection as an Antireflux Procedure for Refractory Laryngopharyngeal Reflux: A First Case Report of Innovative Autonomic Regulation." *Innovations in Clinical Neuroscience* 13.11-12 (2016): 32.

[34] Fedorko, L., E. G. Merrill, and J. Lipski. "Two descending medullary inspiratory pathways to phrenic motoneurones." *Neuroscience Letters* 43.2-3 (1983): 285-291.

[35] Chaitow, Leon, Dinah Bradley, and Christopher Gilbert. *Recognizing and Treating Breathing Disorders E-Book*. Elsevier Health Sciences, 2014.

[36] Jundt, Katharina, Ursula Peschers, and Heribert Kentenich. "The investigation and treatment of female pelvic floor dysfunction." *Deutsches Ärzteblatt International* 112.33-34 (2015): 564.

[37] Dooley, Dr. Kathy and Folckomer, Anna "Immaculate Dissection: Core Concepts" New York, NY

[38] Crombie, Kevin M., et al. "Endocannabinoid and opioid system interactions in exercise-induced hypoalgesia." *Pain Medicine* 19.1 (2017): 118-123.

[39] Masubuchi, Y., et al. "Relation between neck accessory inspiratory muscle electromyographic activity and lung volume." *Nihon Kokyuki Gakkai zasshi (The Journal of the Japanese Respiratory Society)* 39.4 (2001): 244-249.

[40] Moore, Christopher A., and Jacki L. Ruark. "Does speech emerge from earlier appearing oral motor behaviors?" *Journal of Speech, Language, and Hearing Research* 39.5 (1996): 1034-1047.

[41] Gerritsen, Roderik Jan Sebastiaan, and Guido PH Band. "Breath of life: the respiratory vagal stimulation model of contemplative activity." *Frontiers in Human Neuroscience* 12 (2018): 397.

[42] Vagal Sensory Neuron Subtypes that Differentially Control Breathing. Chang RB, Strochlic DE, Williams EK, Umans BD, Liberles SD Cell. 2015 Apr 23; 161(3):622-633.

[43] Koopman, Frieda A., et al. "Vagus nerve stimulation inhibits cytokine production and attenuates disease severity in rheumatoid arthritis." *Proceedings of the National Academy of Sciences* 113.29 (2016): 8284-8289.

[44] Sollier, Pierre. Listening for wellness: An introduction to the Tomatis method. Mozart Center Press, 2005, p. 116.

[45] Powers, Michelle, and Megan Cahill. "Case Study: Unilateral Vocal Cord Paralysis." (2019)

[46] Porges, Stephen W. *The pocket guide to the polyvagal theory: The transformative power of feeling safe*. WW Norton & Co, 2017.

[47] Linderoth, Bengt, and Björn A. Meyerson. "Dorsal column stimulation: modulation of somatosensory and autonomic function." *Seminars in Neuroscience*. Vol. 7. No. 4. Academic Press, 1995.

[48] Entezami, Pouya, et al. "Stabbing injury of the cervical spinal cord resulting in complete bilateral proprioception loss." *World Neurosurgery* (2019)

[49] Flemming, Edward. "24.963 Linguistic Phonetics, Fall 2005." (2005).

[50] Vander Stoep, Carol. *Mouth Matters; How Your Mouth Ages Your Body and What You Can Do About It*. Ianua Publishing, 2012.

[51] Alghadir, Ahmad H., Hamayun Zafar, and Zaheen A. Iqbal. "Effect of tongue position on postural stability during quiet standing in healthy young males." *Somatosensory & Motor Research* 32.3 (2015): 183-186.

[52] di Vico, Rosa, et al. "The acute effect of the tongue position in the mouth on knee isokinetic test performance: a highly surprising pilot study." *Muscles, Ligaments and Tendons Journal* 3.4 (2013): 318.

[53] Vander Stoep, Carol. *Mouth Matters: Healthy Mouth, Healthy Body*. Dripping Springs, TX Ianua Publishing, 2012.

[54] Lear, Cl SC, J. B. Flanagan Jr, and C. F. A. Moorrees. "The frequency of deglutition in man." *Archives of Oral Biology* 10.1 (1965): 83-IN15.

[55] Rosenberg, Stanley. *Accessing the Healing Power of the Vagus Nerve: Self-help Exercises for Anxiety, Depression, Trauma, and Autism*. North Atlantic Books, 2017.

[56] Doidge, Norman. *The brain that changes itself: Stories of personal triumph from the frontiers of brain science*. Penguin, 2007.

[57] Tyler, Mitchell E., et al. "Non-invasive neuromodulation to improve gait in chronic multiple sclerosis: a randomized double blind controlled pilot trial." *Journal of Neuroengineering and Rehabilitation* 11.1 (2014): 79.

[58] Bachmanov, Alexander A., and Gary K. Beauchamp. "Taste receptor genes." *Annu. Rev. Nutr.* 27 (2007): 389-414.

[59] Kuttila, S; Kuttila, M; Le Bell, BY; Alanen, P; Suonpaa, J. Recurrent tinnitus and associated ear symptoms in adults. *Int. J. Audiol*, 44:164-70, 2005

[60] Gibbs, Charles H., et al. "Limits of human bite strength." *Journal of Prosthetic Dentistry* 56.2 (1986): 226-229.

[61] Kibana, Y., T. Ishijima, and T. Hirai. "Occlusal support and head posture." *Journal of Oral Rehabilitation* 29.1 (2002): 58-63.

[62] Tanaka, Shoji, and Eiji Kirino. "Dynamic reconfiguration of the supplementary motor area network during imagined music performance." *Frontiers in Human Neuroscience* 11 (2017): 606.

[63] Simonyan, Kristina, and Barry Horwitz. "Laryngeal motor cortex and control of speech in humans." *The Neuroscientist* 17.2 (2011): 197-208.

[64] Kuhtz-Buschbeck, J. P., et al. "Activation of the supplementary motor area (SMA) during voluntary pelvic floor muscle contractions—an fMRI study." *Neuroimage* 35.2 (2007): 449-457.

[65] Laviolette, Louis, et al. "The supplementary motor area exerts a tonic excitatory influence on corticospinal projections to phrenic motoneurons in awake humans." *PLoS One* 8.4 (2013): e62258.

[66] Trulsson, Mats, et al. "Brain activations in response to vibrotactile tooth stimulation: a psychophysical and fMRI study." *Journal of Neurophysiology* 104.4 (2010): 2257-2265.

[67] Telles, Shirley, R. Nagarathna, and H. R. Nagendra. "Breathing through a particular nostril can alter metabolism and autonomic activities." *Indian Journal of Physiology and Pharmacology* 38 (1994): 133-133.

[68] Aksoy, Fadlullah, et al. "Role of nasal muscles in nasal valve collapse." *Otolaryngology—Head and Neck Surgery* 142.3 (2010): 365-369.

[69] Esiri, MARGARET M., and GORDON K. Wilcock. "The olfactory bulbs in Alzheimer's disease." *Journal of Neurology, Neurosurgery & Psychiatry* 47.1 (1984): 56-60.

[70] *Essential Oils – Health Warning*, healthywa.wa.gov.au/Articles/A_E/Essential-oils.

[71] Fujii, Kiyotaka, Steven M. Chambers, and Albert L. Rhoton. "Neurovascular relationships of the sphenoid sinus: a microsurgical study." *Journal of Neurosurgery* 50.1 (1979): 31-39.

[72] Keir, James. "Why do we have paranasal sinuses?." *The Journal of Laryngology & Otology* 123.1 (2009): 4-8.

[73] Swift, A. C., I. T. Campbell, and TessaM Mckown. "Oronasal obstruction, lung volumes, and arterial oxygenation." *The Lancet* 331.8577 (1988): 73-75.

[74] Durgin, Frank H., et al. "Self-motion perception during locomotor recalibration: more than meets the eye." *Journal of Experimental Psychology: Human Perception and Performance* 31.3 (2005): 398.

[75] Kautz, Steven A., et al. "Comparison of motor control deficits during treadmill and overground walking poststroke." *Neurorehabilitation and Neural Repair* 25.8 (2011): 756-765.

[76] Zelano, Christina, et al. "Nasal respiration entrains human limbic oscillations and modulates cognitive function." *Journal of Neuroscience* 36.49 (2016): 12448-12467.

[77] Friedman, Oren. "Changes associated with the aging face." *Facial Plastic Surgery Clinics* 13.3 (2005): 371-380.

[78] Sabini, Rosanna C., and David E. Elkowitz. "Significance of differences in patency among cranial sutures." *Journal of the American Osteopathic Association* 106.10 (2006): 600.

[79] Sandhouse, Mark E., et al. "Effect of osteopathy in the cranial field on visual function--a pilot study." *Journal of the American Osteopathic Association* 110.4 (2010): 239.

[80] Antony, F. C., and C. C. Harland. "Red ink tattoo reactions: successful treatment with the Q−switched 532 nm Nd: YAG laser." *British Journal of Dermatology* 149.1 (2003): 94-98.

[81] Todd, N. P., Cousins, R., & Lee, C. S. (2007). The contribution of anthropomorphic factors to individual differences in the perception of rhythm. *Empirical Musicology Review*, 2(1), 1–13.

[82] Juntunen, M.-L., & Hyvönen, L. (2004). Embodiment in musical knowing:How body movement facilitates learning with Dalcroze Eurhythmics. *British Journal of Music Education*, 21(2), 199–214.

[83] Madaule, Paul. "Listening training and music education." *Early Childhood Connections* 4.2 (1997): 1-9.

[84] Phillips-Silver, Jessica, and Laurel J. Trainor. "Vestibular influence on auditory metrical interpretation." *Brain and Cognition* 67 (2008): 94-102.

[85] Nandi, Raj, and Linda M. Luxon. "Development and assessment of the vestibular system." *International Journal of Audiology* 47.9 (2008): 566-577.

[86] Bonaz, Bruno, Valérie Sinniger, and Sonia Pellissier. "Anti−inflammatory properties of the vagus nerve: potential therapeutic implications of vagus nerve stimulation." *The Journal of Physiology* 594.20 (2016): 5781-5790.

[87] Smith, Paul F., et al. "Does vestibular damage cause cognitive dysfunction in humans?." *Journal of Vestibular Research* 15.1 (2005): 1-9.

[88] Furman, Joseph M., Rolf G. Jacob, and Mark S. Redfern. "Clinical evidence that the vestibular system participates in autonomic control." *Journal of Vestibular Research* 8.1 (1998): 27-34.

[89] Sailesh, Kumar Sai, R. Archana, and J. K. Mukkadan. "Vestibular stimulation: A simple but effective intervention in diabetes care." *Journal of Natural Science, Biology, and Medicine* 6.2 (2015): 321.

[90] Yates BJ, Bolton PS, Macefield VG. Vestibulo-sympathetic responses. *Compr Physiol*. 2014;4:851–87.

[91] Sailesh, Kumar Sai, R. Archana, and J. K. Mukkadan. "Impact of traditional vestibular stimulation on depression, anxiety and stress in college students." (2016).

[92] Lambert, François M., et al. "Vestibular asymmetry as the cause of idiopathic scoliosis: a possible answer from Xenopus." *Journal of Neuroscience* 29.40 (2009): 12477-12483

[93] Kiefer, D.H. "Unstable Surfaces for Stability Training (aka Clown School)" athlete.io, (2012).

[94] Das, Barshapriya, Indranil Chatterjee, and Suman Kumar. "Laryngeal aerodynamics in children with hearing impairment versus age and height matched normal hearing peers." *ISRN Otolaryngology* 2013 (2013).

[95] Mürbe, Dirk, et al. "Significance of auditory and kinesthetic feedback to singers' pitch control." *Journal of Voice* 16.1 (2002): 44-51.

[96] Sollier, Pierre. *Listening for wellness: An introduction to the Tomatis method*. Mozart Center Press, 2005.

[97] Kenmegne, Romuald, and Qi Lu. "Comparison of 440 Hz vs. 432 Hz Tuning through EEG of Human Brain Waves." *Bulletin of the American Physical Society* 63 (2018).

[98] Calamassi, Diletta, and Gian Paolo Pomponi. "Music tuned to 440 Hz versus 432 Hz and the health effects: a double-blind cross-over pilot study." *EXPLORE* (2019)

[99] Griffiths, T. D., Uppenkamp, S., Johnsrude, I., Josephs, O., and Patterson, R. D. (2001). Encoding of the temporal regularity of sound in the human brainstem. *Nat. Neurosci.* 4, 633–637. doi: 10.1038/88459

[100] Cutting, James E., Jordan E. DeLong, and Christine E. Nothelfer. "Attention and the evolution of Hollywood film." *Psychological Science* 21.3 (2010): 432-439.

[101] Bejan, Adrian. "Why the Days Seem Shorter as We Get Older." *European Review* 27.2 (2019): 187-194.

[102] Lee, Sun Haeng, Byeong-Yeon Moon, and Hyun Gug Cho. "Improvement of vergence movements by vision therapy decreases K-ARS scores of symptomatic ADHD children." *Journal of Physical Therapy Science* 26.2 (2014): 223-227

[103] Rogers, Tracie J., and Daniel M. Landers. "Mediating effects of peripheral vision in the life event stress/athletic injury relationship." *Journal of Sport and Exercise Psychology* 27.3 (2005): 271-288.

[104] Noseda, Rodrigo, et al. "Migraine photophobia originating in cone-driven retinal pathways." *Brain* 139.7 (2016): 1971-1986.

[105] Höfling, Danilo Bianchini, et al. "Assessment of the effects of low-level laser therapy on the thyroid vascularization of patients with autoimmune hypothyroidism by color Doppler ultrasound." *ISRN Endocrinology* 2012 (2012).

[106] Kulekcioglu, Sevinc, et al. "Effectiveness of low–level laser therapy in temporomandibular disorder." *Scandinavian Journal of Rheumatology* 32.2 (2003): 114-118.

[107] Aghamohammadi, Dawood, et al. "Effect of low level laser application at the end of surgery to reduce pain after tonsillectomy in adults." *Journal of Lasers in Medical Sciences* 4.2 (2013): 79.

[108] Jürgens, Uwe, and Steffen R. Hage. "On the role of the reticular formation in vocal pattern generation." *Behavioural Brain Research* 182.2 (2007): 308-314.

[109] Kent, Raymond D., ed. The MIT encyclopedia of communication disorders. MIT Press, 2004.

[110] Gaab N, Gaser C, Zaehle T, Jancke L, Schlaug G (2003) Functional anatomy of pitch memory – an fMRI study with sparse temporal sampling. *NeuroImage* 19:1417–1426

[111] Kleber, Boris, et al. "The brain of opera singers: experience-dependent changes in functional activation." *Cerebral Cortex* 20.5 (2009): 1144-1152.

[112] *Callan DE, Tsytsarev V, Hanakawa T, Callan AM, Katsuhara M, Fukuyama H, Turner R (2006) Song and speech: brain regions involved with perception and covert production. NeuroImage 31:1327–1342*

[113] Louw, Adriaan, and E. Puentedura. "Therapeutic neuroscience education, pain, physiotherapy and the pain neuromatrix." *International Journal of Health Sciences* 2.3 (2014): 33-45.

[114] Schaal, Nora K., et al. "From amusic to musical?—Improving pitch memory in congenital amusia with transcranial alternating current stimulation." *Behavioural Brain Research* 294 (2015): 141-148.

[115] Poeppel, David, et al. "Towards a new neurobiology of language." *Journal of Neuroscience* 32.41 (2012): 14125-14131.

[116] Royal, Isabelle, et al. "Activation in the right inferior parietal lobule reflects the representation of musical structure beyond simple pitch discrimination." *PloS one* 11.5 (2016): e0155291.

[117] Simonyan, K., and Horwitz, B. (2011). Laryngeal motor cortex and control of speech in humans. *Neuroscientist* 17, 197–208. doi: 10.1177/1073858410386727

[118] Kleber, B., Zeitouni, A., Friberg, A., and Zatorre, R. J. (2013). Experience-dependent modulation of feedback integration during singing: role of the right anterior insula. *J. Neurosci*. 33, 6070–6080. doi: 10.1523/JNEUROSCI.4418-12.2013

[119] Nagi, Saad S., and David A. Mahns. "Mechanical allodynia in human glabrous skin mediated by low-threshold cutaneous mechanoreceptors with unmyelinated fibres." *Experimental Brain Research* 231.2 (2013): 139-151.

[120] Schleip, Robert, and H. Jäger. "Interoception." The Tensional Network of the Human Body, eds R. Schleip, WF Thomas, L. Chaitow, and PA Huijing (Edinburgh: Elsevier) (2012): 89-94.

www.ingramcontent.com/pod-product-compliance
Lightning Source LLC
Chambersburg PA
CBHW081106080526
44587CB00021B/3474